Yahweh Is Exalted in Justice

Yahweh Is Exalted in Justice

Solidarity and Conflict in Isaiah

Thomas L. Leclerc

Fortress Press
Minneapolis

YAHWEH IS EXALTED IN JUSTICE
Solidarity and Conflict in Isaiah

Author photo courtesy of Craig Bourque of Bourque's Photography.
Cover art copyright © Reactor 1995.
Cover design: Joseph Bonyata
Interior design: Beth Wright

Translations of biblical passages, unless otherwise noted, are the author's.

Library of Congress Cataloging-in-Publication Data

Leclerc, Thomas L., date–
Yahweh is exalted in justice : solidarity and conflict in Isaiah / Thomas L. Leclerc.
p. cm.
Includes bibliographical references and index.
ISBN 0-8006-3255-9 (pbk. : alk. paper)
1. Bible. O.T. Isaiah—Criticism, interpretation, etc. 2. Justice—Biblical teaching.
I. Title.
BS1515.2 .L43 2001
224'.106—dc21

2001044849

The paper used in this publication meets the minimum requirements of American National Standard for Information Sciences — Permanence of Paper for Printed Library Materials, ANSI Z329.48-1984.

Manufactured in the U.S.A. AF1-3255
05 04 03 02 01 1 2 3 4 5 6 7 8 9 10

To my parents
Arthur and Yvonne Leclerc

To Dad—
whose love for his wife of sixty-three years was never more evident than in his care and solicitude for her throughout her final illness;

To Mom—
whose unfailing love of family and invincible faith in God, in the end, robbed death of its sting.
March 7, 1917–April 4, 2001

Contents

Acknowledgments

The research at the core of this book was undertaken for my doctoral dissertation. I was extraordinarily fortunate to have a distinguished writing committee to guide my efforts. The project was directed by Paul D. Hanson. In addition to the innumerable ways he has assisted me academically, he has been a source of personal encouragement and guidance. Jon D. Levenson and Peter Machinist aided in this project, consistently combining exacting demands for research with exceptional generosity and patience. Their influence hopefully will be evident in these pages; where it is not, I alone am responsible.

I wish to acknowledge with gratitude Professors Jo Ann Hackett, Frank Cross, James Kugel, Gary Anderson, Theodore Hiebert, and Stephen Cole. As is well known, each is an exceptional scholar; what is perhaps less well known is that each is an even more exceptional teacher. I can think of no greater compliment.

My editor at Fortress Press, K. C. Hanson, helpfully suggested a new introduction addressing some contemporary concerns for justice and the addition of lectionary notes.

I am very grateful also to many people who read and commented on various parts of this book, in particular the Right Reverend Gregory J. Polan, O.S.B., Abbot of Conception Monastery, Conception, Missouri; Sr. Joyce Ann Zimmerman, C.PP.S., of the Institute for Liturgical Ministry in Dayton, Ohio; Rev. John R. Donahue, S.J.; and Rev. Charles Collins, pastor of St. John the Evangelist Church in Cambridge, Massachusetts.

I am also grateful to the members of my religious community, the Missionaries of La Salette, who have generously supported me both personally and financially, and Adam C. Barrett, whose friendship and support are a daily joy.

And finally, an acknowledgment of a different sort. Scholarly work on Isaiah proceeds at a breakneck rate. Between the time this manuscript was first submitted to the publisher and its final editing, a number of important commentaries on Isaiah have been published, most notably works by Joseph Blenkinsopp (*Isaiah 1–39*, Anchor Bible 19 [2000]), Brevard Childs (*Isaiah*, Old Testament Library [2001]), and Klaus Baltzer (*Deutero-Isaiah*, Hermeneia, [2001]). I regret that I was unable to incorporate their work into my own.

Introduction: Justice Now and Then

Justice Now

The natural drama of courtroom proceedings has long held a certain fascination. Already in antiquity, the *Dialogues* of Plato chronicled the events that led to Socrates' indictment, trial, imprisonment, and execution. Plato used the judicial setting, the courtroom, and the holding cell to raise profound religious, philosophical, moral, and civic issues. When life or death depends on the administration of justice, the stakes are high, the outcome unsure, and the suspense palpable. The Bible, too, has its stories of judicial decisions affecting life and death: Solomon and the two mothers (1 Kgs 3:16-28), Daniel's cross-examination of the two elders who falsely testified against Susanna (Daniel 13), the contrived cases of the poor lamb-owner presented by Nathan to David (2 Sam 12:1-7), and the case of the widow and her murderous son presented to David by the wise woman of Tekoa (2 Sam 14:1-11).

Centuries later, these matters of justice and of life and death make for compelling reading. In our own day, plays and countless movies exploit the courtroom to great dramatic effect: *Twelve Angry Men, A Man for All Seasons,* and *A Few Good Men* all come readily to mind, as do the television series *Perry Mason* and *The Practice.* Despite the specific allegations or other issues that are raised in courtroom dramas, the very setting alerts the viewer or reader to the underlying and most basic issue of all: Will justice prevail?

The same is true in "real life." The case may be as notorious as the O. J. Simpson trial, as heinous as the Bosnian and Serbian war crimes trials, or as heartbreaking as the trial of a child molester and murderer. The verdict may be guilty or not guilty. Regardless of the particulars, at the outcome of a trial people have a clear and immediate opinion as to whether justice was served or not. They may not be able to give a definition or even a description of "justice," but they know it when they see it; and they know, too, when justice fails. There is something almost intuitive or instinctive about justice. All the clever and compelling arguments of defense lawyers and prosecutors notwithstanding, despite all the intricacies and nuances of the law that may make a particular verdict technically correct, people still know whether or not justice has prevailed.

Throughout the world, particularly in democratic societies, justice is a foundational value, both the guarantor of order and the guiding principle of law. It has a transcendent authority that stands over governments, officials, and legal systems. In the United States, justice enjoys an almost mythic status—mythic, both in the sense of "larger than life" and as something not real. The "larger than life" aspect is captured in the inscription over the Supreme Court building that proclaims "Equal

Justice Under Law," and in the Pledge of Allegiance that promises "liberty and justice for all." Nevertheless, there is a sense that these lofty ideals remain elusive for many people. In courts, it sometimes seems that the justice to which one is entitled is the justice one can afford: with enough resources, a "dream team" of lawyers can almost certainly make the wheels of justice grind out the desired decision. Sometimes the scales of justice are tipped by the weight of political influence or by the expediency of plea bargains. The motions of justice too often make do for actual justice.

Cynicism about the court system, coupled with prohibitive costs and lengthy delays, have given rise to a kind of "populist justice" featured on a variety of televised court shows with celebrity judges and cases selected for their entertainment value. An optimist might argue that the hope for justice, though disappointed in official venues, is strong enough to find an alternative setting in which to survive; a pessimist might observe that justice has become nothing more than a commodity to be manipulated and used for entertainment. Still, whether the courtroom is to be found in government buildings or in television studios, there is a ready and immediate identification of justice with the courts.

But the concerns of justice are not restricted to the courts. Social, moral, and even religious issues are often matters of justice. Though, in the past, laws established a "separate but equal" society or an official policy of apartheid, today racial discrimination is recognized as patently unjust. Still, even after official policies have been abolished and formal laws have been overturned, matters of racial equality continue to be pressing social concerns. Social advancement, educational placements, housing, and employment opportunities are affected, sometimes positively, sometimes adversely, on the basis of race and ethnic identity. Racial discrimination apparently has economic consequences: in the United States, poverty rates for Latinos, African Americans, and Native Americans are more than double the poverty rate of white Americans (*Boston Globe,* July 30, 1999: A23). How is justice promoted in the public policies that affect the lives of racial and ethnic minorities?

The distribution of wealth involves complex issues of justice. A 1999 report in *Time* magazine indicates that the combined assets of the world's three wealthiest individuals total $156 billion, while the total gross national product of the forty-three least developed nations (for a combined population of 600 million people) is $136.2 billion. Approximately 1.3 billion people around the world live on less than $1.00 a day (*Time,* July 16, 1999: 17). The disparity defies imagination. While not so dramatic, the salaries of superstar actors and sports heroes are staggering. Meanwhile, public assistance, welfare, and other social programs become prey both to social reformers who claim that such economic policies are too costly, and to moralists who suggest that the dependency allegedly created by such programs undermines human dignity and self-respect. Ironically, all of this is taking place at a time when the U.S. economy is enjoying unprecedented vigor and growth, and when the upper and middle classes are prospering while the poor are losing benefits, support, and protection. In the period between 1994 and 1999, "welfare to work" programs have reduced the number of people on public assistance by almost 50 percent, but during the same period, the number of those living below 50 percent of the poverty level has grown from just below 14 million people to almost 14.8 million people. Clearly, questions of economic justice are acute and urgent. Do people have an unrestricted right to gain as much wealth as possible? Should justice constrain unbridled capitalism? Do the rich and society have an obligation toward the poor?

On a national and international level, loans from the World Bank and from developed nations to Third World nations, while often helpful and constructive, also create a long-term and debilitating debt crisis that keeps the governments and peoples of struggling nations in virtual thrall to their economic overlords. The promise of foreign aid or the threat to withhold it creates an imbalance of power and reduces recipient nations to a kind of political vassalage. Is such a use of wealth just?

Health care, too, raises issues of justice. Access to treatment is often determined by the coverage provided by insurance programs and benefits packages. But even insurance does not guarantee access to health care. With managed health care and with medicine for profit, medical decisions may be made and treatments may be offered on the basis of cost, putting the insured at risk, and the poor and uninsured at a distinct disadvantage. Nursing homes for the elderly, skilled facilities for those with Alzheimer's disease, rehabilitation centers, and treatment programs are either not covered by insurance or provide very limited coverage and require prohibitive premiums. The result is care for those who can afford it and neglect for those who cannot. The poor and unemployed are at the greatest disadvantage. The cost of prescription drugs makes it impossible for the uninsured, for those with chronic conditions that require multiple prescriptions, and for the elderly on fixed incomes to afford life-sustaining or lifesaving treatments. The costs for researching and developing new treatments and "miracle drugs" are routinely passed on to the consumer in a way that maximizes profits for the drug companies and their investors. Is it just for those who can afford to invest in the first place to grow even more wealthy at the expense of those who must pay for their health and well-being? Is it a matter of justice when pharmaceutical companies choose to develop drugs to treat chronic conditions, thus guaranteeing income from a lifetime of treatment, rather than to invest in finding a cure? Is a stratified health care system, with benefits distributed according to wealth, just?

There are similar concerns about defense spending and military funding. When funds from social programs are diverted to military and defense needs, there is a direct impact on the quality of life of the poor. Do costly defense contracts and the stockpiling of arms, the relentless pursuit of the newest technologies and the most advanced weapons, exact a human cost that is disproportionately borne by children, the elderly, and the poor?

A persistently contentious issue facing society and religious communities is the question of gay rights. Legal protection in housing and employment is seen by gay people and their supporters as "equal rights" but by opponents as "special rights." Advocates of gay rights see the issue as one of basic justice. In one controversial issue, gays and lesbians observe that many rights accorded to married, opposite-sex couples are denied same-sex couples on the grounds that they are not married, but when they try to marry, the law prohibits them. Attempts to change the law have been met in some states by preemptive legislation making it illegal to enact laws allowing same-sex couples to marry. When cities enact domestic-partner policies that provide same-sex couples with economic and legal benefits, they are struck down as discriminatory against unmarried opposite-sex couples—though these couples have a right to marry that they choose not to exercise. To gay people, the very structure of the law is unjust. Some opponents respond that the issue is not justice, but morality: giving gays and lesbians legal rights and protection legitimizes a "lifestyle" some hold as morally wrong. Implied in such arguments is the belief that morality trumps justice.

Churches wrestle with the issue of ordaining gays and lesbians; some denominations struggle with ordaining women. Some advocates of ordaining gay people and women see the issue as one of simple justice: rights accorded to one group are denied another, creating a de facto situation of discrimination and therefore of injustice. Opponents argue that ordination is not an issue of justice, but of doctrine. The Roman Catholic Church, for instance, maintains that the ordination of women is not possible because Jesus chose only men as his apostles, men who eventually became the "college of bishops" of the early church. Even if the church wanted to ordain women, the argument goes, it does not have the authority to do so (*Catechism of the Catholic Church,* §1577). It is not a matter of justice, but of doctrine. In this case, doctrine trumps justice. In both the examples of gay rights and the ordination of women, the claims of justice are subordinated to the claims of morality or of doctrine, implying that justice is somehow subordinate to morality or doctrine, or at the very least, not essential. The questions can rightly be raised, what kind of moral system does not have at its center a concern for justice? What kind of doctrine is it that conceives of a God for whom justice is not a defining quality?

While the Bible does not address many of these particular issues—nor many others besides—it is nonetheless as eloquent as it is insistent about matters of justice and injustice. Religious communities that claim the Bible as their foundational document and canonical Scripture routinely consult the Bible for what it has to say about God and God's will for us—that is, matters of belief and behavior. Bible teachers, preachers, and evangelists who may be able to cite chapter and verse on such matters as salvation and justification, sexual morality, the role of women, tithing, and the use of alcohol are often less vocal about its teachings on justice. Yet, many biblical books and authors—arising from different times and in different circumstances—champion the cause of justice, attesting to the ubiquity of its importance and the urgency of its claims; indeed, it is no overstatement to say that justice is central to the Bible's understanding of God and of God's will for humanity. The pervasive concern for justice throughout the Bible makes it reasonable to assert that moral systems and doctrinal formulations that do not include justice as a constitutive element are intrinsically deficient.

Before pastors, theologians, and committed believers begin to address the varied issues of justice that face us, we might rightly and profitably consult our sacred writings for guidance. It would be naive to think that these ancient texts could have envisioned the complexity of modern life, or that they might address directly some of the concerns that are peculiar to our age. Nevertheless, the Bible's unwavering commitment to justice and its vision of how justice instructs leadership, shapes society, and guides individuals make it indispensable for our reflection and for our moral guidance. Let's begin to lay the groundwork necessary to see the importance of justice in the Bible, and then specifically to understand justice in the book of Isaiah.

Justice Then

The Bible's first explicit mention of justice is linked, tellingly, to a question concerning the nature of God. It comes in that poignant scene in which Abraham and God discuss the fate of the notoriously sinful cities of Sodom and Gomorrah (Genesis 18). In a soliloquy, YHWH first debates whether to disclose his plans to Abraham, but in the end YHWH decides to share his confidences with him because "I have known him in order that he may command his children and his household after him, that they might keep the way of YHWH—to do righteousness and justice" (*ṣĕdāqâ ûmišpāṭ*, Gen 18:19a). This reflective monologue so contributes to the drama and pathos of the story that the reader may well miss a profound point that summarizes the essence of the moral and religious life of the children of Abraham: "the way of YHWH" is "to do righteousness and justice."

In the end, YHWH chooses to reveal to Abraham his intent to visit the "sin cities" of the Plain. A dismayed Abraham intercedes for the cities, beginning with a pointed question that implicitly impugns the very character of God: "Will you really sweep away the righteous with the wicked?" (18:23). Then, as if he had read YHWH's earlier thoughts, Abraham puts to him a question tinged with irony: "Shall the judge of all the earth not do justice *(mišpāṭ)*?" (18:25b). The irony is this: God fully expects Abraham to instruct his children "to do righteousness and justice" but here is God on the brink of "not doing justice." At stake are some vital issues: Does "the way of YHWH" (18:19) mean one thing for God and another for people? Or, stated somewhat differently, is divine justice qualitatively different from human justice? Is there a universal standard for doing "righteousness and justice" that is to be applied impartially or is it determined by the unique circumstances of the concrete situation? Can the demands of compassion and justice be balanced? Which would be the greater injustice: to let the guilty go free in order to spare the righteous, or to punish the wicked even at the expense of the righteous? Given the greatness of Sodom and Gomorrah's sin, at what point do the concerns of morality trump those of justice? In all these concerns, Abraham's ancient questions strike a disturbingly contemporary note.

With this story in Genesis 18, the reader has scarcely begun the very first book of the Bible and has already been confronted by one of life's—and the Bible's—most persistent and problematic issues: the question of justice. Matters of justice and episodes of injustice refuse to quit the stage of history but find their way into every sphere of life. In the Bible, justice demands the spotlight in both the lyrical ruminations of the sages and the strident denunciations and sorrowful soliloquies of the prophets; even the sorry plight of Job is made to serve as foil to the urgency and magnitude of the issue. Indeed, the concern for justice is found almost everywhere in the Bible—in narrative material,[1] prophecy,[2] laws,[3] psalms,[4] and wisdom.[5] It is found in the some of the oldest material (Covenant Code, Exod 20:22—23:33) and in some of the latest writings (Sirach). In short, it is not the isolated concern of a few authors at a particular time; and, most significantly, it is presented as a matter about which God is urgently and personally concerned.

While the Bible tells the story of Israel, there is a sense in which YHWH, the God of Israel, is the main character of the Bible. Whether YHWH is present as actor, as lawgiver, judge, or plaintiff, as aggrieved lover, as celebrated hero, as worshipped sovereign, or whether he is in the wings, far from the obvious notice of the storyteller and the audience, YHWH stands behind and above the entire history of Israel. Wherever the concern for justice moves to the center of the stage, YHWH, "the God of justice" (Isa 30:18), is rarely far behind. The combination of these two elements, God and the concern for justice, makes for an irresistible and compelling drama. This is true whether justice is considered under its divine, legal, human, or social aspects.

This book sets out to examine one part of the Bible's story of justice, namely, justice in the book of Isaiah. The endeavor sounds deceptively simple; the reality is quite the opposite. There are two major issues to be clarified before the actual study can begin. The first is the vocabulary for "justice" in the Bible. There is a variety of terms and related concepts that must first be sorted out and clarified. To anticipate the outcome of this first issue, we will be studying the Bible's principal term for "justice," namely, *mišpāṭ* (pronounced "mish-PAHT"). The second issue is what is meant by the "book of Isaiah." While both ancient and modern Bibles contain a book called "Isaiah," it is by no means clear that we are dealing with one book written by one author. These two issues—"justice" in the Bible, and the "book of Isaiah"—will be addressed in the first two chapters of this study. These chapters lay the foundation upon which the rest of the book will be built. Admittedly, foundations are not particularly exciting, and the technicalities and mechanics that are part of laying a good foundation are not always easily understood. But to neglect the foundation puts the entire building at risk. Taking the time to prepare the ground will be well worth the effort.

chapter 1

The Study of Justice in the Bible

Problems of Method

As suggested in the introduction, the concern for justice is found throughout the Bible. For those who wish to understand biblical concepts of justice, this is both fortunate and problematic. It is fortunate that there is lots of evidence to examine and plenty of material to study. As it turns out, the very abundance of material creates its own problems.

It will be helpful first to discuss and clarify some of the problems that affect the method of studying justice in the Bible.

Difficulties Intrinsic to the Study of Justice

1. The Complexity of the Concept. Justice is a complex topic, and its complexity is evident first in the choice of vocabulary. Both the Hebrew words *mišpāṭ* and *ṣĕdāqâ* (righteousness) can, depending on context, be translated by the English word "justice." The concept of social justice is also implied in the term *mêšārîm* (equity). One scholar, Rolf P. Knierim (1995), includes the following terms in the word-field of "justice": *ʾĕmûnâ* (steadfastness); *ʾĕmet* (faithfulness); *ḥesed* (kindness); *šālôm* (sufficiency, peace); *ḥōq* (statute); *miṣwâ* (commandment, ordinance); *tôrâ* (instruction, law); *mûsār* (correction, warning); and *tōm* (completeness). As will be seen below, the choice of terms will lead to different conclusions. For our purposes, the complexity on the level of vocabulary can be minimized by focusing this study primarily on *mišpāṭ*.

Even so, complexity is evident in the wide range of meanings conveyed by *mišpāṭ*. By way of example, Osborne Booth (1942) classifies the meaning of the term in eleven categories, with more than one-third of the occurrences falling into more than one category; Even-Shoshan's concordance (1990) classifies the meaning under seven headings; Robert Culver (1980) describes thirteen "distinct but related" meanings; Rolf Knierim (1995) discusses sixteen "aspects of justice in the horizon of the Old Testament"; and J. L. Mays (1983) delineates three broad spheres within which the term "justice" functions. These studies point both to the multivalence of the term and to the lack of critical agreement as to even the semantic range of the term. Among its nuances, *mišpāṭ* may refer to social custom; to specific laws and ordinances; to court cases, types of proceedings, or the verdict; it may mean the principle or virtue of justice or the specific implementation of a social reform.[1] A careful study of the term in its contexts—both literary and historical—will be critical for accurate understanding.

Further complicating the discussion is a tendency to understand the term by setting it within a conceptual framework, for example, to understand justice as an "extrinsic norm" or to see it functioning in the context of "relationship." In addition to the problems of privileging one framework at the expense of others, and of reducing the multivalence of the term to a more manageable sameness, there are two further difficulties here. One is methodological: extracting terms from their literary and historical contexts and placing them in another interpretive framework does violence to the native environment of the terms. The other danger is the likelihood of importing uncritically into the biblical milieu notions from the interpretive framework. An example may help illustrate this. Because justice pertains to dealings between persons, an interpreter may seek to understand "justice" primarily in terms of how it regulates or functions in relationships, in which case the notion of "relationship" is used as the governing interpretive paradigm. Not untypically, the more biblical term *covenant* is used as the equivalent for "relationship." This poses a serious difficulty. While the English term *covenant* can describe a relationship between equals, biblical covenants more often involve parties of different ranks, as is obvious in the covenant between God and Israel. The problem is this: because moderns tend to understand "relationship" in personalist terms, the biblical notion of "covenant" may be made to conform to those preconceptions. While it is true that the biblical "covenant" does establish a relationship between parties, covenants based on the model of international suzerainty treaties (such as the covenant between God and Israel) establish relationships that codify the authority and power of the suzerain (overlord) on the one hand and, on the other hand, the duties and obligations of the vassal. The fact is that the stern demands of such a covenant are loyalty and obedience, not the mutuality and equality sometimes implied by "relationship." Interpreting "justice" in the context of a broader category such as "relationship" risks distorting the very meaning of the term. In terms of method, it is more sound to interpret each occurrence of the term *mišpāṭ* in the literary and historical context in which it is found. Thus both the multivalence of the term *mišpāṭ* and the necessity of interpreting its every occurrence with attention to its native environment complicate any study of this term.

2. The Distribution of the Term. As mentioned above, the problem of the complexity can be addressed in part by focusing on the particular term *mišpāṭ*. Still, its very frequency makes a comprehensive study of the term *mišpāṭ* somewhat unmanageable: the word occurs 425 times in the Hebrew Bible[2] and is found in 31 of its 39 books.[3] With such a wide distribution, it is evident that the term is to be found in a variety of literary contexts and genres. Further, the sources cover the entire historical range of the literature, from the earliest (tenth century B.C.E.?) to the latest (second century B.C.E.?). Account of these factors must be made in any discussion. Attempts to proceed historically, charting an evolving meaning from early to late sources, suffer from two handicaps: a neglect of literary concerns (Booth's article is an example), and the growing difficulty of dating sources with confidence. Attempts to proceed semantically may neglect social, literary, and theological contexts. Bovati's book (1994) is an example of this latter problem. Bovati examines the vocabulary of legal proceedings, often to the neglect of literary forms, social developments over time, and the actual social institutions that are charged to reestablish justice.

Range of Texts Selected for Study

Treatments of the theme of justice in the Bible typically suffer from one of two problems. On the one hand, the theme is treated globally, in which case an array of relevant texts is marshaled to make a point. In the process, the modern author's ideology may unintentionally drive the selection of texts, leading to a tendentious interpretation. Further, the sheer vastness of the subject requires a selection which, even if rigorously representative, is still only partial. Knierim (1995: 87) estimates that in his semantic field for justice, there are over 3,800 references. Clearly, a study of all such terms would be a monumental undertaking. Treatments that attempt to present "Justice in the Old Testament/Bible" (for example, Nardoni 1997) or, more narrowly, "Justice in the Prophets" (for example, Gossai 1993) have not, as yet, paid adequate attention to the questions of tradition history and literary context, social setting, and theological significance for this array of material.

On the other hand, too narrow a focus, for example, "Justice in the Book of Micah" (Candelaria 1983), does not allow one to extrapolate a broad understanding of justice. Such studies are indispensable for an informed understanding of *mišpāṭ* in a particular setting, but they afford too narrow a base from which to provide a more comprehensive understanding of justice.

Generally, "Justice in Isaiah" is found in surveys of the prophets where it is treated in a few paragraphs, such as in Mays's and Gossai's kaleidoscopic treatments of eighth-century Judean prophets, or in broad summaries, as in Heschel's treatment (1969) of "Justice in the Prophets." An exhaustive study of justice *(mišpāṭ)* in the book of Isaiah that is sensitive to both literary and historical concerns is as yet lacking.

Aspects of Meaning

The wide range of distribution and the multivalence of the term *mišpāṭ* result in widely varying treatments evident in the staggering number of articles and books dealing with justice in the Bible or in its various parts. It would be neither possible nor particularly profitable at this point to survey all of the biblical scholarship on justice or to describe the variety of approaches with all their nuances. Readers who may be more interested in such a perspective can turn to the introduction to Hemchand Gossai's 1993 book, which reviews some of the important scholarship up to 1985.[4] Because of the amount of material available and the broad range of approaches to the topic of justice, it will be helpful to schematize the variety of approaches under three general headings.

Two final comments about this schema. First, a caveat: none of these three approaches to *mišpāṭ* is to be found to the exclusion of the others. For the most part, individual authors tend to emphasize one aspect without explicitly denying others. Second, as indicated above, the word *ṣĕdāqâ* is closely related to *mišpāṭ* and can also mean "justice." It is not surprising, then, that discussions of each of the particular aspects of justice will be affected by which of the two terms is chosen as the point of departure.

1. Political/Social Aspects of Justice. Especially in contemporary discussions of justice, interest focuses on the social, political, and economic aspects.[5] Particularly in liberation theologies, injustice is understood as oppression, and justice as liberation. Often, religious and spiritual concerns are yoked to social programs. The biblical concern for "the widow, the orphan, and the poor" is taken as a cipher for all present-day forms of oppression that demand liberation. While such contemporary approaches are susceptible to ideological manipulation and may sometimes use religious concerns as a front for other agendas, we hasten to point out that the understanding of justice enacted in the political and social realms has an ancient pedigree and a venerable cross-cultural heritage, as shown by the work of Moshe Weinfeld, to which we now turn.

In *Social Justice in Ancient Israel and in the Ancient Near East,* Weinfeld (1995) tracks the vocabulary and social institutions of justice both in the Bible and in extrabiblical sources. His study crosses the historical and geographical terrain from Sumer in the third millennium B.C.E. to Greece and Rome of the classical period and finally into early Christianity and rabbinic Judaism. In the Bible, he traces the language and practice of social justice across the social spectrum from the individual to the just king, and in the religious world from the eschatological king to the deity. Throughout, historical and chronological considerations are secondary to Weinfeld's interests in the cultural and linguistic evidence.

His analysis depends in large measure on understanding the ubiquitous word pair *mišpāṭ ûṣĕdāqâ* not as individual words, for example, "law and justice" or "justice and righteousness," but as a single concept that refers to "social justice." There are two parts to this argument; each will be considered in turn. This discussion is crucial both to the proper understanding of the vocabulary and to our discussion of justice in the remainder of this book.

The first part of Weinfeld's argument is grammatical. To appreciate it, we must digress into a brief, and simplified, discussion of Hebrew grammar. It is a peculiarity of Hebrew that there is a "shortage of adjectives" (Weingreen 1959: 167) and a preponderance of nouns. To make up for this lack, nouns are sometimes used in a variety of ways to modify other nouns. One way this is done is through the "construct" in which one noun is used in a genitive ("of") relationship with another noun. So, for example, there is no adjective in Hebrew for "wooden"; the noun "wood" must be used, as in "idols of wood" for "wooden idols" (Isa 45:20); similarly, there is no adjectival form of "stone," so the noun is used, as in "tablets of stone" for "stone tablets" (Deut 4:13). Another way in which one noun modifies another is through a hendiadys, that is, two nouns joined by "and" to express a single thought. A few examples will help illustrate this. In Genesis 19, God destroys

Sodom and Gomorrah by sending "brimstone and fire," which is a hendiadys for "burning brimstone" (Gen 19:24; Myers 1986: 98). To understand this phrase as a hendiadys means that God does not send two different things, some brimstone and some fire; the two nouns together signify one reality, namely, "burning brimstone" or "sulfurous fire" (JPS, NAB) or "burning sulfur" (NIV). Waltke and O'Connor (1990: 70, #4.4.1b) offer as an example Jer 6:7—"*violence and destruction* resound in her"; they helpfully compare the italicized hendiadys to the English equivalent "assault and battery," which are not two separate acts, but a particular kind of assault. For a final example, consider Job 4:16, in which the Hebrew reads "I heard *silence and a voice*," which means "I heard a whispering voice" (Weingreen), or a "hushed voice" (NIV), or a "still voice" (NAB). All these are examples of two nouns used together to express one thing.

According to Weinfeld, the word pair *mišpāṭ ûṣĕdāqâ* ("justice and righteousness") is to be understood as a hendiadys. Weinfeld bases this judgment on the work of E. Z. Melamed, Y. Avishur, and his own research.[6] While Weinfeld accepts the conclusions of these arguments and cites their references, he does no more than assert them. As this point is of significance to the analysis of justice in Isaiah that follows, a brief examination of his sources here will be helpful.

Summarizing the findings of his first article, "Hendiadys in the Bible" (1945), Melamed writes: "The prophets and poets of the Old Testament were in the habit of breaking up compound linguistic stereotypes and distributing their component elements between the first and second members of the verse; and that, of the two parallel sentences thus formed, some can only be understood by re-writing them into a single prose sentence" (1961: 115). This takes the grammatical points made above a step further. Melamed is saying that the two nouns that comprise a hendiadys can be separated for poetic purposes—but they still refer to only one reality.

At this point, an example may help to clarify the main points. Isaiah 16:5 reads as follows:

Line 1:	(A) A throne shall be established in *kindness*
	(B) and upon it shall sit in *faithfulness* in the tent of David
Line 2:	(A) a judge who seeks *justice*
	(B) and is quick [to do] *righteousness*.

This is a two-line verse, each line being divided into two parts (called "cola")—A and B. It is a common technique in Hebrew poetry to express the same idea using parallel terms in each part (A and B) of the same line. In this verse, there are two sets of word pairs, or what Melamed calls "compound linguistic stereotypes": (line 1) kindness and faithfulness, and (line 2) justice and righteousness. The poet has taken the hendiadys and divided it, placing one element in each half of the verse. Even though the hendiadys is "broken," the two terms express one concept, that is, though *kindness* and *faithfulness*, or *justice* and *righteousness*, each occurs in different parts of the line, each element of the pair nevertheless refers to the same thing. It would be a serious misunderstanding of both the poetry and the grammar to think that "justice" refers to something different from "righteousness." To avoid confusion and to obtain the proper sense, Melamed suggests rewriting the poetic line in a single prose sentence. Weinfeld rewrites this verse as follows: "A throne shall be established with *kindness and faithfulness,* and a devoted judge, who seeks *justice and righteousness* shall sit upon it in the tent of David" (1995: 29, n. 17). The important point is this: even when a hendiadys is broken for the sake of poetic parallelism, the terms are to be understood as signifying one referent. Further, because both terms in a hendiadys have but one referent, the order of the terms can be reversed with no change of meaning.

Avishur's study of "Pairs of Synonymous Words" (1971–1972) confirms the work of Melamed. Avishur agrees that the appearance of correlative terms in two cola is the result of the hendiadys being broken for poetic parallelism. H. A. Brongers (1965), building on the work of Honeyman (1952), cites examples in which the combination of abstract nouns in hendiadys results in something more concrete (in Ps 97:2, *mišpāṭ ûṣĕdāqâ* are the foundation of YHWH's throne).[7] Weinfeld's analysis comports with Brongers's findings: in the word pair *mišpāṭ ûṣĕdāqâ*, the somewhat general qualities are combined to concretize a practical and realizable program of social justice.

The work of all these scholars—Melamed, Avishur, Brongers, and Weinfeld (see also Bazak [1989], Honeyman, and Myers [1986])—contributes to our understanding of *mišpāṭ ûṣĕdāqâ* as a hendiadys. Thus, when we encounter the terms *mišpāṭ ûṣĕdāqâ,* whether in that sequence or reversed, and whether joined by the conjunction or split for parallelism, we will consider them as a hendiadys. Indeed, according to Melamed's study, two cola that are joined by parallelism are even more "tightly interlocked" when the parallel terms are the two terms of a hendiadys (1961: 152).

The first part of Weinfeld's argument is that the *mišpāṭ ûṣĕdāqâ* is a hendiadys; the second part of his argument is that the hendiadys refers to "social justice." He begins by examining the Akkadian evidence—Akkadian being the East Semitic language used by the ancient Mesopotamian peoples from the third to the first millennium B.C.E., especially in the Babylonian and Assyrian empires. Weinfeld documents royal decrees by which inequities in society were righted, debts canceled, lands reapportioned, slaves liberated, and the like. Such decrees were expected upon the accession of a new king, but could be undertaken at other decisive times as well. Weinfeld's point is that such decrees were a matter of *social policy,* not narrowly conceived *legal reforms.* Thus "to do justice and righteousness" (Hebrew *ʿăśôt mišpāṭ ûṣĕdāqâ* = Akkadian *kittam u mīšaram šakānum*) is to address social inequities and wrongs, and to ameliorate the situation of the destitute. These kinds of actions "cannot be aided by righteous judgements in court alone, but by the elimination of exploitation and oppression on the part of the oppressors" (1995: 7). He later explicitly asserts that "*[mišpāṭ]* in this word-pair should not be understood in the juridical sense" (1995: 35).[8]

The task of maintaining social justice so that equity and freedom prevail is the particular responsibility of the king. Unfortunately, because it was so rarely achieved in Israel, it came to be expected as the defining quality of the eschatological king. But social justice was equally the task of the individual: having enjoyed the benefits of freedom from slavery, the Israelite similarly extends "justice and righteousness" to the neighbor, both in refraining from doing harm (for example, Ezek 18:5-8), but especially in caring for the needy, particularly orphans, widows, and the poor (for example, Jer 7:5-6; Zech 7:9-10). We will have occasion to return to and expand on these points in the course of this study of Isaiah.

This concern for "justice and righteousness" is also reflected in the Israelite understanding of God, the divine sovereign, who, in creation, established the world in justice; who at Sinai established laws of justice; and who will one day reveal himself as the just and righteous ruler of all nations. Weinfeld's study shows both the pervasive reach of "justice and righteousness" in Israelite tradition, wisdom, and law and the eminently pragmatic expression of this concern in the practice of social justice.

2. Theological and Moral Aspects of Justice.[9] General articles sometimes approach justice theologically, treating "justice" under "Just" (Mafico 1992) or even under "Justness of God" (Steinmueller and Sullivan 1956). This, in turn, goes in two directions. In Christian exegesis, consideration of justice is most often a discussion of justification.[10] The point of departure is the New Testament and the Greek word *dikaiosynē,* which is then traced back to Hebrew *ṣĕdāqâ*. Or, the concern is to show how God is just, in which case the discussion begins with *ṣĕdāqâ* and moves towards a philosophical consideration of theodicy; in such discussions, the book of Job figures prominently. In either approach, religious and theological considerations eclipse concerns for the enactment of justice in the social sphere and its guarantee in law.

Another approach understands justice in moral terms, that is, as a virtue expressed in action. Debate often centers on whether the basis of morality is to be found in laws and external norms or in "relationship" with God and community. As we shall see, these theological and moral aspects of justice are well represented in the biblical text.

3. Legal Aspects of Justice.[11] The term *mišpāṭ* derives from the verbal root *špṭ (šāpaṭ),* meaning "to exercise the processes of government" (Culver 1980: 947), processes that include our notions of executive, legislative, and judicial functions. Not unexpectedly, then, the legal overtones are particularly pronounced. In fact, the plural form *mišpāṭîm* means "ordinances" and is frequently found in parallel with "statute" *(ḥōq/ḥuqqâ)* and "commandments" *(miṣwōt)*. Bovati's extensive bibliography shows the widespread attention this area of research has generated. His book well represents the legal aspects of justice.

The above survey has highlighted three major approaches to justice—the social, the moral (relational), and the legal aspects. Just as no one of the above approaches adequately addresses the full range of meanings, no individual approach fails to bring something significant to the discussion. The a priori exclusion of one or more possible ranges of meaning is as unwarranted as the exclusive approach of any one. In approaching a topic so unwieldy as justice/*mišpāṭ* in the Bible, it is understandable that interpretive frameworks be employed to bring some order to the discussion. The strength of these approaches is that they provide maps through some very rough and varied terrain; the weakness is that each one directs the reader down a main road without the pleasure of scenic detours on the more interesting side roads and byways, or without a consideration that theirs may not be the only path. The drawback, in short, is to sacrifice the varied nuances of the subject for the cohesion of the interpretive schema. The study we are about to undertake is a modest approach, and the scope of the work is limited. This will allow the luxury to examine each text in some detail with the hope of "doing justice" to the rich, varied, and complex subject that is a central concern to the prophets generally, and to the book of Isaiah in particular.

Justice in the Book of Isaiah

The task we set for ourselves is to examine one portion of the biblical story of justice, namely, justice/*mišpāṭ* in the book of Isaiah. The value of this endeavor comes clearly to light in the context of the book's structure.

As we will show in the next chapter, there is wide scholarly consensus that the book is divided into three main parts, each originating from different authors and distinct historical and social settings; these divisions are commonly called First Isaiah (chs. 1–39), Second Isaiah (chs. 40–55), and Third Isaiah (chs. 56–66). For now, we merely note that since the nineteenth century, scholarship has focused on these distinct collections of material gathered under the one name Isaiah.

The concern for justice/*mišpāṭ* figures prominently in each of the three sections of the book. The importance of *mišpāṭ* is attested by the frequency of its occurrence, its thematic centrality, and its structural placement. The term *mišpāṭ* is found twenty-two times in First Isaiah, eleven times in Second Isaiah, and nine times in Third Isaiah, for a total of forty-two occurrences in the book; forms from the root *špṭ* (*šāpaṭ* = to judge, to which the word *mišpāṭ* is related) occur another fifteen times throughout. The theme of justice or the act of judging is prominently placed in the editorial framework, chs. 1 and 66, as well as at the opening of each division: 2:2-5; 40:12-31; 56:1-8. The theme's significance is heightened and extended through its frequent alliance with the related terms *ṣĕdāqâ* (righteousness) and *yĕšûʿâ* (salvation). The expectation that justice be upheld is associated with key figures in each section of the book: in First Isaiah, with the leadership in general, that is, elders, magistrates, priests, and princes, and particularly with the reigning and the eschatological king; in Second Isaiah, with the Servant of YHWH; in Third Isaiah, YHWH himself is the guarantor of justice for the dispirited community.

A further factor commends itself to this study. In recent years, there has been growing interest in addressing the final stage of the book of Isaiah as a whole rather than focusing primarily on its reconstructed earlier sources. Increasingly, attention has focused on how the three separate parts can be regarded as a single book.[12] Editorial intentionality, literary structure, and thematic or theological concerns have all been advanced as rubrics by which the book's unity can be better appreciated. Because *mišpāṭ* is one of three key terms in the book of Isaiah (the other two being *ṣĕdāqâ*/righteousness and *yĕšûʿâ*/salvation; Coggins 1996: 367), this study will suggest that *mišpāṭ* and the theme of justice can provide another such connecting thread. For all these reasons, a systematic study of the term *mišpāṭ* in the book of Isaiah should shed light both on the understanding of justice itself and on a key theme in a major prophetic book.

The Goal of This Study

In seeking to come to an understanding of justice, this study will examine every occurrence of the term *mišpāṭ* in the book of Isaiah and will refer to *ṣĕdāqâ*/*ṣedeq* and related terms when appropriate. By selecting a large and clearly defined corpus of material, the book of Isaiah, we can examine *mišpāṭ* over a significant period of time and in sufficient depth to be context-specific and productive, while at the same time avoiding the danger of narrowness. Further, this study will offer some concluding observations on how the term *mišpāṭ* and the language of justice intersect with other major themes throughout the Isaian corpus.

Before we can take up the study of *mišpāṭ* in the book of Isaiah, however, it is necessary to come to an understanding of the book itself. To do this, we will review a variety of approaches to the book of Isaiah taken by scholars today.

chapter 2

Isaiah: The Prophet(s), the Book, the Commentators

As difficult as the book of Isaiah may be to read on its own, reading it with the assistance of commentaries can be even more difficult. Especially if one consults a variety of commentators, one is likely to become even more perplexed by the very divergent views and varied interpretations of scholars. The book seems to generate as many theories as it attracts commentators. In a sense, the book of Isaiah is the Gordian knot of biblical studies, challenging armies of commentators and expositors, generations of readers and believers to unravel its mysteries. Its tangle of sources and editorial layers, of historical references and timeless insights, defy confident commentary and frequently humble the creative labors of scholars as the interpretive maneuvers of one generation are revealed as inadequate or incomplete by the labors of the next generation. Each hard-won insight is a tribute to the determined diligence of scholarship, to the sometimes profound and passionate commitment of religious belief, and to the still greater genius of the authors who now stand anonymous behind the name Isaiah. The book's obvious signs of complex growth and development over time are more transparent in Isaiah than in any other book of the Bible; indeed, its extraordinary complexity rivals that of the Pentateuch. It is perhaps this very complexity and inherent mystery that continue to invite the interest of scholars and to speak to the searching hearts of believers.

Here I describe the wide variety of approaches taken by scholars to understand and explain the book of the prophet Isaiah. Readers without much experience in modern study of the Bible and newcomers to the book of Isaiah may well be amazed at how one book can generate such a variety of proposals and offer so many different understandings. The following overview will introduce beginners to the broad strokes of various modern proposals. For experienced Bible students and scholars, this overview will provide a snapshot of the present state of affairs in Isaianic studies. This overview will end with a statement of the understanding upon which this book will proceed.

Overview

Common to most modern approaches to the book of Isaiah is the recognition that it is not the work of one author. This recognition dates back more than two hundred years. Already in the eighteenth century, Johann G. Eichhorn (1783) and Johann C. Döderlein (1789) had observed that the historical and geographic references, as well as the vocabulary, of Isaiah 40–66 were distinctly different from those of chs. 1–39. Both scholars argued that chs. 1–39 could be assigned to the eighth-century prophet, Isaiah of Jerusalem, but that chs. 40–66 presumed the Babylonian exile of the sixth century as their setting. With Isaiah of Jerusalem beginning his ministry around 742 B.C.E., and the exile ending some two hundred years later, it was obvious that the book was the work of more than one author, perhaps even several authors. The modern critical assessment of the book of Isaiah as a work of many authors was most forcefully presented by Bernhard Duhm, who in 1892 argued that, with the exception of the "Servant of the Lord Songs," chs. 40–55 should be attributed to an unknown prophet working during the period of the exile (587–539) and that chs. 56–66 should be attributed in their entirety to yet another prophet working in Jerusalem around 450 B.C.E.. These proposed authors are anonymous and are labeled "Second Isaiah" and "Third Isaiah," respectively, because their prophecies have been added to the book of the "First Isaiah." Though aspects of Duhm's proposals, notably the dating and the unity of chs. 56–66, continue to be debated, his three-part division of the book has been firmly established and widely accepted in modern critical study.

In our day, two related concerns have shifted the attention of scholars away from the historical reconstruction of biblical texts in general, and of the book of Isaiah in particular. One is the awareness that the individual books of the Bible belong to a "canon," that is, an authoritative collection of books recognized by the church or synagogue as normative for teaching and believing. Interpretation of a passage depends ultimately on its context in the canonical book and in the complete Bible, not on its supposed and reconstructed "original" setting. "Canonical criticism," as it is sometimes called, arises from the concerns of a particular faith community for the way in which the biblical text functions normatively for that faith community.

The other concern that has affected modern interpretation of the Bible is more secular or academic in its interests. "Literary criticism" approaches each book as a literary unity. It contends that each book has been preserved and presented to us *as a book*. While it may be interesting to speculate on how, when, and why passages or parts of the text came to be, what matters is how the book actually exists for readers today. Both canonical and literary criticism, for different reasons, focus on the final form of the text. These approaches do not reject the historical settings or origins of the biblical books, but they do relativize the importance of historical and redactional research.

In keeping with these developments, interest in the book of Isaiah has also shifted away from historical criticism and toward unitary readings. For the most part, the historical assumptions behind the three-fold division of the book are still widely accepted, but many scholars, for either literary or canonical reasons, have directed their efforts primarily to a unitary analysis. Even within these two broad approaches—historical and unitary—there is a wide array of opinions and interpretations. It will be helpful at this point to cite some examples of these various approaches to the book of Isaiah. It is not our purpose to examine each approach in detail, but to offer examples to illustrate some of the main trends.

Approaches in Isaianic Studies

"Isaiah" as Author

Historical evaluations of the material in the book of Isaiah run the gamut from those that attribute the entire book to the eighth-century prophet, Isaiah of Jerusalem, to those that assert that none of the book originates with him, and finally to those that hold that some but not all is attributable to the eighth-century prophet.

1. The Entire Book Is Early and Original. In a 1993 introduction and commentary on the prophecy of Isaiah, the evangelical commentator J. Alec Motyer argues that the book is exactly what it says it is: from first to last, it is the work of Isaiah of Jerusalem. Rejecting the findings and claims of critical scholarship, Motyer believes that the eighth-century prophet Isaiah is responsible for the written work in its entirety and in its present arrangement: "The whole book is a huge mosaic in which totally pre-exilic material is made to serve pre-exilic, exilic, post-exilic and eschatological purposes" (31) and is "the product of one mind" (25). The sections dealing with the Babylonian exile and the postexilic resettlement are the prophet's predictions of that far-distant future uttered under divine inspiration. According to Motyer, the nineteenth-century rationalism that undergirds the historical-critical method unfortunately dismissed out of hand the possibility of predictive prophecy and thus set critical scholarship down the erroneous path of fragmentary composition and multiple authorship. Motyer refutes the grounds on which the conclusions of historical criticism allegedly rest, namely, arguments from geography, history, and literature; he supplements his attack with arguments based on his understanding of prophecy and theology.

In discussing the various elements that point to the unity of the book and its authorship, Motyer gives the Memoirs (chs. 6–8) an important role. In the call narrative in ch. 6, the holiness of God overwhelms the prophet in an intensely personal religious encounter; indeed, the holiness of God comes to dominate the prophet's consciousness, his ministry, and his writing. The "Holy One of Israel" is a title of singular importance in Motyer's assessment of the prophet and his book. Motyer's conclusion of a single author, Isaiah of Jerusalem, producing a unified, integral work means that the work of canonical and literary criticism is collapsed into the historical endeavor.[1]

In general, evangelical scholars and those who believe the Bible is to be interpreted literally accept the reality of predictive prophecy, that is, God inspires a prophet to know the future and enables him to predict what will come to pass. Thus, it is entirely credible that Isaiah living in the eighth century B.C.E. can speak with precise knowledge of people and events some two hundred years later and can even provide the name of the Persian king, Cyrus (Isa 45:1), despite the fact that the Persian Empire isn't even known in the eighth century. By contrast, modern historical critics of the Bible, regardless of their personal religious beliefs and theological convictions, try to understand and explain biblical texts in the same way historians understand and explain other texts—on the basis of verifiable data that are subject to examination and rational explanation, that is, without recourse to supernatural causes. Because private divine revelation cannot be verified, it is not accepted as an explanation for the appearance in an eighth-century text of a sixth-century name. Only someone living at the time of, or after, Cyrus could know of him. Such "secular," or more properly, "historical," beliefs make possible theories about the book of Isaiah such as those that follow.

2. The Entire Book Is Late and Anonymous. The 1983 commentary for the Old Testament Library by Otto Kaiser argues that the book in its entirety is an anonymous work from the exilic and postexilic periods. "The foundation of the collection may be seen as a smaller collection of prophetic sayings, presumably first made at the beginning of the fifth century, and influenced by the theology of the Deuteronomistic History. It begins with the earliest sayings, contained in ch. 1, and is continued in the basic material of chs. 28–31" (1983: 1). For the anonymous author(s), the past was used to foreshadow the author's present reality in the sixth century. Thus, the crisis faced by Isaiah and Hezekiah in 703–701 (recorded in 2 Kgs 18:17—20:19) provides the theological lens through which to understand the destruction of Jerusalem and the exile of the people in 587/586. According to Kaiser, because that earlier crisis showcased the prophet Isaiah, his name came to be associated with this anonymous collection composed in the sixth century.

For Kaiser, too, the Memoirs of 6:1—8:19 (+ 9:2-7 [MT 1-6]) are pivotal. The nucleus of the Memoirs, found in 7:1-9, is a theological narrative that attempts to respond to the demise of the Davidic dynasty and the decimation of the people. The first-person narrative material in chapters 6 and 8, which frames this nucleus, is a fictitious way of transposing the entire account into the time of Isaiah. Thus, the book as a prophetic collection is not datable to the eighth century nor attributable to the historical figure of Isaiah mentioned in 2 Kings.[2]

The Historical-Critical Approach to Isaiah 1–39

Between the all or none positions represented by Motyer and Kaiser, most critical scholars recognize that the book is built around a nucleus of authentically Isaianic material. Modern critics believe that anything that can be attributed to the historical figure, Isaiah of Jerusalem, is to be found exclusively in chs. 1–39. These chapters, rather than the entire book, will be the focus of the discussion that follows. Many modern critics believe that the "nucleus" of Isaiah's prophecies was later subjected to extensive revisions. Once such a nucleus is posited, the question naturally arises, "What can be attributed to Isaiah of Jerusalem?" The effort to identify what is "authentic" or "genuine" was a major critical concern of Isaianic studies for most of the twentieth century, and varying opinions on virtually every line are not wanting.

1. The Eighth-Century Isaiah as Author. Broadly speaking, on the one hand, there are those who hold that almost all of chs. 1–39 are authentically Isaianic. John H. Hayes and Stuart A. Irvine maintain that "with the exception of Isaiah 34–35, practically all of the prophetic speech material in what is traditionally called first Isaiah—that is Isaiah 1–39—derives from the eighth century B.C.E. prophet" (1987: 13). Similar views are held by Y. Kaufmann (1970: 382), who believes that not even a single non-Isaianic verse can be found in Isaiah 1–33.

2. "Authentic Core" and Literary Development. Among historical critics, the majority position holds that at the heart of Isaiah 1–39 lies a collection of prophecies that originated with Isaiah of Jerusalem and that underwent subsequent editing and additions.

Ronald E. Clements (1980) is fairly representative of this position. He attributes to Isaiah of Jerusalem the bulk of chs. 2–12, which record prophecies uttered by Isaiah during the Syro-Ephraimite crisis (735–733 B.C.E.; see Isa 7:1-8:15 and 2 Kgs 16:1-20) when Ahaz was king of Judah. The command in Isa 30:8 to write his words in a book for a future time suggests that his prophecies uttered during King Hezekiah's attempted revolt against Sennacherib in 705–701 B.C.E. were perhaps also gathered together, forming an important supplementary collection now found in chs. 28–31. All of these prophecies were assembled as part of a major written collection of the prophet's words, namely, 2:1—32:20. Clements posits that the collection underwent a major redaction in the period of Josiah (640–609 B.C.E.). There were two further redactions: one after 587 B.C.E. designed to interpret the event of the fall of Jerusalem in light of Isaiah's prophecies, and a fifth-century redaction responsible for most of the "apocalyptic" material in chs. 24–27 and 34–35. Chapter 1, for the most part authentically Isaianic, was later gleaned from his prophecies and prefaced to this collection sometime during the exile or later to serve as an introduction. Despite evidence of extensive editing and a complex and protracted history of transmission, the process of recording, preserving, and interpreting Isaiah's prophecies began in his own lifetime. Clements finds it altogether reasonable that "a significant body of written prophecies from Isaiah came into being during the prophet's own lifetime. That these were edited and collected together with other prophecies before the prophet's death is then a reasonable assumption" (1980: 4).

In much the same vein, but with attention focused on the literary forms, their structure, setting, and intention, Marvin Sweeney's commentary (1996) attends to the historical development and literary growth of the Isaianic corpus with even greater precision. He identifies the authentic material of Isaiah and assigns those texts to four different periods in the prophet's career. Like Clements, he sees evidence for three subsequent redactions: one each in the late seventh, sixth, and fifth centuries. For each of these redactions, Sweeney identifies the purported setting that the text addresses and suggests the intentions of the redactors. The bulk of his work contributes to a reconstruction and understanding of the redactional history of the book. Still, it is based on the presumption that the "authentic" words of Isaiah of Jerusalem are recoverable and identifiable.

Isaiah as a Unified Literary Work

For traditional commentators like Motyer and Young, the unity of the text is found in the author himself: one man, Isaiah of Jerusalem, wrote the entire text. Motyer's starting point is the final ("Isaian") form of the text. Unlike Sweeney and other redaction critics, he places "the originating and organizing mind at the beginning rather than the end" (1993: 30) of the compositional process. Though Motyer is committed to a reading of the book as a unitary work, his accounting of the book's unity brings him to a different starting point and leads to different conclusions from those reached by most others who also share concern for the unity of the book, but do not posit single authorship as the source of that unity.

For modern critical scholars, the focus of Isaianic studies has shifted in recent years. Just as the multiple sources and authorship of the book of Isaiah excited the curiosity of previous generations of scholars, the question of the book's final unity occupies much of this generation's intellectual energy. Growing interest in the final shape of the book is so intense that Sweeney can rightly claim that "the final form of the book has clearly established itself as the central issue of Isaiah studies" (1993: 140). This turn of events, as Seitz notes, does not discredit earlier historical-critical research but in an ironic way confirms it: "it could be said that the recent search for unity and coherence in the book of Isaiah, along literary and theological lines, has become a concern of the newer redaction-critical studies precisely because it is now taken as settled that the message of the larger book has moved far beyond the original eighth-century setting of the historical Isaiah" (1988a: 18). Seitz then suggests that the critical question to be faced now is, "what are the internal features that enable the book to be read as a coherent whole?" Or, even more basically, how did various collections of oracles, sayings, and narratives, originating from different authors at different times, come to be united in one book which we now call the book of Isaiah? It is to this concern that we now turn.

1. Redactional Unity. As was the case in discussing the historical origins and development of the book of Isaiah, there is a wide variety of approaches to understanding how the book of Isaiah attained its present unity. H. G. M. Williamson (1994: 3–17) conveniently summarizes the scholarship from Duhm until the present and describes six approaches.

a. The two major portions of the book (chs. 1–39 and 40–66) developed independently of one another and were combined at a late date, perhaps (so some suggest) to conserve precious scroll space or to create a scroll of approximately the same length as those of Jeremiah, Ezekiel, and the Twelve.

b. The unity of the book is due to the work of an Isaianic school of disciples who conserved the original material while adding commentary, updates, and wholly new material in the spirit of Isaiah.

c. Redaction and composition were closely associated processes. Perhaps as Second Isaiah composed his own work, he undertook a redaction of First Isaiah. Or, alternately, a late redaction of chs. 1–39 and an independent but originally shorter Second Isaiah were combined, and in the process Second Isaiah was expanded in order to link it more closely with First Isaiah.

d. Unity is to be found in the editorial work most clearly evident in broad themes which link the three portions of the book, themes such as blindness and deafness, divine election, God's plan, former and latter things, the Holy One of Israel, and so on.

e. Some studies find unity in the overall structure of the book, seeing, for example, conscious parallels in chs. 1 and 65–66, and in chs. 5–6 and 36–40, or verbal, thematic, and historical connections between chs. 39 and 40.

f. Finally, canonical, new literary, and reader-response criticisms look for unity not in its history of composition, but in the context, whether ancient or modern, in which the text is read.

Williamson's own approach seems to be a variation on the third scheme described above. He holds that it was Second Isaiah himself who "included a version of the earlier prophecies [First Isaiah's] with his own and edited them in such a way as to bind the two parts of the work together" (1994: 241). Rolf Rendtorff suggests that First Isaiah was edited in view of Second Isaiah, though he doesn't specify whether Second Isaiah was himself aware of, or influenced by, First Isaiah (1993a).

All these competing redactional theories have turned scholarship 180 degrees in its assessment of the book of Isaiah. Earlier scholarship was concerned with the "original Isaiah" and debated the existence of a Second and a Third Isaiah. Now interest is focused on later redactors and editors who were responsible for structuring and preserving the book as we know it. Interest in these last stages of development and composition have led some scholars to question whether it is even possible to talk about a "book" attributable to Isaiah of Jerusalem. Seitz, for example, says:

> So-called Second and Third Isaiah are far more coherent and temporally locatable than First Isaiah, which has its own complex history, extending in some cases into a much later time period. The whole notion of Second and Third Isaiah depends in no small part on there being a clear First Isaiah. *Such an Isaiah is not to be found.* Isaiah 1–39 is an extremely complex collection of material, with a diverse background. (1988b: 111, italics added)

Peter Ackroyd, too, has serious "doubts about the propriety of a method which makes this assumption, as so many commentaries and works of introduction do, that it is possible to consider Isaiah 1–39 as a book separate from the whole in which it is now contained" (1987: 79). He does not think it is possible to reconstruct a life and times of the prophet Isaiah from the book, which is geared instead, through the labors of its editors and redactors, to "the presentation of the prophet as authoritative spokesman" (1987: 94) announcing oracles of doom and salvation.

The main concern of the book, according to Ackroyd, is not the messenger, but the authority of the message, which is to be found not "in the reconstruction of the original moment . . . [but] in the continuing process by which prophetic word and receptive hearing interact" (1987: 104). Thus, for some, the very existence of a "First Isaiah," and for others, the priority of a "First Isaiah" as the "core" or bedrock of the Isaianic tradition that earlier scholarship had taken as the starting point for discussing the book of Isaiah, can no longer be assumed. Whatever the historical origins of chs. 1–39, their present form, structure, and inclusion as part of a larger book constitute the essential context for their interpretation.

This last point is made forcefully by a number of commentators. Sweeney, for example, believes that exegesis must begin with the final form of the book, its final perspectives and literary character that, in turn, "provide the basis for analytical work designed to identify earlier textual stages." Even then, this analytical work has as its goal determining "the hermeneutical perspectives and influence of the text's redactors in shaping the final form of the text" (1993: 147). In his most recent commentary, Sweeney (1996a) follows this method rigorously, granting priority to the structure of the book as a literary work. He discerns the following structure for the book:

1. 1:1—33:24	Concerning YHWH's plans for worldwide sovereignty at Zion
a. 1:1-31	Prologue
b. 2:1—33:24	Prophetic instruction concerning YHWH's plans: announcement of the Day of YHWH
2. 34:1—66:24	Concerning realization of YHWH's plans for worldwide sovereignty at Zion
a. 34:1—54:17	Prophetic instruction concerning the realization of YHWH's plans
b. 55:1—66:24	Prophetic exhortation to adhere to YHWH's covenant

Each section is first subjected to minute structural analysis, then its genre determined. Only then is its setting, both historical and redactional, considered and finally its intention explicated. With his focus on structure, Sweeney gives priority to redactional concerns. Historical references and clues, though addressed, are subordinated to literary, structural, and thematic concerns. In this light, Sweeney suggests that Isaiah 1–39, rather than being a collection of words stemming from Isaiah ben Amoz and others, is better understood as "the preface that looks forward to Isa 40–66, and Isa 40–66 is presented as the completion which presupposes Isa 1–39" (1988: 7).[3]

Similarly, Christopher Seitz maintains that interpretation should favor the final form of the text over the separate blocks of material determined by textual deconstruction. The warrant for the priority of the unified book is found in the text itself, which is presented with one superscription for the entire book (1:1) and one call narrative (ch. 6), and which shows no literary markers signaling the boundaries between First, Second, and Third Isaiah (1988b: 109–12). In addition, the complex network of cross-references and themes not only recommends but requires that each unit be read in light of the whole book.

Though Seitz and Sweeney work with the book as a whole as the primary context for interpretation, each nonetheless recognizes the importance of the historical context in understanding the meaning of the text.[4] As Williamson states succinctly, "a properly synchronic reading depends on a prior, rigorous diachronic analysis" (1995: 214). In the end, diachronic and synchronic concerns work together in bringing to light various meanings of the text.[5]

2. Literary/Canonical Unity. Some practitioners of canonical and literary criticism take the text as it stands in its present form without endeavoring either to recover its original literary or artistic unity on the one hand or, on the other hand, to recover the historical contexts that gave rise to the text's reconstructed prior traditions. In the case of Isaiah, Childs, for example, maintains that historical references, particularly in Second and Third Isaiah, have been deliberately suppressed in order to give the material its distinctive and purely theological shape, allowing it to be a prophetic word unencumbered by specific historical referents (1979: 326).[6] The entire book, presented under the title "The Vision of Isaiah," stands as a literary and theological work with its own integrity, preserved in its present form for a purpose; reconstruction of its historical context or redactional history not only serves little theological purpose, but runs directly counter to the book's (obvious) intention.

The canonical approach is taken by Walter Brueggemann in his recent two-volume commentary on the entire book of Isaiah (1998). Brueggemann accepts the scholarly consensus of the "Three Isaiahs" and recognizes the literary complexity of the book. He comments, however, that the canonical approach "seeks to understand the final form of the complex text as an integral statement offered by the shapers of the book for theological reasons" (1998a: 4). At almost every turn, he acknowledges the historical circumstances that possibly gave rise to the text, but then moves on to comment more substantively on the significance of the text for the interpretation of the book.

For Brueggemann and canonical critics, each individual textual unit finds its meaning neither in original history nor in redactional history, but primarily in the context of the book itself and its theological function for the community of the synagogue or church.

As the discussion above suggests, this turn in scholarship from original historical setting to final literary context has proved to be a fertile ground for exegesis and has yielded significant and illuminating insights into the book as a whole and its constitutive parts. Yet this focus on the final shape of the book and its unity as a literary or canonical work is not without its own problems. Indeed, this literary approach has given interpretive priority to the text's final voice in the same way that historical criticism had given final authority to the original words of the prophet. Unitary readings assert that the text's final form is the primary arbiter of meaning and that reconstructed historical or literary settings that predate the final redaction are of secondary interest, belonging as they do to a no longer extant or recoverable context. What is in danger of being lost in this approach is the "originating genius" (Boadt 1997)[7] to which the "final form" ostensibly owes its identity.

All of this shows the difficulty facing present-day commentators on Isaiah. Is it possible to speak meaningfully or confidently of each or any of the three "Isaiahs"? Is each of these three merely a cipher or convenient peg on which to hang this or that text or theme? Are the reconstructed original words or the final redacted words the controlling factor in interpretation? Is it even possible or desirable to speak of "original words" or an "authentic core"? Attempts to isolate the authentic words of Isaiah, which the previous generation of scholars staked out with such certainty, prove to be a shifting landscape to some present-day commentators. An approach like that of Motyer, who takes the entire text as authentic, seems naive in light of the historical and literary evidence. The same evidence suggests that Ackroyd's view, that the present shape of the text has been so profoundly affected by its redactors that all we can glean from it is their "presentation of the prophet," seems too agnostic. Between these two poles stands Sweeney, who, sensitive to redactional concerns and the text's final literary shape, assigns with great precision texts to Isaiah in four specific periods.[8] At present, a wide range of competing methods is available simultaneously to scholars: recent years have seen the production of both massive historical-critical commentaries (three volumes on Isaiah 1–39 by Hans Wildberger [1982, 1991, 1997] and three volumes on Isaiah 40–55 by Jan L. Koole [1997, 1998]) as well as a canonical commentary by Brueggemann (two volumes); in addition, there are numerous articles and studies that approach all or part of the book of Isaiah through literary and reader-response methods. Such interpretive diversity makes it difficult to know how to proceed.

A Proposed Approach

The questions raised above indicate the volatile but fertile state of Isaianic studies today. In order to proceed clearly, it is both desirable and necessary to stake out one's position on the issues. Stating clearly what this study hopes to accomplish and how it will proceed is an important starting point.

Rendtorff has advocated thematic study as a profitable direction in Isaianic research (1996: 44), the value of which can be seen in the many such studies undertaken in recent years.[9] Surprisingly, a comprehensive study of the term *mišpāṭ* in the book of Isaiah has not yet been undertaken, even though, as Coggins points out, it is, along with *ṣĕdāqâ* (righteousness) and *yĕšûʿâ* (salvation), one of three key terms in Isaiah (1996: 367). This study seeks to address that lack by examining, as noted earlier, the concept of justice *(mišpāṭ)* in the book of Isaiah. We will address those passages that deal with the word *mišpāṭ* as well as its verbal root *špṭ* (*šāpaṭ* = to judge), and the verbal noun *šōpēṭ* (judge). In addition, this study will consider, as appropriate, other words closely associated with *mišpāṭ* such as *ṣĕdāqâ/ṣedeq* (righteousness) and *yĕšûʿâ* (salvation). Attention will also be given to those people who are routinely deprived of justice, namely, orphans, widows, and the poor, as well as the social manifestations of injustice such as corrupt legal practices, land-grabbing, economic exploitation, oppression, violence, and so on. Each of these terms and concepts will be examined within the larger context of the literary limits of the passage in which it occurs. Obviously, this selective interest at once limits the number of passages to be considered in detail. In part, this study will address the thematic use of the term *mišpāṭ* in the book as a whole and will treat the term synchronically.

However, because the composition and redaction of the book cover such a long time—from the eighth to the fifth century or later—it is natural to wonder whether the meaning of the term evolved or changed over that time. It will thus be helpful to study *mišpāṭ* not only in its particular literary unit and in the book as a whole, but also in its historical context as best it can be recovered. Given the complex compositional and redactional history of the book, and the debate about both the validity of such an enterprise and the specific dating of individual passages, it will be helpful now to set out the structural and historical assumptions under which this study will proceed.

Despite the range of approaches to the book of Isaiah described in the first part of this chapter, it is nonetheless possible to begin with some widely held beliefs about the book of Isaiah, beliefs so widely held, in fact, that it is possible to speak of a consensus. First, there is general agreement as to the broad divisions of the three works designated First, Second, and Third Isaiah. Seitz, citing what he affirms to be one of "the assured results of critical scholarship," summarizes this consensus, which he calls perhaps "the greatest historical-critical consensus of the modern period" (1988a: 14):

> In the case of the Book of Isaiah, three basic historical situations can be reconstructed: (1) for (much of) chapters 1–39: Judah in the Assyrian period, especially during the critical years of Ahaz and Hezekiah; (2) for chapters 40–55: Israel in exile, in the mid-sixth century B.C.E., during the period of waning Babylonian strength; and (3) for chapters 56–66: Judah/Jerusalem in the late sixth century, back in the homeland, concerned with the reestablishment of the community along social and religious lines. (1988a: 19)

I agree with Seitz in his description of that consensus and will operate within those most general historical and geographical frameworks.

While some passages provide detailed historical settings (for example, Isaiah 7; 36–39), often the text is simply too laconic to allow the kind of precision with which some commentators proceed, and the disagreement among scholars over precise details makes almost any consensus unlikely. To make interpretation dependent on precise conjectural historical reconstructions is precarious. We can proceed validly and profitably by situating passages either in preexilic, exilic, or postexilic periods and by appropriately noting their corresponding address to people in the land of Judah or in Babylon. While this is somewhat easier in dealing with the material in Second and Third Isaiah, the varied material in First Isaiah is obviously more complex. We will make some attempt to determine those texts that can, with some plausibility, be attributed to Isaiah of Jerusalem. Nevertheless, even passages that some commentators attribute to a Josianic redaction in the late seventh century arise in circumstances that share a great deal of similarity to the material originating in the eighth century: in both centuries, the key institutions—monarchy, priesthood, and temple—are all intact; social and economic conditions are broadly similar; and Judah's political status as a vassal of Assyria is unchanged, though by the end of the seventh century, Assyria is in decline and the rise of Babylon is on the horizon. The major change comes when the king is taken as a prisoner to the Babylonian court in 597, when the temple of Jerusalem is destroyed in 587/586, and when the people of Judah are deported in three waves—597, 586, and 582. These are the circumstances that will shape the message of Second Isaiah.

Appreciating the book as an integral and unified work with its own literary and theological merit is an indispensable part of the work of a biblical theologian. After all, it is the biblical book—not its reconstructed historical core—that addresses the church and synagogue. But it is not a freestanding book that addresses faith communities of today. The book of Isaiah is part of the faith community's religious heritage, and this larger context gives the text a distinctive voice. As Boadt explains:

> Because these books are part of the sacred canon of communities of faith, prophetic texts are not "texts in themselves" alone but are *embedded* texts which of their very nature testify, celebrate, proclaim, and seek to persuade hearers of the religious truth of a historical experience that has grown and has been fashioned and further interpreted within a specific set of religious convictions and presuppositions. To neglect the essential characteristic of the Bible as *Bible* threatens to reduce its authority to the same level as that of Dante or Shakespeare. (1997: 4)

This, too, is an assumption that lies behind the present study. The book of Isaiah is more than its antecedent historical core, and more than a literary document. It is accepted as a text with authority and so its interpretation is of vital importance. Situating the exegetical enterprise in both the larger academic and faith communities requires the interpreter to engage those communities in meaningful discussion and helps to curtail individualistic or exclusively sectarian interpretations.

While historical criticism tends to give priority to the "original" text, and canonical and literary criticism the final text, we need to recognize that the entire process of composition, collecting, editing, redacting, and transmitting—in short, all the human activity that goes into the production of the biblical text—is integral to the formulation of the document the church and synagogue recognize as the word of God. An exclusive focus on either "original" or "final" texts shortchanges not only the literary complexity and multivalence of the text, but needlessly circumscribes the role of Divine Providence in the production of the text. At every stage, these prophetic words have been accepted as the word of God. Granted, it is possible to say that "original" words can only be reconstructed while the final text is more assured, nevertheless it is suspect theologically to assert that one phase of the text's development is more the word of God than another. Historical origins, textual developments, and final forms are all instructive and testify to the vitality of the religious convictions of the communities that live by these words. In short, the meaning of the text is not exhausted by its historical meaning, nor is the literary context alone always sufficient to lay bare the possible meanings of the text.

Finally, we should not confuse the "final form" with the final destination of the text. As preserved and cherished texts, the most significant ambiance of the Bible is not the academy but the liturgy. The liturgical proclamation of texts relativizes both the historical and canonical approaches by placing texts in a new interpretive context—that of a liturgical calendar and in explicit and purposeful dialogue with other selected texts for the liturgy of the word. This, too, will be part of our study and reflection: those texts in Isaiah that we are examining for their importance to the theme of justice and that also appear in the Roman Catholic and Revised Common Lectionaries will be discussed in sections titled Lectionary Notes. Our approach, then, will attempt to address historical, literary, and liturgical concerns.

chapter 3

Isaiah 1–39

Introduction

Whether the grounds are historical or literary, most commentators see a structural divide at chapter 40. Representing traditional historical criticism, the Old Testament Library series sees not only a divide between chs. 1–39 and 40–66, but so great a divide that these works are treated by two different scholars, Otto Kaiser writing on the former, Claus Westermann on the latter; similarly, the Interpretation commentary assigns Isaiah 1–39 to Christopher R. Seitz and Isaiah 40–66 to Paul D. Hanson. Among contemporary scholars who acknowledge the multiple authorship of Isaiah but who argue for the unity of the entire book, both Seitz and Sweeney offer several compelling arguments for treating the book of Isaiah as an integral work, but nonetheless each has published a commentary on Isaiah 1–39.

Even those who argue that Isaiah of Jerusalem is the book's sole author see a pronounced shift in the tone or outlook of the material. Motyer, for example, sees chs. 38 and 39 as the prologue to "The Book of the Servant" (Isaiah 38–55). Similarly, Edward Young sees the overall structure of the book as divided between chs. 1–35 and 40–66, with 36–39 serving as a bridge between the two sections (1992: vol. 3, 540–49).

These latter views, though theologically at a great remove from historical criticism, correspond to modern criticism's interest in Isaiah 1–39 as a discrete section within the larger book of Isaiah. Regardless of one's views on authorship and historical provenance, there is ample precedent for beginning this discussion of justice in Isaiah by focusing on Isaiah 1–39.

Scholarship is fairly well agreed, too, that within these first thirty-nine chapters there are clearly defined subsections, namely, chs. 1, 2–12, 13–23, 24–27, 28–33, 34–35, and 36–39. Of these, chs. 34–35 are widely taken to be from Second Isaiah, a matter that will be taken up in the discussion of these chapters below.

Our goal is to treat the relevant texts in their historical and literary contexts; as appropriate, we will also offer some comments on the liturgical use of these texts. As described in the previous chapter, our historical and literary examination will involve describing what may be inferred about the social conditions reflected in texts set in the preexilic period somewhat broadly or in the late eighth century when it is possible to determine, and the overall effect of their literary arrangement in this first major section of the book. It is not our goal to provide an exhaustive exegesis of each pertinent passage, but rather to study each passage in order to glean from it what may be learned of the theological meaning, social context, and literary function of the theme of justice. As the occasion arises, we will also address some comments to the canonical context of a particular passage.

Isaiah 1

The individual units in ch. 1 that are of relevance to this study are vv. 10-17 and 21-28. There are, however, particular aspects of ch. 1 that affect the interpretation of the individual units. It will be helpful, therefore, to address some of the issues before turning to vv. 10-17 and 21-28. As it happens, these preliminary issues offer specific examples of the somewhat theoretical discussions of the previous chapter, namely, the historical-critical and literary or canonical approaches to the text.

From the historical-critical perspective, Isa 1:7-8 has garnered considerable attention for the clues it may yield on the question of the historical setting for chapter 1.

1. Isaiah 1:7-8. In attempting to ascertain when the material in ch. 1 might have been composed, scholarly interest has focused on the description of the country in vv. 7-8 (for example, Emerton 1993; Ben Zvi 1991; Willis 1984, 1985).

The most widely accepted explanation for the widespread devastation is a military invasion, as the vocabulary in 1:7-8 indicates: land devastated and devoured, cities burned with fire and besieged, the taking of plunder, the presence of foreigners. According to Peter Machinist, the language in 1:7 *(ʾereṣ šĕmāmâ, śārap ʾēš,* and *ʾākal)* is particularly common throughout the Bible and in Assyrian sources to describe the destruction caused by warfare (1983: 724, n. 25). Machinist carefully examines these three terms and finds not only their usage but even their consecution (unique in biblical usage to Isa 1:7) particularly close to the royal Assyrian annals. Clearly, the language in Isa 1:7-8 is the language of warfare. Three major proposals for military actions against the land have been advanced: the period of the Syro-Ephraimite conspiracy, c. 735;[1] the aftermath of the events of 597–587;[2] the third suggestion and majority view is that these verses are written with Sennacherib's siege of 701 in mind. According to those who hold this view, Sennacherib's campaign as recorded in his annals accords well with the image presented by Isaiah; and the survival of Jerusalem as a hut in a vineyard or a lodge in a field better describes Jerusalem's survival than its destruction. Further, Judah's continued rebellion in v. 5 is better identified with her survival after 701 than her destruction in 587. The threat implied in vv. 5-6 is that more bruises are on the way; the prophetic assessment of the nation's exile is that judgment has been rendered and that the nation has paid double for all her sins (Isa 40:1-2). It seems best to see 1:7-8 as a reference to the events of 701.

With such lively debate about the historical references, Ben Zvi (1991) offers a considerably more circumspect position. He believes that the ambiguity of the text both prevents certainty about the actual historical circumstances and also allows the text to speak to a variety of situations. This historical evaluation overlaps with the canonical assessment. Brueggemann, for example, notes in passing the majority opinion that these verses refer to the Assyrian invasion by Sennacherib. He goes on to say, "At the same time, in the larger scope of the book, the text looks beyond Assyria to the ultimate devastation of the Babylonians. Both devastations and all devastators are present to the imagination of the poet" (1998a: 17). Thus, from a canonical perspective, all the historical arguments and counterarguments are subordinated to the determinative perspective of the canonical editors. The reader is invited to stand neither in the eighth century nor in the sixth century, but sometime after it all, and there to discern the overall sweep and pattern of God's sovereignty over history. Both perspectives are productive: the canonical perspective gives us the bigger, theological picture, while the historical-critical approach, when taken theologically, roots divine activity not merely in broad sweeps and general perspectives, but in the realia of historical engagements. Both approaches enhance interpretive insights.

2. Isaiah 1 and the Concern for Justice. Susan Niditch, reviewing the work of major historical-critical commentators of the last seventy-five years, summarizes the generally accepted assessment of Isaiah 1: it originates in large part from Isaiah of Jerusalem; it was placed at the head of the book by an editor at a later time to draw the reader's immediate attention to some of Isaiah's principal concerns; and it is composed of several originally independent sayings, though the precise identification of these units varies somewhat.[3] Verse 1 is commonly accepted as a redactional addition. The typical introductory language that begins vv. 2, 4, 10, and 21, together with v. 20 which signals the close of a unit, is strong evidence for seeing separate and discrete sayings that may have originated from different periods of Isaiah's prophetic career. Many believe that vv. 27-28, and possibly 29-31, are exilic or postexilic additions.

Niditch rejects the supposition that there are four or more separate compositions artificially strung together by a redactor. Applying principles of oral composition proposed in the work of A. B. Lord, Niditch argues that definable units do not imply separate composition. She suggests instead that the structure of ch. 1 can be better explained by common techniques of oral speech, seeing just two discrete units, one framed by the other. These are discernible by differences in style (syntax, tone, and point of view) and differences in theology (for example, the views of who is blessed and who is cursed). The original core from Isaiah is found in 1:4-20 which, in turn, is composed of stock elements from traditional oral speech, namely, a woe oracle (vv. 4-9) and a cult polemic (vv. 10-20). These are distinguished by their sermonic qualities and tone. Verses 4-20 are framed by 1:2-3 and 21-31 from the exilic or postexilic period and are identifiable by their simple declarative tone.

As suggested above, most modern historical-critical commentators (for example, Sweeney, Clements, Wildberger, Kaiser, Jensen, and Stacey) agree on the following distinct units: vv. 2-3, 4-9, 10-17, 18-20, 21-28, 29-31. Only vv. 21-28 are analyzed in various ways, a matter that will be addressed in the discussion to follow.

Because the units that are of interest to this study (vv. 10-17 and 21-28) stand in obvious relation to what precedes, reference to vv. 2-3 and 4-9 will be made as needed.

Seek Justice! Isaiah 1:10-17

Isaiah 1:10 begins by echoing and expanding the classic summons found in v. 2. The coordinated imperatives *hear! (šimʿû)* and *give ear! (haʾăzînû)* are a familiar pairing: Judg 5:3; Jer 13:15; Joel 1:2. In Isa 1:2, the heavens and earth are summoned to bear witness to Israel's two-sided sin, namely, rebellion and ignorance. Taken together, these represent complete estrangement from God (v. 4), by which the yoke of obedience is thrown off and the knowledge of God is abandoned.[4] It is therefore significant that when Isa 1:10 repeats the summons of 1:2, it specifies the content to be heard and heeded: the *word of YHWH* and the *torah of God.* The ignorance that results in rebellion is to be ameliorated by the *word* and *torah* of God.

Verse 10, having echoed and expanded 1:2, shifts the focus from summoning *heaven* and *earth* to serve as witnesses, to calling the *leaders of Sodom* and the *people of Gomorrah* to account for their sins. This reference to *Sodom* and *Gomorrah* is the climax of vv. 4-9, which include both an expansive list of the evil done and a comprehensive list of those who perpetrate it. The whole populace is accused of *abandoning* YHWH and *despising* the Holy One of Israel, resulting in a state of *estrangement* (v. 4). The prophet rhetorically asks why they continue to be *beaten* and to *turn aside* (v. 5). Their pitiable state is diagnosed in a medical metaphor (v. 6). Their bruised and battered condition has resulted from the punishment described in vv. 7-8. But for God's determining otherwise, they would have been effaced like Sodom and Gomorrah (v. 9).

It is frequently remarked that the mention of Sodom and Gomorrah in v. 9 is what attracted the independent oracle in vv. 10-17 to its present location, beginning as it does with the same word pair. While this may indeed be a factor, the present arrangement seems to be more than merely mechanical. As suggested above, v. 10 seems to be calling on and expanding vv. 2-3. Similarly, the stunning scope of evil in v. 4 naturally evokes the image of those notorious ciphers for "sin city," Sodom and Gomorrah. And just as the listing of those who do evil in v. 4 is comprehensive, in v. 10 it spans the social structure from *leaders (qĕṣînîm)* to the common *people (ʿam).*

Verse 11 echoes the pattern found in v. 5 in which questions follow the introduction. Both sets of questions address the issue of repeated actions (vv. 5, 13), namely, continuing to *turn aside* and continuing to *bring vain offerings.* Just as v. 10 expanded and specified the terse introduction in v. 2, the questions in vv. 11-12 are similarly more expansive, iterating YHWH's response to the cultic offerings (vv. 11-15), with which YHWH is *sated* and in which he does not *delight* (v. 11), which he finds *abominable*, cannot *bear* (v. 13), and indeed *hates* (v. 14). So abhorrent is Israel's cult-with-iniquity that YHWH will *close his eyes* to their *outspread hands* and will *not hear their prayers* (v. 15). These last acts of piety clearly move the indictment beyond that of the public cult to include all religious acts by which one might be tempted to assert godliness. The summary indictment is dramatic: "your hands are full of blood." The plural form "bloods" (*dāmîm,* 1:15) often refers to bloodshed by violence (Gen 4:10). This seems to refer not only to the blood of cultic sacrifices (v. 11), but to the blood later specified as the blood of murderers (v. 21) and social evil (5:7, *miśpāḥ*). The following command in 1:16 to "Wash! Clean yourselves!" thus refers both to the blood of unacceptable sacrifice and to the social crime with which the people have become sullied and polluted.

While the prophecy in vv. 4-9 ended with a description of the punishment inflicted on Israel for their rebellion, vv. 16-18 conclude with a string of nine imperatives detailing what must be done to avoid further punishment. The evocation of Sodom and Gomorrah in v. 10 suggests that this time, the punishment will be complete and irrevocable. The unit ends as it began, with imperatives addressed to social classes: having begun with princes or leaders (v. 10, *qĕṣînîm*), it concludes at the opposite end of the social spectrum—with the orphan *(yātôm)* and widow (*ʾalmānâ,* v. 17).

The question whether Isaiah is here rejecting the cult per se need not unduly detain us. It seems clear that what is at issue is not "the cult as cult" but the voluntary, as opposed to prescribed, offerings[5] that are made without regard for the fulfillment of the social obligations detailed in vv. 16-18 and taken up again in vv. 21-23. The close link between cultic observance and ethical conduct is signaled by the terms "Wash! Clean yourselves!" These are actions at home in the cultic sphere, but here they serve to make the transition to the ethical conduct that will reinvigorate cultic practice with the integrity of a moral social life (Wildberger 1991: 48). The impurity that nullifies cultic offerings is "washed away" by a change in conduct. Cult and conduct are not separate spheres of life: they are concomitant realities of authentic religious life. This close connection between cult and conduct is hardly an Isaianic innovation, as the entrance liturgies of Psalms 15 and 24 (among others) suggest. Among extrabiblical sources, Kaiser (1983: 31–33) traces at some length antecedent traditions that, as early as the third millennium in Egypt, relate ethics and worship. Fensham, too, examines ancient Mesopotamian and Egyptian sources, and concludes, "As in Mesopotamia the religious ethics are closely intertwined in Egypt with the social ethics" (1962: 133–34). Thus, the corrective social actions that Isaiah specifies in some detail are an appropriate correlative to cultic acts and a fitting climax to this oracle. It is these social acts to which we now turn.

Following the double command to wash are two commands dealing with evil: "put aside the *evil* of your deeds" and "cease to do *evil*" (*rʿʿ* in both instances). Balancing the command to cease evildoing is the command "learn to do good." The language of "good" and "evil" finds its home in the wisdom tradition, as the accompanying imperative "learn" suggests (Jensen 1984: 43–46). These general principles are then specified in a staccato series of four two-word imperative phrases. Their impact is reinforced by their asyndetic coordination, their balanced components, and their assonance, characteristics that apply also to the two preceding imperative phrases (1:16b-17):

> Cease to do evil. Learn to do good.
> Seek justice; set aright the ruthless.[6]
> Do justice for the orphan;
> argue the case of the widow.

The text specifies the meaning of justice in classic, even stock, terms: defending the *orphan* and the *widow*.[7] A brief digression on this important biblical and prophetic concern will prove fruitful.

Excursus: Concern for the "Orphan and Widow"

Concern for the orphan and the widow is an ancient tradition. H. Eberhard von Waldow (1970: 182–204) argues that the earliest biblical legislation protecting the orphan, widow, and sojourner (the Covenant Code, Exod 20:22—23:33) reflects the concerns of nomadic peoples and most probably arose in the tribal period. Moreover, this concern is not peculiar to Israel or Yahwistic religion. As Fensham has pointed out, it is attested in the legal and wisdom writings of both Egypt and Mesopotamia, where it dates back to the third millennium. There, protection of the orphan and widow is frequently found as an expectation of the gods and as the boast of kings. Fensham goes on to say that "the plea of prophets for restoration of morality and protection of the weak points to times of absolute decay and negligence of the commonly accepted policy of the gods and strong kings" (1962: 130). He argues that in Israel the cause of decay is straying from "the principles of the religion of Yahweh."

In his study, however, Fensham seems content to point out the similarities between Israelite practice and the practice enshrined in the laws and wisdom texts of Mesopotamia, Canaan, and Egypt. The only significant difference he discusses is in the divine patronage of justice: while elsewhere the concern for justice is shared among the gods, in Israel the focus is on the one God to the exclusion of all others (1962: 135). Otherwise, the expression of social concern, its origin in the will of the gods, its identification with the virtuous king, and its practice in the life of the common people are all shared characteristics in the various cultures he studies (1962: 138–39). He does not regard the ubiquity of this concern for the orphan, widow, and poor to be a matter of "borrowing" but of a common cultural stock.

By contrast, in examining much of the same material, Hammershaimb argues that Israel's prophetic concern for the orphan and widow is derivative, quite clearly influenced by Canaanite concerns (1966: 71). In this, he seems more at pains to counter the efforts of some to find what is distinctive about the religion of Israel in contrast to the religions of her neighbors (1966: 66).[8] According to Hammershaimb, the emergence of concern for the welfare of the widow and orphan suggests both the disintegration of the old family-based culture which is distinctive of agricultural society and the disenfranchisement of the vulnerable that accompanied the emergence of advanced urban culture (1966: 74–75). Hammershaimb believes that the prophets "have taken over a formulation of the duties towards widows, orphans and others in distress, which were already firmly established among the Canaanites long before the invasion of the Israelites" (1966: 75).

These two literary and social studies have been expanded by two theologically sensitive analyses. Richard D. Patterson examines the theme of the orphan and widow primarily from an apologetic point of view. After examining a number of extrabiblical sources and comparing them to similar passages in the Old Testament, he suggests that the early predominance in the ancient Near East of this concern for the orphan and widow may be understood as "a primeval reflection of God's own self-disclosure as being the Redeemer of the helpless. Its very antiquity may be accounted for because it speaks of man's helpless position before God right from the beginning. Its localization in the Near East may be occasioned by direct contact within the area of God's revelation" (1973: 233). He argues that "although the Old Testament partakes of that international culture and even utilizes it in the presentation of God's life giving message, its concept of God, its high ethical standards and its objective verifiability make it distinctively unique among the writings of the pre-Christian world" (1973: 224). In Machinist's terms, Patterson seems to make a doctrinal argument for Israel's distinctiveness both in terms of "pure traits" and in the distinctive "configuration" of traits shared in common with other cultures (Machinist 1991: 197–200). Patterson's recourse to confessional assertions is unsatisfying in two ways. First, it assumes that Israel's tradition is valid only if it is indeed distinctive. The moral "superiority" of the biblical tradition is somehow linked to its being demonstrably different from neighboring traditions. In any case, these alleged differences are asserted rather than demonstrated. Second, Patterson's argument does not engage other sources on their own terms: ancient Near Eastern cultures are merely unwitting receptacles of a transcendent revelation of *Israel's* God. The moral value, social worth, and cultural similarity of these traditions are explained only in reference to spiritual realities extrinsic to those cultures. Patterson bypasses entirely the social, historical, and literary matrices of the shared traditions in favor of a facile doctrinal explanation.

More recently, Paul D. Hanson (1994a) has examined a broader range of biblical and extrabiblical sources than Fensham, Hammershaimb, and Patterson, and has done so with theological and sociological interests in the fore. By understanding laws and social structures as societal expressions of a cultural worldview, Hanson contrasts Mesopotamian, Egyptian, and Canaanite legal and social institutions, which are founded on myth and royal ideology, to those of Israel, which are founded on epic and covenant. For Israel's neighbors, society's institutions—royal and sacral—are founded on timeless myths of order and chaos: kingship itself descends from the gods as a bulwark against chaos. In these hierarchical societies, stability and order are social goods because they secure the power and wealth of the ruling class; policies of care for the vulnerable serve a pragmatic goal of maximizing royal authority and guaranteeing social order, stability, and productivity. Poverty and social neglect are undesirable to the degree that they pose a threat to good social order or represent a loss of productivity.

The biblical record, by contrast, presents Israel as a tribal organization founded on historical deliverance from social oppression by the act of a compassionate God. Israel's earliest legal practices and social structures addressing the welfare of the vulnerable are, therefore, embodiments of divine mercy and justice expressed in historical and social terms. Hanson summarizes:

> Our observations relating to earliest Israel identify two principles upon which its notion of social welfare was based: (1) a theological principle that located the source of community in divine grace and the norm for human behavior in the nature of the God encountered in the deliverance and empowerment of slaves, and (2) a sociological principle that generated laws and structures from the perspective of a community of equals rather than from the vantage point of the privileged few. (1994a: 18–19)

When the monarchy emerged, and with it the notions of a stratified society, the centralization of power, and recrudescence of the mythic foundations of court and temple, the prophets arose to keep calling Israel back to its theocentric, covenantal, and egalitarian perspective. Hanson observes, "Though early Israelite law addressed many of the same specific areas as had the laws of Mesopotamia and Egypt, the thrust of the law was transformed by the interpretive framework of the epic. Righteous compassion replaced authoritative ordering as the intention of the law" (1994a: 27). Where Fensham and Hammershaimb focused more on the commonality of concerns and the social structures and norms that embody those concerns, Hanson looks to the religious foundations and the social function of laws and institutions. This is a significant contribution to the discussion.

For the purposes of this study, it is helpful to understand both the care for the "orphan and widow" as part of a tradition that prevailed throughout the ancient Near East (Fensham 1962) and the sociological factors that occasioned the need for attention to their plight (Hammershaimb 1966). Both these factors affect our treatment of Isaiah. Clearly, Isaiah is also attentive to changing patterns of land ownership and social configurations (5:8-24), just as he is heir to a firmly established ancient tradition of social concern for the orphan and widow. But as that tradition comes to Isaiah, it is already shaped by the particularly historical and theological grounding of Israel's experience of YHWH as the very foundation and source of Israel's life (Hanson 1994a). The historical bedrock of Israel's confession is the foundation upon which is built Isaiah's message and even his political counsel. Isaiah's engagement with the international and political issues of his day (chs. 7–8; 36–39) stands in continuity with Israel's founding experience of a God who acts in history for Israel's deliverance and security. The nation's peace and security are rooted not in shrewd politics, but in God alone (cf. 7:9b; see also 33:6).

Similarly, concern for the orphan and widow expresses the nation's fidelity to YHWH, who, according to Isaiah, is a "God of justice" (30:18). Thus, when Isaiah expresses concern for the orphan and widow, he does so not only from the point of view of Israel's common tradition with its neighbors or from sociological astuteness, but from a particularly Yahwistic and prophetic point of view. When society at large or the leadership in particular failed to care for the orphan and the widow, Isaiah spoke not as an agent of the state or as a proponent of an economics of prosperity, but as a defender of the divine concern for the "orphan and widow" that finds expression in historical and social realities. Given the cultural ubiquity and antiquity of the concern for the orphan and widow, it is doubtful that it must always be understood as an expression of YHWH's covenant with Israel. While the covenant context is clear in the traditions in Exodus and Deuteronomy, for example, the same is not apparent in First Isaiah. There is remarkably little explicit attention to the covenant in First Isaiah or, for that matter, in Second Isaiah either. We will come back to this when we discuss Third Isaiah, where the covenant makes its first prominent appearance. For now, we note that care for widows and orphans is not in itself an indication of a covenant context.

These two groups of people, the "orphan" and the "widow," are to be understood both literally, that is, as specific individuals whose social and legal status is made precarious because of their peculiar circumstances, and symbolically, that is, as representative of all people who are socially disadvantaged. Hence, these terms are either individually or together linked to other terms such as "the poor" (*dal,* Isa 10:2; Ps 82:3; Job 31:16; *ʿānî,* Isa 10:2; Job 24:9; 29:12), "the needy" (*ʾebyôn,* Jer 5:28), and "the stranger" (*gēr,* Pss 94:6; 146:9; Deut 16:11, 14; 10:18).[9] These terms are dramatically clustered in Zech 7:10: "Widow *(ʾalmānâ)* and orphan *(yātôm),* stranger *(gēr)* and poor *(ʿānî)* do not oppress; / do not plot evil in your heart, one against another." Later in Isa 10:2 we will see the common word pair *dal* and *ʿānî* set in parallel to "widow and orphan":

> [Woe to those who] turn aside the poor *(dallîm)* from judgment
>   and rob the oppressed *(ʿănîyîm)* of my people of justice;
> widows *(ʾalmānôt)* become their spoil,
>   and orphans *(yĕtômîm)* they plunder.

While this cluster of terms in fact refers to people in specific and different circumstances, they are also used to describe the socially disadvantaged as a class who share the condition of their common vulnerability. As such, their plight both demonstrates the nation's hard-hearted negligence and motivates Isaiah's passion for justice. Division along economic lines is an affront to the nature of the community and fractures the solidarity of a people God had chosen to be his own. Injustice is a threat, not only to those who are its victims, but to the very theological foundations of the nation as Isaiah understands it.

Isaiah, it seems, follows the lead set by Amos. Isaiah's admonition to "seek justice" comes after his own critique of the cult and empty religious observances.

Whereas Amos admonished people to "seek" YHWH (Amos 5:4-6), Isaiah adjures the seeking of justice. With Amos as a background, the verb *dāraš* now takes on a specifically theological hue: to "seek" God, to know what God wants and desires in this particular situation, to know what one should do, is concisely and compellingly enunciated in two words—"seek justice." Amos had enunciated the theological principle: "Seek YHWH and live." Isaiah spells out its practical program: "Seek justice." Isaiah's assertion is bold: the "seeking" of God takes place in the seeking of justice. In the specific context of eighth-century Judah, justice means the social and legal care of the widow, orphan, and poor. Doing, establishing, and enacting justice, all firmly rooted in eighth-century prophetic tradition, are elevated one step further by Isaiah. "Seeking justice" is as much at the center of authentic religion as "seeking YHWH." The latter is clearly impossible without the former; and conversely, the former is prerequisite to the latter.[10] This insight or instruction may well be the fullest meaning of *torah* in 1:10. The religious use of the term *dāraš* in Isaiah[11] argues persuasively for understanding the command "seek justice" as the social and moral equivalent of the religious and cultic act of "seeking God."

Just as a pilgrim seeks out God in order to discover what to do, one who seeks justice is informed by Isaiah to set right oppression, to do justice for the orphan, and to argue the case of the widow. Whether these verses are approached from the point of view of their social,[12] forensic,[13] or theological[14] demands, the practical result is the same: the socially oppressed, here represented by the orphan and widow, are to be saved, defended, and have their suffering redressed. This is the sine qua non for acceptable worship: true worship proceeds from a true heart acting in justice. For God to accept worship without justice would make God no better than an unjust judge who accepts bribes against the innocent (Bovati 1994: 205; see Sir 35:11-15)—an unthinkable and intolerable situation for the Judge of all the earth whom Israel knows and expects to act justly (Gen 18:25). The unit thus comes to an abrupt end with a startling and uncompromising imperative to act with justice.

There is no consensus as to whether vv. 18-20 belong to the preceding prophecy. Many suggest that these verses were placed here by the attraction of the legal terminology that concludes v. 17 and the summons to court that opens in v. 18. While vv. 18-20 are not directly relevant to the present discussion, two observations may be made. First, there is a close verbal connection between vv. 17 and 18. The verbs *šāpaṭ* (to judge) and **yākaḥ* (Hiphil: to decide) are a word pair found in Isa 2:4 and 11:3, 4. Their occurrence across 1:17 *(šāpaṭ,* to judge) and 1:18 (**yākaḥ,* to decide) provide a familiar link between sections. Second, as it stands, the closing statement in 1:18, "for the mouth of YHWH has spoken *(*dbr)*" forms an inclusion with the opening "Hear the word *(*dbr)* of YHWH" (1:10), and provides a conclusion that is otherwise entirely lacking in vv. 10-17. Thus, both internal verbal links and the overall structure created by this inclusion urge the interpreter to consider the larger unity of vv. 10-20 as the context for understanding the individual verses. The forgiveness offered in v. 18 and the choice between the blessings of v. 19 or the dire consequences of v. 20 are thus made dependent on the change in behavior required in seeking justice, setting aright the oppressor, doing justice for the orphan, and arguing the case of the widow. In this way, vv. 16-17 serve a pivotal role in the interpretation of what precedes and follows these verses: both an acceptable cult (vv. 11-15) and the possibility of forgiveness (vv. 18-20) are structurally and theologically dependent on vv. 16-17.

Lectionary Notes

Common Lectionary: Proper 26 [C]: Isa 1:10-18 / Ps 32:1-7 / Luke 19:1-10 [Roman Lectionary: 31 C—Wisdom 11:22—12:2 / Psalm 145 / Luke 19:1-10. The Common Lectionary substitutes the reading from Isaiah for the reading from deuterocanonical Wisdom and assigns a different psalm.]

Introductory Comments. To this point, we have examined texts primarily in two different interpretive contexts: the historical and the canonical. We observed earlier that these two approaches are neither mutually exclusive, nor do they exhaust the possibilities for interpretation. One of the more significant uses of Scripture is as proclamation in a worship context. For both the church and synagogue, biblical texts may take on a new meaning when interpreted in the context of worship. The liturgy often situates particular passages in relation to other readings and in a variety of liturgical feasts and seasons that cast them in a different light and open up the possibilities latent in multilayered texts.

The proclamation of Scripture in a worship context is the occasion for liturgical preaching that should be built on solid and careful exegesis of the text; but liturgical preaching is not primarily expository or didactic. The task of the preacher in a liturgical setting is not the same as that of a professor of biblical studies in a classroom. In preaching, the primary task is not to set the text in its historical or even its canonical context, but to address the assembled faith community in such as way as to provide an encounter with the living word of God.

In the Christian lectionaries (both the Roman and Common lectionaries), this new context for Scripture is twofold: first, each passage is set within a service of the word, that is, as part of a coordinated set of readings; second, the readings themselves are part of a liturgical cycle of seasons and feasts that is structured on the unfolding of salvation history. The festal seasons of Advent-Christmas and Lent-Easter, together with Ordinary Time (called Proper Sundays in the Common Lectionary), unfold progressively the paschal mystery from its past realization, to its present actualization, to its future consummation. Interpreting biblical passages from the vantage point of the church's liturgical life casts each passage in a new light and invites understanding from a new perspective.

The structure of the Christian lectionaries gives priority to the progressive reading of the Gospel assigned to the Sundays in Ordinary or Proper Time, one Synoptic Gospel being assigned for each of the three years in the lectionary cycle. On Ordinary/Proper Sundays, the first reading is chosen to coordinate with the Gospel.[15] During festal seasons, the Gospel and other readings are geared to the general themes of the season. The responsorial psalm bridges the two readings.

In the lectionary notes that follow, we will address only those texts from Isaiah that are examined in this book and that appear in the lectionaries as coordinated readings.

The readings from the Common Lectionary for Proper 26 [C] exemplify the principle of the Old Testament reading placed in parallel to the Gospel (*Revised Common Lectionary*, §20). The Gospel states, literally, that Zacchaeus was "seeking *(zēteō)* to see who Jesus was" (NRSV, "trying to see"). The Greek verb "to seek" in the Gospel is the same Greek verb that the Septuagint uses for "seek justice" in Isaiah 1:17 *(ekzēteō)*. While on the level of plot, Zacchaeus is merely "seeking out" Jesus, the terminology is redolent with other meanings: in both Isaiah and Luke, what is "sought" will lead to salvation.

The identification of Zacchaeus as a "sinner" (Luke 19:7) would have been based both on the general assumption that tax collectors were crooks and thieves, and on his ritual impurity for his dealings with unclean Gentiles. He tacitly acknowledges the graver sin—defrauding and depriving the poor. The corrective action he undertakes is exactly what Isaiah recommends. In the same way that the wicked and sinful leaders of Judah must "wash and make themselves clean" (Isa 1:16) through caring for the orphan and widow (1:17), Zacchaeus manifests his conversion in the economic realm where the injustice had been perpetrated when he restores what was unjustly taken. This he does most generously: while the law required full restitution plus one-fifth (Num 5:7), Zacchaeus restores fourfold. In response, Jesus announces that "salvation" has come to the "lost" (Luke 19:10). Salvation comes from an encounter with Jesus, which moves the sinner to "cease doing evil and learn to do good." As grave as the sin may be—whether it be scarlet or crimson—it can be washed away by the costly and difficult change of life God requires. Repentance is not merely a matter of acknowledging the wrong done, but of correcting it. The primary arena in which the conversion of the Israelites and of Zacchaeus takes place is the social realm: restoring the rights and property of those who have been neglected, defrauded, and deprived. In this way, not only are the victims of injustice delivered from oppression and want, but the "sinners"—for such social neglect is sinful—are "found" and "saved." For Isaiah, such justice will remove sin (1:18) and "redeem" Zion (1:27). By placing the reading in dialogue with the Gospel, the mystery of salvation is unfolded. The kind of radical change in life that Isaiah urges for his people and that Zacchaeus manifests is actualized by a zealous seeking of what God requires and of what God reveals—for Christians—in Jesus Christ.

Zion, City of Justice: Isaiah 1:21-28

The original unit, 1:21-26, is a tightly structured composition. On the one hand, its boundaries are set by the inclusion formed by the phrase "faithful city" (vv. 21 and 26), while its two constitutive parts, the indictment of vv. 21-23 and the judgment of vv. 24-26, are linked by the repeated image of "dross" for Israel's sin (vv. 22, 25). Verses 27-28 are widely taken as a later addition or commentary made by a disciple or redactor. While it is impossible to know with certainty when these verses were added or by whom, it will be shown that vv. 27-28 are thematically, theologically, and structurally a fitting conclusion to vv. 21-26.

The indictments made in vv. 21-23 are among the most graphic in the book of Isaiah. The controlling metaphors speak of dissolution and vapid decay: silver is tarnished and devalued by dross, liquor has been watered down, weakened to a cheap semblance of the real thing. In both cases, the unwary might be taken in by a cheap alloy or a diluted drink, but not the prophet who knows better. This lamentable situation is dramatically revealed in the first word, *ʾêkâ* ("How!"), and reinforced by the *qinah* meter (3 + 2) of vv. 21, 22, 23a (see Wildberger 1991: 62–63)—this is the outcry of a dirge, the wail of a lament. Something has been lost and the response is a grief-stricken lament.

The generic situation is stated in v. 21: The faithful city has become a whore; the longtime residents, *justice* and *righteousness,* have been evicted by a new citizenry, *murderers*! Whoring and murder—strong language! Hayes and Irvine (1987: 80) find a specific reference behind the accusation of murderers: the political assassinations of the previous three rulers—Athaliah (2 Kgs 11:1-16), Jehoash (2 Kgs 12:20-21), and Amaziah (2 Kgs 14:19-21). Clements (1980: 36) enlarges the accusation to include broader acts of physical, street-type violence. The imagery of Israel as a whore is familiar, but Isaiah's nuance is new. In Hosea, and later again in Jeremiah and Ezekiel, the imagery of whoring is used to describe Israel's idolatry as infidelity to her "husband," YHWH. Isaiah makes no reference in this passage, or to this point in ch. 1, to idolatry. "Whoring," as will soon become clear, refers to forsaking YHWH by abandoning the demands of justice. The indictment of infidelity is initially leveled at the entire city. Though these charges will later focus on the leadership (v. 23), the scope of the accusation encompasses both, as it had in v. 10.

While the characterization of any city as a whore would be a stinging indictment, against a temple city it is particularly shocking. Throughout the ancient Near East, temple cities are sacred to the gods and enjoy special privileges such as exemptions from corvée (conscripted labor), from military service, and from the imposition of certain taxes. ". . . In a divine city or holy precinct man is subservient to the god alone, and the kingdom of man has no authority over him" (Weinfeld 1995: 97). In the Bible, Jerusalem as a temple city is designated by such terms as "the holy city" (Isa 48:2; 52:1), "the city of righteousness" (Isa 1:26), or "city of truth" (Zech 8:3). Weinfeld sees an equivalent designation in the title "the faithful city" (Isa 1:21; see v. 26, where "the righteous city is a faithful city"). Thus, the catalogue of crimes that follows in 1:21-23 is made all the more odious because these crimes take place in the temple city, in which justice and righteousness are supposed to be inviolable. As v. 21 indicates, this used to be the case, but no longer.

In v. 21 we find the first of eighteen instances in the book of Isaiah where the terms *mišpāṭ* and *ṣĕdāqâ* are paired as a hendiadys meaning "social justice." Zion, as YHWH's temple city, is to be a city filled with *justice* and in which *righteousness* dwells, that is, a city built on the practice of social justice. This ideal sets up the contrast which follows. The complete breakdown of good civic order and of a just society is represented by its most scandalous antithesis, murder.

The term *ṣĕdāqâ* is a freighted term for Isaiah, with his keen interest in Jerusalem. It perhaps evokes names particularly associated with Jerusalem: Melchizedek, the "priest of God Most High" in Salem (that is, Jerusalem; Gen 14:18), and Zadok, the priest at the time of David. These ancestors of the faithful city evoke memories of a city in which righteousness once dwelt, but now they stand in mute testimony against a city from which righteousness has fled. In light of the previous discussion about the relationship between justice and the cult, the possible evocation of two righteous ancestors who are associated with the cult should not be overlooked.

After the analogy of tarnished silver and diluted liquor, the general accusation that social justice is gone from the faithful city is further specified: accusations of collusion, graft, and negligent use of office are laid at the feet of the leadership. However, while the indictment is directed against the leadership, it is the city as a whole that is being addressed. The second feminine singular endings indicate that the addressee is Lady Zion and it is she who has become a whore. While injustice is most obvious in the courts, it is not confined there. The specifics are now entered into evidence (1:23):

> Your rulers are rebels and accomplices of thieves;
> every one of them loves a bribe and solicits gifts.
> The orphan they do not defend *(*šāpaṭ)*,
> and the cause *(*rîb)* of the widow does not come to them.

Using the same language found in 1:16-17 *(*šāpaṭ, yātôm, *rîb, ʾalmānâ)*, the prophet, acting as the prosecutor, lays out the accusation. To accuse the leaders of being "accomplices of thieves" and accepting, even soliciting, bribes describes a patently unjust society in which corrupt magistrates engage in extortion. When court cases and favorable judgments are for sale to the highest bidder, it is the poor who become all the more vulnerable and easily exploited. Without the means to offer bribes and "gifts," what chance have they for a favorable ruling? Though the leadership is singled out, they stand for the whole community, and in their failure Isaiah sees the failure of the entire city, which now comes under sentence.

In vv. 16-17, the practice of social justice was made the condition for reprieve from judgment and the sine qua non for acceptable worship. The indictment in vv. 21-23 makes it clear that those conditions have not been met. And so God, the personal deliverer of the oppressed (Exod 3:7-9) and the protector of widows and orphans (Deut 10:17-18), arises to enact judgment. In Isa 1:24, the language shifts to divine first-person speech, and God introduces himself in a rather elaborate series of epithets. "YHWH of Hosts" and "Strong One of Israel" are particularly noteworthy as epithets for the Divine Warrior (Hayes and Irvine 1987: 81; Cross 1973: 68-71). That "my people" (1:3) have become "my enemies" is a biting and bitter development. It is noteworthy that it is God who personally acts: in this instance he does not raise up another kingdom or send another agent but in a series of six first-person verbs (vv. 24-26) acts decisively to deal with the situation detailed above. Because the offense has become personal (*my* enemies and *my* adversaries), God arises to enact the sentence. This depiction of the Divine Warrior exercising judicial functions is an ancient motif: the Divine Warrior serves as judge, and the lawsuit is how the battle is waged (Kang 1989: 14–15; see also Patrick Miller 1968: 104).

Though God seeks to *take revenge* and *avenge Godself,* the intent of the Divine Warrior in moving against his enemies is not destruction but purification and restoration: the impurities will be *smelted* away and *removed* (v. 25), and then judges and counselors will be *returned* (v. 26). The corruption represented by tarnished silver in v. 22 finds a fit remedy in the purifying fires of the foundry where what is corrosive is removed (v. 25). The imagery here is evocative of the prophet's call in ch. 6, where he comes to recognize his own impurity as participating in the impurity of the people at large. In both 1:21-28 and 6:1-8, YHWH of Hosts acts (1:24; 6:3, 5), the sins of one are associated with the sins of the people at large, and the removal (**swr,* 1:25; 6:7) of the wrong is accomplished by fire (**ṣrp,* 1:25; **śrp,* 6:6). The root metaphors, the fundamental understanding of Jerusalem's condition, and the corrective treatment (viz., impurity, removal of impurity, fire), all seem to derive from the prophet's own experience. In both cases, remedial measures are the first steps taken.

In order to redress the abhorrent social conditions that have adulterated the once faithful city, God will return "judges as at first" and "counselors as in the beginning." Clearly, integrity in these two social offices is key to reestablishing justice. While the smelting away of dross, that is, the destruction of evildoers, is a sentence carried out by YHWH (vv. 25, 28), the establishment of justice is something to be carried out by judges and counselors on behalf of society at large. God's sweeping away the evildoers sets up the conditions that make it possible for just judges and counselors to be restored, but justice enacted in the social realm is an activity carried out by people for people.

YHWH, having completed his purging of corruption, will guarantee justice by installing judges like those he had earlier raised up—heroes who take decisive action to deliver from oppression. While the judges of old most often fought against an outside enemy, here YHWH clearly identifies his enemies as those who turn aside the most vulnerable and oppressed members of society. When justice is once again exercised on behalf of the orphan and widow, then shall the city reclaim its former glory and be recognized again as a righteous and faithful city (v. 26).

Verses 27-28 are a powerful summary statement, not only of this preceding oracle but of ch. 1 as a whole. Indeed, in the entire Hebrew Bible there is perhaps no more compelling statement about the centrality and efficacy of justice and righteousness.

Three points about vv. 27-28 may be observed. First, the heretofore unnamed city is now specified as Zion, forging a link between vv. 21-26 and vv. 27-28. Second, a motif common to both wisdom and prophetic traditions brings the prophecy to a conclusion by enunciating the two sides of judgment: deliverance for the just (v. 27), destruction for the wicked (v. 28). Third, and most importantly, the redemption of Zion is accomplished by justice and righteousness, the same word pair encountered at the beginning of the oracle in 1:21 and which in both instances signifies social justice.

Verse 27 presents an interesting interpretive and theological problem: whose "justice and righteousness" is meant—YHWH's or the city's? The grammar, it must be admitted, does not clarify the problem. The verb here, the Niphal of *pādāh* ("redeem"), is of little help in resolving the issue. This Niphal occurs in just two other instances in biblical Hebrew, both in the Holiness Code (Lev 19:20; 27:29); they are used with no modifiers or agents specified and thus shed no light on the construction found in Isa 1:27.

Contextually, however, a strong case may be made that the justice and righteousness described are those of Zion. So far in ch. 1, the people and the leadership have been instructed to enact social justice (1:16-17). The acceptability of their cultic worship (1:11-15) and, indeed, their ultimate fate as blessed or cursed (1:19-20) are made contingent on their doing justice. Then an indictment details the gross corruption of the leadership (1:23a) and their callous neglect of justice for the orphan and widow (1:23b). After YHWH purifies the city, he then restores just judges and wise counselors. Presumably, a restored and just leadership cultivates that climate and culture of justice—not merely in the courts, but throughout society at large—that allow Zion to reclaim her former glory as a *faithful* and *righteous city*. Just as the people's failure to do justice and to enact righteousness hastens judgment, now their walking in the ways of justice will guarantee the city's redemption.

It is wholly consistent with the theology of the Hebrew Bible that it is in one's power to secure a blessing by faithfulness or to incite a curse by sinful ways. The justice of the city and the righteousness of her repentant ones result in redemption in the same way that the actions of sinning, rebelling, and forsaking result in destruction. Both redemption and destruction are divine responses to human action. The desire to attribute the city's redemption to the righteousness and justice of God (Young 1992, 1:89) seems an intrusion of Pauline theology read through Luther.

One final point on this issue. To understand the word pair "justice and righteousness" as a hendiadys for "social justice" moves the discussion away from consideration of the abstract theological qualities of God and focuses more properly on the realm of human activity. Thus, Zion is redeemed by enacting justice in the social sphere and proving her fidelity to God in her care for the orphan and the widow. Just as her harlotry consists in her neglect of justice, her redemption consists in her doing justice. Bovati confirms this meaning in his examination of the forensic use of the term *mišpāṭ*. He suggests that the term *mišpāṭ* with the prepositions *bě* ("in, with"; as in Isa 1:27) or *lě* ("to, for") refers to a "fair sentence" (1994: 210). Thus, Zion will be redeemed by its restored judges enacting right judgments in the courts. Though this is a more restricted sense than the concept of social justice conveyed by the hendiadys, this technical use of *běmišpāṭ* nonetheless moves along the same lines of understanding the justice involved in Zion's redemption as that enacted by its people.

Verse 28 serves as a conclusion to both the judgment announced in vv. 24-25 and the larger section, 1:2-28. In v. 25, YHWH threatened to remove Zion's slag or cheapened alloy, and this metaphorical purification finds its more realistic accomplishment in the breaking of rebels and sinners, and the destruction of those who forsake YHWH. This is the other side of judgment, the destruction of the wicked as counterpoint to the reward of the righteous. Verses 27-28 serve as a fitting summary statement to the preceding prophecy of judgment and redemption.

Further, the extraordinary recapitulation of terms in v. 28 clearly signals the end to a composition that now stands as a unified passage beginning in v. 2.[16] Those who rebel (**pšʿ*, v. 2), who are sinners (**ḥṭʾ*, v. 4), and who forsake YHWH (**ʿzb*, v. 4) are all recalled, and in the same order, in v. 28:

> But he shall shatter[17] rebels *(*pšʿ)* and sinners *(*ḥṭʾ)* together,
> while those who forsake *(*ʿzb)* YHWH will be destroyed.

This summarizing verse in a powerful and unequivocal way draws together the entire passage into a unified whole. For our purposes, one of the more important effects of considering 1:2-28 as one large passage is that it clearly identifies the miscarriage of justice detailed herein as acts of rebellion and sin, acts by which the people as a whole, the city at large, and the leadership in particular have abandoned YHWH. The basis for the coming judgment is not so much cultic infidelity and idolatry (concerns taken up elsewhere) but initially and most prominently sins of injustice, both governmental and societal.

What may well have been five originally separate prophecies from Isaiah of Jerusalem (1:2-3, 4-9, 10-17, 18-20, 21-26) have been drawn together into a greater single unit by the addition of vv. 27-28. It is not possible to say with certainty who added these crucial verses or when. But the effect of these verses is twofold: verse 27 brings the chapter to a climax and heightens the significance of social justice as the means to a secure future; verse 28, by recapping the key terms culled from the two initial oracles, purposefully imposes a unity on the material now comprising vv. 2-28. The two separate prophecies in vv. 10-17 and 21-26 are each impressive in their demand for justice. Structurally and theologically, vv. 16-17 conclude vv. 10-15 and establish the criteria by which blessing or curse in vv. 18-20 will be determined. If we take, then, vv. 27-28 as the conclusion to the entire unit, vv. 2-28 sound an insistent demand for the kingdom to realign its social, civic, and religious life by the practice of social justice.

The urgent call to justice suggests its lamentable absence in society. The accusation of injustice is directed to the people at large, the city in general, and the leadership in particular. Conversely, the expectation to act with justice is demanded of all, though the courts and civic leaders bear an appropriately greater responsibility. The kind of justice the prophet adjures is social justice, as indicated both by the hendiadys *mišpāṭ ûṣĕdāqâ* and by the specific actions commanded. The corrective measures that Isaiah specifies imply that the basic requirements of a just society—care for the needy, integrity in public office, right judgment in the courts, freedom from violence in the streets—are so egregiously lacking that the cult has become not only ineffective, but loathsome in its hypocrisy. The threat of judgment is an inducement to a reform of life and society, the absence of which will result in a judgment like that on Sodom and Gomorrah—complete and irrevocable. Blessing or curse, redemption or destruction is God's action; the performance of social justice is the act of the entire community, and the particular responsibility of its leadership.

By demanding that the people "seek justice," Isaiah imbues the pursuit of justice with theological and cultic resonance. It is not possible to say with certainty that Isaiah is using the word *dāraš* in its technical, cultic sense, but the data are suggestive. To "seek justice" may well stand as both the corrective to, and the fulfillment of, cultic life, bringing into unbreakable unity the liturgical and social demands of religious life. The seeking of God is to take place in the temple *and* in the streets: worship finds its legitimacy in the protection of the orphan and the widow. As if to underscore this point, Zion, tellingly identified as a temple city, then comes under indictment precisely for its corrupt civic and social life (vv. 21-26). Her harlotry is identified as injustice rather than by the more traditional charge of idolatry, that is, cultic infidelity. In this way, too, the cultic aspects of life are yoked to the social demands, just as the seeking of God in a cultic sense had earlier been tied to the seeking of God in social justice. Finally, what had been implied in vv. 16-17, 19-20, and 25-26 is made explicit in vv. 27-28: redemption or destruction depend on the (re)establishment of a just society.

Particularly when ch. 1 is taken as an introduction to the book of Isaiah, the significance of justice as a theological concern and a social blueprint comes into striking relief. Israel's rebellion, ignorance of God, corrupt civic life, and vain cult are all manifest in her fundamental injustice. Conversely, and stated most simply and eloquently, "Zion shall be redeemed by justice, and her repentant ones by righteousness" (1:27).

Isaiah 2–12

Chapter 2 begins what is considered to be the core of the "authentic" words of Isaiah, namely, chs. 2–12. While some commentators deny the possibility of recovering the historical Isaiah, the more hopeful maintain that if the eighth-century prophet is to be found anywhere, it is in these chapters, together with a second collection of words in chs. 28-31. Chapters 2–12 begin with a majestic scene of YHWH, the universal Judge, issuing effective decrees and exercising authority over all the earth from atop Mount Zion, and they conclude with a hymn of thanksgiving praising God for salvation and celebrating the presence of the Holy One of Israel in Zion. In between are oracles of indictment and doom and of promise and salvation. Key to the indictments are charges of injustice; essential to the coming of salvation is the restoration of justice.

YHWH Shall Judge from Zion: Isaiah 2:2-4

Before turning to the content of this oracle, we must examine three preliminary issues that affect its interpretation: (1) the limits of the unit; (2) the authenticity of the unit's Isaianic authorship; and (3) the relationship of this unit to the surrounding material.

1. The Limits of the Unit. Verse 1 is widely conceded to be a redactional addition and need not detain us. Frequently, the unit is defined as 2:2-5 (so Clements, Stacey, Jensen, Hayes and Irvine, Wildberger). Sweeney, however, makes a compelling argument for seeing the break after v. 4, with v. 5 serving as the introduction to 2:6-21.

> The boundaries of this unit are determined by its future orientation, its focus on Zion and the nations, the 3rd-person descriptive language employed throughout the passage, and the absence of any specific indication of its addressee. Although many scholars maintain that 2:5 is part of this unit because of its lexical similarities and its idyllic contents, this view must be rejected. The lack of a syntactical link between vv. 4 and 5, the use of an imperative address to the "house of Jacob," and the explanatory *kî* in v. 6 (which links vv. 5 and 6ff. together) demonstrate that v. 5 introduces a new structural subunit within chs. 2–4. (1996a: 97–98)

This seems to be a compelling analysis, which we accept.

2. The Authenticity of the Unit. Apart from a few small details, this oracle is almost identical to the oracle in Mic 4:1-3. The obvious question is—whose oracle is this? The older position that the oracle originates with Micah is now largely rejected. We begin instead with the majority position that this oracle is in some way related to the Isaianic tradition.[18] Still, there is no consensus as to whether the oracle originates with Isaiah of Jerusalem (for example, Wildberger, Jensen, von Rad) or is an exilic Isaianic redaction (for example, Sweeney, Clements, Williamson). There are some, too, who hold a kind of middle ground that acknowledges the impossibility of determining its exact origin but points out its congruence with authentically Isaianic material (for example, Seitz, Stacey). The impossibility of deciding this issue with certainty warrants a cautious approach in this study. The congruence of the concerns of 2:2-4 with those of Isaiah and its prominent position in the structure of the book invite our attention at this point.

3. The Relationship of 2:2-4 to the Surrounding Material. Stacey asserts that 2:1-5 is "unrelated to what goes before it and what comes after" (1993: 15). The latter part of this statement has been shown by Sweeney to be untrue, due in part to Stacey's wrongly defining the unit: v. 5, taken by Stacey as the end of 2:1-5, is clearly linked to vv. 6ff. Further, this introductory passage (2:2-4), taken together with the conclusion, 4:1-6, sets the intervening oracles of judgment within a framework of redemption and ultimate salvation. As for Stacey's contention that 2:2-4 is unrelated to the contents of ch. 1, a closer examination shows a number of lexical and thematic points of contact.

a. Three Verbal Links

i. The *torah* and *word of YHWH* that go forth from Zion/Jerusalem (2:3b) recall the *word of YHWH* and *torah* of God in 1:10. These two passages contain the only joint occurrences of these terms in the book of Isaiah. It is also significant that the *word* and *torah* go forth from Zion/Jerusalem, which, in the preceding passage (1:27-28), is a Zion purified and redeemed. It is significant, too, that the locus on the poetically lofty Mount Zion is the "house of the God of Jacob" (2:3): the temple, earlier the site of unacceptable worship (1:11-13), is now foreseen as the place from which God's effective word issues forth. The city, once again properly a temple city established on the mountaintop, regains its centrality as the place where decrees are promulgated with integrity.[19] The terms *word, torah*, and *Zion* all evoke the preceding material.

ii. In the next verse, 2:4, the verbs **špṭ* (to judge) and **ykḥ* (Hiphil: to decide) are paired as they had been linked earlier by the combination of 1:10-17 and 18-20 (**špṭ* in v. 17; the Niphal of **ykḥ* in v. 18). Apart from the sister text in Micah, these terms are found together in the Hebrew Bible only here in chs. 1 and 2, and in both Isa 11:3 and 11:4 (both verses employing the Hiphil of **ykḥ*). The rare pairing of these two verbs in the Hebrew Bible and its concentration in these texts are suggestive.

iii. Finally, the expression "they shall not learn war again" *(wĕlōʾ-yilmĕdû ʿôd milḥāmâ)* occurs only here and in the parallel text in Micah.[20] When the verb **lmd* (to learn) is elsewhere used with *milḥāmâ*, it is always in the Piel—to teach or train (Judges 3:2; 2 Sam 22:35; Pss 18:35 [Eng. v. 34]; 144:1; Song 3:8; the Qal passive participle is found in 1 Chr 5:18). The use of **lmd* (Qal) with *milḥāmâ* is therefore highly unusual and catches the attention of the reader. The verb **lmd* was used previously in Isa 1:17: "Cease doing evil; *learn* to do good." The "good" that people are to "learn" is spelled out in terms of justice on behalf of the orphan and widow (1:17). Perhaps the unusual use of the verb **lmd* in 2:4, "they shall not learn war again," can be better understood in light of its earlier occurrence in 1:17. In fact, when taken together, "they shall not learn war" is the inverse of the earlier command, "learn to do good." Doing "good" on the domestic scene requires the practice of social justice, while on the international stage, doing good is *not learning war.* When the national concerns of ch. 1 are transposed to the international context of 2:2-4, the domestic concerns for justice are writ large in the ways in which nations deal with one another, that is, international disputes are not settled by war, but by the rule and decree of YHWH (2:4a). As in the case of **špṭ* and **ykḥ*, the use of a relatively rare term in two proximate passages, and in ways that are complementary, invites the reader to understand 2:2-4 in relationship to ch. 1.

b. The Meaning of *špṭ

The key term and concept in 2:2-4 for this study is the verb **špṭ* (v. 4). The expression "to judge between" *(šāpaṭ bên)* is a simpler form of the fuller idiom *šāpaṭ bên . . . ûbên*,[21] which implies that the basic meaning of "judging" is "an authoritative act of discerning, separating, deciding between what/whom is just and what/whom is unjust, between the innocent and the guilty" (Bovati 1994: 185). The general situation envisioned is judging between good and evil, right and wrong. Such a judgment implicitly lies behind the command found in 1:16b-17a, "Cease doing evil, learn to do good." This "deciding between" function is the proper activity of judges in court vis-à-vis individual petitioners, and exclusively the prerogative of YHWH in his role as Judge of all the earth.

In 2:4, the subject of the verb "to judge" is YHWH, whose *word* and *torah* are described in the previous verse, and the object of the verb is the *nations*, anticipating already God's sovereignty in judgment as explicated in chs. 13–23 (Seitz 1993a: 38–40). This picture is the cosmic counterpart of the domestic description found in ch. 1: there, judges "judge" the oppressed, while in ch. 2, YHWH "judges" the nations and arbitrates for many peoples. The judgment YHWH issues is the *word/torah* of the previous verse, and the effect is immediately evident: weapons of war are recast into the tools of peacetime with the result that there are no swords left to be raised and no need to learn the science of warfare.

YHWH's conduct toward the nations sets the standards for their relationships among themselves: just as YHWH settles disputes without resorting to warfare, henceforth nations, subject to him, will no longer have recourse to warfare to settle their disputes. This peaceful situation is not a tribute to the voluntary, goodwill decision of humble nations; it is, rather, testimony to the sovereignty of the Divine Judge who can compel nations by his word and effect sentence as needed (see chs. 13–23). Or, as Levenson summarizes, "recognition of YHWH's lordship is the basis for universal peace" (1992: 1101). While in some traditions the Divine Warrior "makes wars cease to the end of the earth, breaks the bow, and shatters the spear; he burns the shields with fire" (Ps 46:9 [MT 10]), in Isa 2:2-4 YHWH accomplishes the same end without violence. His mere word is effective (Isa 55:10-11). As Wildberger nicely summarizes, "the justice of God is in force among the nations" (1991: 95).

The verbal and thematic links between ch. 1 and 2:2-4 cast these two passages as a diptych, two scenes that may be profitably considered together: the human and the divine, the earthly and the cosmic. On the macrocosmic level, YHWH exercises worldwide rule so that all the nations live in peace and walk in his ways. On the microcosmic scale, the temple city, established in justice and righteousness, cares for all members of society so that the orphan and the widow can live free from oppression and want. In both realms, YHWH's *word* and *torah* are instructive, Israel learns to do good, all the nations stop learning warfare, and "judging" rightly leads to a society living in justice and a world at peace. In the temple city, its counselors, leaders, and courts are to be the most conspicuous defenders of justice; on Zion, YHWH himself issues effective decrees. Zion, the faithful and righteous city (1:26), is the suitable place for YHWH's worldwide reign to become manifest.

Lectionary Notes

Common Lectionary: First Sunday of Advent (A): Isa 2:1-5 / Psalm 122 / Matt 24:36-44
Roman Lectionary: Same, except Matt 24:37-44

In seasonal time, such as in Advent, the readings are related more to the season than explicitly to one another. The First Sunday of Advent is eschatological in perspective. Indeed, the Gospel reading for the First Sunday in all three years is apocalyptic. As a season, Advent begins by directing the attention of the church to Christ's future coming, even more than to his historical coming celebrated in Christmas (*Revised Common Lectionary* §25).

The previous Sunday's liturgical enthronement of Christ as King leads nicely to this Isaian vision of YHWH exercising universal rule from the exalted mount of Zion (Isa 2:1-4). This scene of divine sovereignty, though set in the future, seems to envision a transformation of the present order: it describes a specific geographical place, the Lord's sovereignty over all nations, and peace among all peoples. This alone offers an important alternative to the apocalyptic perspective of some of the New Testament readings for this season. The Bible does not speak with one voice about the future. For example, the book of Revelation presents the cataclysmic destruction of the world that leads to a "new heaven and a new earth" (21:1). In today's Gospel reading from Matthew, the coming of the Son of Man is compared to the total destruction brought by the flood in the days of Noah. The chaos that Matthew describes is the prelude to the coming of the Son of Man. But such scenes are not the only possibility. This passage from Isaiah, along with images of the natural order restored to *šālôm,* where the wolf and lamb lie down together (Isa 11:6; 65:25), are also visions of the future. These strands of tradition envision the peaceful transformation of the present order. Canonically, these different traditions stand side by side and serve to contextualize, and even relativize, each other. What all visions share, however, is the establishment of the universal rule of God.

As a reading in the Christian Lectionary, the universal rule of God that Isaiah envisions is linked to the return of Christ in glory. As the Roman *Lectionary for Mass* states, on the Sundays of Advent, "The Old Testament readings are prophecies about the Messiah and the Messianic age, especially from the Book of Isaiah" (General Principles, §93). By explicit intention, the Lectionary casts the first reading as a prophecy of the *messianic* age. Hence, the Liturgy for Advent interprets the Isaian vision christologically, and transfers that vision from the indefinite future to the end of time. The coming in glory of the Son of Man serves as the prelude to the establishment of God's worldwide sovereignty, that is, the reign of God. Though we argued in the exegesis above that Isa 2:5 belongs to the next unit, the lectionary includes it as part of the reading and thus suggests that the establishment of God's reign is furthered when God's people walk in God's ways.

Corruption and Confusion in Zion: Isaiah 3:1-12

In 3:2 we find the term *šôpēṭ* ("judge"), first seen in 1:26, where it was in parallelism with *yôʿēṣ* ("counselor"; note the occurrence of this term in 3:3). In ch. 3, it is listed with an expansive, if somewhat eclectic, roster of the leadership of Jerusalem and Judah, with the notable exceptions of the king and priests.

The term *šôpēṭ* is in use in both the tribal and the monarchical periods, and its meaning, though frequently judicial, enjoys a much wider range. Bovati summarizes the broadest range of meaning: *šôpēṭ* "is used to describe a post of public interest: it normally refers to the function of a magistrate, but there is no lack of texts in which the participial noun refers in general terms to authority, a chief, a notable, and the like, and therefore where the juridical connotation is no longer clearly observable" (1994: 173; Cross 1973: 220, n. 3). In the period of the monarchy, the term could be used somewhat restrictively to describe royal appointees to judicial and administrative posts. The functions of "judges" may have evolved; "tribal" and "royal" functions and structures seem to have existed simultaneously in the monarchic period (Stager 1985: 24). The presence of the term in this long list of civic leaders makes it difficult to decide with greater precision what is meant by "judges." What is clear from the overall intent of 3:1-3 is that all persons of authority are to be removed.

Wildberger reads the social instability of 3:4-5 as evidence of an internal revolution that results in the loss of the above-mentioned leadership. He explicitly denies the role of any foreign enemy (1991: 127–28). The more widely accepted interpretation is to understand the removal of the leadership (3:1-3) as part of Assyria's standard operating procedure against rebellious vassals; the leadership vacuum results in the social chaos described in 3:4-7.[22]

The cause for this chaotic situation is summarized in 3:8:

> For Jerusalem has stumbled and Judah has fallen,
> for their speech and their deeds were against[23] YHWH,
> rebelling in his glorious sight.

This generic accusation is then further specified in 3:9:

> Their partiality *(hakkārat pĕnêhem)* testifies against them,
> yet they proclaim their sin like Sodom—they do not hide [it]!
> Alas for them! For they have contrived harm to themselves.

The opening phrase of this verse has been traditionally translated as "the look of/expression on their faces" (NRSV, NAB, KJV, ASV, NIV). But the grammar[24] and the context here favor a charge of judicial partiality: such a judicial miscarriage is followed by another legal technical term, *ʿānâ bĕ,* "to testify against." Further, their sin is likened to that of Sodom, which in 1:10-17 is specified as corrupt legal practices. The traditional translation, "the look of/expression on their faces," is nondescript and generic by comparison. The leadership's partiality, as we have seen, refers to their neglect of the concerns of the orphan and widow (1:23) and their active obstruction of justice when the cause of the widow and orphan comes to them (10:2). The charges leveled in this passage are continuous with concerns already encountered, specifically judicial corruption.

YHWH's Day in Court: Isaiah 3:13-15

Taking 3:10-11 as a late addition and v. 12 as an independent saying of Isaiah placed here editorially (Sweeney 1988: 177–81; Wildberger 1991: 127; Gray 1912: 66) leads directly into the courtroom (3:13-15) and sets up a telling contrast: YHWH, unlike those who show partiality in judgment, stands to give just judgment:

> YHWH takes his place to argue his case,
> and he stands to judge peoples.[25]
> YHWH will come in judgment *(bĕmišpāṭ)*
> with the elders of his people and his princes.
> "You! You have burned the vineyard;
> the spoil of the poor is in your houses.
> What do you mean by crushing my people
> and grinding the faces of the poor?"
> says the Lord YHWH of Hosts.

From a technical point of view, the legal idiom in this passage is somewhat imprecise. Bovati makes a distinction between a "two-party dispute" and a trial before a judge: "the former has its own juridical character and can proceed to a resolution without outside mediation; on the other hand, the intervention of a judge can in certain circumstances bring about a reasonable conclusion to proceedings that originally involved only the two parties in dispute" (1994: 33). In the first stage of the dispute *(rîb)*, the injured or wronged party, taking the role of "prosecutor" or "avenger," presents the accusation and makes a demand for justice. If the accused party acknowledges guilt, the two can then come to some reconciliation. If, however, the accused does not confess to wrongdoing, the dispute may be brought to a judge, who will pronounce sentence (Bovati 1994: 30-32). This is the second stage to which the term *mišpāṭ* in 3:14 refers: it is the actual procedural action taken in court (Bovati 1994: 208). We may infer, therefore, on the basis of the legal language involved, that in 3:13 YHWH initiates a dispute or *rîb* that goes unresolved. The next step, begun in v. 14, is to go to court (Hayes and Irvine 1987: 93). The two distinct phases described by Bovati appear to be conflated in 3:13-15, perhaps because YHWH is both prosecutor and judge.

A closer look at the parties involved and the accusations being made is needed.

1. The Injured Party. Though the ones who actually suffer the wrong are "my people" (3:15), specifically the "poor," it is YHWH who enters the plea. Two points may be made. First, the poor who have already been wronged by the legal process are powerless to act on their own behalf. As Abraham Heschel observes, "those who know how to exploit are endowed with the skill to justify their acts, while those who are easily exploited possess no skill in pleading their own cause" (1969: 204). And so it is that YHWH, the well-known champion of the powerless, must arise: "When God arises for judgment, [it is] to save the poor of the earth" (Ps 76:9 [MT 10]). Second, though the poor have suffered, it is YHWH who is wronged; an offense against the vulnerable is a sin against YHWH (von Waldow 1970: 189). As it says in Prov 14:31, "The one who oppresses the poor profanes his Maker."

2. The Accused. Those addressed are "the elders of his people and his princes" (3:14). The "elders" reflects the older, tribal ideal of governance in which the family or clan elders dispensed justice in legal, economic, and moral disputes. Their particular role was to defend the common people. The "princes" reflect the newer, centralized form of royal government: they are professional civil servants answerable to the crown and entrusted with both administrative and judicial functions. These are not to be understood as having replaced the tribal structures entirely, but the two seem to coexist in their own proper spheres. In short, both the formal and the informal structures of government, as well as the older and the newer officers of justice, all come under indictment. The very ones to whom recourse would normally be made are the ones responsible for perpetuating the injustice that grinds the faces of the poor into the dust. There is no one to whom the injured poor can turn.

The elders and princes are addressed abruptly, without any introduction to YHWH's direct speech. The first word is an emphatic, direct address: "And you! You have burned the vineyard!" YHWH's eagerness to confront and his urgency in reproaching the evildoers signal his outrage and lead directly into the accusation.

3. The Accusation. In 3:14b, the accusation is phrased in both metaphorical and literal terms. The accused "burn" or "devour"[26] the vineyard. Especially in light of Isa 5:1-7, the vineyard is readily taken as a metaphor for the people Israel. What should be tended with care so that its fruit grow bountifully has been ransacked for the personal benefit of those who are charged with its care. The extent of the harm inflicted is indicated by the term **bʿr*, which, however translated, seems to imply wholesale devastation.

But there is a legal/literal sense, too, in which "vineyard" is employed. In the ancient Covenant Code, the vineyard, like fields and olive groves, is to lie fallow and rest every seventh year so that the poor of the land, and after them the beasts of the fields, may eat whatever grows there (Exod 23:10-11). This humanitarian concern is later expanded in the Deuteronomic Code, which prohibits, on a yearly basis, the overgleaning of the fields, olive trees, and vineyards so that something may be left behind for the sojourner, orphan, and widow (Deut 24:19-22). In this light, the image used by Isaiah of a vineyard "devoured," "depastured," or "burned" presents the owners of the vineyard greedily grabbing and gleaning all that can be had in callous disregard for the poor, who are deprived of even the leftovers of the harvest. The owners' rapacity is so consuming that they leave nothing behind for the needy. Whether the vineyard of 3:14 is understood metaphorically for Israel or literally as an overgleaned agricultural holding, the stripping bare of the vineyard reveals its caretakers as greedy and self-concerned.

Their greed is further specified in the second part of 3:14b—"the spoil of the poor is in your houses." The term *spoil (gāzēl/gĕzēlâ)* usually refers to that which is robbed or stolen (Ezek 18:7, 12, 16, 18; Mal 1:13), what Stacey calls "simple robbery" (1993: 26). Its occurrences in other texts, however, suggest something that is at once both more sinister and violent. When Lev 5:21, 23 (Eng. 6:2, 4) lists various sins *(*ḥṭʾ)* against one's neighbors, **gzl* is used with the terms *deceive (*kḥš)* and *defraud/oppress (*ʿšq)*. In Isa 3:14, then, it may be that these sinful acts against the poor are not merely "simple robbery," but more likely acts of fraud and deceit accomplished under the guise of legal means (see the accusation in Isa 10:1 against those who "decree iniquitous decrees and who write oppression").

There is another sense in which *spoil (gāzēl/gĕzēlâ)* is sometimes used—that which is plundered or seized as spoil in warfare (for example, Deut 28:29, 31). Indeed, in the only other occurrence of this term in First Isaiah, this is exactly how it is understood (10:2):

> [Woe to those who] turn aside the poor from judgment *(dîn),*
> and who rob *(ligzōl)* the oppressed of my people of justice *(mišpāṭ),*
> widows become their spoil *(*šll),*
> and orphans they plunder *(*bzz).*

To rob the people is comparable to making widows and orphans their *spoil* and *plunder,* both terms that are commonly found to describe the aftermath of warfare. The nuance this context imparts to 3:14 is as frightening as it is subtle. What is suggested is a kind of class warfare that pits the powerful against the weak, the privileged against the disadvantaged. The orphan and the widow are no better than vanquished victims of war given over to plunder. In the face of such violent oppression, YHWH himself arises as judge and defender (Exod 22:20-23 [Eng. vv. 21-24]).

The personal nature of this economic assault upon the poor is indicated tersely: what has been robbed is *in your houses.* The oppressors are confronted directly and the evidence of their sin is found "in hand," as it were. That their ill-gotten goods are found not only in their houses is suggested by what appears to be the companion piece to this oracle. In Isa 3:16-24 (a passage some commentators consider a later addition), the haughty daughters of Zion are excoriated for their obsession with fashion and finely coifed hair, their love of fine jewelry and trinkets. Indeed, the text lists some twenty-one fashion and luxury items, from earrings to anklets: these wealthy women are bedecked, literally, from head to foot (Lang 1982: 54). The contrast is both shocking and appalling: the faces of the poor are ground into the dust while the nouveaux riches prance about with enticing eyes and extended necks. Isaiah and Amos are equally vituperative; but while Isaiah is more incisive in his attention to detail, Amos is more personal in his invective—"You cows of Bashan!" (Amos 4:1-2).

The wanton exploitation of his people moves God to anger. The outrage of God is reflected in the nearly apoplectic, elliptical exclamation, *mallākem,* which has the effect of "What's wrong with you!" This in turn leads to a summary description of the effects of the injustice afflicting the poor: "You are crushing my people and the face of the poor you are grinding [into the dust]." The direct divine discourse, introduced so abruptly, comes to a rather solemn conclusion with the words being attributed to "the Lord YHWH of Hosts" (3:15), thus directing the offense of the people against the sovereignty of God.

In these three short verses (3:13-15), Isaiah indicts those who should be responsible for the defense of the poor. He goes on to detail the scope of social oppression that leaves nothing for the poor, the economic warfare that plunders and robs the underclasses, the manipulation of the legal system that puts a good face on their crimes, and the outrage of God who arises to defend his people and who moves quickly from a dispute to a formal legal proceeding. Surely the God who judges the nations (2:2-4) will not long delay to bring judgment against the corrupt leaders. The sentence is anticipated and awaits only its execution.

Purifying Judgment in Zion: Isaiah 4:2-6

This section of Isaiah, chs. 2–4, concludes with an apparently late redactional scene of judgment, purification, and redemption, 4:2-6. The term *mišpāṭ* is found in 4:4, where it means "judgment." This unit seems closely tied to 3:16—4:1 in that the "daughters of Zion" are the subject of both (3:16; 4:4). Reading the latter in terms of the former reduces all the carefully inventoried wardrobe and jewelry to "filth" *(ṣōʾâ),* a term vile in its literal sense, and impure in its cultic sense. When "YHWH enters into judgment with the elders of his people and his princes" (3:14), his "spirit of judgment" will be "a spirit of burning" (4:4). There is a fitting irony in how the purification literally takes place: "the Lord has washed away the filth of the daughters of Zion, and the blood of Jerusalem he cleanses from her midst with a spirit of judgment *(mišpāṭ)* and a spirit of burning *(*bʿr)*." The term "burning" in 4:4 is the same term used in 3:14 (both Piel) to describe how the corrupt leaders dealt with the vineyard. What they inflicted on the poor shall be meted out to Jerusalem, but with different effect. Their action was one of oppression, while YHWH is acting to purify so as to glorify. But for that purification and glorification to take place, there must first be judgment *(mišpāṭ).*

Seeds of Corruption, Harvest of Injustice: Isaiah 5:1-7, 8-24

That these two undisputed Isaianic passages are companion pieces is widely acknowledged. Sweeney convincingly argues that "a number of features demonstrate their interdependence and indicate that they were composed to function together as two parts of a larger unit" (1996a: 128). From the point of view of the thematic concerns of this study, this is evident structurally in two ways. First, both passages come to an end with dramatic indictments of injustice. This is more evident in 5:7b:

> He expected justice *(mišpāṭ)* but found bloodshed,
> righteousness *(ṣĕdāqâ)* but found an outcry.

In the second unit, the concluding pronouncement of sentence, 5:24, depends on the series of preceding woes (vv. 8, 11, 18, 20, 21, 22), which is epitomized and brought to a head in the summary indictment in 5:23:

> [Woe to those] who acquit the guilty for a bribe,
> but the just cause of the righteous they turn aside from him.

The second structural feature common to both units is this: these summary statements become the launching point for what follows. Though 5:7b is the "punch line" of the preceding oracle, its generic indictment is followed by a bill of specifics in 5:8-24. Similarly, the final woe in 5:23 leads to the announcement of sentence: the "fire that consumes stubble" so that "hay sinks down in flame" (v. 24) is realized in the destroying advance of the implacable Assyrian army (5:25-30).

1. The Bitter Fruit of Injustice: Isaiah 5:1-7. Most commentators, with the notable exception of Kaiser, locate the parable in the ministry of Isaiah either just before the fall of Samaria or shortly after it. Though the conditions described in the following woe-prophecies could apply to either the northern kingdom or to Judah, it is difficult to be more precise in situating this passage. The caution of Motyer against allegorizing the details of the parable so as to find referents to Israel's history (1993: 68) and Gray's acknowledgment that "the year in which the poem was either written or recited cannot be even approximately determined" (1912: 83) are judicious warnings against seeking too precise a historical setting for the parable. We must be content to describe the general social conditions of the last third of the eighth century reflected in the material rather than attempt to tie the interpretation to specific historical circumstances that cannot be determined with confidence.

The first term that requires our attention is found in 5:3, in which the voice of the Owner of the vineyard overtakes the friend/spokesman:

> So now, inhabitants of Jerusalem and people of Judah,
> judge between me and my vineyard.

The Owner of the vineyard instructs the people to "*judge (*špṭ)* between me and my vineyard." This is a textbook example of the full and classic form of the expression earlier described by Bovati, "to judge between . . . and . . ." (*šāpaṭ bên . . . ûbên;* cf. 2:4). It expects both a decision that distinguishes between the complainant and the accused, and an assessment of who is in the right and who is in the wrong. While not a legal verdict in the strict sense, forensic imagery is applied to heighten the urgency in assigning culpability. Even this sluggish people should be able to make a proper determination: indeed, as presented, the facts of the case are so self-evident that this is more a rhetorical exercise than a procedural one. If the people engage the prophet's rhetorical question, there is only one possible answer. The term *šāpaṭ* here functions in its expected manner.

The parable finds its climax in v. 7b, which is perhaps the single most graphic and severe indictment against the perversion of social justice in the Hebrew Bible, and employs striking wordplays: "[YHWH] expected justice *(mišpāṭ),* but found bloodshed *(miśpāḥ)*; righteousness *(ṣĕdāqâ),* but found an outcry *(ṣĕʿāqâ).*" The significance of this stunning conclusion, however, is not its clever rhetorical effect, but its function in summing up the specific image used in the parable. Surprisingly, very few commentators make the connection between the paronomasia and the image of grapes and wild grapes.

First, it may be observed that the problem is not that the vines failed to produce. The fact is that the vines produced wild grapes. Though *bĕʾūšîm* (found only in Isa 5:2, 10) eludes exact definition, the suggestions "wild" or "sour" or "stinking" grapes come close to the intent. The point is that they looked like the real thing but upon closer inspection were not desirable at all, "stinking" and "odious." The paronomasia thus provides the aural counterpart to the visual image of the grapes. Just as grapes and wild grapes may at first look alike to the untrained eye, so, too, *mišpāṭ-miśpāḥ* and *ṣĕdāqâ-ṣĕʿāqâ* sound alike but are radically different. The deceptive likeness between the good and bad grapes is essential to the parable as it heightens both the vintner's eager expectation and then his bitter disappointment.

The interpretive significance of this crucial connection between the agricultural image of the parable and the summary indictment of v. 7b is that while the outward forms of "justice and righteousness" (social justice) are there for the eyes to see, closer inspection reveals the most rank forms of injustice. That the enactment of "justice" results in "bloodshed" and the life of "righteousness" produces an "outcry" confirms what we have seen above, namely, that judicial and social structures intended to protect the poor have been corrupted and perverted to exploit and oppress them. The outward machinery of justice is there but it produces injustice. This is more insidious than overt evil or brazen exploitation because it is masquerading as virtue—the same complaint Isaiah made about hands raised in prayer but covered with blood (1:15), zealous sacrificial offerings accompanied by evil deeds (1:11-16), wine diluted with water, and silver corrupted with rust (1:22). All of these images speak of outward appearances hiding inner corruption (whitened sepulchers housing dead men's bones, Matt 23:27), and they all come to a powerful, concise exposé for what they are in 5:7b.

This compact statement is powerful and shocking, and is tantamount to an accusation of a capital crime (Boadt 1997: 15). But because it is somewhat generic, the specifics will be entered into evidence in 5:8-24.

Lectionary Notes

Common Lectionary: Proper 22 (A): Isa 5:1-7 / Psalm 80 / Matt 21:33-46
Roman Lectionary: 27 (A): same, except Matt 21:33-43

After Jesus' Palm Sunday entry into Jerusalem (Matt 21:1-11) and the cleansing of the temple (21:12-17), the Gospel according to Matthew details the escalating conflict between Jesus and the religious authorities. This pericope is part of a series of conflicts and controversies in Matt 21:23—23:39 (the Two Sons [21:28-32], the Wicked Tenants [21:33-46], and the King's Wedding Feast [22:1-14]), which depicts those unwilling to do what is commanded. This lack of fidelity merits judgment. The setting of these controversies in the temple suggests that what is at stake is the nature of true worship. Jesus, like Isaiah and other prophets, links worship to living a life of fidelity. The message inferred from the setting is that what takes place in the temple must correspond to what takes place in daily life—a very Isaian theme.

The points of contact between the Isaiah and Matthew readings are obvious, as are their differences. The care the landowner lavishes on the vineyard (Matt 21:33-34) echoes that of the "beloved" for his vineyard in Isa 5:1-2. The remainders of the two stories move in different directions. In Isaiah, the fault is in the vineyard itself, which produces bitter fruit; in Matthew, the vineyard produces the desired fruit, but those in charge of the vineyard prove disloyal and corrupt. The rest of Matthew's parable seems to be a thinly veiled allegory of Israel's history, culminating with the death of the owner's son and the retributive destruction of the tenant farmers. The result is that the vineyard will be given into the care of others. The intent of the parable is to move the hearers to repentance: as spoken by Jesus, it is a threat that *will be carried out* if the required fruit is not given over to the owner; for Matthew's readers, the destruction of Jerusalem and the growth of the church are now familiar realities. In Isaiah's story, depending on when and where historical critics situate it, the destruction of the vineyard itself refers to the destruction of either the northern kingdom of Israel (722/721), or the southern kingdom of Judah (587/586), or of both in retrospect.

Reading the two stories together suggests that Matthew had already contemporized Isaiah's story. In taking up the well-known image of the vineyard, Matthew suggests that however the historical references to Isaiah's song are read, the judgment rendered in it is provisional: the destruction of the vineyard is not definitive. Indeed, Matthew "updates" the history of the vineyard to his own times. The survival of the vineyard is testimony to the enduring graciousness of God, whose activities of election and redemption are ongoing. The Gospel parable equates the vineyard not with national entities—neither Judah nor Israel—but with the kingdom of God (21:43). This explains its enduring fruitfulness and its ability to withstand opposition and even mismanagement.

As Scripture proclaimed in the gathered worshipping community, neither the historical reconstruction of Isaiah's song nor the allegorical interpretation of Matthew's parable is the final word. Placing them together in the liturgical setting relativizes their historical components and invites reflection in light of one another and of the church's ongoing experience. This is one of the salutary aspects of the psalm: the vineyard does not refer to a past "them" whose fate can be observed dispassionately; this vine is "us," their sin is ours, as the first-person plural forms attest—"we will no more withdraw from you; give us new life and we will call upon your name."

Finally, the proclamation of these readings toward the end of the liturgical year, with the eschatological enthronement of Christ the King in sight, suggests that the themes of judgment so prominent in Isaiah, Psalm 80, and the Gospel are not merely past actualizations but will be final resolutions. Judgment is in the hands of the only One to whom it is proper. We, to whom presumably the vineyard/kingdom has been given, are under the same expectation as the original tenants: it is rightly expected of us to "give him the produce at the harvest time" (Matt 21:41). The produce the owner expects, a feature the Gospel does not allegorize, is supplied by the reading from Isaiah: "he looked for justice . . . and righteousness" (Isa 5:7). The Gospel does not support a smug Christian supersessionism of Judaism. In both cases, the vineyard belongs to God; in both cases, the Owner has expectations—that the vineyard produce fruit and that those in charge yield the harvest to the Owner. In both cases, judgment is rendered on the failure to meet the expectations. With such expectations, the prayer of the psalmist becomes the urgent prayer of believers—"take care of this vine and protect what your right hand has planted." But, in the end, prayer without produce is fruitless.

2. Land-Grabbing and Wanton Luxury: Isaiah 5:8-24. The economic and social situation this passage presumes points to the breakdown of traditional systems of property ownership. While the tribal period was characterized by clan ownership, economic and social conditions were emerging that favored individual ownership (Wildberger 1991: 197–98; Kaiser 1983: 100–101). Two social factors contributed to this transformation: the monarchy and urbanization. On the one hand, land acquisition undertaken by the crown, either corruptly (for example, Naboth's vineyard, 1 Kings 21) or legally (for example, through the confiscation of the estates, fields, vineyards, and orchards of traitors or other criminals), made it possible to bestow land grants on favored "servants of the king." In this way, a man's inherited patrimony could be augmented by a royal grant (1 Sam 8:14-15). The recipient of this royal largesse would live in the capital city and was expected to eat at the king's table, all the while enjoying the produce of his land holdings. Thus, important officials and nobles, especially those who had ingratiated themselves to people in power, were well placed to acquire, by both illegal and legal means, the property of those vulnerable to oppression (Stager 1985: 25–28; Johnstone 1969: 308–17).

On the other hand, growing urbanization created new ties of interdependence between peasant farmers and the propertied merchant class, which usually resided in the towns and influenced public affairs (Lang 1982: 48). When an individual peasant farmer suffered economic setbacks—for example, illness, marriage payments, crop failure due to droughts or locusts, and so forth—he would turn to an urban moneylender or merchant. He would either be charged interest for a loan or "be forced to cultivate the soil of others on a share-cropping or tenant basis" (Lang 1982: 49). Lang calls this the *mercantile system*, or *rent capitalism*. In his discussion of peasant poverty in biblical Israel, Lang recounts the situation described in documents from the fifth-century B.C.E. community in Elephantine that tell of Jews who had to pay interest rates of 5 percent per month. When unpaid interest is added to the capital, the average annual rate is 60 percent. To illustrate his point further, Lang turns to Gen 47:13-26, which, he says, does not correspond to known Egyptian practice and must therefore reflect the practice of the Israelite author and his day. Lang explains how the poor Israelite peasant becomes dependent on a rich lord: "It is reported that in a time of famine the Egyptians had to convey everything to the Pharaoh—first their cattle, then their land and even themselves, so that they were in bondage, owing the king 20% of their annual yield" (1982: 49–50).

As agricultural parcels become the property of a single owner (perhaps an absentee city dweller), as peasants become virtual slaves or indentured serfs, and as their goods and services are received as payments on loans, the gap between rich and poor widens. Because land ownership translates into economic and civic power, issues of taxes, property rights, foreclosures, and related matters increasingly fall into the hands of the rich, thereby widening the power gap (von Waldow 1970: 195–97).

It is perhaps a similar situation that lies behind the land-grabbing described in 5:8 (see also Mic 2:2-5). The greed of the wealthy and the vulnerability of the poor make for a volatile situation, one that apparently erupted in the eighth century and occasioned the condemnation of Amos, Isaiah, and Micah. In addition to the economic factors described above, there were corrupt courts with which to contend. If, as Isa 10:1-2 attests, the courts were promulgating laws and rendering decisions that favored the rich at the expense of the poor, then the situation Isaiah condemns is graphically portrayed: large estates amassed by adding field to field on which sit "large and beautiful" homes (5:9b). The acquisition of land comes as debts are foreclosed and the property is expropriated. Because this is presumably done according to the laws of the marketplace and by statute, it is all strictly legal—but utterly immoral. This is a powerful demonstration of the parable of the vineyard at work: the outward form of the land acquisition is all legal but perfectly corrupt—the productive harvest upon closer inspection is rotten.

And so the wealth and luxuriant lifestyle of the upper class grow even as the poor get poorer. The punishment therefore fits the crime: the fine homes will become desolate and uninhabited (5:9), and the fields so ravenously acquired will be blighted (5:10).[27]

Lang (1982) describes the lifestyle of a growing upper class. The accumulated wealth frees the gentry from the necessity of working and allows them to indulge la dolce vita. After the property and fine homes, perhaps the most conspicuous sign of this detached and carefree life is feasting and drinking, both of which are bitterly decried by Isaiah. Excessive drinking—drinking literally from morning to night—is twice decried (5:11, 22; cf. Amos 2:8; 4:1; 6:6). Their fine feasts are accompanied by small orchestras—lyre, harp, tambourine, and flute (Isa 5:12; cf. Amos 5:23; 6:5). Again, the punishment is directly targeted to the offense: "their nobility are dying of hunger and their multitude are parched with thirst" (Isa 5:13).

The summary statement, "my people go into exile for lack of knowledge" (5:13), is reminiscent of the very first complaint raised in the book of Isaiah: "Israel does not know, my people do not understand" (1:3). What they don't know is the "deed of YHWH . . . the work of his hands" (5:12). Though they protest, "let his work hasten that we may see it, let the counsel of the Holy One of Israel draw near and come so that we may know it" (v. 19), the truth is, the only wisdom they seek is that which is good in their own eyes (5:21). Thus, they call good evil and evil they call good; they call bitter sweet, light darkness and so on (5:20). To continue the metaphor of 5:1-7, they see the rotten grapes and declare them good; they see bloodshed and call it justice. What is true in society is true also in the courts: they "acquit the guilty for a bribe, but the just cause of the righteous they turn aside" (5:23).

All of this corruption and evil surrounds a passage that demands our attention. Commentators assess 5:14-17 differently, some seeing it as authentic, others as a later addition. There is no compelling reason to excise this passage from its present location or assume a different author. Verses 14-15 describe a typical Isaianic theme: the humbling of the proud (2:9-18; 3:8; 3:16-17; 3:18—4:1). This leads up to the remarkable statement in 5:16:

YHWH of Hosts is exalted by justice,
and the Holy God is sanctified in righteousness.

Commentators who see these verses (5:15-16, or even 5:14-17) as later historicizing additions tend to translate *mišpāṭ* as "judgment" (Kaiser, Gray, Wildberger, Stacey) and view these verses as a reflective assessment of the events of 587. Sweeney argues just as plausibly that the punishment described refers to the Assyrian invasion of Israel in the aftermath of the Syro-Ephraimite War.

The term *mišpāṭ* frequently has the meaning of "judgment," for example, as the final stage of a legal procedure. Indeed, the sense of judgment enacted against Israel is not inappropriate in the present context, as the Masoretic pointing for the definite article *(bammišpāṭ)* in the preposition seems to confirm.[28] The context here, however, argues that "justice" is the preferred meaning, and this for two reasons. First, as was the case in previous instances, the paired terms *mišpāṭ ûṣĕdāqâ* seem to be a hendiadys broken for poetic parallelism, as it had been in 1:27 and 5:7. The coordination of these terms provides the primary parallelism in this verse; the coordinated verbs in these two bicola—**gbh* ("to exalt") and **qdš* (Niphal, "to be sanctified")— are not otherwise found paired in the Hebrew Bible. Second, the entire unit, 5:8-24, is concerned primarily with violations of social justice. As in 1:27, the enumeration of social injustices is balanced by a focus on the dynamic importance of justice enacted in the social realm. In 1:27, social justice results in the redemption of Zion, while here (5:16) it serves to exalt God. In both instances, social injustice is catalogued as the reason for punishment, and social justice is highlighted for its salutary effects.

The cohesion of 5:16 within this entire unit is evident in the contrast formed between v. 7 and v. 16: justice and righteousness are the virtues both by which the kingdom is judged, condemned, and humbled, and by which God is sanctified and exalted (Jensen 1984: 78). In this way, the contrast between God and humanity is further heightened: the absence of justice and righteousness results in human abasement while their presence results in divine exaltation. This cohesion further argues for understanding *mišpāṭ* as "justice" in v. 16. In order for the term to produce its antithetical results, it must convey the same meaning or the contrast is lost.

But what does it mean to say that "the Holy God is sanctified by righteousness"? To be sure, the association here of "justice" and "righteousness" with holiness is significant, especially in light of the Inaugural Vision in ch. 6 to which this verse serves as a fitting entrée. What must be avoided, however, is precisely the route Motyer and Young take in discussing righteousness and holiness as theological attributes of God. Motyer begins by asserting that "*Holy (qāḏoš)* is the divine nature itself." He then discusses the meaning of the term *qādôš* as "separated," which, in reference to God, refers to his moral purity. He explains: "What made Israel's God *holy* was his moral purity (6:3). This was his 'separateness.' *Righteousness* is holiness expressed in moral principles; *justice* is the application of the principles of righteousness (cf. 1:21). Both *justice* and *righteousness* are the outshining of holiness" (1993: 72). Young similarly asserts that God "possesses holiness as an attribute." He goes on: "the God who is holy reveals or declares that holiness is the accomplishment of his righteous judgments" (1992, 1:215). Holiness is equated to God's divinity and is revealed in his just judgment of sin (1992, 1:216). In both Motyer and Young, the verse in question has been decontextualized and has become a kind of "proof text" for their theological assertions. As has already been suggested above, the text cannot support these assertions. First, both commentators have broken the hendiadys; Motyer has given the now separate terms distinct spheres of operation—principles and action. The inherent complementarity has been ruptured.

Moreover, I think Motyer's understanding of holiness as "separateness," while both semantically and culturally accurate, misses the very inventiveness of Isaiah's usage here. To be sure, the holiness of God will be revealed in his separateness from sinful humanity (ch. 6), but in 5:8-24 God's holiness is honored[29] as he himself is exalted by justice *in the human realm*. In both halves of the verse, the action of the verbs should be understood as directed to YHWH, rather than the first verb *(wayyigbah)* understood as passive ("YHWH is exalted") and the second *(niqdāš)* as reflexive ("God shows himself holy"). The semantic parallelism is better preserved by translating "YHWH of Hosts is exalted, the Holy God is sanctified" (that is, honored as holy). The exaltation and sanctification of God are accomplished through the enactment of a just social order,[30] the precise remedy to the conditions described throughout 5:8-24. This is in keeping with the pattern established earlier in which the excesses perpetrated by the unjust are undone: the overindulged eaters and drinkers suffer hunger and thirst, the acquired fields are ravaged, and the magnificent homes abandoned. Here, the same course is charted: God who has been aggrieved and dishonored by injustice will find exaltation and will be sanctified by justice.

Isaiah, whose call story will soon provide one of the Bible's most compelling descriptions of God's transcendent otherness, does not shy away from immersing God in the realia of social life. The injustice so vividly presented in this prophetic book moves God to act in the historical realm. Similarly, the exaltation and celebration of God's holiness are to be found in the historical realm: they are not restricted to the paeans of heavenly seraphim but are taken up by his own people acting with justice. This is a stunning and challenging assertion, possibly even a bit discomfiting. It is perhaps easier to keep separate the sinful world of humanity and the holy realm of God than it is to acknowledge that the holiness of God is revealed in something so immanent as a just social order. This separateness, which Motyer is at pains to defend, is belied by the text under discussion. The placement of vv. 15-16 between vv. 8-12 and 18-23 is suggestive: YHWH of Hosts is exalted and the Holy God is sanctified in the midst of injustice whenever justice and righteousness make their appearance as social justice, and injustice is itself overturned in the abasement of the proud and haughty. Thus, the destruction of the proud (5:15) is the converse of the exaltation of God (5:16), and both occur in the same social-historical situation.

The Holy One of Israel Calls Isaiah: Isaiah 6–8

This portion of the text, frequently called the Memoirs, is lacking both the vocabulary and content that are our concern. Given the prominence that this section has in the overall structure and meaning of the book of Isaiah (Vriezen 1962: 131–42), this lack is notable. However, the contents of ch. 6 are not without relevance to this study. Isaiah's profound experience of the holiness of YHWH has far-reaching consequences throughout the book, not the least of which is the distinctive and pervasive use of the title "the Holy One of Israel." The holiness of God celebrated in this classic passage (6:1-4) is sharply contrasted to human sinfulness (6:5-7). On the sin side of the equation, images from ch. 6 recall the earlier discussion of Isa 1:2-28, in which Isaiah's understanding of Israel's sin and rebellion is tied to his participation in the sin of his people (6:5): just as his sin (*ḥṭʾ, 6:7; cf. 1:4) and iniquity (*ʿwn, 6:7; cf. 1:4) are purged by fire (6:7), so Israel's sin must be smelted away (1:25). On the holiness side, we have seen that the God who is called "Holy" *(*qdš)* in 6:3 is "sanctified" *(*qdš)* by justice and righteousness in 5:16. Later, that same God will be explicitly identified as "the God of justice" (30:18). The intersection of justice and holiness grounds Isaiah's understanding of holiness not only in the transcendence of God but in the immanent realm of social justice. Holiness and justice emerge as concomitant realities. The God whom ch. 6 honors as transcendentally holy is honored as holy by a people who live in justice. Indeed, it is only by the restoration of justice that Israel's worship will have value (1:10-17) and God's holiness will be vindicated. This distinctively Isaianic interaction of holiness and justice will be taken up by Second Isaiah.

His Kingdom Founded on Justice: Isaiah 8:23—9:6 (English 9:1-7)

Those who argue for and against the authenticity of this passage are conveniently listed in Wildberger (1991: 389–90). It seems that more recent scholarly opinion has been shaped by Alt's influential work on Isa 8:23—9:6 (Eng. 9:1-7) (1953), so that many commentators today attribute this passage to Isaiah and locate it in the aftermath of the Syro-Ephraimite War. Some go further and see the birth of the child in v. 5 (Eng. 6) as referring, in all probability, to Hezekiah. In this case, the birth language is used metaphorically to describe, not the physical birth, but the accession of a new king (see Pss 2:7; 89:27-30 [Eng. 26-29]; 2 Sam 7:14).[31] I accept the authenticity of the passage and agree with the general assessment that it refers to the events immediately following the Assyrian invasion of Israel precipitated by the Syro-Ephraimite War. While it may not be possible to say with certainty that Isaiah had Hezekiah in mind, we will not be far off the mark in agreeing with Vawter's assessment:

> . . . Whether or not Isaiah was thinking of Hezekiah, his perspective is rather of what the king should be—the antithesis of what the kings had been—than of any specific bearer of the royal title. It was allowable for him at least to hope that Hezekiah would embody in himself all that Yahweh had promised as the issue of the Davidic kingship, but it was the promise itself with which he was most concerned. (1961: 184)

Particularly in light of the catalogues of injustice that have preceded, it is no surprise that Isaiah looked for the throne and kingship to be established "in justice and righteousness" (*bĕmišpāṭ ûbiṣdāqâ*, 9:6 [Eng. 9:7]). This was the Davidic ideal, specifically invoked in the beginning of this verse and recalling 2 Sam 8:15. In the context of First Isaiah, these qualities are not merely abstract virtues; they represent a longing for the reestablishment of social justice. The accession of a new king, announced in 9:5 (Eng. 9:6) and accompanied by a series of titles bestowed at his coronation (Weinfeld 1995: 72; Goldingay 1999: 239–44), was a time to redress wrongs and establish the right. This practice is also found in Mesopotamia, where the social institution of righteousness/freedom *(= mīšaram/andurāram šakānum)* was associated with the coronation of a new king[32] and other pivotal moments in the life of the kingdom. The Mesopotamian enactment of social reforms (see our earlier discussion of *kittam/mīšaram šakānum* in ch. 1) is equivalent to the practice of the Sabbatical Year and the Jubilee in Israel, though there it was ideally institutionalized cyclically. The institution of these social reforms sought to secure the "liberation of slaves, restoration of land to their original owners, and cancellation of debts," all designed to "establish social justice and equity and to assist the weaker members of society" (Weinfeld 1995: 9). This impulse toward social reforms on the part of a new king (Weinfeld 1995: 59) lies behind the prophetic expectations and hopes articulated in Isa 9:2-6 (Eng. 3-7).

In 9:6 (Eng. 7), the hendiadys, as we have seen, represents social justice, not just as an ideal but as the very foundation of the royal throne. Weinfeld, drawing on a wide range of texts, makes the case that a throne established on *mišpāṭ ûṣĕdāqâ* is interchangeable with a throne established on *ḥesed weʾĕmet* ("kindness and truth," Prov 20:28; cf. also Ps 89:15 [Eng. 14]). Indeed, this very alternation of descriptions is found in Isa 9:6 (Eng. 7) and 16:5. Weinfeld goes on to suggest that the social reforms implied by "justice and righteousness" refer to acts of kindness and mercy on behalf of the weak (Weinfeld 1995: 9). That Isaiah would attach such expectations to a new king, given the social inequities he decries so vociferously, is perfectly appropriate.

In this regard, the title "eternal father" (*ʾăbîʿad*; Cross 1973: 15–16) in Isa 9:5 (Eng. 6) is of interest. Bovati, in discussing biblical terms used to describe the role of a judge, includes the term *father (ʾāb)*. Among the various ways in which the term is used (for example, master of a company of craftsmen, spiritual leader of a prophetic brotherhood, priest in charge, political superintendent), "father" sometimes means "the guardian of a socially or juridically disadvantaged class such as orphans, widows and the poor" (Bovati 1994: 174). Bovati cites in particular Job 29:12-16, in which Job, acting in the gates of the city (29:7), tells how he "delivered the poor who cried, and the orphan who had no helper" (29:12). Job goes on, "I was a *father* to the needy, and I championed the cause of the stranger" (29:16).[33] Because Bovati's focus in this section is on the titles of administrators of justice, he fails to point out the presence of the broken hendiadys in Job 29:14: "*Righteousness* I put on and it clothed me; like a mantel and a turban was my *justice*." The entire context in Job speaks of a compassionate, judicial execution of justice for the oppressed, the orphan, and the needy under the title "father."

Bovati also points to the use of "father" to describe a political functionary, particularly a king. He acknowledges that this is more widespread in surrounding cultures, but he adduces a few examples in the Bible (Deut 10:18; Pss 10:14, 18;

72:12-13; 82:3-4) and suggests that the title in Isa 9:5 (Eng. 6), *ʾăbîʿad,* may indicate "the king's constant care for this people, especially the poor, a care which is typical of good government" (1994: 175). This is consonant with Isaiah's perspective on social justice; his repeated indictment of those in leadership roles makes his designation of the king as *ʾăbîʿad* and his attention to a royal throne founded on justice and righteousness particularly poignant.

Finally, it should be noted that the divine throne is similarly founded on "justice and righteousness" (Pss 89:15 [Eng. 14]; 97:2). God himself is the ultimate Judge who judges justly, and the care of the weak and needy is his special concern (for example, Exod 22:21-23 [Eng. 22-24]; Job 34:28; Pss 10:17; 140:13 [Eng. 12]; 146:7; Prov 22:22-23; 23:10-11). This symbiotic relationship between God and his earthly surrogate, the king, is common both in biblical Israel and in its neighboring cultures, and is reflected in this text. Both the heavenly throne and the Davidic throne are founded on "justice and righteousness." Thus, the congruence between the heavenly and earthly realms, evident in Isa 2:2-4, is highlighted again in this passage.

Lectionary Notes

Common Lectionary: Christmas Proper I (A, B, C): Isa 9:2-7 / Psalm 96 / Luke 2:1-14 (15-20)

Roman Lectionary: Christmas Mass at Midnight (A, B, C): Isa 9:1-6 / Psalm 96 / Luke 2:1-14

Note: Despite the different versification system in the two lectionaries, the Isaiah reading is the same in both.

The identification of this passage from Isaiah with the birth of Jesus, due in part to its very familiar musical rendition in Handel's *Messiah,* is so firmly etched in Christian awareness that its Christian interpretation is often taken as its primary and most obvious meaning (see Brueggemann 1998a: 81-85). This tendency is reinforced by "historicizing" v. 5 (Eng. 6), "a child is born to us": Christmas worshippers reflexively turn their minds to the manger in Bethlehem. Yet the lectionary chooses to emphasize the royal aspects of this reading by using a psalm of royal enthronement for the response. This reinforces the exegetical argument that "birth" here refers to the accession of a new king to the throne. The lectionary's use of this passage from Isaiah highlights the meaning of the event rather than the fact of the event: what is significant about the "birth" is that the divine covenant made with David (2 Samuel 7) is being fulfilled and a new Davidic heir is taking the throne in "justice and righteousness"[34] to establish a reign of peace.

Though the Lukan Gospel is often taken to highlight the poverty and simplicity of the birth of Jesus, one should not lose sight of the royal themes. This is established in the opening verse, which sets Roman royal rule and messianic royal rule in a conflict that will find its climax in the Roman execution of Jesus. The mention of Caesar Augustus in v. 1 is not coincidental. Monuments set up by Augustus in 9 C.E. and placed in Roman temples throughout the empire to inaugurate a new calendar herald the beneficent rule of the emperor. The decree recounts how under

Caesar Augustus, the empire was at the height of its *glory* and enjoyed the Pax Romana—the great Roman *peace.* Augustus, hailed as the *god* and *savior* of the empire, reformed the calendar so that the new year would begin with his *birthday,* a day which signaled *good news* for all the world. All the capitalized words are found in today's Gospel from St. Luke. A knowledgeable historian in his own way, Luke was no doubt aware of this Roman propaganda. He seems deliberately to have framed the birth story of Jesus as a rebuttal to the claims of imperial Rome. It is of Jesus who is *born* this *day* that the angels announce as *good news:* they hail Jesus as the *savior* and *lord* who brings *peace* on earth and *glory* to God (Crossan 1994: 73–74). To complete the argument against Rome, Luke presents Jesus as born of the house of David, heir to a proud and ancient royal heritage. Thus it is fitting that Joseph and Mary travel to Bethlehem—the town of David's birth—to be enrolled there and so to stake their claim that Jesus is a royal descendant. This point is reinforced by the angels who indicate to the shepherds that Jesus is born in the city of David.

The lectionary readings taken together make a powerful statement about Jesus as the heir of David's throne and describe the qualities of his rule, both from the positive assertions made by Isaiah and Psalm 96, and from the negative critique of Roman rule implied by Luke's account. While popular celebrations of the feast tend to sentimentalize the birth of "Baby Jesus," the lectionary emphasizes the royal prerogatives and mission of Jesus. Jesus, the Savior who brings peace, takes up rule from the throne of David, a rule of "justice and righteousness." Luke, throughout the Gospel, is particularly conscious of the mission of Jesus to those whom Isaiah also defends—the poor, the outcast, and the socially vulnerable.

Corrupt Courts: Isaiah 10:1-4

The close thematic and structural ties with the preceding woes in ch. 5 bring us back to Isaiah's concern for the corruption of justice in the social realm. In 10:1-2, he addresses the miscarriage of justice in legislation that has a direct impact on the needy:

> Woe to those who decree iniquitous decrees,
>   writers who keep writing[35] oppression,
> to turn aside the poor from judgment *(dîn),*
>   and to rob the oppressed of my people of justice *(mišpāṭ),*
> widows become their spoil,
>   and orphans they plunder.

The situation envisioned has deteriorated from that described in 1:23, where negligence and avoidance was the issue: "the orphan they do not defend, and the cause of the widow does not come to them." Here, the leaders are actively obstructing justice—turning aside the poor (cf. Isa 29:21), robbing the oppressed, despoiling and plundering them.

The issue described in 10:1 is clearly an issue of unjust legislation (Isa 29:21; cf. Ps 94:20) that gives the appearance of legality to immoral acts that oppress the poor (Bazak 1989: 7). This appears to be more than unjust verdicts in criminal cases but probably refers to civil disputes dealing with land and property (Clements 1980: 61; cf. 5:8; 3:14). As discussed above (5:1-7, 8-24), while the outward appearance conforms to the dictates of law, the law itself is corrupt. Bovati indicates that the Hiphil of **nṭh* ("to turn aside") used with *mišpāṭ* (or its synonyms, here *lĕhaṭṭôt middîn*) refers to injustice in the courtroom (1994: 191–93).[36] Thus, the very forum to which the poor would turn for protection and vindication—the courts—has become the refuge of the oppressor. Justice perishes, the widow and orphan are legally despoiled. Clements speculates that this situation was possible because active membership in ruling bodies was probably determined by owning property (1980: 61), thus excluding de facto the non–property owners and rendering them voiceless in the decisions that most affect them.

The wartime imagery of 10:2—vanquished foes being victimized and plundered—is the very antithesis of what the law was designed to ensure, that is, protection of the vulnerable. The image evoked in 3:14—"the spoil *(*gzl)* of the poor is in your houses"—comes back in 10:2, but what is robbed is not merely the goods of the poor, but the essence of equitable existence—justice itself is robbed: "to rob *(*gzl)* the oppressed of my people of justice"! This, again, represents an escalation of the wrongdoing and a deterioration of the social situation.

In 10:3, the speech turns to second-person direct address.

> What will you do on the day of visitation,
> when the storm from afar comes?
> To whom will you flee for help,
> and where will you leave your wealth?

The "you" stands in pointed contrast to "my people" in 10:2. The "us against them" mentality evoked by the despoiling imagery of 10:2 is now turned on the perpetrators of evil: the "us" stands as "them" before God—no longer his people, but those to be turned upon by God.

The earlier image of 3:14 is further evoked in the rhetorical questions of 10:3-4: speaking of all these stolen goods that are in their houses, God asks, "Where will you leave your wealth?" The more general and ominous question is hurled at them as an accusation: when the day of punishment comes, "What will you do?" The implied answer, of course, is that there is nothing that can be done to escape. The very One to whom they would turn for protection and vindication—YHWH—has become their enemy (1:24).

With this scene of legal and social chaos and a threat of certain reprisal on the wicked, Isaiah's denouncement of injustice comes to an end in the first major section of the book, chs. 2–12. All that remains is a vision of a more equitable and secure future under the protection of a just king.

Clothed in Justice: Isaiah 11:1-9

The historical setting, and therefore the authenticity, of this section is usually tied to an understanding of the term "stump of Jesse" (11:1). As Clements argues, "the prophecy clearly presupposes that the Davidic dynasty had been severely judged and reduced to a mere 'stump,'" that is, after 587 (1980: 121–22). Sweeney also relies on the image of a "stump" to reconstruct the setting (1996a: 203–5). Unlike Clements, however, he does not look to the exile but rather points to the assassination of Amon, the abortive coup, and the restoration to the throne of the eight-year-old Josiah ("the small boy" of 11:6b; see 2 Kgs 22:19-26).[37] However, Seitz, Jensen, Wildberger, and Hayes and Irvine, among others,[38] argue that the imagery is consistent with the tree/forest imagery found both in ch. 10 and elsewhere in chs. 5–12, and that the reduced, stumplike condition of Judah can be descriptive of situations other than the aftermath of 587. Both the conditions surrounding the Syro-Ephraimite War, which left Ahaz in control of little more than just Jerusalem proper, and the situation after 701, as a result of which Isaiah described Jerusalem as a "booth in a cucumber field" (1:8), have been appropriately suggested and fit the description in 11:1. This is an instance when a determination of the historical setting seems elusive (see Brueggemann 1998a: 99). Though the precise political conditions of the eighth-century setting proposed by many authors are different than the seventh-century setting plausibly argued by Sweeney, the overall social conditions are continuous enough in both periods to interpret this passage profitably in the context of preexilic Judah.

The relationship between 11:1-5 and 6-11 has occasioned much discussion. It is an issue that need not be addressed directly in this discussion because the material that is relevant to our interests is found exclusively in vv. 1-5. The vocabulary that requires comment is the presence of the verb *šāpaṭ* in both vv. 3 and 4 (both times parallel with the Hiphil of **ykḥ*, "to decide"). The twofold appearance of **ṣdq*, first parallel with *mîšôr* ("equity," v. 4), then with *ʾĕmûnâ* ("faithfulness," v. 5), also requires our attention. The verses in question read:

3b But not by appearance shall his eyes judge,
nor by hearing shall his ears decide.[39]
4 He shall judge the poor with righteousness,
and decide with equity for the afflicted of the earth;
4b and he shall strike the ruthless[40] with the rod of his mouth
and with the breath of his lips he shall kill the wicked.
5 Righteousness shall be the belt[41] of his waist,
and faithfulness the belt of his loins.

First we note that the pairing of *šāpaṭ* and **ykḥ* found in vv. 3 and 4 is the same pairing encountered in 2:4 (and 1:17-18). The function of "judging" and "deciding" that YHWH will exercise "in the last days" (2:2) is to be exercised more proximately by the spirit-endowed ruler. Verse 3 describes *how* this judging will be accomplished: it will be accomplished without regard for appearance or hearsay, that is, it shall be impartial. This, says Bazak, means that the ruler "will not be entrapped by crafty litigants who attempt to delude the judge by feigning innocence and truthfulness" (1989: 9). The importance of impartiality is not merely good advice but a principle of law in Israel (Lev 19:15; Deut 1:17; 16:19).

Next, these verbs are used to describe *who* is so judged: the poor and the afflicted. This informs us of two important points. First, the protection of the underclass, earlier described by the terms "orphan and widow," continues to be a concern. The justness of the king's rule is assessed in terms of his protection of the weakest members of society. Second, the poor and afflicted turn to the king when they are in need of deliverance from unscrupulous oppressors. "Judging" is more than rendering legal decisions; it is also delivering and saving those whose lives and well-being are threatened. Bovati explains how the term *šāpaṭ* and its equivalents are "developed, on the one hand, by positive terms suggesting benevolence, attention, a saving intervention for someone in the right, and on the other hand, by terms with a negative value, suggesting punishment, towards the evildoer and violator of justice" (1994: 202). This is precisely how the oracle continues: the just king destroys the ruthless and the wicked. The "ruthless" and the "wicked" are not just semantic opposites of the "poor" and "afflicted" employed for literary effect: they represent those who use power—violently and immorally—for their own gain at the expense of those who are unable to withstand them (Wildberger 1991: 477). Weinfeld suggests that the ensuing destruction of the wicked by the "rod of his mouth . . . and the breath of his lips" (11:4) refers to a royal decree, like the *mīšarum* (the decree of social reforms) in Mesopotamia, by which the poor are aided while oppressors are destroyed (1995: 190–91).

The term **ṣdq* appears in 11:5 with *mîšôr* (equity) and describes the manner in which the poor are judged and the afflicted have their cases decided. According to Weinfeld, the vocabulary of "equity" is found also in Ugaritic and Phoenician passages in connection with the coronation of kings, and in Israel with the enthronement of God (Ps 98:9). When used of God in the enthronement psalms (96–98), judging the nations with "equity" means "saving" them (1995: 190–91).

As for the garments of "righteousness and faithfulness/truth" (11:5), Weinfeld also finds parallels with Akkadian *kittum* ("truth") and *mīšarum* ("righteousness"; 1995: 63). Again, these terms are not merely descriptive adjectives, but represent proscriptive actions to be taken on behalf of those threatened by injustice. The confluence of terms in these Isaianic texts (see Weinfeld for references to Jeremiah, Ezekiel, and the Psalms), as elsewhere in the ancient Near East, points in the direction of social reforms and measures taken to protect the weak, redress inequity, punish evildoers, and establish justice. In this passage, it is the particular responsibility of the king to renew the social justice that had been associated with David from of old (2 Sam 8:15). As Wildberger pointedly observes, "if Isaiah attaches such great importance to establishing justice, for the poor and the lightly esteemed, that is clearly because the entire system of justice had, in plain words, gone to the dogs" (1991: 475–76).

The accouterments of royal power and responsibility taken together from 9:2-6 (Eng. 3-7) and 11:1-5 are impressive: a throne established on justice and righteousness (9:6 [Eng. 7]), on which is enthroned a king clothed with righteousness and truth/faithfulness, wielding a (verbal) scepter that slays the oppressor, all in service of judging the poor with righteousness and the afflicted with equity. As we indicated in the discussion of 9:2-6 (Eng. 3-7), there is a noteworthy parallel between the descriptions of God and the just king. It is entirely fitting that the same throne, garments, and scepter that are used of God should characterize the just king (who is the Divine King's surrogate on earth). The outrageous injustice, social oppression, economic exploitation, and judicial corruption that Isaiah has so vividly catalogued and decried is thus thwarted and held in abeyance by the righteousness of a king who will act with justice. Such a king, in his person, stands as an implicit indictment against the corrupt leadership who have been excoriated throughout chs. 1–12. At this point in history, Isaiah still nurtured a hope that a just leadership would lead to a just society. The double effect of such pervasive justice is that Zion is redeemed (1:27) and God is exalted (5:16).

Lectionary Notes

Common Lectionary: Second Sunday of Advent (A): Isa 11:1-10 / Psalm 72 / Matt 3:1-12
Roman Lectionary: Same

The readings are once again directed to seasonal themes. As on the First Sunday of Advent, the first reading is taken as a messianic prophecy fulfilled in Christ. The Gospels for the Second and Third Sundays of Advent focus on the ministry of John the Baptist. Images of apocalyptic judgment precede his words of the coming of one "mightier than I" who also brings a judgment in fire. The very structure of the Matthean passage reiterates the apocalyptic unfolding of the end times—judgment leading to the coming of the Son of Man.

Isaiah once again offers an alternative vision of "that day." And, once again, the lectionary relativizes the historical settings—whether of Hezekiah in the eighth century or Josiah in the seventh—in favor of a christological interpretation. This is a distinctive lectionary development not anticipated elsewhere in the canon. The only explicit New Testament use of this Isaian passage is Paul's citation in Rom 15:12 of Isa 11:10 as a proof text for a Gentile mission. (The "seven spirits" in Rev 5:6 may be an oblique reference to Isa 11:2.) Neither historical nor canonical exegesis of the Isaian passage unlocks the explicitly christological interpretation that the lectionary proposes. The original vision of Isaiah of some future Davidic heir who will so judge with justice as to reestablish peace and harmony throughout creation is liturgically specified: that future time is the messianic age, and that heir is the Christ, whose way John the Baptist heralds and prepares.

Isaiah 13–23 and 24–27

These sections, normally headed "Prophecies concerning Foreign Nations" and "The Apocalypse of Isaiah," respectively, are almost entirely lacking in vocabulary and content relevant to this study, which itself may be suggestive. Though Seitz contends that the ultimate destiny of the foreign kingdoms is conversion and obedient worship (1993a: 16), the major concern of these sections is God's judgment of these kingdoms. For the purposes of this study, it is regrettable that the actual word for "judgment," *mišpāṭ*, is found only in a lament over Moab (16:1-5), and the plural of the term, *mišpāṭîm* ("precepts" or "ordinances"), occurs only in a brief post-Isaianic passage describing the Lord's righteous ways (26:7-10). Both these oracles will be discussed below in the literary context of Isaiah 1–39.

We may begin with a few general observations about judgment. In these chapters of Isaiah, divine judgment is executed against the enemies of YHWH (both foreign and domestic) for a variety of reasons, most frequently pride and arrogance (13:11; 14:13-14; 16:6; 23:7-8; 25:11; 26:5), but also for unspecified iniquity (13:11; 26:10), idolatry on the part of Jacob (17:7, 10; 27:9), Jerusalem's failure to repent (22:12-14), the shedding of blood (26:21), and breaking of the law and the covenant (24:5). It is significant that the typical prophetic indictments against Israel and Judah that result in their eventual destruction, namely, idolatry, rebellion, and social injustice, are not leveled against any of the foreign nations in these sections of Isaiah.

"A Judge Who Seeks Justice": Isaiah 16:1-5

The verse that requires our attention also provides most of the interpretive problems:

> A throne shall be established *(wĕhûkan)* in kindness
> and upon it shall sit in faithfulness in the tent of David
> a judge who seeks justice
> and is quick [to do] righteousness. (Isa 16:5)

Some commentators (for example, Clements, Jensen, and Barton) take the verb "shall be established" *(wĕhûkan)* as indicating that the house of David has collapsed; therefore, this oracle must come after the events of 587. Sweeney, in our judgment, correctly sees the establishment of Davidic rule to refer to the extension of Judean hegemony over Moab, not to the reestablishment of a moribund Davidic house. Sweeney plausibly sets this prophecy in the period of the Syro-Ephraimite War. Ahaz, having asked Tiglath-pileser's help against Syria and Israel, is in a position to ask that the Assyrian army not attack Moab any further. The Moabites, who have been pushed back to their traditional borders, are urged by the prophet to seek the Judean king's intercession (16:3) at the cost of submission to the Davidic throne (1996a: 240–52). The plausibility of this argument, in addition to a particularly Isaianic expression, inclines us to accept the authenticity of this prophecy.

The terms found in 16:5 have all been previously encountered. We note especially the recurrence of the peculiarly Isaianic expression, *wĕdōrēš mišpāṭ* ("one who seeks justice"; cf. 1:17). As discussed earlier, the occurrence of *mišpāṭ* as the object of the verb *dāraš* is found only in these two passages from Isaiah. While in itself insufficient to establish authorship, it is a bit of contributing evidence.

The overlapping meanings of the expressions *ḥesed weʾĕmet* (kindness and faithfulness) and *mišpāṭ ûṣĕdāqâ* have also been discussed (cf. 9:2-6 [Eng. 3-7] and 11:1-5). Addressing the issue of these two split hendiadys in 16:5, Weinfeld suggests that the proper sense can be determined by rewriting the poetic line in standard prose and by reuniting each broken hendiadys; he offers this paraphrase: "A throne shall be established with kindness and faithfulness *[ḥesed weʾĕmet]*, and a devoted judge, who seeks justice and righteousness *[mišpāṭ ûṣĕdāqâ]* shall sit upon it in the tent of David" (1995: 29, n. 17). While the terms of each hendiadys are used for parallelism in their respective bicola, the entire hendiadys "kindness and faithfulness" stands in a parallel relationship to "justice and righteousness."

The images in 16:5 seem somewhat confused. The mention of a "throne" and the "tent of David" certainly evoke monarchical images. But the mention of a *šōpēṭ* ("judge") rather than a "king" or "prince" is jarring. Bovati points to the judicial terminology in this verse, noting in particular that the verb *yāšab* ("to sit," v. 5) is a specifically courtroom posture (1994: 232). Bazak, too, highlights the judicial overtones when he describes the actions of a judge who does not delay in judgment and who is quick to reach the correct verdict (1989: 8). But while the language is from the courtroom, the context better pertains to royal rule and protection of fugitives and refugees. As we have seen before, the meaning of *šōpēṭ* is wide ranging and can properly describe any number of people who exercise authority. The king is one who is especially charged with giving right judgment. In this regard, Z. Falk understands "throne" as a symbol for the king's responsibility to administer justice (1960a: 350–54). The language in this verse, then, should be understood in its widest sense of just rule rather than in its limited and literal sense of court decisions.

The characteristics of just rule are extended to the fugitives and refugees from Moab who turn to Judah in their distress. Similar concern is evident for an Arabian tribe in 21:14-15 (nonauthentic): "To the thirsty bring water; O dweller in the land of Tema, meet the fugitive with bread." As *personae miserabiles*, the fugitives and refugees from Moab look for protection and help, though here it comes with a price: submission to Judean rule. It is significant, however, that in the prophet's view, such rule is tempered by the same qualities that characterize domestic rule. The exercise of authority over subjects, whether domestic or foreign, is restrained by the prophetic expectation that justice and righteousness be observed. All the vocabulary with which this study is concerned functions in ways that are consistent with what has preceded.

Ordinances from the Just One: Isaiah 26:7-10

This unit, together with its larger context (26:1-21), is universally taken to be post-Isaianic. Its relevance to this study is minimal: the term *mišpāṭêkā* ("your ordinances") occurs only in 26:8 and 9 (and just once more in 58:2). The absence of this term in the authentic passages and its rarity in the rest of the Isaianic corpus minimize the importance of this passage to this study. Only a few comments are needed.

In the plural, *mišpāṭîm* means "judgments, ordinances" (Gossai 1993: 176–78). When *mišpāṭîm* occurs with terms such as "way" (*ʾōraḥ,* 26:8) and "path," it carries the nuance of proceeding in conformity to law (Bovati 1994: 192, n. 52). In these verses, the ordinances are YHWH's, and so proceeding in conformity to his law leads to righteousness. It is YHWH himself, the "Just One" (v. 7), who instructs the world in the ways of righteousness by means of his judgments. The sentiments of these verses—the contrast between the righteous and the wicked, the way of righteousness, the activity of learning, the universal appeal ("inhabitants of the world")—all point to the wisdom concerns of this passage. Thus, even this decidedly legal term takes on a particular flavor of wisdom. We may note, once again, the close relationship between *mišpāṭ* and *ṣĕdāqâ* in v. 9b: "when your judgments *(mišpāṭîm)* are in the earth, the inhabitants of the world learn righteousness *(ṣĕdāqâ)*."

What is perhaps most significant is the apparent disinterest of these chapters (chs. 13–27) in the concerns of justice prophetically conceived. It is difficult to assess at this point whether such disinterest is a sign of the (later) times or whether the audience addressed, viz., the foreign nations, is responsible for the shift in interest. This portion of Isaiah stands in continuity with other prophets in not indicting the foreign kingdoms for breaches of social justice. This different kind of accountability for Israel as opposed to the foreign kingdoms is particularly striking, for example, in Amos 1:2—2:16. There, the six foreign kingdoms are indicted for excessive cruelty in warfare, for taking men for the slave trade, and for desecration of the bones of the dead, that is, acts that the mores of the time and region would consider questionable (Mays 1969: 28). Yet, the indictment against Judah turns immediately to violations of the covenant law and idolatry, and those against Israel to disregard for, and exploitation of, the poor. So, too, in Isaiah, the foreign nations may be judged for general immorality such as murder, or for arrogant presumption and abuse of a divinely appointed role as YHWH's instrument of judgment against his people, but they are not judged for crimes of social injustice against the poor and the needy, the widow and the orphan, the sojourner and the alien. Their folly and ultimate demise may be the result of their disregard of YHWH and their dim-witted worship of blocks of wood and statues of stone, but their idolatry per se is not the cause of their destruction, as it is in the case of Israel and Judah. It seems that the standards of justice, especially social and economic justice, are applied with particular rigor to Israel and Judah but are of less concern in Isaiah's evaluation of the conduct of foreign nations.

Isaiah 28–32 (33) and 34–35

After a span of some fifteen chapters of diverse materials, we encounter a block of material (28–32) many commentators believe is, in large part, genuinely Isaianic. As for the remaining chapters of First Isaiah, namely chs. 33–39, chs. 34–35 are attributed all or in part to Second Isaiah, and chs. 36–39 are viewed either as an historical epilogue to First Isaiah, or as an introduction to Second Isaiah.

While the assessment of the authenticity of material in chs. 28–32 is based on a number of different considerations, from the point of view of the present examination, the return to stinging, even vituperative, denunciations of social injustice strikes a familiar chord. The reader, having been taken to a number of Israel's neighbors in the prophecies of chs. 13–23, and given an apocalyptic preview in 24–27, is back in Judah of the preexilic period, almost certainly towards the end of the eighth century. The very familiarity of the material is sad. Though the intervening chapters have presented awesome displays of divine sovereignty over the nations, over history and time, little has changed in Judah: the nation is still held in the grip of debilitating social and judicial corruption. Indeed, this section opens with a disturbing portrayal of social chaos, the response to which is a prophetic vision of a coming reign of justice.

The vocabulary of justice meets the reader almost immediately. We note in particular that the hendiadys occurs four times in these chapters, twice split (28:17; 32:1); once divided over an *athnaḥ* (that is, a punctuation mark indicating a division in the verse; 32:16); and once unbroken, as the object of the verb (33:5). Each of these will be addressed. Some passages, however, are of only passing interest (for example, 28:26; 32:7; 33:22; 34:5) and can be treated briefly.

Only a comment is needed about the material in chs. 33 and 34–35.[42] It is widely agreed that the material in ch. 33 is a later addition made to end an earlier edition of the Isaianic collection (Sweeney 1996a: 428–33). Similarly, chs. 34–35 have long been recognized, and increasingly accepted, as post-Isaianic. Indeed, Duhm dated it to the period of John Hyrcanus (135–104 B.C.E.), though the majority opinion associates this material with Second Isaiah (Seitz 1993a: 203) or the work of a redactor bridging chs. 1–33 with 40–66 (Sweeney 1996a: 46–48). Our interest in this passage is limited to the occurrence of *mišpāṭ* in 34:5, where it clearly refers to "judgment" as the verdict in a legal proceeding. The meaning of the term here is narrowly defined. Though associated with the work of Second Isaiah, both this passage and the material in ch. 33 will be treated in the literary setting of First Isaiah.

A Spirit of Justice for One Who Judges: Isaiah 28:5-13

Chapter 28 is usually divided into four units: vv. 1-4 (5-6), 7-13, 14-22, 23-29. While the chapter as a whole is considered authentically Isaianic, most commentators regard vv. 5-6 as an editorial addition to vv. 1-4. Because the term *mišpāṭ* occurs twice in these disputed verses, a few comments are required.

The judgment that vv. 5-6 are an editorial addition is usually based on two factors: (1) the shift in meaning of the "garland" *(ʿăṭeret)* in v. 1 and v. 5: in the former it refers to the arrogance of the leaders in Ephraim, while in the latter it refers to the Lord himself as the crowning glory of his people; (2) the mention of the "remnant of his people" is taken by some to refer to the returnees from exile.

1. The "Garland" (ʿăṭeret) *in Verses 1 and 5.* Sweeney addresses these objections in part by defining the units differently. He first notes that the expression "on that day" (v. 5) introduces a new unit and provides no apparent syntactical connection between vv. 1-4 and vv. 5-6. On the other hand, vv. 5-6 are tied to vv. 7ff. by the connecting "and these also" *(wĕgam)* of v. 7. Verses 5-6, therefore, serve as the introduction to vv. 7ff. This analysis provides a different structure to the material and with it a new understanding. Verses 1-4 announce a general woe directed against Ephraim. Verses 5-29 then describe YHWH's purpose in bringing Assyria against Israel and Judah, namely to remove their leadership. To this end, vv. 5-6 announce that YHWH will assume leadership of the remnant people, vv. 7-13 indict the leadership of Ephraim, while vv. 14-22 inveigh against the Judean leadership; vv. 23-29 are an instruction on the duration and purpose of the punishment. Understanding the structure in this way directly ties the shift in the meaning of "garland" to the major theme of this chapter: just as YHWH had swept away the incompetent leadership of Ephraim (vv. 1-13), he intends to do the same with Judah (vv. 14-22), making himself the "crown" of the remnant of his people. For both structural and thematic reasons, Sweeney therefore divides the unit as vv. 1-4 and vv. 5-29 (1996a: 361–62, 367). With this analysis, the jarring shift from vv. 1-4 to vv. 5-6 is obviated.

2. The "Remnant of His People" (šĕʾār ʿammô). The "remnant of his people" need not refer to the events of 587. In context, Isaiah is counseling Hezekiah to wait until the Assyrians (the **šṭp* = "flooding waters" of vv. 2, 15, 17; see also 8:8) have passed from the scene and the house of David once again asserts its rule over all Israel (Sweeney 1996a: 370). As vv. 23-29 make clear, the limited scope and duration of the punishment do not envision something so final as the destruction of 587. Thus, it is not necessary to assign vv. 5-6 to a post-Isaianic editor.

This study accepts this analysis of structure but disagrees with points of the interpretation. Sweeney understands vv. 5-6 as describing YHWH's new role: "YHWH will become the crown of the remnant of the people (v. 5), YHWH will become the spirit of justice (v. 6a), and YHWH will become the strength of the defenders (v. 6b)," all of which indicates that "YHWH will assume leadership" (Sweeney 1996a: 362). What is absent from Sweeney's analysis is that YHWH will be a spirit of justice *(rûaḥ mišpāṭ)* "for the one who sits in [presides over] judgment" *(layyôšēb ʿal-hammišpāṭ),* and "strength for those who turn back war from the gate." Those who exercise these offices seem to be just rulers, unlike the incompetent and drunken rulers of Ephraim (vv. 1-4), the errant, drunken priests and prophets (v. 7), and the scoffing rulers in Jerusalem (vv. 14-22). YHWH may indeed become the spirit of justice and the strength that Sweeney describes, but these are attributes imparted to an unspecified individual or individuals ("the one who sits" and "those who turn back"). These governing and military functions indicate leadership status. Such longings for Spirit-endowed leadership are familiar from Isaiah's earlier words in 9:2-6 (Eng. 3-7) and 11:1-9.

Because the issue is leadership, it is important to understand those whose leadership is condemned. The description of both the leaders of Ephraim (v. 1) and the priests and prophets (v. 7) as drunkards is variously interpreted (see Asen 1996: 73–87). Hayes and Irvine begin their discussion by setting vv. 1-14 "in the months following Hoshea's initial submission to Shalmaneser (probably in 727) but prior to Ephraim's sending of ambassadors to Egypt to secure aid (726). Late in 727 or early in 726 would seem to be the historical horizons" (1987: 323). Hayes and Irvine understand the image of drunkenness as a metaphor "describing the foolishness of their [that is, the leadership's] participation in the planning of rebellion." They conclude that "political matters, not rowdy drunkenness, are the real issue" (1987: 324). Thus, "the one who sits upon the judgment," according to Hayes and Irvine,

> is not a reference to a judge or to one who lives a particularly just pattern of life. Here the phrase refers to those who favored adherence to the principle of justice—that is, in this case, adherence to the terms of the vassal treaty instituted earlier between Hoshea and Shalmaneser. The second [phrase], "those who turn back the battle in the gate," does not refer to warriors but to those who opposed rebellion in the deliberations about revolt. (1987: 324)

The meaning of the verse in question is thus wholly dependent on a historical reconstruction that, in the text, is entirely opaque.

Similarly, Sweeney ties his interpretation to a specific cultural reconstruction. For him, the image of drunkenness alludes to the *marzēaḥ,* which Ugaritic accounts describe as "an extended feast of the gods in which El becomes so drunk that he falls into his own excrement" (1996a: 369). The *marzēaḥ* is also associated with the Canaanite funerary practices and other occasions, such as concluding contracts (a reference to the "covenant with death" in vv. 15, 18), which can involve excessive drinking. "In the present instance, Isaiah associates the funerary character of the *marzēaḥ* with its use by northern Israel to conclude a covenant with an ally (perhaps Egypt?) to oppose the Assyrians" (1996a: 369).

Without denying this as a possible background, we find a more accessible understanding of the charges of drunkenness that ties the image directly to the issues of justice and judgment in v. 6. In the context of Isaiah, the image of excessive drinking and rich foods (28:1, 4) has been encountered earlier in the drinking bouts and musical feasts of 5:11-12, 22. There, such extravagance was associated with the wanton lifestyles of those grown wealthy by unjust economic and judicial practices (5:8, 13, 18, 20-21, 24). The remedy was to return to a life of social justice by which YHWH would be exalted (5:16).

The image in ch. 28 describes haughty leaders adorned with flower garlands who are, literally, "hammered by wine" (*hălûmê yāyin,* v. 1) and bloated with fat (*gêʾ-šĕmānîm,* "rich food," v. 4); it continues in v. 7:

> These, too, with wine reel
>   and with strong drink go astray:
> priest and prophet reel with strong drink
>   and become confused from the wine;
> they go astray from the strong drink:
>   they err in vision, they stumble in [rendering] decision.

Excessive wine and rich food—hallmarks of wealth[43]—insulated the leadership from the concerns of others and incapacitated them in doing what they ought.

Chapter 28 describes leaders who do not lead, prophets whose visions are erroneous, and priests who give poor decisions. This chaotic situation is addressed with two remedial measures, one corrective, the other punitive. Punitively, the drunken gibberish the priests and prophets spout in v. 10 will be matched by the gibberish of foreign conquerors (v. 13a) under whose power the culprits will "stumble backwards, be broken, snared, and taken captive" (v. 13b). As a corrective, their incompetent leadership will be replaced when YHWH gives "a spirit of justice *(mišpāṭ)* to the one who sits over the judgment *(hammišpāṭ)* and of strength to those who turn back battle in the gate" (v. 6).

In v. 6, the term *mišpāṭ* is used in two related but distinct ways. The first occurrence refers to the attitude or "spirit" that characterizes judicial conduct, namely, "justice." This is both a legal requirement and a moral norm. The second occurrence indicates a specific legal action, as the reference to "sitting" indicates. The verb **yšb* ("to sit") describes the posture of an official presiding over a legal matter (Bovati 1994: 232). The king, seated on the throne, exercises his role as executor of justice (Falk 1960b: 72–74). The legal action may be either the judicial procedure as a whole or, more specifically, the verdict. Though the present context makes it difficult to determine which is being indicated, the general setting is clearly the exercise of justice in an official decision-making capacity.

Verses 5-6, with their vocabulary recalling vv. 1-4 and their form introducing vv. 7-13, function as a kind of hinge text. Both the arrogant and drunken leaders of Ephraim (v. 1) and the drunken, errant priests and prophets (v. 7) will be swept away to be replaced by one who "sits in judgment" and "those who turn back battle in the gate." Drunken arrogance alone does not warrant the destruction of the nation. No, drunkenness is emblematic of a wealthy and unconcerned leadership whose neglect gives rise to injustice (Beuken 1995: 34) and whose self-absorption produces a power vacuum. The prophet asks tauntingly, "Whom will he [YHWH] teach knowledge, and to whom will he explain the message? Those weaned on milk? Those removed from the breasts?" (v. 9). There is no responsible adult available whom YHWH can address. This same chaotic lack of leadership was earlier bemoaned in 3:1-12, in which YHWH threatens to appoint women, children, and infants as rulers of Judah (3:4, 12a). There, too, the same terms are used to accuse the leaders of "leading astray" the people (**tʿh,* 3:12b; cf. 28:7), and "confusing the ways of your paths" (**blʿ*, 3:12b; cf. 28:7). The punitive action in 3:1-3 was the removal of the leadership, and that same fate is decreed in 28:13b. That the redressing of this deplorable state involves YHWH's becoming "a spirit of justice for the one who sits in judgment" eloquently and succinctly indicates that the heart of the political, international, economic, and social crisis is fundamentally a lack of justice. Unjust leadership, variously depicted as arrogant, drunken, greedy, and corrupt, results in a society riddled with chaos and ripe for punishment.[44] While the punishment for Israel is final and punitive, the parable in 28:23-29 (see below) suggests that Judah's punishment will be limited and corrective.

Justice as a Measuring Line for Zion: Isaiah 28:14-22

The fate of Ephraim in vv. 1-13 is a warning for Jerusalem. Though the leaders scoff (v. 14) that what has happened in Israel shall bypass them because of their shrewd political alliances (v. 15), YHWH has decreed that not by political covenants and pacts will Jerusalem be saved, but by trust alone will the people be spared (28:16b; cf. 7:9b). The basis for trust is to be found in the sure foundation and cornerstone that YHWH establishes in Zion (v. 16). Though the waters surge all around it—reflected structurally in the surging waters *(*šṭp)* of vv. 15 and 17—Zion proves to be a tested stone. The foundation has been carefully laid by YHWH, who uses "justice for a measuring line and righteousness for a plummet" (*mišpāṭ lĕqāw ûṣĕdāqâ lĕmišqālet*, v. 17).

The controlling image in vv. 16-17a is architectural. Some commentators detach v. 17a from v. 16 because they see "justice and righteousness" somewhat generically as the measuring standards for judging behavior. I take v. 17a as YHWH's description of how he is laying the foundation stone.[45] The tools YHWH the architect uses are the measuring line of justice and the plummet of righteousness. This describes how the very foundation of Zion is set in place and built with the assistance of justice and righteousness.

This reappearance of the hendiadys *mišpāṭ ûṣĕdāqâ* in 28:17 is significant in three ways. First, it confirms the point made above that the underlying issue in vv. 1-4, 5-13 is injustice. Because the fate of Ephraim/Israel in vv. 1-13 functions as a warning to Jerusalem in vv. 14-22, the situations are best taken as analogous. Thus, the prominence given to social justice in vv. 16-17 as the measure by which the sure foundation of Zion is set serves as a pointed contrast to the injustice in vv. 1-13 that warrants destruction.

The second point of significance to the reappearance of the hendiadys *mišpāṭ ûṣĕdāqâ* is its close ties to Zion, whose foundation stone is set in place by "justice and righteousness." As discussed above in 1:21-28, Zion as YHWH's temple city is particularly distinguished by its "justice and righteousness." Indeed, Zion and its citizens are redeemed by the practice of social justice (1:27). Now in 28:16-17, "justice and righteousness" are not only characteristic of Zion and the agents of its redemption, they are very foundation upon which Zion is built. The importance of the expression "justice and righteousness" in Isaiah finds its apogee in Zion.

Third, the hendiadys "justice and righteousness" serves to link together four important Isaianic concerns. We discussed its identification with, and importance to, Zion (1:21-27) in the preceding paragraph. Recall that in 5:16 YHWH is exalted and sanctified by "justice and righteousness." Then, in 9:6 (Eng. 7), the royal throne is established upon "justice and righteousness." Now, in 28:16-17, the very foundation stone of Zion, the temple city, is measured out and squared away by "justice and righteousness." Thus, the expression "justice and righteousness" ties together four key Isaianic complexes: Zion as a temple city, the foundation stone of Zion, the exaltation of God, and the royal throne. In 28:16-17, the fate of the city and the nation is as dependent upon social justice as a structure is upon its foundation, as earlier the royal throne was dependent upon its pedestal (9:6) [Eng. 7]. Just as "justice and righteousness" are the tools by which the cornerstone is measured and set, so, too, justice and righteousness are the foundation upon which the people and the nation stand firm or not at all (cf. 7:9b). How terrifying, then, is the indictment sounded earlier in 5:7, where violence is found in place of justice, and an outcry in place of righteousness. Making the same substitution of violence and outcry for justice and righteousness in both the vineyard of Israel and the foundation stone of Zion produces a terrifying image of social chaos. The ruling class, however, seems unconcerned and so comes under indictment. But how impotent are the lies and deceit in which the leaders find refuge (28:15b, 17b) compared to the rock-solid foundation established in "justice and righteousness." When the surging torrent (the Assyrians) overwhelms the land, Jerusalem's paltry refuge will be swept away but Zion will stand secure, built as it is on "justice and righteousness."

God, the Wise Farmer: Isaiah 28:23-29

In 28:26, *lammišpāṭ* functions almost adverbially. The phrase *wĕyissĕrô lammišpāṭ* is commonly translated "he instructs him rightly" or "well." Understanding *mišpāṭ* against the history of its semantic development confirms this translation. One of the earliest meanings of *mišpāṭ* is "custom" (Booth 1942: 108). Applied to the agricultural metaphor of the preceding verses, the instruction on correct planting proceeds according to customary practice in the proper technique. The occurrence of *mišpāṭ* in this context is primarily of semantic interest, indicating as it does one more facet of the term's many possible meanings.

The point of the parable is that there is a limit and a purpose to threshing. In the same way that farmers who are instructed in the proper technique neither plow nor thresh continually, but also plant, harvest, and crush the grain without pulverizing it, so God's punishment of Jerusalem is measured and purposeful. Just as any farmer who is "instructed aright" knows his craft, now the people who are instructed by the prophet's word know the purpose of God's plan.

YHWH Is a God of Justice: Isaiah 30:18-26

The verse that requires our attention is v. 18:

> Therefore, YHWH waits to be gracious to you;
>   and therefore he is lifted up to be compassionate to you;
> for a God of justice is YHWH *(kî-ʾĕlōhê mišpāṭ YHWH)*;
>   blessed are all who wait for him.

Many commentators, indeed most, take v. 18 as a later editorial comment on the preceding verses that also serves as an introduction to vv. 19-26. Stacey's assessment is representative:

> There is every reason to see this verse as a later addition, but a very constructive one. In vv. 1-17 Isaiah or his editor used "therefore" as a keyword to introduce a promise of punishment. Here the same word introduces a promise of grace which hardly flows from the preceding oracles. (1993: 187–88)

Clements argues similarly: v. 18 dates from after 587 and vv. 19-26 from the late fifth century (1980: 249–50).

As was the case in 28:1-4, 5-13, the questions of the oracle's date and structure are related and resolved by Sweeney in a way that takes issue with prevailing views. Sweeney believes that vv. 1-18 are Isaiah's original words, while vv. 19-26 originate from the Josianic redactor. Originally, v. 18 rounded out the judgment of vv. 1-17 with a promise of eventual salvation (just as 28:23-29 did for 28:1-22). This is expanded by later hands and linked to v. 18 by the causative *kî*. Sweeney argues that, structurally, v. 18 is no longer the conclusion to vv. 1-17, but the introduction to vv. 19-26.[46] Thus, the original Isaianic verse is given a new structural function to introduce a unit (vv. 19-26) that is indeed, as almost all commentators acknowledge, a later addition (Sweeney: Josianic; Clements: late fifth century; Duhm: Maccabean period).

I agree with Sweeney in accepting the Isaianic authenticity of v. 18, but I think that the verse functions better as a hinge verse between the two sections. The "and therefore" (*wĕlākēn*) of v. 18 serves not merely as a conjunctive link to what precedes (Sweeney 1996a: 391), but also summarizes all that has come before: in punishing the rebellious overtures of his people to establish foreign alliances (vv. 1-17), God acts with justice. But justice is also described as being gracious and compassionate in bringing salvation, even if it must be delayed. That promise of delayed salvation becomes the basis for the unit that follows and leads into a new unit that is signaled by the causative *kî* (v. 19). The "justice" of God in verse 18 is thus expressed in both punishment (vv. 1-17) and salvation (vv. 19-26).

In the context of promised punishment and delayed salvation, what does it mean to say that God is a "God of justice"? Most commentators stumble on this issue and revert to a rather generic understanding of *mišpāṭ* as "right order" (Jensen), "all around rightness" (Stacey), "good order" (Clements), "the right way" (Motyer). While these definitions are within the range of meaning for the term, how do they fit the present context? To find a more satisfying answer, we must look to the context.

In discussing 30:18, most commentators are rightly concerned with the themes of "waiting" and the delay of salvation, but they frequently glance over causative *kî* (v. 18b), which links the divine title "God of justice" to the preceding clause in which the divine activities are described as being gracious and showing compassion. The verse as a whole, which describes the divine advent in graciousness and compassion, provides the first context for understanding *mišpāṭ* as more than merely "the right thing." The meaning of justice in 30:18 is illuminated by God's graciousness and compassion.

In earlier discussions, Weinfeld demonstrated the correspondence between acts of "justice and righteousness" and acts of "kindness and mercy" on behalf of the oppressed (cf. Isa 16:5). The words "justice and righteousness," he points out, are frequently found with the words for kindness *(ḥesed)*, truth *(ʾĕmet)*, and mercy *(raḥămîm)*: Pss 33:5; 89:15 (Eng. 14); Jer 9:23 (Eng. 24); Hos 2:21 (Eng. 19); 12:7 (Eng. 6); Mic 6:8 (Weinfeld 1995: 29). Social reforms that enact "justice and righteousness" are described as acts of "kindness and compassion." In the present context, it is precisely because God is a God of justice that he promises to be gracious and compassionate, and, conversely, in being gracious and compassionate God demonstrates his justice.

In Isa 30:18, this gracious and compassionate justice will come after judgment on the rebellious (30:1-17; cf. 1:28). Punishment, the conclusion of the "woe" announced in v. 1 of this chapter, yields to deliverance (30:18ff.). As Bovati demonstrated, justice rightly executed is two-sided in its effects: evildoers are punished while the oppressed are vindicated (Bovati 1994: 201–2; cf. Isa 11:3-4). In this passage from Isaiah, the two-edged sword of justice strikes and separates those who are punished from those who will eventually be restored. While the nation as a whole will suffer, those who wait will experience God's justice expressed in compassion as surely as the evil have experienced his justice as punishment. The punishment aspect is easy to see in 30:1-17. It is in this very sense that Young translates the divine title in v. 18 as "a God of judgment is the Lord" (1992, 2:350). While the justice of God in vv. 1-17 is more evident in punishment, the graciousness of God's justice is the theme later editors developed in vv. 19-26. God, who graciously hears the cry of his people (v. 19), sends rain, fecundity (vv. 23-26), and light (v. 26a). The passage ends with divine compassion finding tender expression in binding *(ḥābaš)* the wounds *(makkâ)* that have been struck (v. 26b; cf. 1:6).

In this sense, Isaiah's description of YHWH as a "God of justice" succinctly and eloquently summarizes the discussion of justice to this point. First, justice is something so close to the heart of God that he is described as its primary patron: Who safeguards, enacts, and promotes justice? YHWH does. In turn, justice is as characteristic of God as elsewhere is his holiness. What attributes describe YHWH? In Isaiah, "holiness" is now augmented by "justice": the Holy One of Israel is a God of justice. Justice means two things simultaneously: on the one hand, it is a gracious compassion extended toward the widow and orphan, the poor and the oppressed; on the other hand, it is punishment and destruction for those who fail to act with that same gracious compassion on behalf of the needy who are in their care. The failure of the leadership to enact justice has been graphically described and bitterly decried. God's justice demands punishment, which was first threatened and then imposed in the destruction of Ephraim and later in the events of 701. Because punishment enacted in history proves God's commitment to justice, it also provides hope for those who wait. The God of justice who destroys evildoers will also vindicate those who trust in him. The accomplishment of the former is the pledge of the latter. The carefully catalogued injustice, which merits punishment, moves the God of justice to act with fierce compassion, to break (30:26, *šeber*; cf. 1:28) his people and then bind them, to inflict a punishing blow and then to heal it (30:26; cf. 1:6).

The remaining prophecies that deal with the terms and themes of justice are all taken to be post-Isaianic, though most likely from different redactional and editorial hands. As has been the practice thus far, these will be considered in their present setting.

A King Shall Rule in Justice: Isaiah 32:1-8

With the exception of Hayes and Irvine among historical critics, 32:1-8 is universally judged to be post-Isaianic,[47] but the wide-ranging assessments of this passage argue against making the interpretation of the verse dependent on historical circumstances and individuals. It seems best to examine the unit thematically for its understanding of justice and just rule.

We begin by noting that the term "king" *(melek)* in 32:1 is surprising.[48] Usually in Isaiah, whenever a successor from the royal house of Judah is mentioned (for example, 9:2-6 [Eng. 3-7]; 11:1-11), the term "king" is avoided: unidentified righteous rulers in Isaiah are not called "king." The same reticence to use the term "king" is found in the many attacks on the leadership of both kingdoms: *melek* is studiously avoided and in its place we find a wide variety of terms, perhaps implying that such corrupt leadership is unworthy of "kingly" rule. If *melek* in 32:1 is meant to refer to Hezekiah or Josiah, it would be the only time the term is used without a proper name or specific kingdom indicated (on 33:17, see below). The uniqueness of this usage makes it difficult to draw conclusions. It is not possible to determine, for example, whether this reflects a time when kingship was still in existence and its purification was earnestly desired or a time when kingship had passed from the scene and its revival was anticipated. A nonreferential meaning of "king" in this passage is reinforced by its context. The "king" in v. 1a is paired with "princes" *(śārîm)* in v. 1b. These parallel terms immediately shift the focus from a particular king to encompass the entire ruling class. The office of governance, particularly just governance, is not the task of the king alone but equally of those around him (Stacey 1993: 196). The rule of these leaders is described by the hendiadys *mišpāṭ ûṣĕdāqâ*, which is here split for the sake of the parallelism.[49] The quality of their just rule, elsewhere described as care of the orphan and the widow, the poor and the oppressed, is here described metaphorically as shelter from the wind and storm, as streams in the desert, and as shade in a parched land (32:2). These are all images of protection from threatening forces. The threat is further described in wisdom terms that pit the fool against the noble, and the villain against the honorable (32:5-6). Fools and villains are not merely inconvenient; they represent a real threat. The confusion they introduce into society is described in vv. 6-7 by the terms "folly" *(nĕbālâ)*, "iniquity" *(ʾāwen)*, "godlessness" *(ḥōnep)*, "error" *(tôʿâ)*, "villainy" *(kîlay)*, "wickedness" *(zimmôt)*, and "lies" *(šeqer)*. This confusion has been encountered earlier in 5:20, where the wicked call evil good and good evil, exchange darkness for light and light for darkness, and call bitter sweet and sweet bitter. It is not unlike the corrupt legal practices that have the appearance of justice but conceal bloodshed, that look like righteousness but provoke an outcry (5:7). The confusion of fundamentally opposed realities (that is, what is honorable and what is villainous) is a serious threat to the moral and social orders.

Once again, the targets for corrupt exploitation are the vulnerable in society: the hungry and the thirsty (32:6b) who are put aside and denied, and the afflicted and poor (*ʿănāwîm . . . ʾebyôn*, 32:7b) who are victimized or "ruined" (*ḥabbēl*, 32:7a) by deceitful words. The Hebrew of v. 7b is very difficult and many suggestions have been offered. Young's suggestion is somewhat wooden but close to the sense: "to ruin the afflicted with words of falsehood, and when the poor man speaks *[bĕdabbēr]* judgment" (1992, 2:388). I would suggest repointing *bĕdabbēr* (a Piel infinitive construct) as *bidbar* (a noun in construct), that is, "in the matter of the poor." Thus: "to ruin the afflicted with deceitful words, and, in the matter of the poor, [to ruin] justice." Against Young, it seems better to understand *mišpāṭ* as "justice"; this provides a broader context than the judicial setting implied by "judgment."[50] But whatever the exact nature of the act, its intent is specified in the first part of the verse: "The villainies of the villain are evil; he plans evil plots." The afflicted and the poor are targets for evil plans.

The actions of the fool and the villain in 32:5-7, while ultimately contrasted with the values of the noble person in v. 8, are also a foil to the righteous king and his princes. Leaders who are righteous and just are a bulwark for the poor and a refuge for the needy, while the unscrupulous seek to exploit them by evil machinations. Whoever the king may be, and whenever he may reign, this passage expects that his rule will be characterized by social justice, particularly on behalf of the afflicted and the poor.

All of this is general enough to be appropriate in the literary context of the eighth-century prophet. Even though the focus on social justice and oppression of the poor is at home in Isaiah, the images of 32:1-8 are more generalized and neutral than the more pointed and incisive accusations that typify Isaiah's earlier indictments.

Creation Bears the Fruit of Justice: Isaiah 32:15-19

Many commentators date this passage to the postexilic period (Kaiser 1974: 333; Wildberger 1982: 1273–81; and Jensen 1984: 252). But, according to Sweeney, the original Isaianic core of ch. 32 (the judgment in vv. 9-14) is surrounded by a Josianic framework: vv. 1-8 announce the new royal savior (that is, Josiah), and vv. 15-19 describe the effects of his just rule as a time of peace (1996a: 418–20). In effect, Sweeney ties his interpretation of the two framing passages to the person of Josiah and, in the process, unfortunately conflates the ruler and his reign: Sweeney attributes the time of peace described in vv. 15-19 to the actions of the righteous king in 32:1. However, there is nothing in vv. 15-19 that requires royal agency for the promised time of peace. Indeed, Sweeney seems to overlook that the "spirit from on high" in 32:15 is poured out "upon us" and not specifically the adduced "new king." A more careful reading of the text shows that it is the "spirit" (v. 15) that is the source of this age of peace and justice. Read within the context of the eighth-century prophet, however, the mention of the "spirit" immediately evokes two earlier passages, both of which link the spirit to the royal ruler. First, Isa 11:2-9 had described seven attributes of the spirit that would rest upon the royal heir. Second, in 28:6 YHWH imparts a "spirit of justice" to the ruler. In light of these earlier passages, Sweeney is not far from the mark in linking 32:1-8 and 15-19, but in attributing the age of peace restrictively to the new king, he misses a new element that 32:15 adds to the discussion: in 32:15-19, the spirit is poured out more generally on the populace.

In 32:15b-16, the effect of the spirit on creation is described in terms that evoke the justice of the king announced in 32:1. In the same way that the just king's reign was earlier described with images from the natural realm (32:2), now the effects of the spirit are similarly described with the transformation of the natural world: the wilderness will become an orchard that is extensive enough to be considered a forest (32:15). The "justice and righteousness" that are established by the king and his princes (32:1) take up residence in this transformed natural habitat: "*Justice* will tent in the wilderness, and *righteousness* will dwell in the orchard" (32:16).[51] The chaos, confusion, and anarchy that accompany injustice (3:1-12) are thereby replaced with peace *(šālôm)*, quiet *(hašqēṭ)*, and security (*beṭaḥ*, 32:17). The peace and security described as dwelling in the wilderness in 32:17 are then applied to "my people" who "dwell in a peaceful *(šālôm)* habitation, and in secure *(beṭaḥ)* dwellings, and in quiet resting places" (33:18). Peace and security are the result of "justice and righteousness," which, in turn, are the preconditions for all blessings (Jensen 1984: 256). The injustice of corrupt leadership that has been so central to the harsh judgments of Isaiah finds its remedy in the social justice of the righteous king, which has its origin in the spirit from on high.

Zion and Justice: Isaiah 33:5-6, 17-24

While Seitz is inclined to date ch. 33 to the period of Isaiah (1993a: 233–34), the majority of commentators situate it sometime after Isaiah, though the proposed settings run the gamut from the time of Josiah to the Hellenistic period. I agree that the passages in question are non-Isaianic but am reserved with regard to a more precise dating. The focus on the kingship of YHWH with no Davidic king in sight suggests a postexilic date when hope for the restoration of the house of David had waned. However, it seems clear that ch. 33 was composed with the prophecies of Isaiah in mind, as evident from the extensive use of Isaianic themes and images found throughout the chapter (Clements 1980: 264).

1. YHWH Fills Zion with Justice: Isaiah 33:5-6. The verses of interest can be treated briefly, their themes having been discussed already. The themes of the exaltation of YHWH in justice and righteousness (5:16) and Zion as a city of justice and righteousness (1:21-28; 28:16-17) come together explicitly in 33:5:

> YHWH is exalted, for he dwells on high;
> he filled Zion with justice and righteousness.

The city that once was filled *(*mlʾ)* with justice and righteousness (1:21b) has been restored to that condition, apparently not through human agency (1:27) but through YHWH's own act on its behalf. The ambiguity that surrounded the interpretation of 1:27—Whose justice and righteousness redeem the city?—is here resolved: any justice and righteousness that are to be found in the city have their source in YHWH.

As we saw in 32:15-19, social justice (v. 16) is the basis for peace and security (vv. 17-18). The same point is made in the relationship between vv. 5 and 6 in ch. 33. Once the temple city has its justice and righteousness restored (33:5), it then becomes worthy of God's blessings. In 33:6, YHWH himself "will be the stability *(ʾĕmûnâ)* of your times, abundance of salvation, wisdom, and knowledge; the fear of YHWH is his treasure." Earlier, the same term *(*ʾmn)* had been used in 1:21 and 26 to describe Zion as a "faithful city" *(qiryâ neʾĕmānâ)*. As history has demonstrated, that fidelity was erratic at best. Zion will no longer depend on the fidelity of its leaders and citizenry for its faithfulness or stability. YHWH himself is its stability (33:6). The last three qualities of 33:6, wisdom, knowledge, and fear of YHWH, had earlier been associated with the sprout from the stump of Jesse (11:2); now they are associated with YHWH's presence in Zion.

In 33:5-6, not only do these three Isaianic themes—the exaltation of YHWH, Zion, justice and righteousness—come together, they are realigned. The qualities and virtues that were to be characteristic of the city of Zion and by which both the people were redeemed (1:27) and YHWH exalted (5:16) had been realities accomplished or compromised by people in the social realm. In 33:5-6, YHWH is the chief actor, the one responsible for filling Zion with justice and righteousness. All the qualities that Isaiah had attributed to Zion and the royal ruler have been appropriated by YHWH. This direct divine agency is a distinct development of the Isaianic tradition. This notion of YHWH as chief actor, taken together with the more generalized and diffuse images of justice encountered in post-Isaianic passages such as 32:15-19, will come together to present a distinctly different notion of justice that will move to center stage in the second half of the book.

2. YHWH Is Our Judge: Isaiah 33:17-24. Just as the qualities and virtues required of his people and the characteristics of his city are attributed to YHWH (33:5-6), so also society's leadership roles are now assigned to him. The failure of the judges, lawmakers, and kings to secure that justice which brings peace and guarantees security moves the author to assign those roles to YHWH. And so 33:22 proclaims that

> YHWH is our judge, YHWH is our lawgiver,
> YHWH is our king; he will save us.

YHWH's sovereignty over the foreign kingdoms, expressed in terms of judging and arbitrating in 2:2-4, is reprised and explicitly expanded in 33:22 to include lawgiving and kingship. Although 33:22 seems to apply nationally to Israel, YHWH's rule extends beyond the borders of Israel to include all the peoples on earth, as chs. 13–27 had demonstrated, and as ch. 34 is about to make clear.

The structure of 33:22 is emphatic: the threefold repetition of the divine name makes it clear that YHWH alone is the supreme ruler who appropriates all offices of social authority. The verse comes to a climax with the personal pronoun in emphatic position before the inflected verb, "*he* will save us" *(hûʾ yôšīʿēnû)*. Not only does this last statement bring to a climax the exaltation begun with the first words of 33:5 ("YHWH is exalted"), it implies that salvation comes from judging, law-giving, and kingly rule finally exercised properly. The equivalency between "judging" and "saving," inferred earlier, is now made explicit.

The kingship of YHWH in 33:22 is the context within which to understand the mention of "a king in beauty" in 33:17. This verse has occasioned much discussion: does it refer to the future messianic king, any future righteous king, or YHWH himself? Two points argue for understanding it as a reference to YHWH. The first is the point discussed above: verse 22 emphatically asserts that YHWH is "our king." The second point serves to confirm this assertion. Contextually, 33:17-24 follow upon the "entrance liturgy" of 33:14-16. The questions are asked of those who seek admission to the sanctuary (cf. Pss 15:1-5; 24:3-5 [requirements listed, without the initial questions, Ps 118:19-20]); gaining admission, one seeks a vision of God (cf. Pss 11:7; 42:3 [Eng. 2]). As Clements points out, the language in Isa 33:16, "he shall dwell upon the heights," is an expression that means "to worship in the sanctuary" (cf. Ps 148:1), and suggests that the prospective worshipper has gained admittance to the sanctuary. Further, the mention of "bread" and "water" in Isa 33:16 (cf. Ps 23:5—"you spread a table before me") draws on the belief that the sanctuary is a source of blessing and prosperity for the worshipper (Clements 1980: 268–69). In context, upon completing the "entrance liturgy" and gaining access to the sanctuary (Isa 33:14-16), one sees the "king in beauty" (33:17). As 33:22 had made abundantly clear, "YHWH is our king."

Chapter 33, like ch. 32 before it, marks a dramatic shift in perspective in the book of Isaiah. The prophet had once looked forward to a time when YHWH would "restore your judges as in the beginning" (1:26). He had seen the house of David as the divinely approved ruler of God's people (9:6; 16:5; 37:35; 38:5). The evils within Israel and Judah that Isaiah catalogued were evils he hoped their leaders and people would set aright (1:17). The concerns of Isaiah—both the sins of the nation and the required corrective measures—were firmly situated in the sociopolitical world. The justice Isaiah demanded was a justice enacted in the social realm. Even the necessary punishment God would inflict on the people was meted out through the human agency of the Assyrian army. But the optimism of Isaiah (for example, 1:27; 5:16; 9:2-6 [Eng. 3-7]; 11:1-9) that the security of the city and the kingdom could be guaranteed by the justice of their citizens and leaders has collapsed under the weight of human pride and frailty. Though the kingdom is in ruins and the kingship dissolved, this post-Isaianic passage does not look for the restoration of judges or of the monarchy. Instead, the offices of judge, lawmaker, and king are now exercised by YHWH. There is only one hope and that is summarized in the last phrase of 33:22: "[YHWH] will save us." This is a worldview that is more typical of the exilic and postexilic authors of Isaiah; this perspective will become a central concern of the next portion of this study.

Judgment on Edom: Isaiah 34:5-17

Even Hayes and Irvine, otherwise stout defenders of the Isaianic authorship of almost all of chs. 1–39, concede that chs. 34–35 are not the work of the eighth-century prophet (1987: 13, 67). Because our interest is limited to 34:5, a protracted discussion of the authorship, redaction, and structural relationship of chaps. 34–35 to chaps. 1–33 and 40–66 is not warranted.[52] A few brief comments will get to the heart of the matter.

Structurally, ch. 34 begins in vv. 1-4 with a summons to all the nations, the peoples, the earth and those who fill it, the world and those who go about in it (34:1). They are called to witness the wrath and burning anger of YHWH expressed in devoting *(*ḥrm)* them to destruction and giving them over to slaughter (v. 2).

The destruction announced generically in vv. 1-4 is specified in more precise terms in vv. 5-17. Edom, for reasons not specified in this text and only inferred elsewhere (cf. Obadiah), is singled out as the first doomed to destruction (v. 5): YHWH's sword will descend upon Edom and upon the people he has devoted *(*ḥrm)* to judgment *(lĕmišpāṭ)*. Verses 6ff. describe in grisly detail the specifics of that destruction. As the context makes clear, *mišpāṭ* in v. 5 means "judgment" and includes "the punishment following the judgment" (Bovati 1994: 189). In this instance, judgment involves punishment for Edom (34:5-17) as a prelude to redemption for Zion (ch. 35).

Overall, the judgment in ch. 34 is the inverse of the picture painted in chs. 32–33. The natural images used for peaceful prosperity in 32:15-20 are undone in 34:9-15: the land that was once densely covered with fruitful trees (32:15) is now overgrown with thorns and thistles (34:13). In ch. 33, YHWH rules Israel as judge and king in justice and righteousness; in ch. 34 his sovereignty over the nations, announced in 2:2-4 and proved in chs. 13–23 and 24–27, is demonstrated in wrath against the enemies of his people. Implied in this reversal of conditions are the two sides of judgment as vindication for his people and punishment for his enemies.

A telling detail links the perspective of ch. 34 to that discussed above in 33:17-24—YHWH himself is the apparent agent of the terrible carnage described in 34:5-17 (Jensen 1984: 264). In these late passages, both just rule and destroying judgment are executed by YHWH's unmediated actions.

Conclusions about *Mišpāṭ*/Justice in First Isaiah

In this first part of the book of Isaiah, we have examined carefully each passage in which the term *mišpāṭ* or the verb *šāpaṭ* and its nominal form *šōpēṭ* ("judge") are found. In the course of this analysis, we have judged which passages are from the prophet Isaiah and are reflective of his historical setting in the second half of the eighth century, and those that are later than Isaiah. We have also taken note of those instances in which *mišpāṭ* occurred as part of the hendiadys *mišpāṭ ûṣĕdāqâ*. The distribution of these terms can be conveniently presented in chart form (see page 88).

In no small part, the understanding of the term *mišpāṭ* that emerges from this study is colored by its occurrence with *ṣĕdāqâ* in almost half of all the cases and in fully half of the authentic passages. We have agreed with Weinfeld's study of the hendiadys in its larger ancient Near Eastern and biblical settings that the expression, even when divided for poetic purposes, refers to social justice, that is, justice enacted in the social realm on behalf of the oppressed and poor. This may be expressed in official royal acts of liberation and benevolence ("kindness and mercy"), or correcting unjust legal acts that result in exploitation. Bovati's careful study of legal language, terminology, and practice demonstrates that *mišpāṭ* and other terms from the forensic sphere are used both in a specifically legal way and in a broader social sense. The legal idiom is transferable to nonlegal settings (for example, 16:5; 32:7).

Passage	**Isaiah (c. 742–701)**	***mišpāṭ***	**Verb *šāpaṭ***	**Noun *šōpēṭ***	**Hendiadys *mišpāṭ ûṣĕdāqâ***
1:10-17	Yes	v. 17	v. 17		
1:21-26, [27-28]	Yes [?]	v. 21, 27	v. 23	v. 26	vv. 21, 27 (both split)
2:2-4	No		v. 4		
3:1-12	Yes			v. 2	
3:13-15	Yes	v. 14			
4:2-6	No	v. 4			
5:1-7	Yes	v. 7	v. 3		v. 7 (split)
5:8-24	Yes	v. 16			v. 16 (split)
8:23—9:6 (Eng. 9:1-7)	Yes	v. 6 (Eng. 7)			v. 6 (Eng. 7)
10:1-4	Yes	v. 2			
11:1-9	Yes		vv. 3, 4		*v. 4* verb *šāpaṭ*, with noun *ṣĕdāqâ*
16:1-5	Yes	v. 5		v. 5	v. 5 (split)
26:7-19	No	vv. 8, 9			*v. 9 mišpāṭêkā* with *ṣedeq*
28:5-13	Yes	v. 6 (2x)			
28:14-22	Yes	v. 17			v. 17 (split)
28:23-29	Yes	v. 26			
30:18-26	Yes	v. 18			
32:1-8	No	v. 1, 7			v. 1 (split)
32:15-20	No	v. 16			v. 16 (split over an *athnaḥ*)
33:5-6	No	v. 5			v. 5
33:17-24	No			v. 22	
34:5-17	No	v. 5			
Isaiah, 8th-cent. subtotal		14	5	3	7
Post–8th-cent. subtotal		8	1	1	3
Total		**22**	**6**	**4**	**10**

This social understanding of justice has been confirmed by examining the vocabulary in its context. Isaiah describes "justice" in positive terms only briefly in 1:17—"seek justice: set aright oppression; do justice for the orphan, argue the case of the widow." Equally briefly, its positive effects are described (for example, 11:6-9; 32:15-19). Because the positive description of justice is so cursory, this study has examined the manifestations of injustice in order to add to our understanding of what justice must entail. In doing so, we have examined the situations against which Isaiah fulminated, namely, the gross neglect and exploitation of widows, orphans, and the poor (for example, 1:17, 23; 10:2; 11:4); corrupt legal practices that imparted the appearance of legitimacy to wrongdoing (for example, 3:14; 5:23; 10:1); the greedy accumulation of property and possessions (for example, 2:7; 3:16-23; 5:8-9; 10:2-3); violence and bloodshed (for example, 1:15, 21; 5:7); a public policy of deceit and lies (for example, 28:15); oppression (for example, 1:17; 3:15; 5:7); and a luxuriant, debauched lifestyle (for example, 5:11, 12, 22; 28:1, 7-8; 32:9) lived in neglect of the underclasses (for example, 1:22). As is abundantly clear, Isaiah's sense of "justice and righteousness" is very much centered on the real world of his day. This is a significant point: the primary frame of reference for understanding justice is not as a theological quality or a divine attribute but as a way of life for the individual and society. Both the injustice that demands correction or punishment and the justice that brings redemption to Zion (1:28) and glory to God (5:16) are found in the social life of the people. To say that "YHWH is a God of justice" (30:18) is not an ontological comment on the divine nature but an assertion that YHWH, the compassionate savior of Israel and the historical protector of his people, demands that justice be expressed in the lives of people and in the structures of society. To paraphrase the refrain of the Holiness Code, "You shall be a people of justice, for I, YHWH, am a God of justice."[53]

As documented in the preceding paragraph, the scope of (in)justice is not limited to legal concerns, or matters of economic oppression, or social neglect and marginalization, or moral virtues narrowly conceived. It is not exclusively a private or a public matter. It is all these things. The legal, economic, social, and moral life of individuals, classes of individuals, and society as a whole all fall within the wide embrace of justice. Attempts to discuss "justice in Isaiah" under only one rubric[54] fall short of his breadth of vision and scope of concern. Attempts to understand justice theologically without regard for its social demands are as misconceived as attempts to consider social justice without appreciating both its theological foundation and its religious essence. This last point is, as we saw, characteristic of Israel's practice of justice as described by Hanson: more than just good statecraft or a prop of political propaganda, justice in Israel is rooted in God's compassion for the widow and orphan, the poor and the alien.[55] Those who are beneficiaries of God's saving justice are in turn agents of justice for those in need. Just as God's saving justice for Israel historically meant the crushing of her oppressor, justice in the social realm involves not just acts of charity for the poor and the indigent, but the defeat and overthrow of those individuals and structures that perpetuate injustice.

This fundamentally religious heart of justice is what allows Isaiah to link it so boldly to the cult. Justice is not in opposition to the cult any more than it is meant to replace the cult. The relationship between cult and justice is more symbiotic: true worship finds its expression in justice and justice recognizes its source in the worship of God. The seeking of God usually associated with formal cultic inquiry finds its social counterpart in the seeking of justice (Isa 1:17). The correspondence between worship and justice underlies the Inaugural Vision of Isaiah. The God who is revealed to Isaiah as thrice holy sends him out to announce judgment, which, as we saw, involves both the punishment of evildoers and the deliverance of the oppressed. The holiness of God, so clearly expressed in Isaiah's use of the divine title "the Holy One of Israel," animates his entire ministry. The impressive emphasis on justice in Isaiah is easily understood, not merely as one individual's sensitivity to society's underclasses, but as impelled by the holiness of God, which demands justice. The words of Heschel on this point are as insistent as they are eloquent:

> Justice is not an ancient custom, a human convention, a value, but a transcendent demand, freighted with divine concern. It is not only a relationship between man and man, it is an act involving God, a divine need. Justice is His line, His plummet (Isa. 28:17). It is not one of His ways, but in all His ways. Its validity is not only universal, but also eternal, independent of will and experience.
>
> People think that to be just is a virtue, deserving honor and rewards; that in doing righteousness one confers a favor on society. No one expects to receive a reward for the habit of breathing. Justice is as much a necessity as breathing is, and a constant occupation. (1969: 198–99)

The religious component of justice is underscored in yet another way. By understanding the structural unity of ch. 1, injustice falls under the rubric of "sin" and "rebellion" (1:2, 4). Thus, failures in the social realm are not merely bad public policy or unfortunate lapses of social institutions: they are sins against YHWH and evidence of the people's rebellion against God. This is cast into sharp relief when Isaiah calls Zion a "whore" (1:21), a term other prophets use to denounce Israel's infidelity expressed in idolatry. Isaiah's description of Zion's neglect of the orphan and widow (1:23) as whoring broadens the particular nature of Israel's infidelity to include injustice. Thus, to serve the appetites of greed and luxury to the neglect of the poor is not merely a matter of selfishness and corruption run amok; it is an abandoning (**ᶜzb*, 1:4, 28) of God and is tantamount to idolatry. The corresponding action to redress the abandoning of God that takes place in social neglect is to "seek justice" (1:17), wherein God is found.

The demand for justice is made of everyone in society: the people at large (for example, 1:4-6, 10; 5:3) and the kingdom as a whole (for example, 1:5-6), judges (for example, 1:26; 16:5), elders (for example, 3:14), princes (for example, 1:23; 3:14; 32:1), rulers (1:10; 28:14), and kings (9:6 [Eng. 7]; 16:5; 28:6). All are called to act with justice and are condemned in the strongest terms whenever they fail. In

Isaiah's mind, the leadership bears a particular responsibility and is therefore singled out for particular attention: because the head is sick and the heart is faint, the whole body, from the sole of the foot to the very head, lacks soundness (1:5-6). The failure of the leadership to set the pace for the nation to follow made Isaiah long for a day when the house of David would be renowned for its practice of justice (9:2-6 [Eng. 3-7]; 11:1-11; 16:5; 32:1). In the present, however, the serious consequences of injustice, measured in terms of the punishment inflicted first on Israel, then on Judah, are eloquent testimony to the surpassing importance of justice. Justice is not of incidental importance: it is literally a matter of life and death.

The tendency in later passages to describe justice more as a quality proper to God (for example, 33:5-6) or originating in God (32:15-19) and to look to God as its primary executor (for example, 2:2-4; 14:28-32; 33:5-6, 17ff.) will emerge as an obvious concern in the next part of our study. The effect of distinguishing such later passages in First Isaiah highlights a difference in perspective and understanding of justice. For the eighth-century prophet working in Judah, justice is enacted in the social realm and is done by both the people as a whole and the entire leadership class. By contrast, later Isaianic writers will look to God to guarantee and secure justice, and will understand justice more as an expression of God's sovereignty than of his compassion.

While a diachronic study of the book casts these nuances into sharp relief, a synchronic study of these passages in their literary context as part of First Isaiah provides a more comprehensive understanding of justice as a work of God, the human community, and its leadership undertaken mutually, and enacted in the social realm as a tangible manifestation of the transcendent and compassionate sovereignty of God. What may have been discernible as distinct aspects of justice are now understood as complementary parts of a more complex social and theological matrix. However, before we can address these synchronic concerns, it is necessary to continuing tracking the understanding of justice that emerges in the changed social and historical circumstances of the people now exiled to Babylon.

chapter 4

Isaiah 40–55

The chapters known as Second Isaiah[1] contain some of the best-known, most beloved, and theologically significant texts in the Bible. With the exception of the book of Psalms, no Old Testament book is more widely quoted in the New Testament than the material in Isaiah 40–55. The christological interpretation of these texts reaches its artistic zenith in Handel's *Messiah,* in which fourteen selections come from this portion of Isaiah. Even taken on its own terms, apart from its use by other authorities, this material in Second Isaiah is widely and rightly celebrated for its lyrical poetry and profound theology. From the point of view of our own study of justice, these chapters represent a distinctive and crucial development in perspective and understanding.

The difference between the understanding of *mišpāṭ* in Isaiah 1–39 and chs. 40–55 can be highlighted in three general observations. First, the hendiadys *(mišpāṭ ûṣĕdāqâ)* that occurred ten times in the first thirty-nine chapters does not occur even once in chs. 40–55. This is true even though the relative frequency with which the term *mišpāṭ* occurs is slightly higher in Second Isaiah: 11 times in the 333 verses of Isaiah 40–55 compared to 22 times in the 766 verses of Isaiah 1–39. In Second Isaiah's context of exile and return, the term that is more frequently paired with *ṣĕdāqâ* is not *mišpāṭ* but *yĕšûʿâ* (salvation): 45:8; 45:21;[2] 46:13; 51:5, 6, 8. Second, the social aspect of justice recedes entirely into the background. Indeed, the orphan *(yātôm)* and widow *(ʾalmānâ)* are not even mentioned. Third, in Isaiah 40–55, the idiom of the courtroom moves to center stage (for example, 41:1-5, 21-29; 43:8-15, 26; 45:20-25; 50:1-3, 8). In such a setting, the forensic aspect of the term *mišpāṭ* is particularly prominent, and the term is redeployed in a strikingly different way from how it was in Isaiah 1–39. The impact that this change in setting has on the understanding of *mišpāṭ* will be tracked in the examination of the passages that follows.

Preliminary Issues

Two questions must first be addressed: the issue of the so-called Songs of the Servant, and the geographical and historical setting of chs. 40–55. While both of these are topics that could profitably be explored at length, only a few comments are needed to relate them to the present discussion.

The "Songs of the Servant"

In his seminal study on Isaiah, Duhm distinguished between passages that identify the Servant of YHWH as an individual and those that describe Israel as YHWH's

Servant. Duhm isolated four poems in Second Isaiah that he believed describe an individual, unnamed servant: 42:1-4; 49:1-6; 50:4-9; and 52:13—53:12. He argued that these passages are not integral to their present settings and that the author of these poems was not Second Isaiah. Subsequent scholarship pursued with great interest first the identity and fate of that mysterious figure,[3] and then, despairing of any satisfactory resolution to that quest, scholars turned their attention to his function or significance. One "regrettable casualty" of scholarly interest in the identity and fate of the Servant has been a disregard for "the actual literary contexts in which the theme [of the Servant] appears" (Eissfeldt 1965: 336).

Each of Duhm's three assertions—that "these 'Songs' are remarkable in that they are only loosely related to their contexts, they speak of a different 'Servant' than do the rest of Isaiah 40–55, and they are secondary to their present situations"[4]—has been seriously challenged over the years. The most sustained attack against Duhm's assessment is that of Mettinger, who makes three counterarguments: (1) the four Songs are of different literary forms *(Gattungen)* and therefore do not constitute of themselves a separate unified block of material; (2) chapters 40–55 are carefully structured and the four songs are integral to that structure; and (3) there is no material difference in how the Servant is conceived in those passages that are alleged to deal with an individual and those that identify the Servant as Israel.[5] Barstad agrees that Duhm's distinction can no longer be supported by positive argument, and suggests that the impulse to distinguish an individual Servant from Servant Israel has enjoyed currency mostly because of the desire to interpret these texts in a christological context (1994: 261–70). Barstad wishes to do more than merely say "farewell" to the songs: he concludes that "the myth of the 'Servant Songs' is long, long overdue for demolition" (1994: 270).

In a sense, Mettinger's and Barstad's arguments are directed against a straw man: Duhm's pure position is rarely advocated today, though aspects of his analysis continue to be compelling. Among recent scholars, some are inclined to agree with Duhm's assessment that these songs constitute a separate strand of material, but they are less convinced that these songs come from a different author. Westermann, for example, agrees that the first three songs seem to rest uneasily in their present settings, and that they represent a separate strand of material that was added later; but he argues that these songs were composed by Second Isaiah himself (1975: 20, 29), though the Fourth Song presupposes the Servant's death and was therefore written by someone else. Clifford, too, believes that Second Isaiah is the author of the Servant Songs, and argues that Duhm's distinguishing between those songs that describe an "individual" and those that refer to "Israel" as the Servant is an invalid distinction (1984: 57–58; 1992: 499ff.).[6] Yet, Clifford nuances his position more than does Mettinger. Mettinger argues that all references to the "Servant" are to "Israel," that is, the Servant is Israel.[7] Clifford upholds the distinction of identity, but not of function: there may be a real individual, but both the individual and Israel are described in royal and prophetic terms, and are called to obedience and mission. The role of the one informs and illumines the role of the other.[8]

Though scholars continue to differ on many of these issues—whether the Songs are distinct or integral, original or later, and whether the Servant is an individual or Israel—the trend in interpretation is to treat the Songs in their literary context and in relation to chs. 40–55. This study accepts the close connection between the Songs and their literary context.

In a sense, the issue of the Servant Songs is representative of a larger issue that has emerged in recent years, namely, the unity of the material called Second Isaiah. In addition to the Servant Songs, other passages have been identified as constituting distinct redactional layers, thus challenging the traditional unity of Second Isaiah. Among the suggested later redactional layers are the anti-idol passages[9] and the *qārôb* material, which argues that the longed-for but delayed salvation is "near."[10] Surveying these and other arguments challenging the unity of Second Isaiah, Williamson concludes that "we are not yet in a position where we can with confidence abandon the usual understanding of Isaiah 40–55 as an essential unity" (1994: 24). He documents a number of recent studies that collectively argue that the Songs of the Servant (and other material discussed above) "must be regarded as integral, and indeed indispensable, parts of their present literary contexts" (1994: 21). Rendtorff, too, argues that "these chapters are homogeneous to such a degree that they have to be taken as a more or less deliberately shaped literary unit" (1993b: 184). This will be the assumption of the present study.

The Geographical and Historical Setting

Apart from those who hold to the authentic Isaianic authorship of the entire book, or who hold for an entirely postexilic composition, the majority position maintains that Isaiah 40–55 is set in Babylon during the sixth-century exile.[11] McKenzie (1978: xvi–xviii) argues more narrowly that Second Isaiah can be dated between the years 550 and 540 B.C.E.. Others, like Stuhlmueller (1980: 5), believe that chs. 41–48 were written before the fall of Babylon, and chs. 49–55 were written after the fall of Babylon and the initial return—but both sections were written by Second Isaiah in Babylon. While the general assessment that Isaiah 40–55 is set in Babylon during the sixth-century exile is occasionally disputed, it remains the majority opinion.[12] As indicated earlier in ch. 1 of this study, Seitz[13] and Rendtorff refer to this assessment as part of a near-consensus view of the book of Isaiah. It is a view we accept.[14]

Passages in Isaiah 40–55

Justice, Creation, and Kingship: Isaiah 40:12-31

There are three terms in this unit that require attention: *mišpāṭ* in v. 14, *mišpāṭîm* in v. 23, and *mišpāṭ* again in v. 27. These last two will be treated briefly in the course of the discussion of *mišpāṭ* in v. 14.

As is almost universally recognized, the series of questions begun in 40:12 signals a new unit. Yet 40:12-31 is related to vv. 1-11 in at least two significant ways: by the presumed setting and by the content.

1. The Setting in the Divine Council. Second Isaiah opens magisterially in the Divine Council (40:1-11),[15] which also provides the presumed setting for the first part of vv. 12-31. The questions in vv. 12-14 about YHWH's potential counselors, instructors, or teachers seem to imply heavenly beings who could fulfill those roles (Whybray 1971: 39–53, 78–84). Hanson summarizes succinctly: "verses 12-17 probe the divine assembly and the nations over which its members preside to determine whether Israel's God is merely one actor under the command of others" (1995: 27). It seems, then, that vv. 12ff. are a continuation of the goings-on in the Divine Council begun in vv. 1-11.

While the Divine Council is familiar from Israel's theological and cultural traditions (for example, 1 Kgs 22:19-22; Isa 6:1-8; Psalm 82; Job 1–2), it becomes acutely problematic in polytheistic Babylon. The traditional notion of YHWH's Divine Council faced the danger of contamination from the religious and cultural environment of the exiles' new home in Babylon. Is YHWH merely the Israelite equivalent of Marduk (Bel)? Does he take counsel, advice, and instruction? Whybray explains this danger:

> It may be that there were those among the exiles who, while accepting Yahweh as the supreme god, were inclined to understand this concept in Babylonian terms by transforming the hitherto innocuous concept of the heavenly council into something like a pantheon in which that supremacy was in fact a limited one. (1971: 81)

Thus, the questions in vv. 12-14 are apparently both occasioned by the setting of the Divine Council in vv. 1-11 and initially addressed to the members of that council in vv. 12-14.

2. The Content. Whether 40:1-11 is understood as the commissioning of a new, unnamed prophet[16] or the commissioning of the word of YHWH for a new age (Seitz 1990; also 1996: 219–40), the effectiveness of the prophet or the efficacy of the word must overcome an immediate challenge: the prophet and his word are met by a dispirited, doubtful people (40:27). For the prophet and message of 40:1-11 to get off the starting block, the issue of a people grown faint (**yᶜp*, vv. 30, 31) and weary (**ygᶜ*, vv. 30, 31) had to be addressed before a message of comfort, expiation, and redemption could find a receptive hearing. The content of vv. 1-11 will not advance unless it first addresses the lament of this crestfallen people.

Both the setting and the content, then, argue that vv. 12-31 are continuous with vv. 1-11, and specifically address some issues that both stem from the initial verses of ch. 40 and confront the community in their exilic setting. Building from 40:1-11, vv. 12-31 introduce some of the key themes of Second Isaiah: creation and divine sovereignty (vv. 12-17), the incomparability of YHWH (v. 18), anti-idolatry polemics (vv. 19-26), and God's power to redeem the discouraged people (vv. 27-31).

As has been often observed, the questions that are posed and the issues that are raised in vv. 12-26 are all directed toward the dramatically delayed lament found in 40:27,

Why do you say, O Jacob,
  and declare, O Israel:
"My way is hidden from YHWH,
  and from my God my cause *(mišpāṭî)* is passed over"?

To answer these complaints (see also 49:14), the disputations of 40:12-26 are advanced.

The relationship between the complaint and the answer is underscored by a subtle verbal link that is frequently overlooked: the terms *derek* ("road, way") and *mišpāṭ* are found in both v. 14 and v. 27. In v. 27, Jacob's way *(derek)* and cause *(mišpāṭ)* stand in a very particular relationship to YHWH's way *(derek)* of understanding and path of justice *(mišpāṭ)* in v. 14. Jacob's pitiful way and paltry cause are to God's cosmic justice and sovereign way as God's relationship is to humanity in general—as insignificant as grasshoppers (v. 22). What seems of paralyzing magnitude to Israel is negligible to YHWH. The use of the same terms in two contrasting ways ironically highlights the disproportionality between God and humanity.

The word *mišpāṭ* in v. 27, as also in 49:4, refers to the cause or right of the plaintiff in a legal preceding. This is a common usage, and this specific aspect of the term is confirmed by such passages as Ps 35:23, where "my cause" *(mišpāṭî)* is parallel to "my lawsuit" *(rîbî)*, and Ps 140:13 (Eng. 12), where "the case of the needy" *(dîn ʿānî)* is paired with "the cause of the poor" *(mišpaṭ ʾebyōnîm)*.

3. Mišpāṭ *in 42:14.* The first portion of the argument responding to Jacob's complaint is found in v. 14:

With whom did he exchange counsel, and he gave him understanding,
  and who taught him the path of justice *(mišpāṭ)*;
[And who taught him knowledge,][17]
  and the way of understanding made him know?

The phrase that is of singular interest to this study, "path of justice" *(ʾōraḥ mišpāṭ)*, suffers from two problems in discussion: (a) translation: there is a diversity of opinion as to how *mišpāṭ* should be translated and understood; and (b) treatment: most commentaries pass over it entirely or make comments so brief as to be negligible.

a. Translations

The translations of *mišpāṭ* can be grouped under three headings. A sampling of translations from both Bibles and commentaries shows the main trends:

A. "Path/way of justice": NRSV, REB; Hanson 1995; Clifford 1984; Watts 1987
B. "Path of judgment": KJV, NAB, NJB; McKenzie 1978; Motyer 1993; Young 1992
C. "Right" in the sense of "correct":
  1. "The right way": NIV; Westermann 1975
  2. "The right path": Stuhlmueller 1970
  3. "The way of right": JPS
  4. "How things should be done": TEV
  5. "Way of order": Whybray 1975; Scullion 1990

The differences in understanding arise from the range of meanings inherent in the term: all these suggestions are lexically possible. The question is: which is contextually appropriate? Most commentators understand *mišpāṭ* in terms of the context of the creation imagery found in v. 12, but overlook the more immediate context: *mišpāṭ* does not stand on its own but is part of a construct chain, *ʾōraḥ mišpāṭ*. Whybray is sensitive to this and properly pairs this with its parallel expression, *derek tĕbûnôt* ("way of understanding"). Unfortunately, he breaks both construct chains and considers first *ʾōraḥ* and *derek*, and then *mišpāṭ* and *tĕbûnôt* together.[18] Whybray concludes that *ʾōraḥ mišpāṭ* in Isa 40:14 is "the way of achieving a proper order (in what one does)" (1971: 16–17).

Whybray is correct in seeing the parallels between *ʾōraḥ* and *derek*, but he errs in breaking the construct chains. The prior line of inquiry should be the expression *ʾōraḥ mišpāṭ* itself. The expression occurs in only three texts: Prov 2:8-9; 8:20; 17:23. A detailed discussion of these passages can be found in the endnotes.[19] What is significant for our purposes is that all three passages from Proverbs are found in contexts that clearly point to a concern for justice, rather than judgment or right order.

In Prov 2:8-9, the unbroken hendiadys *ṣedeq ûmišpāṭ* is determinative. God's guarding the paths of justice makes it possible for those faithful to him to understand justice. In Prov 8:20,[20] the pairing of *ṣĕdāqâ* and *mišpāṭ* again makes the translation "justice" obvious. Riches, honor, wealth, and prosperity (8:18-19, 21) accrue to those who love Wisdom and seek after her diligently (8:17). She is to be found in the ways of righteousness and justice. Wisdom as a way of life is manifest in conduct marked by justice. In Prov 17:23, two factors argue for the translation "justice." First, the context of bribery points to corrupt practice in the social realm. Second, the expression *lĕhaṭṭôt mišpāṭ* (Hiphil of **nṭh* + *mišpāṭ*) is a technical term that means "to pervert justice" (Bovati 1994: 191–93). All three texts support an understanding of *mišpāṭ* as "justice" rather than "judgment" or Whybray's more generic "way of achieving a proper order (in what one does)."

Finally, a more general observation can be made about the congruence of wisdom concerns in both Isa 40:14 and the three passages from Proverbs. It is interesting that the only instances of *ʾōraḥ mišpāṭ* outside Isa 40:14 are all found in Proverbs, a collection of wisdom sayings directed to teaching the ways of righteousness and instructing the reader/hearer in right conduct. The metaphor of the road or way is a typical wisdom motif for a way of life and a course of conduct. As Prov 2:8-9 makes clear, it is God's special concern to guard and watch over those ways so as to ensure safe and virtuous passage for those who seek wisdom. The occurrence of this same expression in Isaiah 40 also finds itself surrounded by vocabulary from the world of wisdom. In Isa 40:13-14 we find words from the roots **ʿṣh* ("counsel, advice"; 2x), **ydʿ* ("know"; 3x), **byn* ("understand"; 2x), **lmd* ("learn, teach"; 2x), and the words *ʾōraḥ* and *derek*.[21] Both the specific expression *ʾōraḥ mišpāṭ* and its exclusive place in wisdom environments argue that its meaning in Isa 40:14 should be the same as that found in Proverbs. It would seem, then, that the expressions *ʾōraḥ mišpāṭ*, *ʾorḥôt mišpāṭ*, and *nĕtîbôt mišpāṭ* are all equivalent and should be translated as "the path(s) of justice." What this refers to in the context of Isaiah will be taken up shortly.

b. Treatment

Of the principal commentators mentioned so far, the following offer no comment on the term *mišpāṭ* whatsoever: Westermann, McKenzie, Whybray, Stuhlmueller, and Scullion. Watts makes no explicit comment on *mišpāṭ,* but directs the reader's attention to Isa 11:2-5, which also uses many of the same terms found in 40:14—*perceptiveness, justice, knowledge,* and *understanding.* Watts says only that these are "characteristics which a king needs and which God has" (1987: 91). Motyer merely notes that "judgment" means "making the correct judgment or decision at the correct time" (1993: 303). In the larger context of Motyer's discussion, these decisions have to do with the work of the Creator. Young similarly relates the "path of judgment" to creation: "As judgment is the revelation of God's counsel in the wondrous disposal of the creation and formation of the universe, so knowledge has reference in particular to the creation" (1992, 3:46). Hanson is equally brief: "'the path of justice' . . . in Israel's moral universe is the 'straight highway' that will permit the people to cross the wilderness on their homeward journey" (1995: 28). Though Hanson's focus is on the metaphor of the path/highway and the context of return and redemption, he implies that "justice" refers to Israel's moral conduct.

Berkovits maintains that God's ways with man are God's law for man, that is, human/religious life is essentially *imitatio Dei.* Having described God's ways in terms of loving-kindness, compassion, and charity, he attempts to define with greater precision the material content of *mišpāṭ*. For this, he begins with Isaiah 40:13-14 which he interprets in the immediate context of vv. 11-12, that is, in the context of creation: "measuring and weighing is the establishment of the principle of balance between the various parts of the universe; it is the introduction of the right proportion between the contending forces, without which God's creation could not last but would tumble back into *tohu vabohu* ['emptiness and void,' Gen 1:2] again" (1969a: 202). Thus, the poetic images used of the creative activity of God become for Berkovits the material content of the term *mišpāṭ* about which he is very specific:

> *[Mišpāṭ]* is the measuring and the weighing, the establishing of balance by which alone the universe is able to stand, the bringing together of the various universal forces in harmony so that in mutuality they may constitute the cosmos. This is the way God made the universe, and His way of doing it is the law of the universe. We should then say that *mišpāṭ* here is the cosmic principle of balance and harmony that is required for the preservation of God's creation. (1969a: 203)

More succinctly, he describes *mišpāṭ* as "the cosmic principle of universal appropriateness" (1969a: 209). This is close to the translations (C.1) and (C.4) above: God's acting in the right way, or creating in the way things should be done. Thus, according to Berkovits, God the Creator established the world rightly; *mišpāṭ* is a principle embedded in creation and universally applicable. One virtue of this approach is linking *mišpāṭ* with one of Second Isaiah's most important themes, viz., creation. There are, however, three apparent shortcomings. First, Berkovits takes the poetic images of God's creative activity somewhat literally to determine the meaning of *mišpāṭ*. Second, he understands *mišpāṭ* on its own, when, more properly, the phrase under consideration is *ʾōraḥ mišpāṭ*, "the path of justice," as we saw above. Third, he takes creation as the determinative context without relating vv. 12-14 to what follows.

Thus, the arguments of both Berkovits and Whybray (presented above) depend on the relationship of vv. 13-14 to v. 12, which alone supplies creation as the interpretive context. There is little in vv. 13-14 that requires their interpretation in light of creation exclusively. Ironically, in his monograph, *The Heavenly Counsellor in Isaiah xl 13-14*, Whybray argues at some length (1971: 4–9) that variously proposed larger contexts, for example, Isaiah 40–55, or 40:12-31, or even 40:12-17, are of no help in understanding 40:13-14. In fact, he concludes that "we are unable to use the immediate [context] any more than the general context to determine the sense of verses 13f." (1971: 9). It is for this reason that he can devote his entire monograph to just these two verses, 40:13-14, in relative isolation. His avowed assessment of the immediate context notwithstanding, the argument he makes for his translation and interpretation in fact depends on the context of creation found in v. 12.

The context of creation is helpful and, no doubt, sheds light on many valuable aspects of Isaiah's complex argument. Creation, however, is neither the exclusive nor the determinative context for understanding the expression under discussion. According to Westermann's analysis, the reference to creation in v. 12 is part of a larger argument: "The divine incomparability and immeasurability consist in the fact that nobody possesses the measures for pronouncing judgment on the divine planning and acting; as a result, nobody can give advice, or say to him in this or in that he ought to have acted rather differently (exactly as in 45:9ff.)" (1975: 51). In effect, if no one but God can perform the acts of creation, then a fortiori no one can direct God's Spirit, instruct him, or serve as his counselor. The point of v. 12 is that God is lacking in nothing and no one is superior to God: God is sovereign and unequaled. Though Westermann does not elaborate on his reference to 45:9ff., it is clear that that passage establishes the same relationship between creation and sovereignty: God's dealings with the foreign kingdoms, and choosing Cyrus in particular (45:13), are solely within his divine competence as Creator. Thus, creation is the basis for the more daring claim—sovereignty over the destiny of kingdoms and the course of history. In 40:12, then, creation is prelude to sovereignty.

This is the point further developed by Stuhlmueller in his detailed study of creation and redemption in Second Isaiah. Arguing against the creation context of 40:12-14, he concludes:

> *Directly,* these lines [vv. 12-14] are an argument against Israel for her pessimism and wavering faith. Dt-Is [Deutero-Isaiah] challenges Israel first to tell the measurement of the mountains and oceans, then she can question Yahweh

> about his handling of something still more mysterious, human affairs throughout the universe. The other part of the message is presented more *indirectly*. The passage implies that God's lordship extends to everything on earth and in sky. Human events like massive mountains are but tiny substances in a delicate scale.
>
> The principal thrust of v 12-14, therefore, is not in the direction of creation but of lordship, not primarily over the material universe but over world affairs, especially as these affect Israel. (1970a: 146; italics his)

This perspective is in keeping with an ancient Near Eastern mythic pattern of creation, which culminates in kingship. In the Babylonian creation story, *Enuma Elish*, Marduk's victory over Tiamat leads to creation and propels the story to its climax in Marduk's accession to the throne and the proclamation of his royal titles (see Dalley 1991: 228–77; also Cross 1973: 91–111). In the Bible, Psalm 24 reflects the familiar pattern of creation (vv. 1-2) culminating in kingship: "YHWH of Hosts—he is the King of glory" (v. 10). This pattern is also found in Psalms 89[22] and 93:1-4. Creation is prelude to kingship. The reference in Isa 40:12 to creation, therefore, should be seen not as determinative in itself, but in service to the larger theme of YHWH's sovereignty.

Clifford provides an effective analysis of YHWH's sovereignty in relation to creation in 40:12 and to the nations in 40:15-16:

> Israel has nothing to fear, for *Yahweh is master over all* [italics added], as is shown by his effortless weighing of the world and its inhabitants on a scale. Isa 40:12-16 makes this especially clear.

Weighing of the world (v 12)	*Weighing of the nations* (vv 15-16)
waters	drop of water
heavens	cloud
earth	dust of earth
mountains and hills	Mount of Lebanon

> The entire exhortation assumes that the world is a system in which the inhabitants of each tier (kings and princes on earth, heavenly beings in the heavens) are under God. The people, therefore, need not fear from the inhabitants of heaven and earth; all stand under the power of Yahweh. (1994: 169)[23]

Seen in this way, Isa 40:12-14 leads directly into a description of how the kingdoms are as insignificant as a "drop in the bucket and as dust on the scales" (v. 15). Indeed, "all the nations are as nothing *(ʾayin)* before him" and are accounted as emptiness (*tōhû*, v. 17). God is so vastly superior to the kingdoms and their inhabitants that the peoples look like mere grasshoppers (v. 22). All of this leads to the main assertion in vv. 23-24 that the princes *(rôzĕnîm)* and rulers *(šōpĕtîm)*[24] and their kingdoms are also nothing *(ʾayin)* and emptiness (*tōhû*, v. 23). Though it appears as if the nations have had their way with Israel and that God has either neglected, or is powerless, to come to her rescue (v. 27), the nations and their rulers are nothing before him. God's sovereignty is unequaled and immeasurable.

This focus on the sovereignty of God is further confirmed by a look at the specific vocabulary of vv. 13-14. Watts alluded to this point but did not develop it: the vocabulary in 40:13-14 is directly evocative of Isa 11:2.

Isaiah 40:13-14 reads:

> Who has meted out the Spirit of YHWH,
>   or what man made him know his counsel?
> With whom did he exchange counsel, and he gave him understanding,
>   and who taught him the path of justice;
> And who taught him knowledge,
>   and the way of understanding made him know?

Isaiah 11:2, in describing the attributes of a just ruler, says:

> And upon him shall rest the spirit of YHWH,
>   a spirit of wisdom and understanding,
>   a spirit of counsel and strength,
>   a spirit of knowledge and the fear of YHWH.

The two passages contain these terms in common: "spirit of YHWH" (*rûaḥ YHWH*), "counsel" *(ᶜēṣâ),* "understanding" *(tĕbûnôt/bînâ),* "knowledge" *(daᶜat).* Both from the point of view of vocabulary and the specific context of kingly rule, the two passages should be considered together. There is yet another verbal link between chs. 11 and 40: both contain the very rare word *gēzaᶜ* ("root" or "stump," 11:1; 40:24). It is found only once more in the Hebrew Bible, in Job 14:8. The two Isaian passages each use the term figuratively of royal descendants: of Jesse in 11:1, and in 40:24 of the "princes and rulers" mentioned in the previous verse. The presence of this word, even if accidental, is surely evocative and, together with the other vocabulary, invites the reader to consider these passages in light of one another. The clear focus in both passages is on the exercise of sovereign authority, by YHWH in the cosmos and by his surrogate on earth, the Davidic king.

The "path of justice" in Isa 40:14, then, is associated with God's rule of the kingdoms and is a distinctive feature of his incomparability. "Justice," soon to be personalized by YHWH as "my justice" (51:4), has its source in YHWH, who alone is its origin and patron: no one taught him how to rule justly. Like counsel, understanding, and knowledge, justice is a divine attribute, which Second Isaiah enters into evidence as proof for YHWH's superiority over the gods of Babylon and by which they are revealed to be nongods. As many commentators have noted, this polemic against the gods lies behind the wisdom language of 40:12-13. The emphasis on YHWH's knowledge and understanding (40:13-14) seems to be directed against Ea, the Babylonian god of wisdom who assisted Marduk in creation.[25] Just as YHWH's wisdom, creative power, and cosmic sovereignty will be marshaled in evidence for the incomparability of YHWH, justice is now added to that list as a distinctively divine attribute, which not only sets YHWH apart from others but argues for his uniqueness (Strolz 1981: 257–66). "Justice," then, is not so much a cosmic principle by which creation is established as it is distinctive of YHWH's sovereignty and characteristic of his divine rule of both the natural order of creation and the political realm of the nations. This passage proclaims in unequivocal terms that YHWH rules the kingdoms (40:12-17), princes and rulers (40:18-24), and the heavenly hosts (40:25-26). This assertion is in service of the specific argument that YHWH has the power to redeem Israel; more specifically, a

God who is the sole executor of *mišpāṭ* (justice, v. 14) is uniquely suited to respond to Israel's *mišpāṭ* (cause, v. 27). The redressing of Israel's complaint is now taken up in 41:1-5.

YHWH Takes the Gods to Court: Isaiah 41:1-5

The complaint raised by Israel in 40:27 moves from the disputations of ch. 40 into the courtroom setting of ch. 41.[26] As the form and structure make clear, 41:1 is a summons to trial, which comes to its concluding judgment in v. 5 when the questions asked in vv. 2 and 4 are answered—YHWH alone has done these things, with the result that the coastlands and ends of the earth tremble and obey the summons.

In this setting, *mišpāṭ* is a precise legal term: "Let us draw near for judgment *(mišpāṭ)*." Watts's translation is even more plain: "Let us assemble for the trial!" This is confirmed by Bovati (1994: 338–40), whose description of the formal request for a hearing (typically composed of three parts) is demonstrated in 41:1:

1. An imperative demand for a hearing, normally including an invitation to listen or a demand for silence: in 41:1, this is explicit: "Listen to me in silence!"

2. The recipient to whom this request/demand is addressed: "coastlands and peoples."

3. Reference to the speech that is about to be made: this is suggested in the phrase, "they draw near and speak together."

Of these, the demand for silence is particularly important. On the one hand, it is the hope of anyone arguing a case that the argument and evidence will be so compelling that the opposing party is reduced to silence. On the other hand, the silence in this case is somewhat ironic, as mere manmade idols are incapable of speech (for example, Ps 115:5).

The argument for YHWH's sovereignty, which was made somewhat generally in ch. 40, is now made more specifically. Universal sovereignty is demonstrated in historical acts and is detailed in specific political and military action as YHWH raises up a champion from the east to rule kingdoms and subdue kings (41:2). This champion's sword and bow bring victory; his progress is like that of a devastating storm wind (Clifford 1984: 84–85, n. 5)—not confined to established paths (v. 3b) and powerful enough to pass unimpeded (v. 3a). Who directs these events of history and determines the fates of nations? Consult the generations of long ago, for they, too, will reveal the only possible answer: it is YHWH, the First and the Last, who does these things. This argument reduces those who had been hauled into court, the coastlands, and the ends of the earth to fear and trembling. The coastlands and the ends of the earth themselves confirm YHWH's authority, for having been summoned by him in v. 1, they have obediently drawn near and come to him in v. 5. With YHWH's case uncontested, the court, for the time being, stands adjourned.

Though the rest of ch. 41 does not concern this discussion directly, the context it establishes will be of pivotal importance to the discussion of 42:1-4, which follows. Jerome Walsh argues that this poem in 41:1-20 is "a preparation for the one that follows: in this passage the parties to the trial are summoned and arrive on the scene" (1993: 352, n. 6). Verses 21-29 present the trial. Once the parties are assembled, YHWH confronts the gods directly:[27]

> "Advance your case," says YHWH;
> "present your proofs," says Jacob's King. (41:21)

It is not coincidental that in this context the divine title Second Isaiah uses directly affirms the very point being made, namely, that YHWH is the true King (cf. also 43:15; 44:6). In his presence, the gods are unable to speak of things past or future, and so YHWH pronounces sentence against them in 41:24:

> See! You are nothing *(ʾayin)*!
> And your work is nothing *(ʾāpaʿ)*!

After presenting the case for his own sovereignty (41:25-26), YHWH speaks to Zion (v. 27) and declares in 41:28-29:

> I looked, but there was no one;
> and among these there is no counselor.
> When I asked them, they turned away [my] word.
> See! All of them are a delusion.
> Nothing are their works;
> wind and emptiness are their images.

Thus, ch. 41 opens and closes in court. The case argued in both instances is two-sided: on the one hand, YHWH's sovereignty is established as demonstrated in his control of history; on the other hand, the impotence, and therefore the nonreality, of the gods is proved. The verdict is in: YHWH is God of the nations and of history; the gods of the nations are nothing (41:24).[28]

Servant of Justice: Isaiah 42:1-4

In these four brief verses, the term *mišpāṭ* occurs three times, accounting for more than a quarter of its total appearances in Isaiah 40–55. Clearly this is a pivotal passage that requires close scrutiny.

As we approach what has been traditionally called the first Song of the Servant, and through it, the other Servant passages, we must address two major interpretive concerns that have dominated critical discussion, namely, whether the language evokes a royal or prophetic context, and whether the Servant should be understood in individual or corporate terms. Addressing the first issue, Beuken's comments provide a judicious assessment with which we can agree:

> The royal traits of the Servant, unmistakable in view of the passage's literary genre and the catch-word for his message, do not exclude the existence of other features, like those of a prophet, of a torah teacher, i.e., Moses, and of a suffering individual.[29] They certainly interfere with the dominating king motifs to the extent that the Servant cannot simply be identified with the traditional Israelite king nor with the expected Messiah. . . . It suffices to call attention to the setting-in-life of the Servant's *mišpāṭ* mission: Jhwh points out someone to his people, he designates a man who much like a king is to bring *mišpāṭ* to the nations. (1972: 4)

Because the language in 42:1-4 is so richly evocative and lacks the specificity to make a precise determination, it seems unwarranted to impose upon the interpretation of this passage a constraint that the text itself plainly does not provide. The inherent multivalence of the text can, in this instance, be seen as a prism that refracts a wide spectrum of possibilities rather than the monochrome of certainty.

The second issue, individual versus corporate, admits of no easy solution. Well-reasoned and carefully documented arguments for both possibilities can be found in abundance. Even within these broad categories there are intermediate positions. Wilcox and Paton-Williams, for example, argue that in chs. 40–48, the Servant is to be understood as corporate Israel, while in chs. 49–55 the Servant is Second Isaiah himself (1988). Watts also argues that in these passages the Servant is sometimes a specific individual and sometimes a corporate personality, and he further argues that variation is characteristic of both: the corporate personality is initially Israel in the Diaspora, but later it is loyal worshippers in Judah and Jerusalem; the individual persona of the Servant is shared among the Persian rulers—Cyrus, Darius, and Artaxerxes (1987: 117, and ad loc.). As even this cursory survey shows, anyone seeking a definitive solution by recourse to such scholars will be disappointed. Childs judiciously observes that

> the canonical process has preserved the tradition of the servant in a form which reflects a great variety of tensions. The polarity remains between the servant as a corporate reality and as an individual, between the typical features and the historical, between a promised new Israel of the future and a suffering and atoning figure of the past. Nowhere is there any effort made to resolve the tension by means of a historical sequence, or by a theological pattern, or by an explanatory commentary (contrast the Targum). This observation implies that in regard to this portion of the message of Second Isaiah the canonical process preserved the material in a form, the significance of which is not fully understood. (1979: 335–36)

While I am not convinced that the inherent tensions can be ascribed to "the canonical process," Childs's observations stand. Nevertheless, one way of dealing with these tensions is the tendency, not uncommon today, to approach the texts that present the Servant as an individual and those that describe Israel as a whole as complementary rather than as opposed to one another. Most recently, the commentary of Hanson points out the linguistic resonance between a passage that describes Israel corporately (41:8-10) and one that describes an individual (42:1-4). He concludes that "the election [of Israel and the Servant] is presented in terms apropos of both an individual such as a prophet or king and the faithful community" (1995: 42).[30] This built-in openness leads him to suggest that "rather than being a biographical description of one person in one place and time, the Servant thus is the description of the human being whom all who love God are challenged to become" (1995: 44). The very lack of specificity allows Hanson to reappropriate an ancient text for a contemporary audience. This theological/pastoral hermeneutical move, however, does not give rise to free flights of fancy, as his detailed exegesis goes on to demonstrate. Still, he has been able to approach a traditional interpretive crux in a theologically productive way.

While we may not be able to resolve these tensions, we must nonetheless be aware of them as we turn to the task of understanding *mišpāṭ* in 42:1-4. From a purely descriptive point of view, *mišpāṭ* is a mission that originates in the command of God and that is entrusted to the Servant who is addressed in 42:1-4. As has been made clear in 40:14, *mišpāṭ* belongs to God alone; now it is to be made known by the work of the Servant. Three general directions must be pursued: (1) the meaning of *mišpāṭ* in this passage and its immediate context; (2) its meaning in the other Servant passages; (3) its relation to the concept of *mišpāṭ* elsewhere in Isaiah 40–55. Discussion of this passage in light of the entire book of Isaiah will be deferred to ch. 5.

1. Approaches to Understanding mišpāṭ *in 42:1-4.* The difficulty of determining the precise nuance of *mišpāṭ* in this passage is ably summarized by B. Renaud:

> The term *mišpāṭ* offers a disconcerting range of possible meanings: an act of deciding or judging; a legal decision; the contents of this decision; the judgment itself; the right (of an individual or a group); a statute; a bond; equity; that which is just and right; the law, commandment, or custom (most often in the plural). We can see that in the case of Isa 42:1-4, critical opinions differ. (1990: 106; translation mine)

In an effort to specify the precise meaning of *mišpāṭ* in 42:1-4, scholars have taken a variety of approaches.

a. Mišpāṭ *in the Bible*

Some commentators, like Giménez, have understood *mišpāṭ* in this passage in light of the general biblical teaching of justice as "the defense of the weak, the liberation of the oppressed, respect for the rights of the poor" (1984: 78; all translations of Giménez mine). Acknowledging the royal overtones present in the passage, Giménez goes on to distinguish between the Servant's and a king's mission, not in terms of content ("liberation from the injustices that the oppressed suffer"; 1984: 79), but in the manner of execution, as specified in 42:2-3. There is no doubt that such an understanding is viable in light of the entire biblical tradition, and, indeed, we shall return to this aspect of "justice" when we consider the term synchronically in ch. 6. But this begs the question: Is there anything distinctive about *mišpāṭ* in the historical/social setting of Second Isaiah? What can we learn about *mišpāṭ* in this passage and in Isaiah 40–55?

b. Thematic Contexts in 42:1-4

Some have looked to the general context implied by the language of the unit (described by Beuken above) and have suggested meanings consonant with the kingly, prophetic, priestly, and other implied contexts. Jörg Jeremias (1972) is representative of this approach in the extreme. He sees a different nuance for each of the three occurrences of *mišpāṭ* in 42:1-4. In v. 1, it refers to the royal sovereignty of the Servant over the kingdoms; in v. 3, *mišpāṭ* refers to the prophetic proclamation of pardon for Israel; while in v. 4, *mišpāṭ* announces the salvific will of YHWH for the world that the Servant, like Moses, is to bring to all peoples (1972: 39). Unfortunately, this approach proves to be a foundation built on sand: it rests entirely on the determination of the implied context, which, as we have seen, has proven to be elusive. As a result, if one shifts the context, the very meaning of *mišpāṭ* changes; in the case of Jeremias, the one word takes on three different meanings in the course of four short verses.

c. Lexical Approaches

Some have either looked more specifically to the linguistic idioms "to bring forth *mišpāṭ*" (vv. 1 and 3; *yôṣîʾ mišpāṭ*) and "to establish *mišpāṭ*" (v. 4; *yāśîm mišpāṭ*) or taken their cue from the pairing of *mišpāṭ* with *tôrâ* in v. 4. This approach is more helpful, but no consensus has been established. Addressing the two idioms, Westermann, for example, argues that the different expressions "to bring forth *mišpāṭ*" and "to establish *mišpāṭ*" are "to be taken in the same sense: making *mišpāṭ* prevail abroad, 'in the earth'" (1975: 95). *Mišpāṭ*, then, has the same meaning in each verse (so also Whybray 1975: 72).

Beuken finds a different meaning for each of the two expressions. After examining texts that use the same or similar expressions as those in Isa 42:1-4, he concludes,

> The foregoing investigation has made clear that in the first Servant prophecy *yôṣîʾ mišpāṭ* does not have the same meaning as *yāśîm mišpāṭ*. The former expression envisages *mišpāṭ* as a situation, an event to be realized, a process and its execution resulting in relations of righteousness, the background obviously being this: that the present situation is devoid of justice. The latter expression sees *mišpāṭ* as an ordinance, a law to be proclaimed, the juridical statute of a new situation of justice. The parallelism of *mišpāṭ* and *tôrâ* in V. 4 adds to this meaning aspect. (1972: 7; so also Lindsey 1982a; and Renaud 1990: 108)

A different interpretation is offered by Bovati, whose study of the legal expressions and institutions of justice in the Hebrew Bible have led him to conclude that the Hiphil of **yṣʾ* with *mišpāṭ (yôṣîʾ mišpāṭ)*, much like **špṭ mišpāṭ* or **dyn mišpāṭ*, is a syntagm for "sentence," or "pronouncing, handing down a sentence" (1994: 208–9). He further argues that the pairing of *mišpāṭ* and *tôrâ* in 42:4 "suggests that both terms refer to a decision with normative value" (1994: 210).[31] Both expressions refer to the sentence or the outcome of a juridical process. The distinction Beuken sought to tease out of the two expressions is collapsed by Bovati into the same semantic field.

To recap: Westermann equates *yôṣîʾ mišpāṭ* with *yāśîm mišpāṭ* and understands them to mean proclaiming justice; Bovati also sees both expressions as equivalent, but understands them in specifically juridical terms; Beuken splits the difference, agreeing more with Westermann on *yôṣîʾ mišpāṭ*, and with Bovati on *yāśîm mišpāṭ*.

It seems that both Bovati and Beuken rest their arguments on rather thin textual support: in addition in Isa 42:1 and 3, the expression *yôṣîʾ mišpāṭ* is found in only one other instance, Ps 37:5-6:

Place upon YHWH your way,
and trust in him—he will act.
He will *bring forth* your righteousness like the light,
and your *justice* like the noonday sun.

In the context of this psalm, the just person, beset by evildoers, is assured that YHWH will both punish the wicked and vindicate the just. The person who entrusts his way—that is, the conduct of one's life—to God will find that God will make his just conduct shine like the sun. In this instance, both *mišpāṭ* and *ṣedeq* are descriptive of the faithful person's conduct, while the verbal action belongs to God. It clearly does not suggest the promulgation of a legal decision. This analysis of *yôṣîʾ mišpāṭ* in Ps 37:5-6 does not vitiate Bovati's argument: even though *yôṣîʾ mišpāṭ* does not mean "to pronounce a legal decision" in this text, it may have that meaning in Isa 42:1-4. That has yet to be determined. However, because examination of Ps 37:5-6 does not confirm the fine distinction Beuken seeks to make between the two different expressions, this analysis does weaken his case. It seems that the analysis of neither Bovati nor Beuken is determinative. Thus, in an effort to understand the meaning of *yôṣîʾ mišpāṭ* in Isa 42:1 and 3, parallel texts are of little help and so we must look elsewhere.

d. Situating 42:1-4 in the Context of Chapters 40–41

It was suggested above that the occurrences of *mišpāṭ* in 40:14, 27 and 41:1, together with the courtroom setting described in ch. 41, establish direct verbal and thematic connections to 42:1-4. There are still other features that tie this passage to what has come before. The introductory particle *hēn* ("behold" or "here") in 42:1 also forges a link to what has preceded (Muilenburg 1953: 110). The dramatic contrast between the verdict "See! You are nothing!" (*hēn-ʾattem mēʾayin*, 41:24) and the introduction of the Servant (*hēn ʿabdî*, 42:1) is powerful and significant: into the void created by the expulsion of the nongods, YHWH sends his Servant. What the gods, and their client nations, are unable to do, YHWH will now accomplish through his Servant. Finally, the link between chs. 41 and 42 is furthered by the contrasting sense of *rûaḥ* ("spirit," "wind"), which, in the idols, is nothing and void (41:28) but which on the Servant is power (42:1; Janzen 1994: 472). All of these features suggest that it will be profitable to read 42:1-4 in light of what has come before.

The larger context of chs. 40 and 41 can be of significant help in two ways. First, it will be important to keep in mind how *mišpāṭ* has been used so far. Second, the two immediately preceding trial scenes, especially with the explicit introductions "let us approach for the judgment/trial" (41:1) and "advance your case" (41:21), provide an important context within which to understand *mišpāṭ* in 42:1-4.

Let us deal with the latter point first. As we saw above, the two trial scenes in which the coastlands and peoples (41:1) and the ends of the earth (41:5) witness the impotence of their patron gods (41:21-23) conclude with the summary judgment: "You [gods] are nothing" (41:24). In turn, Zion/Jerusalem is also informed,

See! All of them are a delusion.
Nothing are their works;
wind and emptiness are their images. (41:29)

Immediately on the heels of that summary judgment, the Servant is commissioned to bring forth and establish *mišpāṭ*. Muilenburg argues that this motif of judgment, which dominates ch. 41, comes "to a triumphant culmination" in the commissioning of the Servant in 42:1ff. (1953: 110). The Servant's mission is to bring forth from the courtroom and to establish throughout the world a two-sided judgment—that the gods are nothing and that YHWH alone is sovereign. The coastlands *(ʾîyîm)*, summoned to court in 41:1, and now disabused of their confidence in their gods/idols, understandably find themselves waiting for his teaching (42:4), namely, that YHWH alone is God of all the peoples. The courtroom proceedings in ch. 41 confirm the argument of Watts, Bovati, and others that understands *mišpāṭ* in 42:1-4 as judgment, that is, as the outcome of the foregoing legal proceedings. Again, the translation of Watts is most direct on this point: the servant extends *(yôṣîʾ)* and confirms *(yāśîm)* the verdict (1987: 111). Watts further supports his interpretation by citing the LXX *(krísin)*, the Vulgate *(iudicium)*, and the Syriac *(dynh)*.

While it seems fairly reasonable that the verdict *(mišpāṭ)* reached in 41:1-5 and 22-28 is the subject matter of the Servant's mission, the term "verdict" or "judgment" alone does not convey the full meaning of *mišpāṭ*. When the focus is on making known the result of the judicial process, that is, the "verdict" or "decision," the Bible prefers expressions such as "declare" (*higgîd* [Hiphil of **ngd*] *mišpāṭ*, Deut 17:9; 1 Sam 8:9), or "announce" (*ʾāmar mišpāṭ*, Deut 17:11), or "make known" the decision (*hôdîaʿ* [Hiphil of **ydʿ*] *mišpāṭ*, Ezek 20:11). The action-oriented verbs "to bring forth" and "to establish" seem directed at more than merely causing the nations to have the information about YHWH's rule. These expressions convey not only the verdict but the consequent reality. This was the sense in which the word was used in 40:14, where we argued at some length that YHWH's path of justice referred to his just and sovereign rule of both the cosmos and history. "Justice" used of God implies his undisputed sovereignty, and that sense is embedded in the present Servant passage as well. Indeed, the overall sweep from ch. 40 to 42:1-4 moves in this direction. The opening scene in the Divine Council established YHWH's uniqueness in creation (40:12, 21-22), his sovereignty in history (40:23), and his potency in redressing Israel's complaint (40:25-31). That majestic tableau laid the groundwork for the subsequent courtroom scenes in which the gods are convicted of impotence in the course of history and in the life of the nations. The case for YHWH's sovereignty, established in the Divine Council and proved in court, is now to be made known to the distant coastlands and to the ends of the earth through the agency of the Servant. The particular *mišpāṭ* or verdict that the Servant must bring forth and establish is YHWH's just sovereignty over the world and its history.

It bears repeating: in Second Isaiah, *mišpāṭ* used of God implies sovereignty. On the one hand, the verdict against the gods confirms the claim of YHWH's sovereignty; on the other hand, YHWH's sovereignty provides the authority for the verdict. In 42:1-4, the term *mišpāṭ* refers to both the formal outcome of the legal proceeding and the consequent reality of YHWH's universal rule.

This meaning is confirmed by the use of the parallel term *tôrâ*, of which Whybray correctly writes, "not the 'Law' in the Deuteronomic or later legal sense, but the will of the sovereign God announced by the prophet" (1975: 73). Clements concurs: "In 42.4 and 21 the term *tôrâ* = 'teaching' is used in a very unusual fashion, since it can hardly be intended as a reference to Yahweh's 'law' in the later sense. Rather it appears to refer to Yahweh's 'purpose', which is shortly to be realized and which has been declared beforehand by the prophets" (1985: 107). That purpose, to be enacted by the Servant, is to bring YHWH's sovereignty to the nations. This is the content of his *instruction*, viz., "that the nations might be given light and come to know Yahweh as God" (Melugin 1991: 30).

From the outset, the Servant's mission of justice is directed to the nations (42:1), and it is there that he will surely encounter the bruised reed *(qāneh rāṣûṣ)* and the dimmed wick (*pištâ kēhâ*, 42:3). Whybray's assessment of this verse is typical of many who understand it as describing the Servant's modus operandi: "Deutero-Isaiah's work will be to handle the bruised reed with great care and to keep the dimly burning wick from going out" (1975: 73). He goes on to suggest that the objects of this tender care are the exiles whose faith and hope have grown weak and dim. But it is also possible to see in it a reference to those among the nations who have foolishly put their trust in their gods and idols. In fact, both terms—*qāneh* (reed) and *pištâ* (flax = wick)—are used metaphorically of other nations. Tellingly, in Isa 36:6 (= 2 Kgs 18:21), the Rabshakeh refers derisively to Egypt as "this staff of the bruised reed" *(mišʿenet haqqāneh hārāṣûṣ hazzeh)*, that is, a staff that is too weak to support the one who leans on it. Egypt's reputation as a bruised or broken reed seems well established[32] and is found also in Ezek 29:6 and allegorically in Ps 68:31 (Eng. 30). As for the image of a dimmed wick that should not be *extinguished* (**kbh*, Isa 42:3), we find the same language in Isa 43:17, which recalls former things, specifically the exodus, in which chariots, horse, rider, and soldier are extinguished, quenched like a wick *(dāʿăkû kappištâ kābû)* before the power of YHWH, Israel's Holy One, Creator, and King (43:15). The images of the bruised reed and dimmed wick in 42:3, then, can plausibly be taken metaphorically. Both images occur in the Isaianic tradition (and elsewhere) and the latter specifically in Second Isaiah. Especially in the case of Isa 43:17, the powerlessness of Egypt is contrasted to the unsurpassed power of YHWH the King (Isa 43:15)—an explicit title of sovereignty. If that is the case, then the weakness of the kingdoms to whom the Servant is sent is due to the impotence of their patron gods. As 41:29 made clear, these gods and idols are nothing and empty, their *rûaḥ* ("spirit") is a delusion. In effect, the source of power in which the nations trusted is no power at all. As a result, with their power turned to wind and emptiness, the clients of these nongods are as fragile and weak as a bruised reed, as faint and dim as a smoldering wick. To these the Servant comes with a new teaching (v. 4) and directs their attention to YHWH, who, in creating (42:5) and redeeming (42:7), demonstrates his sovereignty. When the

Servant brings forth justice faithfully (v. 3), he is bringing forth a judgment that testifies to the truth of YHWH's sovereignty, not that of the gods (42:8-9).

Understanding the bruised reed and the dimmed wick as poetic images for the peoples who had been benighted by their idolatry is further reinforced by the images in 42:6-7. There the Servant is once more sent to the people and the nations, "to open the eyes of the blind, to bring forth *(hôṣîʾ)* the prisoner from the dungeon, [and] from the house of confinement those who dwell in darkness." The controlling image here is not so much the political institution of incarceration, but of blindness and darkness. The images of prison and dungeon are introduced because of their relationship to darkness. The mission of the Servant is not to be literalized as lobbying for prison reform. His concern is for those whose eyes are blind and who dwell in the darkness of their folly and ignorance. To them, the Servant who comes with the judgment and the teaching of YHWH's sovereignty is a light (v. 6). This focus on YHWH and his sovereignty is continued in v. 8: "I am YHWH—that is my name. My glory I do not give to another, nor my praise to idols." Idols produce darkness, not light; they are an empty wind (41:29), not a spirit of power (42:1; cf. 45:20). That spirit of power can come only from the one whose spirit it is to give, as is made clear in 42:5—YHWH is the one who "creates the heavens and stretches them out, who forms the earth and its inhabitants, who gives breath to the people upon it, and spirit *(rûaḥ)* to those who walk on in it."

Those from the ends of the earth and the coastlands (42:10) who accept the teaching of the Servant join in a hymn of praise to YHWH (42:10-12). For them, YHWH does wonders (vv. 13-16), but for those who cling to their idols, YHWH comes as the Divine Warrior (v. 13) to crush them in their shame.

Throughout the first Servant Song, the vocabulary and images are in service to the one issue that has dominated Second Isaiah to this point: Who has power to create, to redeem, to rule the nations and the cosmos? The question asked in 40:13, "Who was his counselor?" is answered by YHWH himself in 41:28: "I looked, but there was no one; among these there is no counselor." There is none equal or even comparable to YHWH. That message, intended as a word of consolation to dispirited Israel, is also a message for the nations who still dwell in the darkness of their misguided faith and their erroneous beliefs. Whether the forum is the Divine Council, the courtroom, or the course of history, YHWH's rule is uncontested, his justice unrivaled. The mission of the Servant is to bring forth to the world YHWH's justice, that is, his just and unrivaled sovereignty.

2. The Meaning of Mišpāṭ *in the Other Servant Passages.* Each of the remaining Songs of the Servant contains the word *mišpāṭ,* and its use in each will be examined. We may anticipate two points to be made in that study. First, we noted above that in 42:1-4 *mišpāṭ* is proper to YHWH, that is, it is YHWH's *mišpāṭ* that the Servant brings forth. By contrast, in all three of the remaining songs, *mišpāṭ* is used in reference to the Servant: either the Servant refers to his *mišpāṭ* ("cause," 49:4; 50:8), or his disciples note that it is by a perversion of *mišpāṭ* that the Servant is taken away (53:8). Second, as a result, *mišpāṭ* in the remaining Servant Songs will not again refer to YHWH's sovereignty or just rule, but will be applied more restrictively to aspects of a legal proceeding in which the Servant is a participant. These points will be explicated below.

3. The Relation of 42:1-4 to the Use of Mišpāṭ *Elsewhere in Isaiah 40–55.* Again, we may anticipate two points that will be discussed shortly. We note, first, that whether or not one wishes to maintain the distinction between the individual and corporate aspects of the Servant, apart from these four songs as originally defined by Duhm, the term *mišpāṭ* does not appear in any other passage that deals with the Servant. Second, in broad strokes, it will be observed that the significance of the term *mišpāṭ* is different when used of or by YHWH than when used of or by any other person in Second Isaiah. Again, these points will be documented and discussed as this study continues.

Lectionary Notes

Common Lectionary: Baptism (A): Isa 42:1-9 / Ps 29 / Matt 3:13-17
Roman Lectionary: Same, except Isa 42:1-4, 6-7

The historical problems that attend this first of the Songs of the Servant—whether the Servant is an individual or the whole people, and if an individual, who?—had already been resolved for Christians by the time Mark committed the Gospel to writing. Mark 1:11 paraphrases Isa 42:1 to describe the heavenly voice that discloses Jesus as the Father's "Son,"[33] the "beloved," the one in whom God is "well pleased." For Mark, this seems to be a private revelation to Jesus; the disclosure of his identity as the "Son of God" will be made public only at the crucifixion (Mark 15:39). Writing some years after Mark, Matthew moves this christological moment back to the annunciation and birth stories (see Matt 1:1, 16, 23; 2:4, 15); the baptism is a public disclosure of Jesus' identity as God's Son (R. E. Brown 1979: 134–37, 181–83). Matthew's use of the title "Son of God" is functional, not ontological, that is, it is not a metaphysical statement about the nature of Jesus such as would be made at the Council of Nicea, but refers instead to his role as Messiah, the one anointed to fulfill a mission entrusted by God (Hare 1993: 20–22). The Synoptics' use of this Isaian passage for the baptism of Jesus, then, is well chosen: as Jesus is about to begin his public ministry, he is anointed by the Spirit and sent to "bring justice to the nations." Applying this Song of the Servant to Jesus as the descendant of the royal house of David broadens the meaning of his mission of justice beyond the theological aspects articulated by Second Isaiah to include the social aspects so forcefully described by First Isaiah. Jesus will "fulfill all righteousness" (Matt 3:15) in his outreach to the poor and the outcast, the tax collector and the sinner.

The use of these texts in the liturgy moves their significance beyond that envisioned by either Isaiah or Matthew. From the vantage point of a centuries-long faith tradition, the church acknowledges Jesus as the Servant of YHWH par excellence, affirms his royal mission of justice, and professes his divinity. The use of this

Isaian passage on the Feast of the Baptism highlights both the nature and the mission of Jesus as the Son of God and as the Servant of YHWH.

In the calendar of the Common Lectionary, the Feast of the Baptism continues the public manifestation of Jesus begun in the Epiphany. In the Roman Catholic liturgical calendar, the Feast of the Baptism marks the transition into Ordinary Time, during which the church is instructed in the meaning and practice of discipleship: the way of the Master is the way for disciples. Thus, to understand Jesus as God's Servant of justice is to understand something, too, of the mission of the church and the meaning of discipleship.

In Court, Again: Isaiah 43:22-28

To this point, Israel has been a witness (43:9-12) to the legal proceedings that YHWH has conducted against the nations and the gods. Now she is hauled into court and stands accused before God. This is the first of two trial speeches YHWH directs against Israel, the other being 50:1-3.

At issue is Israel's complaint against YHWH. Israel accuses God of having profaned the officers of the sanctuary and having given Jacob over to utter destruction and revilement (43:28). As once before, the lament comes toward the end of the disputation. This structure is familiar to us from 40:12-31, where, as here, the case leading up to the complaint is presented first. In this regard, two points are noteworthy.

First, 43:22-25 deal with Israel's worthless worship and her sinfulness. Watts thinks that the issue is Israel's idolatrous worship while in captivity (1987: 143). Most others, however, agree that this indictment stands in continuity with preexilic prophetic condemnation of Israel's unacceptable cult as practiced in the Jerusalem temple. Two points support this view. Because the complaint is, in effect, "Why did YHWH destroy the temple and banish us into exile?" the grounds must be sought in the preexilic period. Second, the evocation of Isaiah 1 seems undeniable. Structurally, both passages begin with a scathing critique of the cult (1:10-17; 43:22-25) that leads to a summons to court (1:18; 43:26). The shared vocabulary of both passages is significant: the common terms from the cult are "burnt offering" *(ʿōlâ)*, "sacrifice" *(zebaḥ)*, "offering" *(minḥâ)*, and "fat" *(ḥēleb)*, and the same terminology for Israel's sin is used: "transgression" *(ʿāwôn)*, "sin" *(*ḥṭʾ)*, "rebellion" *(pešaʿ)*. It may be argued, of course, that the similarity of vocabulary arises from the specialized nature of the discussion at hand: there is a limited range of terms for sacrifices and sins. It is, however, the coincidence of two sets of vocabulary compressed into a relatively brief discussion that is noteworthy. It is difficult to listen to 43:22-28 without hearing echoes of 1:10-18.

The second point to be made about the material before the complaint is that Israel's disregard for the cult is symptomatic of her more generalized sin and rebellion, which YHWH traces back to her first father (cf. Hos 12:3-5 [Eng. 2-4]). It is this history of sin that is the cause for the punishment she has received. Israel's complaint presents the opportunity for YHWH to voice his own complaint, which he does in court.

Once the passage arrives at the actual complaint in vv. 26-28, the trial language becomes explicit.

> Accuse me! Let us enter into judgment [**špṭ*] together.
> You recount it so that you may be vindicated.

Clearly in the forefront of these verses, as in previous passages in Second Isaiah, is YHWH's role as Judge. Just as YHWH has exercised his authority over the nations and the gods, he extends it now to Israel as well. YHWH's "taking on" Israel's political and religious enemies should not lure her into a false confidence: the God who loves her tenderly (43:4) can still take her to court. Like the kingdoms and the gods, Israel can make no response, and YHWH's point stands uncontested.

Particularly in light of the similarity between ch. 1 and 43:22-28—structure, vocabulary, and the courtroom contest between YHWH and Israel—the failure to mention Israel's response to matters of social justice, so carefully rehearsed in First Isaiah, is striking.

The Servant's Cause Is with YHWH: Isaiah 49:1-6

For those who see a structural break between Isaiah 40–48 and 49–55,[34] the presence of the term *mišpāṭ* (v. 4) in this opening unit provides an important link that bridges the two sections of Second Isaiah.

In 49:4 we find the second of four occurrences of the possessive form of the noun, *mišpāṭî*—"my" *mišpāṭ*. It was first encountered in 40:27 when Israel issued the complaint that "my God has passed over *my cause*." Both in 49:4 and later in 50:8, it is the Servant who speaks of his *cause* or *right*. Finally, in 51:4, we will hear YHWH announcing that "*my justice* goes forth as a light for the people." The use of *mišpāṭî* in the mouth of one who raises to God a complaint is not novel, as can be seen in Ps 35:23; Job 27:2; 34:5, 6; 40:8; Lam 3:59. God is also celebrated as one who defends *my cause* in Pss 9:5 (Eng. 4) and 17:2. The significance of the personalized form of the noun in Second Isaiah, then, is not its novelty, but the contrasting use of the same term in the mouths of various speakers.

In this second of the traditional Songs of the Servant, the Servant/Prophet is recommissioned for what Seitz describes as a new task. Seitz argues that the language of 49:1-4 indicates that the prophet, whom Seitz believes to be "an actual historical figure," is recounting his prior call which met with no success, while vv. 5-6 commission him for a new task (1996: 233–34). Between the accounts of his initial call in vv. 1-3 and the new task with which he is entrusted in vv. 5-6 is his appraisal of his work to date. It is a bleak assessment:

> But I thought that in vain had I labored,
> for nothing and vanity have I spent my strength. (49:4a)

All the Servant's efforts have come to nothing. Though endowed with the Spirit (42:1), and though his efforts were tireless, by his own reckoning his mission had apparently failed. It seems as though YHWH has failed to come through. Would it not be possible to conclude that, all YHWH's lofty words notwithstanding (for example, 42:1-4), his power was not equal to the task? In the Servant's words we can hear the same plaintive attitude that characterized the complaint of Israel in 40:27. In their bitter disappointment, the Servant and Israel stand together. The use of the same term—*mišpāṭî* —links these passages and invites their comparison. And it is precisely in this comparison that a lesson is to be found. Israel's lack of trust in God finds expression in self-pity: "my God has passed over *my cause*." This necessitates a word of assurance and a demonstration of power from YHWH. By contrast, the Servant, in his lament, turns to YHWH in hopeful confidence:

> But in fact *(ʾākēn)*, my cause *(mišpāṭî)* is with YHWH,
> and my recompense *(pĕʿullātî)* is with my God. (49:4b)

The Servant does not need words of reassurance. The result is that YHWH can instead issue a new commission.

Both subject nouns in 49:4b have been variously translated: *mišpāṭî* is usually understood as "my cause, my right," or, for Motyer, "my judgment" (1993: 387), even "my vindication" (McKenzie 1978: 103). These, as we have had occasion to see, are well within the range of meanings for *mišpāṭ*. The word *pĕʿullātî* is most often "my reward, my recompense, my compensation." This second term *(pĕʿullâ)* occurs only one other time in Second Isaiah: in 40:10 *pĕʿullātô* is parallel with *śĕkārô*, "his wage, his reward," confirming its meaning in 49:4.[35] From the Servant's perspective, then, both his cause and his recompense are with YHWH.

From the point of view of this study, the occurrence of *mišpāṭ* in this passage serves at least two purposes. First, after an absence from six chapters—its last occurrence was in 42:4 (the verb *šāpaṭ* was found in 43:26)—it reestablishes a connection to the foregoing. More specifically, the precise form of the personalized noun directly evokes an earlier lament. This sets up a contrast between doubtful Israel and the faithful Servant. Though both have their grievances—their *cause*—before YHWH, they respond in different ways. Israel's doubt and insecurity require a word of assurance, whereas the Servant's willingness to entrust his *cause* to YHWH and his confidence that YHWH is the ultimate judge of his efforts allow YHWH to build upon that trust and to expand his commission.

Lectionary Notes

Common Lectionary: Epiphany 2 (A): Isa 49:1-7 / Psalm 40 / John 1:29-42
Roman Lectionary: Ordinary Time 2A: Isa 49:3, 5-6 / Psalm 40 / John 1:29-34; the editing of the first reading omits the reference to "my cause."
Roman Lectionary: June 24: The Birth of John the Baptist: Isa 49:1-6 / Psalm 139 / Luke 1:57-66, 80

The use of the second Song of the Servant in conjunction with John's report of the postbaptismal episodes once again makes explicit the christological interpretation of the passage from Isaiah: Jesus is the Servant.

The editing of the Isaian text in the Roman Lectionary serves to highlight the intended points of correspondence between the first reading and the Gospel: the focus is on the public manifestation of Jesus. This is properly an "epiphany" theme, which the Common Lectionary reinforces by maintaining the traditional name of the season; but the epiphany aspects of the readings are evident even in the Roman use of these passages for the beginning of Ordinary Time. While the Roman Lectionary highlights the aspects of election and glorification, its editing of Isaiah 49 omits the consequences of God's choice of the Servant. The salutary effect of the Common Lectionary's unabridged text is its realistic portrayal of the nature of the call to service. Jesus, though the glorious Son of God (1:34), will himself seemingly spend his strength for nothing (Isa 49:4) and in the end will entrust his "cause" to God (see Luke 23:46; John 19:30). When the Common Lectionary extends the Gospel reading to include the call of the first disciples (John 1:35-42), the consequences of discipleship are also made explicit: what is true of the Master will be true of the disciples—service comes to glory only by way of the cross.

On the Feast of John the Baptist, the Roman Lectionary uses this (unabridged) second Song of the Servant is an unexpected way. The christological interpretation of the Servant Songs is, as we have seen, attested already in the New Testament and made explicit in the lectionary. The aspects of being called from the womb and suffering for the sake of his mission are normally and obviously associated with the birth and ministry of Jesus. But the Roman Lectionary makes a bold interpretive move in using Isaiah 49:1-6 for the Feast of the Birth of John the Baptist. The lectionary thereby invites the reader to see the passage from an entirely new perspective, one not adumbrated in the New Testament—John is the Servant, called from the womb (Luke 1:10-17), who suffers for the Lord (Matt 14:3-12; Mark 6:17-29) but who, in the end, is honored (Matt 11:11; Luke 7:28). His mission is not only to the tribes of Jacob, but he is to be a light to the nations (Isa 49:6). While his life seems to have been spent uselessly and for nothing (49:4), his cause is with God, who vindicates him. This feast is a clear example of how the liturgy provides a new interpretive context for Scripture. A text the Christian tradition normally associates with Jesus takes on a new significance when read as referring to John. Not only does the text take on new meaning, but the ministry of John the Baptist is seen in a new light. This reapplication of the text invites the church to take the process one step further by seeing its own life and discipleship in the light of the Servant's ministry.

YHWH Upholds the Servant's Right: Isaiah 50:4-11

That the mission of the Servant has met with no success and that the Servant himself had suffered physical and verbal abuse (50:6) could easily lead to the conclusion that his mission is not from God (Westermann 1975: 230). The Servant has only the assurance of his call and the conviction of his commission upon which to stand. The only one who can settle this dispute between the Servant and those to whom he has been sent is the one who gave the commission, and so the Servant fittingly summons his opponents to court, where previous disputes between YHWH and the nations, their gods, and Israel herself have been contested and resolved. The mechanics of the actual legal procedure are familiar to us from our treatment of Isa 3:13-14, in which the initial stage of a disputation fails to resolve the matter between the parties themselves. Now the disputants must move into the courtroom to seek a binding decision from a judge or official magistrate. The verse in question reads as follows:

> *qārôb maṣdîqî / mî-yārîb ʾittî naʿamdâ yāḥad / mî-baʿal mišpāṭî yiggaš ʾēlāy*
> My vindicator is near:
> Who will contend with me? Let us stand together.
> Who is my accuser? Let him approach me. (50:8)

The structure is clear:

A	B[1]	C[1]
	B[2]	C[2]

As can clearly be seen, v. 8 is filled with legal terminology: invitations to approach the court are issued ("let us stand together," *naʿamdâ yāḥad,* and "let him approach me," *yiggaš ʾēlāy*); the dispute is named in the verbal action ("who will contend?" *mî-yārîb*); three parties in the dispute are named, two with technical terms: the accuser (*baʿal mišpāṭî*; later identified with "one who declares guilty," *yaršîʿēnî*, in v. 9), the defender *(maṣdîqî),* and the plaintiff, in this case, the speaker whose references to himself are found in the three first-person object suffixes (*my* vindicator, with *me, my* accuser) and in the first-person plural form of the verb (*let us* stand together).

Whybray literalizes this language and suggests that the Servant "had been arrested by the Babylonian authorities and put on trial. In view of his public predictions that Babylon would shortly fall to the Persians, it is not surprising that he should have been regarded as a danger to the state" (1975: 151). Westermann's analysis, which sees vv. 4-5a as a description of the history and event of prophecy in Israel (1975: 229), is to be preferred, however. Thus, what the prophet/Servant suffers is a result of his prophetic word to weary Israel (50:4; cf. 40:29-31), not his political interactions with the Babylonian authorities. The Servant's dispute is with his compatriots, not with the Babylonians. The language here is figurative, taken from the court and applied to the Servant's situation vis-à-vis Israel. The idiom of the courtroom has already been used to great effect by Second Isaiah in just this way—an arena to confront the misperceptions and delusions of the nations and of Israel. The legal language functions similarly in this passage.

We encountered the Hiphil participle of **ṣdq* earlier in Isa 5:23 in reference to those who "acquit the guilty for a bribe." In 50:8, it clearly refers to God in a positive sense. These varied possibilities are reflected in the only other two appearances of the Hiphil participle of **ṣdq* in the Hebrew Bible. In Prov 17:15, it is used in the same sense as Isa 5:23; in Dan 12:3 it is used positively of the wise who lead others to righteousness. As a descriptive title for God, its occurrence in Second Isaiah is thus unique. YHWH stands in opposition to those who would attempt to declare the Servant guilty (*mî-hûʾ yaršîʿēnî,* v. 9). YHWH is prepared to defend him in a legal setting just as he is prepared to *help* him (**ʿzr,* vv. 7, 9) in his dealings with others outside the court. The juxtaposing of these terms, *maṣdîqî* and *yaršîʿēnî,* reveals the true nature of the dispute at stake: Israel is not merely rejecting the Servant; Israel is in fact contending with YHWH.

The expression *baʿal mišpāṭî* ("my accuser") occurs only once in the Hebrew Bible. Bovati cites this as a technical term for the accuser (1994: 259, n. 5), and he points to Exod 24:14 for confirmation. There, the expression is found with *dābār*, but is otherwise identical: *mî-baʿal dĕbārîm yiggaš ʾălēhem*. Young (1992, 3:302) helpfully points out the equivalent expressions in Roman (*dominus litis*) and cuneiform texts (*bel dini*). It thus seems to refer to a widely recognized official aspect of ancient legal proceedings. Rendered literally, it reads, "Who is the master of my cause?" While taken idiomatically as the parallel to "who will contend with me," one cannot help feeling the irony of the question. Who, indeed, is "the master of the Servant's cause" but YHWH? The language of the verse itself directs the reader to this very answer. The personalized form of the noun *mišpāṭî* turns the reader back to 49:4, in which the Servant averred emphatically the very answer to this question: "But in fact, my cause (*mišpāṭî*) is with YHWH." And once again, this asseveration stands as a mute indictment against Israel's doubts and lack of trust in YHWH's power to respond to her complaint (40:27). Both these Servant passages serve as a foil to Israel's lack of trust by presenting the Servant as one who grounds his mission, whether successful or not, in YHWH's power.

This contrast between the trusting Servant and the doubtful Israel is further evoked in other terms from this unit. Verse 5 shows the Servant declaring that he has "not turned back," and in v. 7 he asserts that, because YHWH will help him, "I know I shall not be ashamed." These two expressions had come together in 42:17 to describe YHWH's threat against "those who trust in idols, who say to their cast images, 'You are our gods.'" To these YHWH says, "they shall be turned back and utterly put to shame." Thus, while those who put their trust in other gods are turned back and put to shame (42:17), the one who trusts in the name of YHWH (50:10) does not turn back (50:5) and is not put to shame (50:7). By using the same language to contrast the idolaters of ch. 43 with those who stand firm with the Servant in 50:4-9, Second Isaiah implicitly indicts his opponents as idolaters, as people who fail to put their faith in YHWH. Throughout this passage, the language evokes a sharp contrast: the Servant in his own conduct bears testimony to YHWH; his mere presence is an indictment against those who doubt YHWH's word, who give in to weariness of spirit, and who turn to other gods. In all circumstances, even physical assault and verbal abuse, the Servant entrusts his cause *(mišpāṭî)* to the one who will vindicate him *(maṣdîqî)*. He shall not be put to shame. His life is the object lesson Israel needs to learn.

Lectionary Notes

Common Lectionary: Proper 19 (B): Isa 50:4-9a / Psalm 116 / Mark 8:27-38
Roman Lectionary: 24 (B): Isa 50:4c-9a / Psalm 116 / Mark 8:27-35
also:
Common Lectionary: Palm Sunday (A, B, C): Isa 50:4-9a / Psalm 31 / and the Passion account from the Gospel of the Year
Roman Lectionary: Palm Sunday (A, B, C): Isa 50:4-7 / Psalm 22 / and the Passion account from the Gospel of the Year

The third Song of the Servant is used in two contexts. Both contexts, like those of the first two songs and, as we will see, of the fourth song, are explicitly christological. The second of the lectionaries' two contexts, viz., on Palm Sunday, can be dealt with briefly. Its depiction of the mistreatment suffered by the Servant—his back beaten, his beard plucked, his revilement by buffets and spitting—corresponds, and indeed had informed, the Synoptics' portrayal of the abuse suffered by Jesus at the hands of his accusers. The end of the Isaian passage speaks of the confident assurance the Servant has in God's power, if not to deliver him from actual harm, at least to be vindicated in the long run. As an entrée to Holy Week, the reading strikes a balance between the actual suffering and ultimate vindication of Jesus. It is thus a précis of the paschal mystery, which Holy Week celebrates—through suffering to life. In these broad terms, it is an apt first reading for any of the Synoptic Gospels with which it is paired annually.

The choice of this reading to be read with Mark's account of Peter's confession at Caesarea Philippi and the first passion prediction is entirely appropriate. Of all the Gospels, Mark most explicitly ties the identity of Jesus to his suffering and death; indeed, it is finally and only on the cross that his identity is revealed: "Truly this man was the Son of God" (15:39). This essential connection between identity and suffering is adumbrated in the confession of Simon Peter at Caesarea Philippi. While Peter is able to utter the correct words—"You are the Christ"—he has no comprehension of the nature of the Lord's suffering messiahship. When Jesus makes his imminent suffering explicit, Peter protests. It is in that context that Jesus goes on to reveal that not only will he, as Messiah and Son of Man, have to suffer greatly, but whoever wishes to follow him will likewise have to suffer: as the Master's identity is revealed on the cross, the identity of disciples is revealed in carrying the cross. Thus, the passage from Isaiah fittingly describes the suffering of the Servant of YHWH. While the fourth song describing the actual death of the Servant might have been used, this third song highlights the active participation of the Servant in the process: he *gave* his back and his cheeks to his abusers, he *did not hide* his face from their revilement.

It is fortunate that this passage is found in two contexts. The setting of the reading on Palm Sunday puts into sharp relief the unique redemptive sufferings of Christ. As such, Christians might be tempted to read this passage only in light of the crucifixion. But its appearance in Ordinary Time in conjunction with both the revelation of Christ as suffering Messiah and with a description of the nature of true discipleship informs the reader of Isaiah that suffering is an inescapable part of authentically following Jesus, and it invites the reader to place in God the same confidence that God will ultimately vindicate—"uphold the right" of—those who trust in him.

My Justice Is a Light for the People: Isaiah 51:1-8

Though the relationship of this prophecy to its surroundings is a matter of some disagreement, the dispute need not distract us. For the purposes of this examination, we can profitably deal with 51:1-8, and primarily with the second stanza (vv. 4-6), in which are found both terms that concern this study. Here is the translation:

4 Give heed to me, my people;
and my nation, listen to me.
for instruction shall go forth from me,
and my justice (*mišpāṭî*) for light to peoples.
5 Speedily my deliverance draws near,
my salvation has gone forth
and my arms will rule peoples.
For me the coastlands wait,
and for my arm they hope.
6 Lift up your eyes to the heavens,
and look to the earth below:
for [the] heavens, like smoke, are dispersed,
and the earth like a garment shall wear out;
and its inhabitants like gnats will die.
But my salvation will last forever,
and my deliverance shall not fail.

It seems that all that the Servant had been intended to accomplish is now taken over by YHWH. Looking back to the previous Servant Songs, we see that the Servant had begun his address similarly (49:1):

Listen to me, O coastlands;
give heed, O nations from afar.

Now, in 51:4, the Servant's announcement is proclaimed anew by YHWH, and the same audience is addressed ("coastlands" in v. 5b). The Servant's mission in the first song entailed "bringing forth justice" (**yṣʾ*, 42:1); now justice "goes forth" (**yṣʾ*) directly from YHWH (51:4). The Servant was apparently intended to be "a light for the nations" (42:6), but YHWH's own justice is now the light. The coastlands no longer have to wait for the Servant's "instruction" (42:4): instruction now goes forth directly from YHWH. What could account for the similarity between the descriptions of the Servant's mission and the task that YHWH is about to assume? It seems the Servant's involvement with the divine mission, having encountered serious setbacks (50:4-11), has come to an end, as the fourth song (52:13—53:12) is about to make clear. This passage seems to be an interim text between the death of the Servant and the meditation on his ministry that comprises the fourth song. But the death of the Servant does not mean the end of the mission—YHWH steps into the breach and will personally fulfill the task.

Indeed, YHWH in the spotlight is precisely the focus of this passage. He is the speaker and the language points unrelentingly to him, his attributes, and his accomplishments. In these three verses are found nine nouns and four prepositions with the first-person suffix. Everything seems intensely personalized: "my people," "my nation," "my justice," "my deliverance" (2x), "my salvation" (2x), and "my arm(s)" (2x). Even the "instruction" of v. 4 will become personalized as "my instruction" in v. 7; and both "my deliverance" and "my salvation" reappear in v. 9

for the third time. Just as the ear cannot tune out the sound of the repeated long *î* that marks the first-person singular, the eye cannot avert its gaze from the commanding presence of YHWH in these verses. Here, YHWH's speech takes on the cadence of the self-asseveration speeches of the gods of Babylon.[36] But his claims to victory and salvation are augmented by his claim to justice. "My justice" is part of what distinguishes YHWH and establishes the distinctive character of his universal sovereignty.

As had been mentioned in the opening comments to this chapter, the hendiadys *mišpāṭ ûṣĕdāqâ* is nowhere to be found in Isaiah 40–55. Instead, as this passage clearly demonstrates, a far more usual pairing is *ṣĕdāqâ* and *yĕšûʿâ* ("salvation"; 51:5, 6, 8; see also 45:8; 46:13). It is the parallel term *yĕšûʿâ* that pushes the nuance of *ṣĕdāqâ* toward the meaning "deliverance" or "victory" rather than the more common meaning "righteousness."[37] As Scullion has demonstrated, in Isaiah 40–55, "it has been definitely established that the words [*ṣedeq-ṣĕdāqâ*] are used in a salvific sense" (1971: 338).

Though the focus of this passage is on salvation and deliverance, the concern for justice and YHWH's rule are also very much in evidence. In 51:4, *mišpāṭ* is paired with *tôrâ,* a parallelism already encountered in 42:4, where *mišpāṭ* referred to the verdict announcing God's just sovereignty, and *tôrâ* was the instruction concerning that sovereignty. The *instruction* for which the coastlands waited in 42:4 now *goes forth* as *a light* to the *peoples* in 51:4. YHWH's sovereignty is being established.

Sweeney, in his treatment of *tôrâ* in the book of Isaiah, also considers *tôrâ* in the context of sovereignty but approaches the topic somewhat more broadly. After examining all the occurrences of *tôrâ* in Isaiah, he concludes:

> The sum total of these occurrences identifies *tôrâ* as the teaching of YHWH, expressed by the prophet, which stands as the norm for proper conduct by both Israel and the nations, and which stands as the norm for order in the created world. It is likewise identified as something that is not properly understood in the time of the prophet, but the full significance of which will be apparent at a future time in which YHWH's world-wide sovereignty is recognized. As such, *tôrâ* signifies YHWH's revelation to both Israel and the world at large. (1996b: 63)

When *tôrâ* is brought into the orbit of *mišpāṭ,* and more specifically when that *mišpāṭ* is personalized by YHWH, *tôrâ* as "revelation" means the revelation of YHWH's sovereignty. Further, *tôrâ* with *mišpāṭ* is more than a norm for conduct or a principle of order in creation; it is specifically the revelation of God's sovereignty at work in the world. Not merely an announcement, it is the effective accomplishment of YHWH's rule demonstrated in the past through creation and redemption, and enacted now in the restoration of Israel and the submission of the nations to YHWH's effective rule. The relationship between vv. 4b and 5a is causal: YHWH's instruction and justice go forth with the result that his deliverance and salvation are near at hand. Salvation and deliverance, in turn, are the manifestation of his sovereignty.

That *tôrâ* is an instruction about YHWH's sovereignty is supported by v. 5 in which YHWH's arms rule the peoples. This phrase pictures YHWH exercising the sovereignty that is his alone to exercise. When v. 5 goes on to say that the coastlands wait for YHWH and for his arm they hope, we may recall 42:4, in which the coastlands wait for the Servant's teaching. The relationship between these verses seems to be this: when the Servant was still alive, the coastlands waited for his teaching; but now that YHWH is the one fulfilling that mission directly, the coastlands no longer wait for a teaching about YHWH's sovereignty, but long for his actual rule.

Finally, it may be recalled that in 2:2-4, YHWH exercised his worldwide rule *(šāpaṭ)* over many peoples as the instruction and word of YHWH went forth from Jerusalem; in consequence of all this, the house of Jacob is admonished to walk in the light of YHWH. The components of instruction, ruling, peoples, and light all come together to express the notion of YHWH's sovereignty over Israel and all the nations. That sovereignty, characterized by power and justice, is to the governance of the nations as light is to the concourse of creation. However, whereas creation can cease to exist (51:6a), YHWH's salvation and deliverance, accomplished by his arm and exercised in justice, will never fail (v. 6b).

In this passage, the term *mišpāṭî* makes its fourth and final appearance in Second Isaiah. It has now appeared on the lips of the major players: Israel, the Servant, and YHWH himself. Only one other time in the Hebrew Bible is the expression *mišpāṭî* found on the lips of YHWH: in Ezek 39:21 where, in the aftermath of YHWH's defeat of Gog, he announces that "all nations will see my judgment *(mišpāṭî)* which I have done and which my hand has laid on them." While the aspect of judgment meted out as crushing defeat to Israel's enemies is in the foreground, the term's close association with divine sovereignty is also evident. YHWH has executed judgment by his *hand* (a metaphor that is synonymous with his *arm*) by bringing Gog into subjection. Divine sovereignty, whether expressed as judgment or as just rule, is appropriated as a personal characteristic of YHWH. The word *mišpāṭî* spoken by YHWH in Isaiah is synonymous with his divine rule (see also 42:1-4).

In the mouths of the three different speakers, the term *mišpāṭî* reveals something of the essential character of each. For both Israel and the Servant, it is a technical term referring to their complaints. This point should not be overlooked: the Servant and the people are bound together in their shared situation as each gives voice to his complaint (40:27; 49:4). It is their commonality that simultaneously reveals their essential difference. Israel believes her cause has been passed over by YHWH and she gives in to weariness of spirit; the Servant believes his cause is with YHWH and so expresses confidence that, even in the midst of hardship, he will be vindicated. YHWH's use of the same personalized form of the term also shows his link to both the Servant and the people, but his relationship to each is a relationship of power. When his *mišpāṭ* goes forth, it does so with instruction concerning his sovereignty; and as a light, his justice enlightens the ways in which the peoples should walk. *Mišpāṭ* is his just rule, which both guides creation and history and provides the basis for the just interaction of kingdoms among themselves (2:2-4).

Through careful use of vocabulary and thematic development, Second Isaiah presents divine sovereignty as particularized according to the needs of those it addresses: to the entire created order, YHWH's *instruction* and *justice* are manifest most broadly as *deliverance* and *salvation* from chaos; for the peoples, even those as far off as the distant coastlands, *instruction* and *justice* mean *deliverance* from their foolish bondage to idolatry and the imparting of knowledge to worship the one who exercises sovereignty over all kingdoms; for Israel *instruction and justice* mean coming to know that YHWH has power to redeem them from exile and to restore them to their homeland. While the overarching reality of divine sovereignty is particularized according to the needs of those it addresses, each manifestation tends to the same end: that all people (41:20) and all flesh (49:26), Israel (43:10), Zion (49:23), and "my people" (52:6), Cyrus (45:3) and all rulers (49:23) will know that "I am YHWH, and there is no other; besides me there is no god" (45:5).

Lectionary Notes

Common Lectionary: Proper 16 (A): Isa 51:1-6 / Psalm 138 / Matt 16:13-20
Roman Lectionary: 21 (A): Same Psalm and Gospel, but reads Isa 22:19-23—a passage not covered by this study.

The Gospel is the Matthean account of Peter's confession at Caesarea Philippi (for a discussion of Mark's version and its coordinated reading from Isaiah, see the Lectionary Notes for the previous section). As is well known, in the version from Matthew Jesus goes on to designate Peter as "the rock" on which Jesus will build the church. Jesus entrusts to Peter the keys of authority which permit him to "bind and loose" on earth and in heaven. At the risk of understatement, this passage has figured prominently in Protestant-Catholic polemics in ages past. Remnants of the polemic may be evident in the choice of readings from Isaiah: the Roman Lectionary chooses a passage in which Shebna is replaced by Eliakim as steward of the royal household; Eliakim is given the key to the house of David and given the authority to "open and shut." The Roman Lectionary thus reinforces the personal authority of the head of the household. The Common Lectionary departs from its usual practicing of following the Roman Lectionary and instead chooses a passage that, read in light of the Gospel, seems to highlight the church's mission as herald of salvation, but which vests authority in the "arms" of YHWH: his power to rule is revealed in the teaching *(tôrâ)* that goes forth from him, and in his justice *(mišpāṭ)*, which serves as a light to the nations. This is a felicitous description of the mission of the church: to be a herald of God's salvation. When the church is a faithful witness to God's teaching and justice, divine salvation is experienced as comfort for those who mourn and as restoration of creation with the wilderness becoming like the garden of Eden (51:3). Because God's justice is a light by which the nations are to walk, justice is and must be integral to the very mission of the church. The specific notion of justice put forth by Second Isaiah—the just rule of God—contextualizes the debate of authority in the church. Authority has its source in God, its legitimacy in mission, and its effectiveness in establishing God's sovereignty; in the vocabulary of the New Testament, authority and mission are directed toward the building of the kingdom of God.

By a Perversion of Justice, the Servant Is Killed: Isaiah 52:13—53:12

Our interest in this fourth Song of the Servant is very limited and the scope of the discussion can be precisely defined. Structurally, the report of the Servant's suffering and death (53:1-11a) is framed by divine discourse (52:13-15; 53:11b-12). The report itself alternates between first-person plural meditations and third-person accounts. Thus 53:2-3 describe the Servant's beginnings; vv. 4-6 are a confession by those ("we/our") whose sins caused his suffering; vv. 7-9 resume the third-person descriptions, and vv. 10-11a describe God's response to his suffering. The term *mišpāṭ* occurs in v. 8, which is part of the somewhat larger unit, vv. 7-8, to which we now turn our attention.

Though v. 8 suffers from a number of as yet unresolved textual and interpretive problems, most of these problems do not affect our discussion directly and need not distract us. Our concern in v. 8 is with the way in the Servant *was taken* (away); the modifying expression *mēʿōṣer ûmimmišpāṭ* has been variously understood. The preposition *min* (the "*mē-*" in *mēʿōṣer*) can function either separatively (that is, "from" or "without") or causatively (that is, "because of"), and both meanings have been defended. The problem of translation lies not only in the preposition but in the wide range of meanings of which *mišpāṭ* is capable. Motyer ably summarizes both the various meanings of *mišpāṭ* and the varieties of approach to the entire phrase:

> Do we, therefore, say "from justice" (from the court of law, due trial and sentencing) or "without justice" (ignoring rights, without a proper trial)? In other words, we can underline the fact by saying "from arrest and sentence," or the victim by saying "without restraint and without right," or the injustice by saying "without restraint and without justice." All these are contextually satisfactory. (1993: 433–34)

Motyer himself sides with D. F. Payne in seeing the expression as a set phrase meaning "due process of law."

In the end, whether *mišpāṭ* refers to a legal process that condemned the Servant to death or to a miscarriage of justice resulting in the same, what should not be lost is the irony that the preeminent herald of *mišpāṭ* (42:1-4) is done in by *mišpāṭ* as exercised by those to whom he was sent. He who was to bring forth justice is dispatched by those who claim to exercise it. Even more broadly, the courtroom setting that Second Isaiah has used to such great effect in asserting the sovereignty and just rule of YHWH is now the setting in which the Servant's life is unjustly ended. Just as *mišpāṭ* as used previously by Israel and by the Servant pointed to their differences (40:27; 49:4), now the courtroom is used to point out the essential difference between the just reign of God and the unjust practice of the ungodly. The versatility of the term *mišpāṭ* is due not only to its wide range of meanings, as Motyer rightly points out, but also to its incisive deployment by Second Isaiah. Throughout this section of the book of Isaiah, it functions differently depending on who is using it and in what settings it is employed. For this reason, semantic analysis will find itself limited if it fails to take into careful consideration the speakers, the settings, and the contexts of *mišpāṭ*. As this fourth song briefly, almost slyly, suggests, there is a great difference between God's justice and the justice of the world. Between those two worlds stands the Servant, who, in the cause of justice, is simultaneously vindicated by God (*maṣdîqî*, 50:8) and condemned by people (*yaršîʿēnî*, 50:9). His opponents may see his death as the end, but his disciples know differently (53:9-12).

Lectionary Notes

Common Lectionary: Good Friday (A, B, C): Isa 52:13—53:12 / Psalm 22 / John 18:1—19:42

Roman Lectionary: Same

Clearly, the choice of the fourth Song of the Suffering Servant for Good Friday places the interpretation of the passage in a christological context: the mysterious and unnamed Servant is Jesus Christ. This passage together with the passion according to Saint John shows complementary aspects of the death of Christ: the Isaian passage describes the suffering of the Servant while the passion offers a theology of the cross. For John, the cross is Jesus' throne of glory which reveals the kingship of Christ crucified. Religious art that shows Christ on the cross clothed in priestly vestments and wearing a kingly crown depicts this high Christology. The Isaian reading keeps this Christology grounded in the reality of Christ's human suffering and death.

The passage that we discussed above, Isa 53:8, comments on the Gospel in such a way as to highlight the very meaning of the paschal mystery. A perversion of justice leads to the Servant's death, which in turn leads to the justification of many (Isa 55: 5, 8, 10, 12). The perversion of justice at the trial of Jesus is a feature all four Gospels are at pains to highlight; for example, the trumped-up charges made by false witnesses (Matt 26:59-61; Mark 14:56-57; cf. Luke 23:2) and the repeated declarations of the innocence of Jesus by Pilate (Matt 27:24; Luke 23:4; John 18:38; 19:4, 6), Judas (Matt 27:4), the Roman centurion at the foot of the cross (Luke 23:47), and even Herod's wife (Matt 27:19). Nonetheless, Jesus is handed over to death, and in so doing the words of Caiaphas are ironically proved true: "It is better for one man to die for the people" (John 18:14)—and indeed it is, for the injustice perpetrated against one leads to the justification of all. This is a facet of the paschal mystery, which Good Friday celebrates and which is at the very center of the Christian gospel: death leads to life. This core proclamation is expressed in a variety of ways in the Gospels: the grain of wheat must die to bear fruit (John 12:24), one must lose one's life to find it (Matt 10:39; Mark 8:35; Luke 9:24; John 12:25), the first must be last (Matt 19:30; Mark 9:35; Luke 13:30), the greatest must become the servant of all (Matt 23:11; Mark 9:35; Luke 9:48). It comes to clearest expression when Jesus announces that he has come not to be served but to serve and to give his life as a ransom for others (Mark 10:45). These dramatic reversals, which bring unexpected benefit from unlikely sources—life from death—articulate the dynamic that underlies the Good Friday mystery and that ties the Isaiah reading to the Gospel: from injustice to justification.

False Judgment Shall Be Confounded: Isaiah 54:11-17

The God who is able to transform the suffering and shame of the Servant into vindication and honor (53:9-12) now turns to redress the barrenness (54:1-3) and widowhood (54:4-6) of daughter Zion. YHWH's abandonment of Zion is ended in divine compassion (v. 7), and wrath is banished by faithful love (vv. 8-10).

In vv. 11-12, the prophet turns his attention to the glorification of Zion, here rebuilt in jewel-encrusted splendor. This is the architectural equivalent of the verbal self-asseveration that YHWH has indulged throughout these chapters (for example, 51:4-6). Zion, as the temple city, reflects the splendor and majesty of her chief occupant: "the new Jerusalem is God's city in a completely new way, and its glittering splendor points directly to the divine majesty" (Westermann 1975: 278). The life of Zion's citizens reflects the just reign of God, which emanates from the temple city: the children (like the Servant in 50:4) are taught by YHWH and enjoy the prosperity *(šālôm)* that comes from YHWH; they are established in righteousness and live free from fear and terror (vv. 13-14). The opposite is denied: strife and destruction are not from YHWH, and those who stir it up are destined to failure (vv. 15-17).

In this last context—the confounding of evil hatched against Zion—we come to the last occurrence of *mišpāṭ* in Second Isaiah, namely v. 17.

> Every weapon forged against you shall not succeed;
> [and every tongue that rises against you in judgment (*mišpāṭ*) you shall prove guilty;]
> this is the inheritance of the servants of YHWH,
> and their vindication is from me. Oracle of YHWH.

The bracketed portion of the text, v. 17aβ, is missing in 1QIsa[a], and its absence is curiously indicated by a blank line in the text.[38] It is, however, found in the versions, and so we read with the MT.

Verse 15 had indicated that those who stir up strife are not from YHWH. Verse 16 asserts that YHWH creates the artisan who works at the forge, and that it is YHWH who destines both weapons for their purpose and the destroyer for its task. Therefore, weapons and evil machinations vaunted against Zion without YHWH's consent are doomed to failure. This applies equally to weapons (v. 17aα) and words argued in court (v. 17aβ). The expression "to rise in/for the judgment" *(*qwm + mišpāṭ)* is found only here and in Pss 1:5 and 76:10 (Eng. 9). Both are informative. Psalm 1, contrasting the ways of the righteous and of the wicked, concludes that "the wicked shall not rise/stand in the judgment *(lōʾ-yāqumû rĕšāʿîm* *bammišpāṭ)* nor shall sinners [rise/stand] in the company of the righteous." When judged, the wicked will not withstand the accusation and will be deemed unworthy of a place with the righteous. Psalm 76, a hymn that glorifies Zion and exalts YHWH's majesty there, celebrates divine judgment: "when God arises for the judgment, [he shall] save all the afflicted of the earth." Both psalms use the idiom to refer to a formal legal proceeding, and that is the sense also in Isa 54:17. This is confirmed by the technical term by which *every tongue* is confuted: the Hiphil of **ršʿ* means "to declare guilty," as we saw in 50:9, where it is matched against the "defender" *(maṣdîqî)*. There is a nice irony here. Those who sought to declare the Servant guilty in 50:9 find the tables turned: the servants of YHWH will prove them guilty.

A final point may be made about this last appearance of *mišpāṭ* in Second Isaiah. This section of the book of Isaiah began in the Heavenly Council and now ends in a courtroom scene. The opening lofty paean to divine justice and sovereignty finds itself juxtaposed to this rather mundane intrasectarian strife in which the servants of YHWH find themselves embroiled with their opponents. This adumbrates the reality that will emerge more obviously in the next section of the book. This trajectory of *mišpāṭ* from glorious divine sovereignty to pedestrian rancor corresponds to the social and historical movement of the prophet's ministry and the life of the community. Sent as an ambassador of divine justice, the prophet will soon find himself engaged in intramural strife; the stirring visions of divine sovereignty enthroned in the splendor of Zion yield to the reality of Jerusalem in ruins and the community fragmented. The concept of justice can be as lofty as the manifestation of YHWH's unrivaled sovereignty or as pedestrian as the partisan conflicts that find voice in legal proceedings directed at coreligionists. The sovereignty of YHWH, which would govern the nations, has yet to find a home in Israel.

Conclusions about *Mišpāṭ*/Justice in Second Isaiah

First, some statistical observations. The chart on the following page tracks the distribution of the term according to chapters and speakers, and also shades those passages where the term is narrowly defined in a forensic sense. The Servant passages are outlined in a bold border. Verbal and nominal forms of *šāpaṭ* are shown in smaller italics.

Thus, according to the chart, seven of the eleven occurrences are found in direct divine speech; two are spoken by the prophet and two by the Servant. As noted in the chart, Israel's "complaint" is reported as indirect speech by either YHWH or perhaps the prophet. In keeping with Second Isaiah's use of the courtroom to argue his case, seven occurrences refer to specific aspects of the legal process. The distribution between chs. 40–48 and 49–55 is equivalent, six and five occurrences, respectively.

Speakers			
Prophet	**YHWH**	**Servant**	**Israel**
40:14 (?)[39] "path of justice" *40:23 "rulers of the earth"*			
	40:27 (?)[40] (quoting Israel) "my cause"		[40:27] (indirect speech reported by YHWH)
	41:1 "draw near for trial"		
	42:1 "bring forth justice" **42:3** "bring forth justice" **42:4** "establish justice" *43:26 "let us go to trial"*		
		49:4 "my cause"	
		50:8 "my accusers"	
	51:4 "my justice . . . as a light" *51:5 "my arms will rule"*		
53:8—[of the Servant] "by judgment"			
	54:17—tongues that "rise in judgment"		

It is clear that the burden of the discussion of *mišpāṭ* in Second Isaiah is borne by YHWH and his Servant: of the word's 11 occurrences, 7 are found on YHWH's lips and 6 are clustered in the four prophecies traditionally called "Songs of the Servant." The close connection between YHWH and *mišpāṭ* is reflected in this concentrated use of the term by YHWH. This appropriation of *mišpāṭ* by YHWH—no one taught it to him (40:12-14) and it is his (*mišpāṭî,* 51:4)—recalls the earlier assertion that "YHWH is a God of *mišpāṭ*" (30:18). It is YHWH's justice that is entrusted to the Servant. Of all the passages that deal with a/the Servant, only the traditional four songs of the Servant contain the word *mišpāṭ*. YHWH's concern for *mišpāṭ* and the Servant's role in executing it come together in 42:1-4, in which the Servant is commissioned by YHWH to "bring forth" and "establish" *mišpāṭ* (42:1, 3, 4). In the remaining three songs, two of which are spoken in the first-person voice of the Servant, it is a legal term that describes various aspects of the legal process: the *cause* of the complainant (49:4), the complainant's *accuser* (50:8), and, finally, the (corrupt) *judgment* by which the Servant is condemned to death (53:8). The legal idiom is also dominant in three of the remaining speeches by YHWH (40:27; 41:1; 54:17).

The emphasis on the forensic aspect of *mišpāṭ* in Second Isaiah is clearly in keeping with his reliance on the courtroom setting and legal idiom to make his case, whether in disputations, accusations, or in rendering verdicts. The image of "judge" that this setting implies is a manifestation of the prophet's theological assertion that underlies the entire work: authority and power belong to YHWH. Whether YHWH appears initially as accuser or defender, he is always the one who renders the verdict on the gods, the nations, Israel, and the work of the Servant. H. Eberhard von Waldow demonstrates that in all prophetic legal speeches, even when YHWH is identified as either the accuser or the plaintiff, he is always also the judge (1968: 270ff., 280ff.). As the one who renders the verdict, who "judges between nations and renders judgment for many peoples" (2:4), his authority is final and binding. The idiom of the courtroom and the commanding presence of the cosmic Judge are significant expressions of Second Isaiah's argument for the sovereignty of YHWH.

The meaning of *mišpāṭ* differs according to the speaker. For both the Servant and Israel, it refers to their "cause." The shared nature of their plight is suggested by their use of the personal pronoun, *mišpāṭî*; but the same term also points out their differences. For Israel voicing the complaint that "YHWH has passed over *my cause*" (40:27), it is an expression of doubt; for the Servant, it is an occasion to express trust and confidence: "*my cause* is with YHWH, and my recompense is with my God" (49:4). This contrast is ironically reinforced when the Servant asks in 50:8, "Who is *my accuser*?" (literally, "the master of my cause"); the grammatical form of the term directs the reader's attention back to the same term in 49:4 for the answer, "*my cause* is with YHWH."

The same word that points to human need also speaks of divine power. This is particularly clear in 40:12-31. There, the entire disputation is directed toward answering Israel's complaint that her *cause (mišpāṭ)* has been passed over and her *way (derek)* is hidden. In contrast, YHWH's command over the *path of justice (mišpāṭ)* and the *way (derek) of understanding* asserts his sovereign power. The same words *(mišpāṭ* and *derek)* are used to establish a relationship between God and Israel, but the terms of that relationship are spelled out in the contrast of power and need.

The theme of YHWH's power is further developed in 40:12-31. YHWH's unaided, uncounseled work of creation leads to an affirmation of his sovereignty over the nations and the entire created order (40:10-17). In keeping with the widely dispersed mythic pattern in which creation is the prelude to kingship, YHWH's work of creation in 40:12 leads to 40:13-14, where he is presented as a wise and just king. A title of divine kingship comes to direct expression in 41:21, where YHWH is called "Jacob's King," which in turn recalls the assertion of 33:22, "YHWH is our judge, YHWH is our lawgiver, YHWH is our king."

The "path of justice" (40:14) is a key expression in determining the meaning of *mišpāṭ* in Second Isaiah. In the context of the sovereignty argument in 40:12-17, it means that no one has taught YHWH how to rule justly, or how to exercise his rule over creation, history, and the nations. In the context of the prophet's polemic against idols, it serves as a distinguishing and distinctive feature of YHWH's identity. In the same way that YHWH is unsurpassed in *understanding, knowledge,* and *counsel,* there is none who compares to him in directing the *path of justice.* Justice has taken a distinctly theological turn and functions now as an attribute of God's sovereignty.

This theological appropriation is in marked contrast to the understanding of Isaiah of Jerusalem. As we mentioned, the concern for social justice is entirely lacking in Second Isaiah. Even when a suitable context is provided for a reference to social justice—as when 43:22-28 recalls 1:10-17—there is a notable silence. Those passages that deal with issues that might be construed as social concern—release of prisoners, care for the needy, restoration of refugees—do so in service to the larger theological concerns. Release from prison and darkness (42:6-7) is an extension of the metaphor that the Servant, as an ambassador of YHWH's sovereignty, is a light to those confined in the darkness of their idolatrous beliefs (42:6-8). The ingathering of the exiles (43:6-10) is a demonstration that "I, I am YHWH: besides me there is no savior" (43:11). When the "poor and the needy" cry out in their thirst (41:17), YHWH personally responds "so that they will see and know . . . that the hand of YHWH has done this, and the Holy One of Israel has created it" (41:20). Because Israel is robbed, plundered, and hidden away with no one to restore them (42:22ff.), YHWH, who gave them up to such destruction (42:24-25), will personally restore them (43:1-13), once again as proof that "there is no one who can deliver from my hand, and no one besides me who saves" (43:13). Even if one were to construe these as acts of justice enacted in the social realm, it is noteworthy that in every instance, YHWH personally—and no one else—accomplishes them.

The only person in Isaiah 40–55 who is expressly charged to enact *mišpāṭ* is the Servant in 42:1-4. "Justice" is YHWH's alone: the Servant is its herald. In these verses the term identifies both the form and the content of his mission. He is to bring forth God's judgment or verdict, reached in the preceding courtroom arguments, that the gods of the nations are nothing and naught; they have no power and, indeed, no reality. The consequence of this is that YHWH alone is God and to him belongs sole rule of creation, history, and the nations. The verdict announces the just rule of YHWH. This is consonant with the meaning of *mišpāṭ*'s first appearance in 40:14.

Throughout these chapters, *mišpāṭ* points simultaneously to human need and divine power. This contrast is implied in the first and last appearances of the term. Initially, the reader is privy to the goings-on of the Divine Council, in which YHWH's justice is established and his unrivaled rule is majestically defended. By the end of these chapters, the servants are promised defense from those who rise up in judgment against them, implying times of strife and contention (54:14-17). It seems that YHWH's rule, of which the Servant was spokesman and for which he apparently died, has not been established within the community of Israel, which, in rejecting the Servant, has failed to recognize the rule of YHWH in its midst. Just as the mission of the Servant, undertaken in the spirit of the Lord and with full divine authorization (42:1-4), produced "nothing and vanity" (49:4) and ended in the Servant's death (53:7-10), so the rule of YHWH, decisively established in the Divine Council (40:12-31), seems to have foundered on Israel's internal divisions. These divisions will surface for ill in Third Isaiah and will compel YHWH to yet new manifestations and implementations of justice. Because justice is a distinguishing characteristic of YHWH, it can ill afford to meet so unseemly an end. The Judge will become a Warrior and will personally champion the mission that had once been entrusted to the Servant.

chapter 5

Isaiah 56–66

A few preliminary observations can be made that will highlight the major concerns of our examination in this portion of the book of Isaiah. First, the occurrence of the term *mišpāṭ* is proportionally highest in Isaiah 56–66:

Isaiah 1–39	766 verses	22 occurrences (= once every 35 verses)
Isaiah 40–55	333 verses	11 occurrences (= once every 30 verses)
Isaiah 56–66	192 verses	9 occurrences (= once every 21 verses)

Yet in Third Isaiah, 5 of those 9 occurrences are in 59:1-20, accounting for its densest concentration and most uneven distribution in the book of Isaiah. Second, the hendiadys *mišpāṭ ûṣĕdāqâ* makes its reappearance: it occurs five times in the nominal form and also makes one appearance in verbal form. Third, *mišpāṭ* is most prominently and thematically placed in the opening verse, 56:1, sounding an urgent call to action: "Observe justice *(mišpāṭ)*! and do righteousness!" Finally, three of the nine appearances of *mišpāṭ*, and one of the two occurrences of the verb *šāpaṭ*, are modified by the particle *ʾên* ("there is not"), dramatically summarizing the situation in the community of Third Isaiah: there is no justice. Thus, the frequency of occurrence, the prominence of position, and the focus on (the lack of) justice in society all commend our attention in this portion of the book of Isaiah.

Authorship, Unity, and Date of Isaiah 56–66

Most commentators follow Duhm in assessing chs. 56–66 as a distinct portion of the book. Beyond that, we find a wide diversity of opinions about authorship, as well as the unity and date of the composition. There remains some discussion about whether chs. 56–66 as a whole is the work of one or more authors, or whether, indeed, it even has an "author" as such: some believe that it is a collection of disparate sayings and fragments. Today, many commentators hold that chs. 60–62 represents a core of material that is a unified literary and authorial composition, and that other portions of the book may be attributable to the same author. Those who hold for such an individual author are not in agreement as to his identity, whether he is Second Isaiah himself at a later time in his career, or a disciple of Second Isaiah or of the Servant, or someone else altogether. There is no consensus either as to whether the author(s) is a prophet as such, an expositor or exegete of the work of Second Isaiah, or a redactor of the material of others. Most would hold that the material in chs. 56–66 does not represent an independent collection, but was either written or compiled and redacted in view of at least Second Isaiah, and possibly in relation to the book as a whole.

Among those who hold for a separate portion of the book of Isaiah commonly known by the moniker Third Isaiah, most suggest a postexilic date and a setting in Judah. While debate is still lively about references to the reconstructed temple (66:1-2; 56:7) and their significance in dating the material, most are now agreed that datings such as Volz's suggestions spanning the seventh to the third centuries are too broad and too late. A rough consensus favors a dating in the late sixth to early fifth century.

Brooks Schramm, surveying the history of scholarship and its trends, summarizes the state of the question as follows:

> The resulting view is a synthesis of the insights of Duhm, Elliger and Volz. With Duhm, the partitioning off of Isaiah 56–66 from 40–55 is accepted. With Elliger, an early post-exilic dating is accepted. And with Volz multiple authorship is accepted. As is the case with the designation "First" or "Proto" Isaiah, "Third" Isaiah has come mainly to designate a corpus of writings, as opposed to a particular personage. (1995: 21)[1]

The discussion so far has approached the text ("Isaiah" as a whole, or "Third Isaiah" more narrowly) in light of historical, social, and geographical concerns, factors that are largely irrelevant to a literary perspective. From a literary point of view, thematic and theological concerns are the best interpreters of the shape, structure, and message of both the book and its individual sections. Such factors as the destruction and restoration of the temple—decisive factors in historical and social reconstructions—are of secondary significance to the internal dynamics of the book of Isaiah; the central concern is the purification and restoration of Zion, which is nowhere linked to the destruction and restoration of the temple. In such a literary perspective, a major break between 55 and 56 is not at all evident, and the significance of an alleged Third Isaiah is minimal at best (Seitz 1992, 3:501–7; idem 1993b: 265–66).

Concern for the literary character of the book serves as a corrective to an excessive focus on the historical and social situations of the community. This is an especially sobering corrective when dealing with a period that commentators universally acknowledge as being sadly lacking in historically reliable information and yet proceed to reconstruct with unwarranted confidence. Once this cautionary lesson has been learned from the literary approach to the book of Isaiah, however, it is necessary to add that interpretation of the passages dealing with justice must take place within some social and historical context, however tentatively and broadly construed. For our consideration of *mišpāṭ* in this final portion of the book of Isaiah, we will proceed with the understanding Schramm cautiously suggests: Third Isaiah refers to the material in chs. 56–66; it was composed by various authors in the early postexilic period for a community living in Judah and Jerusalem. For ease in discussion, we will continue to use the term "Third Isaiah" to refer to the author/speaker, realizing full well that we may in fact be dealing with a number of different individuals.

Passages in Isaiah 55–66

Observe Justice! Isaiah 56:1-8

There is fairly widespread agreement that 56:1-8 and most of 66:17-24 provide a frame to chs. 56–66.[2] In addition to this framing function, 56:1 provides an important link not only to Isaiah 40–55, but to chs. 1–39 as well. As Rendtorff points out, the two verbal pairings that were distinctive of First Isaiah *(mišpāṭ ûṣĕdāqâ)* and Second Isaiah (*yĕšûᶜâ ûṣĕdāqâ*, "salvation and righteousness") are brought together in 56:1, suggesting that "this verse is intended to establish a deliberate continuity with the other two parts of the book" (1993b: 185). Polan's analysis of the two word pairs *(mišpāṭ ûṣĕdāqâ* and *yĕšûᶜâ ûṣĕdāqâ)* is even more far-reaching. After showing that the former word pair is found only in First Isaiah (1:27; 5:7; 5:16; 9:6 [Eng. 7]; 16:5; 26:9; 28:17; 32:1, 16; 33:5) and the second only in Second Isaiah (45:8, 21; 46:13; 51:5, 6, 8), he shows that the same segregation is to be found in Third Isaiah after 56:1: the pair *ṣĕdāqâ/mišpāṭ* is found in 58:2b, 2c; 59:4a, 9a, 14a; and *ṣĕdāqâ/yĕšûᶜâ* is found in 59:16b, 17a; 61:10b; 62:1b; 63:1c (1986: 58–60). Bringing together these two word pairs in 56:1 not only looks back to the previous two sections of the book, but sounds themes to be developed in the remainder of Third Isaiah.

While Rendtorff's point of interest in 56:1 is the use of *ṣĕdāqâ* with two different meanings—"righteousness" and "deliverance"[3]—our interests move in a slightly different direction: we are interested both in the use of *mišpāṭ* and the reappearance of its pairing with *ṣĕdāqâ*.

Significantly, both terms first appear as the object of divine commands:

1 Thus says YHWH:
"Observe justice and do righteousness,
for my salvation is about to come,
and my deliverance is to be revealed."
2 Happy is the person [lit.: man] who does this,
and the one [lit.: son of man] who holds it fast,
the one who keeps the Sabbath from profanation,[4]
and who keeps his hand from doing any evil.

Thus, like First and Second Isaiah (1:2; 40:1), Third Isaiah begins with a double imperative spoken in the divine voice (56:1). In each section of the book, the spotlight is trained on God's spoken word: "for YHWH has spoken" (1:2), "says your God" (40:1), "thus says YHWH" (56:1). The imperative speaks simultaneously to the sovereignty of God, who has authority to command, and to the urgency of the message which must be heeded. However, unlike First and Second Isaiah, the addressee is not clearly specified. Though the second-person masculine plural direct address of v. 1 shifts to third-person references in v. 2, nevertheless it seems that those intended to fulfill these commands are the "man . . . and the son of man" of v. 2a. The terms employed here are generic, not specific, that is, they apply to every human person, not to particular nationalities or religious adherents.[5] Subtly, then, v. 2a sets the stage for the following discussion: while hearers might be inclined in general to extend blessings to the "man . . . and the son of man" who keep the Sabbath and refrain from evil (v. 2b), does the "man . . . and the son of man" include foreigners and eunuchs? The discussion takes up that question in vv. 3-8.

In examining 56:1-8, we must attend to the use of words to understand the limits of the unit. Westermann's form-critical analysis distinguishes two separate units: vv. 1-2 are "an exhortation to act rightly, especially to keep the Sabbath, while 56:3-8 are a regulation concerning membership of the community that worships Yahweh" (1975: 305). Thus, "Verses 3-8 are independent of vv. 1f., and not their continuation. The word 'and' shows that between vv. 1f. and vv. 3-8 there is similarity of content" (312). Other scholars also argue for the composite nature of vv. 1-8 (P. A. Smith 1995: 50–51). Closer attention to the use of words, however, will show that the unity of the passage seems not to be quite so casual.

Rendtorff examines the language of v. 1 and notes that both the imperatives, "observe justice" and "do righteousness" *(šimrû mišpāṭ* and *ʿăśû ṣĕdāqâ)* "are frequent in other biblical books" (1993b: 184). He asserts this claim without references, merely noting in n. 6 that this is "particularly so in the book of Ezekiel." In fact, however, both expressions are rare.[6] Third Isaiah is not falling back on stock or common expressions, and his use of words is careful, distinctive, and deliberate. Further examination of the verbs and expressions of vv. 1-2 and 3-8 will confirm this.

The focus on "observing/keeping" *(*šmr)* and "doing" *(ʿāśâ)* in v. 1 is continued and amplified in v. 2:

1 Thus says YHWH:
"Keep *(*šmr)* justice and do *(ʿāśâ)* righteousness,
for my salvation is about to come,
and my deliverance is to be revealed.
2 Happy is the person who does *(ʿāśâ)* this,
and the one who *holds it fast,*
the one who keeps *(*šmr)* the Sabbath from *profanation,*
and who keeps *(*šmr)* his hand from doing *(ʿāśâ)* any evil."

As can be seen, *ʿāśâ* and **šmr* are each found twice more in v. 2, where they are supplemented by two additional verbal forms, the Hiphil imperfect of **ḥzq* ("to hold fast") and the Piel infinitive construct of **ḥll* ("to profane"). These four verbs figure prominently throughout vv. 3-8 and forge a strong link to vv. 1-2. Thus the vocabulary and specific expressions found in v. 2 occur in both what precedes and what follows.

In 56:2a, the objects of the verbal actions "doing" and "holding fast" are identified only by pronouns: "this" and "it" are not clearly identified. This "delayed identification" is a rhetorical device (Polan 1986: 62, with n. 35), which serves to bring emphasis to the actions specified in v. 2b,[7] where the "happy" are identified as those who *keep (*šmr)* the Sabbath and who *keep (*šmr)* from doing any evil. Precisely because the identification is delayed, the reader's attention is first and foremost directed to the possible antecedent references, namely, "keeping justice and doing righteousness" (so also Schramm 1995: 119).[8] This reading backward (Whybray 1975: 197) is almost required by using the same verb in v. 2a as in v. 1a: "the one who *does* this" finds a natural referent in the one who *does* righteousness and keeps justice in v. 1. Thus, using the same verbs *(*šmr* and **ʿśh)* in vv. 1 and 2 compels the reader to consider the two verses in light of each other and to broaden the range of meaning. The introduction of two additional verbal forms in v. 2, **ḥzq* (Hiphil: to hold fast) and **ḥll* (to profane), anticipate the same function in what follows: when these verbs appear again with **šmr* (vv. 4 and 6), it is both natural and reasonable to understand them in light of vv. 1-2, as we are about to see.

The lament of the eunuch in v. 3 gets a direct response from YHWH in v. 4, where we find two of the verbs from v. 2: **šmr* (used in reference to the Sabbath) and the Hiphil of **ḥzq,* whose object is specified as "my covenant." This latter expression, "who *holds fast* my covenant," recalls the wording of v. 2: "Happy is the person who *holds it fast*." Because "my covenant" is also feminine singular, it is grammatically possible and conceptually reasonable to understand "the one who holds *it* [fem. sing.] fast" and "the one who holds fast my covenant" as equivalent. Semantically, the vagueness of v. 2a is clarified by v. 2b. Rhetorically, however, delayed identification allows the unspecified expression "holding it fast" in v. 2a, to look backwards to "keeping justice and doing righteousness" (v. 1). At the same time, v. 2a looks forward, both to v. 2b and to v. 4, with its repetition of key vocabulary ("holding fast") and the correspondence of the person/gender of the noun (*bĕrît*/covenant, v. 4) and pronoun (*bāh*/it, v. 2a). Thus, the generalized admonition "do justice and righteousness" finds greater specificity in the description "those who hold fast my covenant"; in short, to "keep justice and do righteousness" is a précis of covenant obligations.

Three remaining features argue that vv. 1-2 and 3-8 are structurally linked. Reading vv. 1-8 together produces a reversal that is difficult to reproduce in translation. The one who "keeps the Sabbath from profanation, and his hand *(yād)* from doing any evil" in v. 2, receives both a "monument *(yād)* and a name" from YHWH in v. 5.[9] This reversal is lost if vv. 1-2 are separated from vv. 3-8.

Second, v. 6 reprises three verbs from v. 2 *(*šmr, *ḥll, *ḥzq)* and repeats verbatim both v. 2bα, "the one who keeps *(*šmr)* the Sabbath from profanation," and v. 4b, "those who hold fast my covenant." This is more than a "catchword" connection; it seems to be a deliberate and purposeful development of ideas contained *in nuce* in vv. 1-2. Finally, the divine speech formally introduced in vv. 1 and 4 ("thus says YHWH") is brought to an equally formal conclusion in v. 8 ("saying of the Lord YHWH").[10] All of this argues that, Westermann's form-critical claims notwithstanding, vv. 1-8 should be considered together.[11]

If we read the passage in this way, three points are significant. First, the reintroduction of the hendiadys *mišpāṭ ûṣĕdāqâ* is a deliberate evocation of past Isaianic concerns. The points Rendtorff made about *ṣĕdāqâ* can be made, by the same token, for *mišpāṭ*. Two factors may account for this renewed interest in *mišpāṭ* as justice. One may well be literary; that is, as Rendtorff suggests, Third Isaiah provides

56:1 as a bridge to the greater Isaiah tradition, forming an explicit connection between antecedent sources and his own work, thus drawing separate traditions into the same interpretive matrix. Polan's analysis also points in the direction of a deliberate literary schema; on the basis of the word pairs he examines, he suggests that "Third Isaiah may be a miniature model of the basic teaching of Isaiah for a new age, the post-exilic community" (1997: 231). The second factor may be social: the historical, social, and geographical situation had changed. The primary threat was no longer the theological incursion of Babylonian religious influences, but the social dislocation, economic insecurity, and religious and political tension that accompanied resettlement. The focus on "justice" as a social reality conforms to the needs and exigencies of the changed situation.

Second, there is an unexpected interest in the covenant. Heretofore in the Isaianic tradition, "covenant theology" has played no role whatsoever (Muilenburg 1956: 405).[12] More specifically, there has been no explicit reference to the Sinaitic covenant and its obligations.[13] While care for the orphan and widow, so prominent in First Isaiah, is part of the covenant tradition, we saw earlier that such concern is so widely diffused through ancient Near Eastern culture that assigning Isaiah's concern specifically to the covenant is unnecessary. By contrast, the explicit references to Sabbath observance and the status of foreigners and eunuchs (Deut 23:2-9 [Eng. 1-8]) suggest that the author has the Mosaic covenant in mind (Westermann 1975: 198; Van Winkle 1997: 238). Westermann is very specific on this point and suggests that the phrase "holding fast my covenant" (56:4, 6) probably refers to "the precepts of my covenant," and that "covenant" in late usage may have the meaning "the law" (1975: 313).

Once reference to the covenant becomes explicit, Eichrodt's point about divergent understandings of the covenant (see note 13) becomes relevant, for in one brief passage, the prophet both affirms the singular importance of the covenant and at the same time supplants some of its provisions. Indeed, controversy over the proper understanding of the covenant moves to center stage in the postexilic period. In whatever way the rival parties in the postexilic period are conceived—eschatologists versus followers of Second Isaiah (Plöger 1968), visionaries versus hierocrats (Hanson), followers of Third Isaiah versus Ezra-Nehemiah (Rofe 1985), Zadokites versus practitioners of an aberrant cult (Schramm), royalists versus priests (see Watts 1987: 198–201)—all would presumably agree on the importance of the covenant. At issue, however, was the interpretation of the covenant and its requirements. One thing seems evident from the passage under discussion: the provisions against foreigners and eunuchs were widely enough understood and disputed as to necessitate a divinely issued prophetic pronouncement to abrogate the old and legitimate a new law (Schramm 1995: 124). That their contested status should require a divine declaration indicates the gravity of the concern and the centrality of the issue.

As suggested above, the backward and forward referencing of the feminine singular pronouns in v. 2a and the strategic repetition of key vocabulary make the command "keep justice and do righteousness" a précis of covenant responsibility.

While this explicit appeal to the covenant may be a new datum in the Isaianic tradition, its formulation is entirely consistent with other witnesses to the covenant tradition, which understand justice and righteousness as characteristic of YHWH's heavenly rule, a mandate for the Davidic king, and an obligation of the people. The general imperative finds its particularization in the specific command addressed to foreigners and eunuchs, namely eunuchs who wish to be included among God's people are to "keep the Sabbath, and choose that in which I delight" (v. 4), while foreigners are "to minister to him, and love the name of YHWH, and become his servants" (v. 6a). Both vv. 4 and 6 conclude with the same expression, "and who hold fast my covenant." Polan suggests that the phrase's placement at the end of the verse serves to emphasize it and to bring to a climax all that precedes it. He supports this literary analysis by a linguistic argument according to which the conjunctive *waw* ("and") is understood as a *waw explicativum*, which allows the phrase to be read as if it were a relative clause: "all who keep the Sabbath, not profaning it, *that is, holding fast my covenant*."[14] Apparently both observant eunuchs and foreigners are then included with all those whom YHWH "will bring to my holy mountain and gladden in my house of prayer" (v. 7).

The imperative verbal forms in 56:1 highlight an essential feature of Third Isaiah's understanding of justice: it is a course of action to be undertaken and enacted. After Second Isaiah's appropriation of justice as a divine attribute that characterizes YHWH's sovereignty, the renewed focus on justice as something enacted by the people signals a change in focus between these two portions of the book of Isaiah. The reason for the need to enact social justice is detailed in the second half of v. 2: "for my salvation is about to come, and my deliverance is about to be revealed." According to Schramm, "Isa. 56:1 expresses the conviction that ethical conduct is determined by eschatological expectation" (1995: 119).[15] This eschatological turn is also in contrast to First Isaiah, for whom justice and righteousness accomplish redemption in history: "Zion shall be redeemed by justice, and her returning ones by righteousness" (1:27). For First Isaiah, the doing of justice is the concretization of salvation; for Third Isaiah, the coming of God's salvation is the motive for enacting justice.

What is unexpected in this decided turn to activism is the nature of the actions that are specified. Leaving aside for the moment the two more generalized and equivalent expressions "to choose that in which I delight and to hold fast my covenant," we are left with these specific actions: to keep the Sabbath, to minister to YHWH, to love his name, and to become his servants. Noticeably absent is any mention of social concern directed toward others. Indeed, all the actions are directed specifically to YHWH in terms that are implicitly cultic. It may be presumed that the social demands of life among YHWH's covenant people are included in "choosing that in which I delight and in holding fast my covenant," but their conspicuous lack of mention is a far cry from Isaiah 1, in which social justice was made the precondition for acceptable cultic service. The closest "keeping justice and doing righteousness" comes to social enactment is found negatively in v. 2bβ, "[happy is] he who keeps his hand from doing any evil" (cf. 1:16b). So while the first verse of Third Isaiah revives the language of First Isaiah and of social justice, its actual articulation is somewhat pale by comparison. However, the trend evident in both First and Second Isaiah to specify the contents of the term "justice" according to the actual needs of the immediate social context is continued. While for First Isaiah the needs of the orphan and widow, the poor and the oppressed were of paramount concern, in this opening section of Third Isaiah the aggrieved groups are eunuchs and foreigners. Their plight is to be addressed both by the actions of the community commanded by YHWH in vv. 4 and 6, and by YHWH's own actions on their behalf, expressed in his intention to bring them to his holy mountain, into his house of prayer and to gather them, as he had gathered the dispersed of Israel (vv. 7-8). Just as 56:1 had incorporated verbal signatures of both First *(mišpāṭ ûṣĕdāqâ)* and Second Isaiah *(yĕšûʿâ ûṣĕdāqâ)*, the rest of the prophecy continues to develop aspects of the antecedent Isaian traditions, namely, First Isaiah's interest in social justice and Second Isaiah's concern for divine sovereignty. Thus the community life of the returnees is to be shaped both by their own enactment of justice in their relationships, and by YHWH's sovereign acts to include among his people those who had been formerly excluded.

To summarize: Third Isaiah begins with a command to enact justice in the social realm. This is specified in terms of the covenant, which highlights the importance of observing the Sabbath. "To do justice and righteousness" is understood as a précis of covenant obligations and is decreed for all who are joined to YHWH; at the same time, participation in the covenant is broadened to include those who had formerly been excluded.[16]

Like his more remote predecessor, Third Isaiah links his concern for justice to an indictment of corrupt civic leaders (56:9-12), whom he characterizes as blind sentinels, mute watchdogs (56:10), and ignorant shepherds (56:11). After criticizing the practice of idolatry in ch. 57, the focus returns to communal behavior and cultic practice in ch. 58.

Lectionary Notes

Common Lectionary: Proper 15 (A): Isa 56:1, 6-8 / Psalm 67 / Matt 15:(10-20), 21-28
Roman Lectionary: 20 (A): Same, except Matt 15:21-28

Those generically described by Third Isaiah as "foreigners" and the "outcasts of Israel" who are considered unfit to offer service on God's holy mountain and in God's house of prayer are described more particularly by Jesus in Matthew's Gospel. The "outcasts of Israel" are represented in the Gospel pericope in the Common Lectionary (but omitted in the Roman Lectionary) by those who have become "unclean" by reason of dietary violations. These are voluntary acts that make one ritually unclean and therefore unfit to join in community worship. Impurity can be corrected by proper rituals of purification and can be avoided altogether by a change of behavior. But Jesus redefines the categories of "clean" and "unclean": what matters more than ritual categories is moral conduct such as murder, adultery, sexual immorality, theft, false witness, and blasphemy (Matt 15:19). Both Isaiah and Jesus attempt to get to the core of what matters. Third Isaiah redefined the essence of "keeping the covenant" not as ethnic origin or physical wholeness but as the command to "observe justice and do righteousness," while Jesus moves from ritual categories to what comes from the heart (vv. 18-19).

Isaiah's "foreigner" is the Gospel's Canaanite woman (in both lectionaries) whom the disciples keep at bay and whom Jesus is at first inclined to ignore. In both readings, those initially excluded from the community are able to find ways of inclusion. Isaiah's outsiders can claim inclusion by keeping the Sabbath and the covenant, and the Canaanite woman finds a hearing by her faith. While the particular means of each is different—the externalized behavior of keeping the Sabbath and covenant, and the expression of faith—the result is the same: outsiders are gathered in. This is the actualization of what the first verse of Isaiah promises: "for my salvation is about to come, and my deliverance is to be revealed." For foreigners and outsiders, salvation/deliverance is experienced as belonging to the community.

This pair of lectionary readings makes a bold proclamation. While both end with the ingathering of outcasts, they are introduced by the same verse that begins the entire collection of Third Isaiah: do justice and righteousness.[17] As a set of lectionary readings, the command to "do justice" comes to a conclusion with inclusion. The inclusion of outsiders was a concern both for the community of Third Isaiah and for the early Christian community that struggled and argued over the admission of Gentiles. These are not merely ancient concerns that can be discussed in the comfort provided by historical distance. The church today continues to struggle with matters of inclusion and exclusion—Who can be ordained? Who can be married? What is more important for membership in the community, right conduct or right belief? The readings contemporize ancient concerns as modern concerns, even as they contextualize the issue of inclusion as an issue of justice and righteousness.

The Justice of God Abandoned: Isaiah 58:1-14

Both the limits of the next unit to be discussed and its overall structure are matters of debate. P. A. Smith argues for considering all of 58:1—59:20 as a unified composition delimited by the inclusion formed by the words **pšʿ* ("rebellion") and "Jacob" in 58:1b and 59:20 (1995: 99–101). For most commentators, however, the unit is confined to ch. 58, and the pressing issue is whether 58:13-14 should be considered as part of 58:1-12. Many find the mention of the Sabbath in vv. 13-14 extraneous to the main theme of fasting. Especially for those commentators who think 56:1-8 forms the opening panel to the framework of Third Isaiah, the recurrence of the Sabbath theme in 58:13-14 is attributed to the same hand as the framework and is taken as evidence of the secondary status of vv. 13-14. However, Polan argues at length that 58:1-14 is a unified text. The chapter is defined by an inclusion of five words found in both vv. 1 and 14, namely, *Jacob*, *day*, *way*, *delight*, and the verb *to do* (**ʿśh;* 1986: 176–85). This inclusion, along with such internal features as microstructures created by the sevenfold repetition of the words *day, fast,* and *YHWH,* and the fivefold repetition of **qrʾ* (to call) and **npš* (self), show that this text is a rhetorical unity. It is an argument we accept.[18] The terms that concern this study are found in v. 2; these terms will be considered in light of the entire unit, which we take to be 58:1-14.

After a stinging indictment of idolatry (57:1-13) and words of consolation (57:14-21), the prophet is commanded in 58:1 to "announce to my people their rebellion *(*pšʿ),* and to the house of Jacob their sin *(*ḥṭʾ).*" Commentators have rightly pointed out the similarity to earlier such prophetic announcements (for example, Hos 8:1; Mic 3:8). What should not be lost sight of, however, is the explicit evocation of Isa 1:2-4, which decries Israel's *rebellion (*pšʿ)* and *sin (*ḥṭʾ).* When 58:2 goes on to talk of *abandoning (*ʿzb)* the ordinance of God, the evocation of the three verbs that were so crucial to establishing the literary unity of Isa 1:2-28 (**pšʿ, *ḥṭʾ, *ʿzb,* 1:2-4, 28) is complete.

After the commission comes the indictment in 58:2. I have divided the verse into three sets of bicola and have provided letters for easier reference to the various units of the verse.

(A) And yet,[19] day by day they seek me,
and to know my ways they delight,
(B) like a nation that has done righteousness *(ṣĕdāqâ),*
and the justice *(mišpāṭ)* of its God it has not abandoned;
(C) they ask of me righteous judgments *(mišpāṭîm),*
in the nearness of God they delight.

For our purposes, the most obvious difficulty comes in deciding the meaning of *mišpāṭ,* which is used twice in this verse. On the one hand, should the first *mišpāṭ* (B) be read with *ṣĕdāqâ* as a hendiadys? Or should it come under the influence of the plural form *mišpāṭîm* (C), which clearly means "ordinances" or "judgments"?[20] This sense would also be supported by the general direction established in section (A): those seeking God and the knowledge of his ways can find their answer in his laws and ordinances. Many translators take the plural form as determinative and so translate even the singular *mišpaṭ ʾĕlōhāy* as "ordinance(s) or law(s) of their God" (for example, NRSV, REB, NAB, NJB, JPS; Westermann 1975, McKenzie 1965). However, I agree with Hanson, Polan, Watts, and others who translate the first occurrence of *mišpāṭ* as "justice." Not only is the immediacy of the hendiadys in section (B) suggestive, but the language of the parallel term, *ṣĕdāqâ ʿāśâ,* explicitly evokes the expression *ʿăśû ṣĕdāqâ* ("do righteousness") in 56:1 and moves the argument toward understanding the first *mišpāṭ* as "justice" (Polan 1986: 194). Further, with Third Isaiah's frequent back-referencing to First and Second Isaiah, the expression "justice of God" evokes remembrance of passages from both previous Isaiahs, namely, "*my justice* will go forth as a light" (51:4), and "YHWH is a *God of justice*" (30:18). The plural form *mišpāṭîm,* as we saw earlier, always refers to statues or ordinances. As suggested above, this accords well with the activities described in section (A): cultic inquiry of God and seeking to know his ways find an appropriate answer in God's righteous ordinances.

We have discussed the cultic meaning of *dāraš* ("to seek") in our treatment of Isa 1:17, where cultic language was applied to the pursuit of justice in the social realm. The same intimate relationship between cult and justice is presumed in 58:2. The relation of parts (A) and (B) explicates the essential connection of cult to the practice of social justice: only the nation that practices righteousness and enacts God's justice has the right to inquire of God and seek his ways. Hanson rightly notes the "exquisite irony" of 58:2: "the accusation that they have abandoned the justice of Yahweh is followed immediately by reference to their cultic activity, 'they ask me for just ordinances.' They have forsaken the *mišpaṭ* of Yahweh ('justice,' in the sense of, for example, Isa 61:8) in their very act of seeking the *mišpāṭîm* of the cult ('ordinances,' in the sense of, for example, Lev 26:46)" (1979: 109). While it is true that v. 2 refers to the cultic seeking of God, I am not convinced that the people are necessarily seeking cultic ordinances, as the parallel term "knowledge of my ways" refers more broadly to right conduct. Still, the tone of irony created by the use of the same word in two senses accords well with the irony discussed by P. A. Smith and Polan with regard to the initial *waw* (and) of this verse.

The prophet's use of irony here is not meant to impugn entirely the cultic and pious acts he describes, all of which seem to be carried out sincerely (Muilenburg 1956: 678). His point, it seems to me, is more nuanced: he argues that religious observance divorced from the practice of social justice is not what God desires. What God desires is discussed in the two cola of section (B), which describe the same reality from different points of view: prescriptively, God's desire is to do righteousness, and proscriptively, it is not to abandon the justice of God. Altogether, the (B) section thus functions both positively and negatively. Positively, it describes in prescriptive and proscriptive terms the conduct of a godly nation; negatively, it implies that Jacob has failed in this regard.

Polan, discussing the structure of 58:2, notes that each of the three parts of the verse ends in a verb. The verbs of the first and third lines are identical (*yeḥpāṣûn*, "they delight"), thus framing and drawing attention to the middle element as the decisive point, namely, the abandoning *(*ʿzb)* of God (Polan 1986: 192). He thus concludes "that the inauthentic seeking and knowing of the divinity is . . . a forsaking of God; though a comparison of this people is made with a just nation that does not forsake its God *(ʾlhyw lʾ ʿzb)*, the point is that when a people claims to seek and know its God and in the end achieves its own pleasures, it strays from its goal, it abandons its God" (1986: 193).

The importance of the verb *yeḥpāṣûn*, however, is not merely structural. All five occurrences of the verbal root **ḥpṣ* in 58:1-14 (vv. 2 [2x], 3, 13 [2x]) point to the people seeking and finding that in which they delight. The problem is not just the incongruity of the people simultaneously fasting and seeking their own pleasure. The use of the verb **ḥpṣ* in 58:2 recalls the language of 56:4, where keeping the covenant is equated with "choosing that in which [YHWH] delights *(*ḥpṣ)*":

YHWH delights in a people who keep his covenant. The use of the same verb thus pits "that in which YHWH delights" against "that in which the people delight." Two points are significant. First, the fact that the people have chosen to pursue their own delights rather than choosing that in which YHWH delights is an implicit indictment that they have abandoned the covenant.[21] In effect, in abandoning the justice of their God (58:2), they have abandoned the covenant. This supports the interpretation above that doing justice and righteousness is a précis of covenant responsibility. Second, while eunuchs and foreigners are striving to be joined to the Lord by holding fast to the covenant and choosing that in which YHWH delights (56:1-8), YHWH's own people ("my people," 58:1) have pursued their own delights. Those who would rule on the admissibility of eunuchs and foreigners into the covenant community themselves fail to meet the minimum requirements.

This charge that Jacob has abandoned the justice of his God is at first explicated obliquely in the discussion of what constitutes true fasting (see Barré 1985: 94–97). Though the people have an apparently active cultic life (v. 2) and augment acts of public piety with the private practice of fasting and asceticism, they nonetheless feel neglected by God (58:3a). Implied in their lament is the question, "What more does God want of us?" YHWH responds, first by pointing out the incongruity of self-deprivation accompanied by self-seeking (58:3ba). In this way, the issue of fasting is the entrée to the larger discussion of the relation of religious observance to social conduct. This is accomplished as YHWH cites three actions that involve others negatively: oppression of workers, strife/contention, and striking (others) with a wicked fist (vv. 3bβ-4a). The violence and strife implied in these verses is deplorable and scandalizing in the covenant community. Though a fast be undertaken with such acts of mortification as humbling oneself, bowing low one's head, and lying on sackcloth and ashes (v. 5), it is unacceptable to the Lord if accompanied by neglect or oppression of others.

YHWH now goes on to describe in positive terms what acceptable fasting involves.

> 6 Is not this the fast that I choose:
> to loosen fetters of wickedness,
> to unfasten the thongs of the yoke,
> to set free the oppressed?
> But every yoke you shall shatter.[22]
> 7 Is it not to break your bread for the hungry?
> But the wandering poor you shall bring into [your] house.
> When you see the naked, you shall cover him,
> and from your own kin you shall not hide yourself.

Similar sentiments are expressed in vv. 9a-10a. In both cases, the language is so compelling that the social life of the reemergent community becomes transparent. In seeking their own pleasure and walking in their own ways, they leave the poor hungry, naked, and homeless; some of them are either oppressed and exploited, or ignored and avoided. As 58:9 further specifies, there is oppression, perhaps even slavery ("the yoke"?), false accusation ("pointing the finger"), and malicious speech. Whatever political, religious, or sectarian rivalries lie behind and give rise to these conditions, the scandalizing fact of unaddressed poverty, oppression, and slanderous strife compels the prophet to bring to explicit attention the expectation of justice, which was presumed in 58:2. The initial imperatives of 56:1, left unspecified, find here a concrete program directed to the poor, the hungry, the homeless, and those unjustly bound. Attention to the plight of these people naturally turns one's gaze from selfish preoccupation: concern for others is, as it were, to fast from seeking one's own delights. Such compassionate concern for the needs of people in miserable circumstances is an eloquent enactment of the justice of God (58:2). It is not possible to "abandon the justice of God" and at the same time seek "seek me and delight to know my ways" (58:2). Instead, to seek the Lord (58:2a) is to find him in the needy members of the community and among one's own kin. When the "justice of God" is articulated in social acts of compassion, cultic acts become productive and the ways of God become manifest. Then, the voice they wished to have heard on high because of their fasting (58:4) will be heard: "then you shall call and YHWH will answer; you shall cry for help and will say, 'Here I am'" (58:9).

This passage, both in vocabulary and content, revives the prophetic concern for justice that found so passionate and articulate a spokesman in Isaiah of Jerusalem. While the theme was introduced in 56:1 and linked to covenant observance, it was not there developed substantively. But now it emerges as a palpable concern. The social context for this emergent interest is significant: matters of social and religious concern not only move to center stage but are drawn together into an inseparable relationship. Just as the returnees to Jerusalem are eager to reestablish their national cultic observance and give fervent expression to their devotional life, the prophetic voice arises to denounce any attempt to identify religious life with cultic life to the neglect of the covenant obligation to care for the poor and needy. From YHWH's point of view, "my ways" (58:2) are at odds with "your ways" (58:13), just as "that in which I delight" (56:4) is opposed to "that in which you delight" (58:13). However, when the conditions set forth in 58:6-7, 9b-10a are met, then the ways that Israel sought to know (58:2) will have YHWH as their perpetual guide (58:11). The disastrous course set out in 58:2, delighting in public religious acts while in fact pursuing one's own delight, finds its corrective in justice enacted compassionately on behalf of others. Refraining from following one's own ways and seeking one's own delights (58:13) make it possible truly to honor the Sabbath, the Lord's holy day (58:13-14). Scullion summarizes that "God's pleasure" is the performance of *mišpāṭ* and *ṣĕdāqâ,* which is authenticated by a combination of true justice and true religious observance (1990: 163). From the prophetic point of view, it is not a choice between cult and justice; it is a matter of cult validated by justice, and justice grounded in worship (see also Hanson 1995: 206).

Lectionary Notes

Common Lectionary: Epiphany 5 (A): Isa 58:1-9a / Psalm 112 / Matt 5:13-20
Roman Lectionary: 5 (A): Isa 58:7-10 / Psalm 112 / Matt 5:13-16

The verse dealing with the words for justice (Isa 58:2) is omitted in the Roman Lectionary. The Common Lectionary's inclusion of "the justice of its God" thereby specifies that the actions described in these verses are acts of justice. The Roman Lectionary's shorter reading, however, adds vv. 9b-10, which reiterate that proper social conduct is the shining of light in darkness—the major theme evident in the Gospel.

The reading from Matthew is a continuation of the Beatitudes and likens the effects of discipleship to the effects of salt and light, metaphors that go undeveloped in the shorter Roman reading. The Common Lectionary attempts to explain the meaning of being salt and light by extending the Gospel reading to include Jesus' command to fulfill the requirements of the law. But this, too, remains generic. When the Gospel is read in conjunction with Isaiah 58, however, the metaphors of light and salt are concretized and particularized by the specific actions Third Isaiah describes. The link between readings is explicit: the light that disciples are called to become is the light Isaiah identifies as right social conduct.

While the passage from Isaiah adds specificity to the Gospel, the Gospel adds scope to the reading from Isaiah, and this in two ways. First, all the second and third-person references in Isaiah are singular, while the forms in the Gospel are plural. It is both individual Christians and the entire church community that must be salt and light. The second point has to do with the end or telos of such conduct. In Isaiah, the actions of righting injustice, feeding the hungry, housing the homeless, and clothing the naked (Isa 58:6-7) are evidence of conversion, which will move God to act on Israel's behalf: "Then you will call and YHWH will answer, you will call for help and he will say, 'Here I am'" (58:9a). These acts are directed to getting God's attention for themselves (58:3). In the Gospel, disciples are called to be light *for the world* and salt *for the earth.* The light that shines is not a spotlight on the church's goodness: it does not call attention to itself for itself. Discipleship is undertaken not so much for individual salvation as for the building of God's kingdom on earth. As Matt 5:16 makes explicit, disciples make their light shine so that others may glorify God. Taken together, the readings provide both the how and the why of the church's mission: acts of social justice lead people to the praise and worship of God.

Injustice Everywhere: Isaiah 59:1-20

The unity of ch. 59, with the exception of v. 21, is widely accepted. For ease in dealing with the text, we will accept the common threefold division, vv. 1-8, 9-15a, 15b-20.

Scullion, who analyzes the structure according to the three-part division just outlined, points to the importance of *mišpāṭ* as a linking device between sections. Section 1, which details the nature of the community's sinfulness, ends with the observation that "there is no [*mišpāṭ*] in their paths"; section 1 begins with v. 9 observing that "[*mišpāṭ*] is far from us." Thus, *mišpāṭ* "clamps" the indictment of sin (section 1) to the confession of sin (section 2). Similarly, section 2 ends by noting that "[*mišpāṭ*] has been driven back" (v. 14); section 3 opens with YHWH decrying the fact that "there is no [*mišpāṭ*]"(v. 15), a lack that moves YHWH to intervene personally. Thus, here again, *mišpāṭ* "clamps" confession of sin to divine response (Scullion 1990: 168). In addition to the thematic, social, and theological significance of the term to be examined below, *mišpāṭ* plays an important role in the literary and structural understanding of the chapter as a whole.

1. Corruption in the Courts: Isaiah 59:1-8. Chapter 59 begins with two significant back-references. First, the people's lament that YHWH's hand is too short to save (59:1a) takes up their lament in 58:3a, in which they complain that God has ignored their fasting and their penitential acts; the result of this divine neglect is evidenced by their continued oppression. Second, 59:1 looks even further back, to YHWH's refutation of the accusation in 50:2 that his hand is too short to redeem. From the people's point of view, the issue in all these laments is divine powerlessness; from the divine and prophetic points of view, however, the issue is human sinfulness that preempts divine response to their plight. The point could not be more clearly made than in 59:2: it is not divine powerlessness, "but rather your iniquities are a barrier between you and your God, and your sins have hidden the Face from hearing you." Verses 3-8 specify those charges in terms that are both general (iniquities and sins, vv. 2, 3) and specific (violent deeds, vv. 3a, 6b, 7; lying speech, vv. 3b, 4b; mischief-making thoughts, vv. 4c, 5, 6a, 7b), as well as literal and metaphorical (for example, the vipers' eggs and spider's web of vv. 5-6). Sometimes it is not entirely clear whether the language refers to specific crimes or is employed to paint generic images of wrongdoing. For example, the indictment of 59:3, "Your hands have become polluted with blood," surely recalls 1:15, where the allegation referred to real crimes, later detailed as assassination and murder (1:21). But Westermann is correct in pointing out that the added colon in 59:3aβ, "and your fingers with iniquity," gives the impression of being a literary artifice, something taken from tradition, devoid of "any trace of a specific allegation" (1975: 346). The same is true in 59:3b of the generic, and psalmic, accusation that "your lips speak deceit (cf. Pss 109:2; 120:2), your tongue mutters mischief (cf. Job 27:4)."[23] It is possible to see actual deeds in these charges, though the literary conventions employed suggest more a climate of wrongdoing than a catalogue of specifics.

Verse 4 points to unjust legal practice; while this is clear in v. 4a, it is less certain in v. 4b, though Muilenburg thinks all the terms in v. 4 should be interpreted forensically (1956: 688). The unusual use of *qārāʾ* ("to call") in the somewhat elliptical expression "no one calls out righteously" (*ʾên-qōrēʾ bĕṣedeq,* v. 4aα) is frequently compared to Job 5:1; 9:16; and 13:22; all three texts are employed to suggest the legal sense of *ʾên-qōrēʾ* (Whybray 1975: 221; Westermann 1975: 346). Though the context of Job 9:16 uses the language of the court (9:15, *ʾim-ṣādaqtî,* "though I am innocent," and *mĕšōpṭî,* "the one who judges me"), those passages are more properly prayer petitions than legal proceedings.[24] The expression in Isa 59:4aα takes on its specifically legal nuance from the parallel phrase, "and no one goes to court honestly" (*wĕ'ên nišpāṭ be'ĕmûnâ,* v. 4aβ), and is thus rendered better as "No one enters suit justly" (Westermann), "No one pronounces suit righteously" (Polan), or "No one pleads justly" (McKenzie). Polan sees a causal relationship between v. 4aα and v. 4aβ: "since no one pronounces suit righteously, the result is that no one is judged honestly" (1986: 264). He goes on to see a progression from the "pronouncement" to "being judged," with the unrighteous suit culminating in a dishonest judgment. While this is plausible in terms of content and progression of thought, there is no syntactical indication for such an interpretation. Further, the argument relies on the thinnest of linguistic evidence to infer two separate stages to the legal proceeding—the "pronouncing" of the suit and the "being judged." Bovati understands *qārā'* here to mean "to take legal proceedings against someone," that is, in the same generic sense as *nišpāṭ* (1994: 315, n. 136). It seems more reasonable to understand the two parts of v. 4a as parallel rather than either progressive or related by cause and effect.

Polan points to the parallel use of *ṣedeq* with the Niphal of the verb *šāpaṭ* in 59:4 as a variation on the word pair we have been treating as a hendiadys (1986: 249, n. 8). As such, v. 4 makes explicit the legal perversion of social justice. The remainder of v. 4, if one follows Muilenburg in continuing the legal setting, would presumably refer to perjury and false testimony (*wĕdabber-šāw',* "telling lies"),[25] and collusion and conspiracy (*hārô ʿāmāl wĕhôlêd 'āwen,* "conceiving mischief, bringing forth iniquity"). The assessment, "no one enters suits justly" (*'ên nišpāṭ),* in 59:4 culminates in v. 8 with the summary judgment, "there is no justice" *('ên mišpāṭ).* The two are obviously related—lack of proper judgment in the courts results in a lack of justice in society.

What comes between vv. 4 and 8, however, is vague to the point of obscurity. Not only is the wickedness implied in 59:2-4 now described metaphorically, but even the metaphors fail to function properly. As Whybray notes, the metaphors of adders' eggs and spider's web in v. 5 "are presumably both intended to illustrate the deliberate, planned wickedness mentioned in verse 4, though only the first in fact is developed along those lines" (1975: 221). Commenting on the phrase in v. 6, "their webs will not serve as clothing," he remarks, "this verse entirely fails to develop the reference to the spider in verse 5, whose web is intended to ensnare the righteous" (1975: 222). Muilenburg seems daunted by these images and lets v. 6 pass with only a quote from Kissane, "the profits arising from injustice are as unsubstantial as a spider's web" (Muilenburg 1956: 698). Hanson, following Westermann, is more generous than Whybray and braver than Muilenburg. He focuses not so much on the problem of the metaphors but on their intended effect: "verses 5 and 6 develop metaphors intended for shock effect more than descriptive accuracy" (1995: 210). Westermann avers that "precise interpretation of the various parts in this description is scarcely possible or worthwhile. They are not intended to indicate specific characteristics of the transgressors, but with as great a variety of words and phrases as possible to give a picture of their flagrant wickedness" (1975:

348). Hanson, however, disagrees with Westermann in arguing that the metaphors are not merely rhetorical but in fact point to the concrete situation of the community. Taking vv. 1-8 as a whole, Hanson notes that "reference to lying, wickedness, shedding innocent blood, and running to do evil are not empty generalities. They describe the disintegration of social order as people embrace deceit and brutality to promote their own power and wealth at the expense of others" (1995: 210).

Watts, too, seeks to bring greater specificity to the somewhat vague language of 59:3-8. Situating this passage in the time of Xerxes' wars with Athens (c. 481–479 B.C.E.), Watts suggests that Palestine and its concerns were neglected by their Persian overlords, and thus the land degenerated into a state of social chaos: "no legitimate government, therefore no peace, justice, or protection from violence" (1987: 281). He takes the references to roads and highways in vv. 7-8 literally and sees in the "desolation and destruction on their highways" (v. 7b) a reference to highway robbery and banditry, thus posing a threat to pilgrims who would travel to Zion for worship and bring their trade with them. Lack of safety sets in motion a disastrous turn of events: "No travel means no trade. No trade in Jerusalem means economic depression and poverty. This is the natural result of crime" (1987: 283).[26] Kendall, too, seeks to find specifics in the generalized descriptions and proposes that the references to blood in vv. 3 and 7, taken together in the legal context established by v. 4, refer to the unjust use of the death penalty (1984: 395).

All these observations are plausible, but the situation must be inferred and reconstructed from the vague references in the text. The overall impression of chaos and the pervasive climate of wickedness are clear, but the particulars are only suggested in the broadest of terms. The most concrete items listed are the miscarriage of justice in 59:4 and the shedding of innocent blood in v. 7, though even there the particulars are not to be found. Apart from these references, allusions are made to lying lips (v. 3), deeds of iniquity and the work of violence (v. 6b), feet running to do evil, thoughts of iniquity, and devastation and destruction in the highways (v. 7). Conspicuously absent are the particulars of First Isaiah: the graphic descriptions of immoral real estate acquisition ("joining house to house, and field to field," 5:8ff.), the mind-numbing cataloguing of extravagant luxury items obtained at the expense of the poor (3:16—4:1), the debauched lifestyle of the ruling class told with a surfeit of realism ("priest and prophet stagger with strong drink . . . every table is covered with filthy vomit," 28:7-13), the exploitation and despoiling of the poor ("the plunder of the poor is in your houses," 3:13-15), the acquittal of the wicked for a bribe (5:23), the enacting of unjust laws (10:1). In their place, Third Isaiah describes vipers' eggs and a spider's web.

Despite the lack of specifics, the result of the general wickedness is abundantly clear. This is rhetorically reinforced by the use of the negative particle of existence, *ʾên* ("there is not"), used 8 times in ch. 59 (vv. 4 [2x], 8, 10, 11, 15, 16 [2x]), 3 times with *mišpāṭ* (vv. 8, 11, and 15) and once with the Niphal of the verb *šāpaṭ* (v. 4). One thing is abundantly clear: there is no justice. The utter lack of justice is simultaneously the cause and the result of the social chaos and the pervasive and abhorrent wickedness described in 59:1-8. Because there is no justice, people do not know the way of peace and all their ways are crooked (v. 8). Even the legal system, charged specifically with the maintenance and administration of justice, is corrupt. In short, a just social order has broken down completely.

2. Justice Has Been Driven Back: Isaiah 59:9-15a. The third-person description of the state of the community—"there is no justice in their paths"—moves directly into a first-person plural acknowledgment of that description (59:9):

> Therefore, justice *(mišpāṭ)* is far from us,
> and righteousness *(ṣĕdāqâ)* does not reach us.
> We wait for light, but here is darkness;
> for brightness, [but] we walk in gloom.

The focus on prevailing social conditions is announced by the use of the hendiadys in v. 9 and by its reappearance at the conclusion of this section (59:14):

> Justice *(mišpāṭ)* has been driven back,
> and righteousness *(ṣĕdāqâ)* stands afar off.

The intervening verses speak of the deterioration of the social life of the community and the appalling lack of justice.

The cause of the present state of affairs is clearly indicated by the introductory "therefore" (*ʿal-kēn,* v. 9) and is further suggested by the repetition of key terms from v. 4, **špṭ* and *ṣĕdāqâ*. Indeed, according to Polan (1986: 275–76), taking these two verses together establishes a cause-effect relationship: "the consequence of unrighteous pronouncements and dishonest judgments [59:4] results in the absence of justice and righteousness [59:9]." In turn, these terms also recall 56:1 in a particular way. With buoyant optimism, 56:1 had linked the doing of *justice* and *righteousness* with the advent of *salvation* and *deliverance.* The essential link between justice and salvation now comes to light negatively: because justice and righteousness are far from us (*rāḥaq . . . mimmennû,* 59:9), so too salvation is far from us (*lîšûʿâ rāḥăqâ mimmennû,* 59:11).

Society without social justice is a society in darkness, images poetically developed in 59:9b-10. This assessment is reinforced semantically: both the vocabulary and the syntactic structure of "we wait for the light" (*nĕqawweh lāʾôr,* v. 9b) are parallel with "we wait for *mišpāṭ*" (*nĕqawweh lammišpāṭ,* v. 11a). Implied in the expectant waiting is the notion that the arrival of the one is tantamount to the arrival of the other, that is, *mišpāṭ is* light.[27] The darkness described is not a relative darkness or even a temporary, transitional darkness, such as twilight or dusk. It is compared to the darkness experienced by the blind and those who have no eyes (v. 10a). For those without eyes, even the noonday sun is perceived as darkness (v. 10b), and those who seek to walk in darkness can do no better than stumble. Such is the lack of justice in society. The darkness of injustice is absolute.

Verse 11a, like vv. 5-6, draws on animal imagery to make its point: the dire straits of the community have reduced them to growling like bears and moaning like doves. While the exact references of these images is debatable, the situation to which they are addressed is clear: "We waited *lammišpāṭ,* but there is none; for salvation—it is far from us" (v. 11b).

There is a grammatical concern to be addressed in 59:11b, one that is universally overlooked. The MT points the object of the first verb as definite, *lammišpāṭ*, which makes the common translation "we wait for justice" difficult. Careful study of the form shows that when a trial or judgment is in view, the definite *lammišpāṭ* is preferred, while the indefinite *(lĕmmišpāṭ)* is preferred for the general exercise of justice. In no instance is the definite used in the abstract sense "justice." In Isa 59:11b, then, the people are not merely describing their situation, "there is no justice"; they are continuing their complaint that God has not yet acted—"We waited *for judgment,* but there is none; for salvation—it is far from us."[28]

The verb used and the structure of the sentence recall an earlier verse in the Isaianic tradition that is also instructive on this point, as the grammar itself signals what is proper to both the divine and human realms. In 5:7, YHWH looks for (social) justice *(wayqaw lĕmišpāṭ),*[29] but finds only bloodshed. Social justice, by definition, is something that only people can enact, and so YHWH expects *justice* from his people. On the other hand, judgment is proper to God as divine judge and cosmic sovereign, and so the people look to God for *judgment.* The same verb (**qwh*) used with both the definite and indefinite forms of the noun makes the comparison appropriate and the argument more reliable.

Understanding the definite singular of *mišpāṭ* in 59:11 as *judgment* keeps the two nouns of v. 11b parallel in the sense that both *judgment* and *salvation* have their origin in God. Otherwise, the restoration of social justice would be identified with God's salvation rather than a prerequisite for it (56:1). In the mind of those crying out, then, the judgment they are awaiting is the punishment of their enemies, the inverse of which is their own salvation. Their enemies, however, seem not to be external, but fellow citizens whose sins, described in vv. 1-8, have resulted in economic hardship, legal oppression, and religious exclusion for those speaking in vv. 9-15a. The reason that God has not acted with judgment against their oppressors or brought salvation to the speakers of these verses is indicated by the connecting particle of v. 12, *kî*, "*because* our rebellions are many before you." This is exactly the same sentiment expressed earlier in 59:1-2: YHWH doesn't act to save because of their iniquity and sins. Their sins are confessed now in v. 13:

> Rebelling against and denying YHWH,
> turning back from following our God.
> Speaking oppression and revolt,
> conceiving and considering from the heart deceitful words.

Commentators (for example, Muilenburg, Westermann, Scullion, Whybray) are fond of noting that the sins of v. 13a are directed against God, while those of v. 13b are sins against humans or sins that are displayed in society. Such an assessment seems to me more schematic than analytical. Examination of the terms produces less agreement about the precise nature of the sins in v. 13a and reveals less certainty about what is involved in v. 13b. For example, of the first group of terms, sins directed against YHWH, Muilenburg is quite certain that they refer not to apostasy or idolatry, but to the sins referred to in chs. 58-59 (1956: 693), which, it may be noted, are mostly "social sins"; this seems to blur the very distinction Muilenburg was attempting to make. Westermann on the other hand asserts that the sins against God are, indeed, apostasy and unfaithfulness (1975: 349; Whybray 1975: 225). While Muilenburg and Westermann do not agree on the precise nature of the sins—vagueness seems endemic to this entire section—they are agreed that the sins are directed against God. Their assessment is confirmed by the language the prophet uses in v. 13a: "rebelling against, and denying *YHWH,* turning back from following *our God.*"

The sin of rebellion (**pšʿ;* cf. 1:2) dominates 59:12-13 (3x), and in its first appearance indicates that "our rebellion is *before you*" (59:12). Though these verses also indicate a profound awareness on the part of the people of their own sinfulness ("our sins testify *against us,* for our rebellion is *with us,* and our iniquities—*we know them,*" v. 12), the one most effected by this sin is God. This sets up a direct correlation between sins *against* God and the delay of salvation *from* God (v. 11b).

The situation in v. 13b is less clear: "Speaking oppression and revolt, conceiving and considering from the heart deceitful words." All the actions in v. 13b are verbal.[30] In discussing "revolt" *(*srh),* Whybray cites Deut 19:16 as an example of revolt, not such as is directed against God, but revolt in the sense of wrongdoing, that is, the "abandonment of honest behaviour" (1975: 224). As it turns out, Deut 19:16 is the only instance of the word's 9 occurrences in which it is used in this generalized sense. When the term is used with the verb "to say or speak" *(*dbr)* (3 other times: Deut 13:6; Jer 28:16; 29:32), the object is always specified as "against YHWH" (*ʿal-YHWH,* Deut 13:6 and Jer 29:32; or *ʾel-YHWH,* Jer 28:16). In two other instances (Isa 1:5; 31:6) the term **srh* is used to mean specifically revolt against YHWH. It seems then that the one on the receiving end of this "speaking revolt" is YHWH. If it is argued that the activity of speaking revolt takes place in a social setting, we may counter that it is unclear whether these are words publicly spoken or are words that, "conceived and considered in the heart," remain in the heart and thus known only to God. Deceitful words *(dibrê-šāqer)* may refer to the perjury and dishonesty in court alluded to in v. 4, but it is not entirely clear.[31] In any event, the *impact* of the sins confessed is considered primarily in religious rather than social terms, and the focus is on confession directed to YHWH rather than on repentance manifested in corrective behavior (cf. 1:16b-17). The *consequence* of the sin is announced in v. 14: *justice is turned back and righteousness stands afar off.* That sin affects the entire salvific plan of God is suggested by the strategic use of the root **rḥq* ("to be far off, at a distance") 3 times in 59:9-14, applied to each of the key terms: standing off at a distance from this sinful community are *justice* (v. 9), *salvation* (v. 11), and *righteousness* (v. 14). Neither the benefits of a just social order nor the blessings that come from God are to be found near at hand.

Overall, it seems that the confession of 59:12-13 is far less immediate and specific than the indictment of vv. 1-8. If the speakers of vv. 9-15a are also those describing conditions in vv. 1-8 (Hanson), we must marvel at their astuteness about the faults of others and their relative vagueness about their own. Significantly, however, the assessment that the sins of others (vv. 1-8) have resulted in the absence of justice and righteousness (v. 9) is also true of their own sins. Because of their sins, confessed in vv. 12-13, the result is that *justice has been driven back, and righteousness stands afar off* (v. 14). In terms of the resultant state of affairs, the sins of both groups produce the same results: *there is no justice* (vv. 8, 15b).

If this analysis is moving in the right direction—the social sins of vv. 1-8 compared to the generally religious sins of vv. 12-13—we are left with a remarkable correlation, one already adumbrated in 56:1. Social and religious responsibilities are not only correlative, they are inseparable: failure in either results in social disintegration and spiritual estrangement. As the use of the terms "sins and iniquities" in both 59:2 and 12 suggests, failure in either social or religious obligations is not merely a matter of neglect or irresponsibility but of sin. Further, right social conduct and true piety ("true fasting," to use an earlier image) are the conditions that alone can realize the advent of God with salvation. This is the significance of 56:1, which linked social life so closely to the religious obligations of the covenant, and made both prerequisite to YHWH's salvation and deliverance.

3. No Justice: Isaiah 59:15b-20. The opening verse in the final section of this chapter reads:

> And YHWH saw, and it was evil in his eyes,
> for there was no justice. (59:15b)

The entire situation described in 59:1-15a comes under divine scrutiny ("YHWH saw") and assessment ("it was evil in his eyes"), and the whole sorry situation is summarized succinctly: "there was no justice" *(ʾên mišpāṭ)*. This divine assessment represents both a confirmation of the prophetic indictment (v. 8) and a broadening of the scope of sin: not only is there no justice *in their paths*, there is *no justice at all.*

Whybray suggests that *mišpāṭ* is used here "in a quite general sense of a properly ordered community life" (1975: 226; so also Scullion 1982: 168). Westermann, too, takes the term broadly, as "well-being" (1975: 350). These understandings, taken in the context described in vv. 1-15a, are adequate, though the language is somewhat colorless to describe a society hatching poisonous and deadly vipers' eggs, and spinning ensnaring spiders' webs, a community in which the blood of the innocent is being shed and the courts are corrupt. To hear the statement "There is no justice" is to envision a society not merely lacking proper order, but a society in chaos that has lost its moorings and has been cut adrift.

Society's dire lack is further detailed in 59:16a and linked to the foregoing by the repetition of the particle *ʾên*:

> He saw that there was *no one (ʾên),*
> and he was appalled that there was *no one (ʾên)* to intervene.

This poignant summary of the changed situation confronting Third Isaiah's community compared to the exilic situation of Second Isaiah evokes a specific passage from that earlier prophet. The divine optimism that pervaded Second Isaiah found confident expression in the two-word announcement, *hēn ʿabdî* (42:1), "Here is my servant." His mission was to inaugurate not only Israel's restoration, but YHWH's worldwide sovereignty. Now, as YHWH sadly notes, *ʾên ʾîš* (59:16), "There is no one." "Here is my servant!" yields to "There is no one." With the death of the Servant, there is no one to carry forth YHWH's work. While the Servant (42:1; 49:3) may have been replaced by the servants (54:17; 56:6; 63:17; 65:8, 9, 13, 15; 66:14),[32] the lack of a specific individual to lead the struggling community is a grievous deficiency. Such a lack of leadership is one more indication of the chaotic state of society: there is no leader, there is no justice. The fearsome prophecy of Isa 3:1-12 has come to pass. Consequently, as many have noted, "Conditions are so appalling that a divine intervention is necessary; the situation is beyond merely human remedy" (McKenzie 1978: 172).[33]

Thus, the lack of justice is what precipitates a divine intervention. Much has been written on the arrival of YHWH as the Divine Warrior and the reappearance of the vocabulary and perspectives of the Israelite tribal league, the use of the "arm of God" motif, the innovative use of metaphorical battle gear, and the relationship of 59:15b-20 to 63:1-6.[34] This is material that need not be rehearsed here. I will make just three further observations with regard to the theme of justice.

First, it may be recalled that 56:1 demanded *justice* and *righteousness* because God's *salvation* and *deliverance* were about to come. In this way, a just social order and the blessings of divine deliverance were yoked together. Though the latter were not explicitly made contingent on the former, their interconnection was implied. That connection seems to have been severed. Social decay has rotted out the very foundations of justice and righteousness, and the restoration of society can be accomplished only by divine intervention. The lack of justice and righteousness is what moves God to act. On the one hand, he comes "to repay them according to their deeds—wrath to his adversaries, and recompense to his enemies" (v. 18a); on the other hand, he comes "to Zion [as] a Redeemer, to those in Jacob who turn away from rebellion" (v. 20). Hanson's identification of the "salvation-judgment oracle" finds a textbook exemplar in the verses just quoted. God's coming in warlike fury will accomplish both ends, revealing that judgment and salvation are concomitant realities.

Second, the personal intervention of the deity on behalf of justice is the single most potent indicator of the importance of justice. Lyrical poetic and powerful prophetic language frequently extols justice; but the surpassing value of justice finds unparalleled validation in the conviction that God is so passionately committed to justice that he intervenes personally on its behalf. The intervention of the Divine Warrior on behalf of his people in the cause of justice places justice in the same category as that other great divine intervention, the deliverance from Egypt, but with a significant difference: whereas the exodus was realized in historical time, the divine war for the restoration of justice is only anticipated. As Westermann says, "Trito-Isaiah finds himself unable to point in advance to a definite historical event, the divine advent is now considerably more dissociated from history" (1975: 357).

Finally, looking back over the course of the book, we have seen that in preexilic Israel, while justice was expected of all, it was particularly the king's responsibility. With the end of the monarchy and the new situation of exile, God raised up a Servant as his ambassador of justice whose mission, tragically and ironically, was cut short by an act of injustice. In the postexilic community, riven by intramural conflict and beset by social chaos, it is YHWH himself who must arise to defend justice. The transfer of agency testifies, on the one hand, to the changing circumstances of the community over time and, on the other hand, to the unchanging importance of justice as a defining element of a people whom God has chosen.

YHWH Loves Justice: Isaiah 61:4-11

With ch. 61, we come to that part of Third Isaiah which many commentators are agreed constitutes the core of the tradition, namely chs. 60–62.[35] In turn, they are agreed that 61:1-3 is an introductory strophe to the entire poem (61:1-11), which describes the ministry of the herald of good news; many further link this prophet to the Servant designated in Second Isaiah.[36] The task to which he is appointed is both spiritual and practical. On the one hand, he is to announce good news to the poor, to bind the brokenhearted, to comfort the sorrowful; on the other hand, he is to proclaim freedom to captives and release to prisoners. The former activities are closely associated with a preaching ministry, or more broadly a ministry of the word; the latter activities have been interpreted both literally (for example, redressing the situation described in 58:6) and metaphorically, "referring generally to the state of frustration in which the community finds itself" (Whybray 1975: 241). As many commentators have pointed out, the language of "proclaiming liberty to captives" is language from the Year of Jubilee (Leviticus 25), in which case the mission of the prophet, while obviously affecting the lives of prisoners and captives, is directed more to the fulfillment of religious law. Yet even Jubilee language is used metaphorically "for the release from the problems of the exile."[37]

The good news the prophet is to announce is further detailed in vv. 4-7 in language that is typical of Third Isaiah's love for the reversal of fortune;[38] thus are the ruins repaired (61:5), and dishonor and shame are replaced by a double portion and joy (61:7). Between these material and existential reversals are listed changes in domestic and international standings: all Israelites are envisioned as priests and ministers (61:6; cf. Exod 19:6), while foreigners will become their domestic help, laboring as farmers and vinedressers (61:5).

Verses 8-9 shift to divine speech, a move Beuken (1989) understands as a divine validation of the prophet's preaching. As such, all that precedes—"salvation" and "deliverance" concretely described in hopeful images of restoration, revival of dimmed spirits, release of prisoners—finds its source in YHWH:

> For I, YHWH, love justice,
>   I hate robbery with iniquity;[39]
> and I shall give their recompense faithfully,
>   and an everlasting covenant I shall make with them. (61:8)

As YHWH sees it, restoration/recompense is a matter both of justice and of faithfulness—justice, in that debts paid are thereby canceled; faithfulness, in that YHWH is true to the terms of the covenant, which requires both punishment and blessing as appropriate. Whybray, explaining that YHWH is unwilling to allow a situation of injustice, robbery, and wrongdoing to continue, interprets the situation politically rather than socially, "that is, the denial to them by their foreign rulers of independence and self-respect" (1975: 244). In Scullion's view, YHWH's love is for "due order," that is, a properly ordered domestic situation (1990: 179). This understanding has the advantage of relating the passage to the more immediate social context described in chs. 58–59. That situation, according to Watts, suffers from "robbery by injustice, that is, depriving anyone of his goods or money by unjust judicial action" (1987: 304).

The antithetical relationship established by the two participles in 61:8 ("YHWH who loves/hates") serves to illuminate the objects of the verbs in terms of one another: the opposite of *justice* is *robbery* and *iniquity.* "Justice" here clearly refers to proper, ethical conduct in the social realm. YHWH's love for justice as practiced in society is also manifest in his restoring Israel (61:1-7) and in faithfully recompensing the people. Thus the divine and human components of justice come together: justice is manifest in a society free from violence, wrong, and corruption (v. 8), and in a country whose ancient ruins are rebuilt and whose ruined cities are repaired (v. 4). Justice, then, is both a state of social relationships marked by ethical conduct and social structures that support community life. More than something that YHWH merely desires, this kind of justice is what he loves.

As was the case in 56:1-8, the passage under discussion, 61:8, links justice to observance of the covenant. The one remaining mention of covenant in Third Isaiah was in 59:21, where covenant seems to be used as a metaphor for conditions that are abiding, namely, that YHWH's words and Spirit will endure through all generations. Scullion thinks that 59:21, which most commentators agree is not part of what precedes, serves in fact as an introduction to chaps. 60ff. (1990: 168–69), and that YHWH's covenant is the restoration that is described therein. The phrase in 61:8, "everlasting covenant," picks up 55:3, which had affirmed that the blessings promised to David continue in effect even though the monarchy has come to an end. In 61:8, the covenant is (re)established with the people by a God who is identified specifically as one who loves justice and hates wrongdoing. By the terms of the covenant, this justice-loving God will *faithfully give recompense* (61:8) to the people according to their conduct, that is, punishment for evildoers, blessing for the righteous (cf. 59:18-20).

This passage, 61:4-11, marks the last appearance of the term *mišpāṭ* in the book of Isaiah. Whether by accident or by design, 61:8 is a felicitous summation of the book of Isaiah's perspective on God and justice. Justice as a thematic concern has been prominent throughout the three sections of the book. The divine self-identification, *I am YHWH,* is particularly evocative of Second Isaiah's affirmation of divine sovereignty. The double-sided nature of the asseveration in 61:8, loving justice but hating iniquity, aptly addresses both Third Isaiah's lamentable social situation and the required corrective action. It is altogether appropriate that the term *mišpāṭ* be last spoken by God, who imparts to the virtue of justice perhaps its highest validation: "I, YHWH, love justice."

Lectionary Notes

Common Lectionary: Advent 3 (B): Isa 61:1-4, 8-11 / Psalm 126 / John 1:6-8, 19-28
Roman Lectionary: Advent 3 (B): Isa 61:1-2a, 10-11 / [Luke 1] / John 1:6-8, 19-28

The readings from Isaiah and John are chosen for their seasonal significance more than for their correlation to one another. In all three lectionary cycles, the Second and Third Sundays of Advent focus on John the Baptist. The first readings generally, as in this case, are interpreted as prophecies of the coming of Christ. Thus, Isaiah's Spirit-anointed figure is the Gospel's "one who is coming after me whose sandal strap I am not worthy to untie." This christological appropriation of the Isaian text is made explicit when Jesus quotes this passage at the opening of his public ministry in Luke 4:18-19.

However, it is possible to read today's Isaian prophecy as descriptive of John's ministry to "bring good news" (Isa 61:1), a theme reinforced in the Gospel's description of John as a "voice crying out." If taken in this way, the closing doxology (Isa 61:10-11) can be read in John's voice as a hymn of praise for God's saving deeds. If read in the voice of Jesus, it is a hymn describing what God accomplished through him.

The Roman Lectionary's shorter reading from Isaiah once again omits the verse that deals with the term for "justice" (61:8). (The translation of Isaiah 61:11 in the NAB reads "the Lord GOD [will] make *justice* and praise spring up before all the nations"; the word translated as "justice" is *ṣĕdāqâ*, that is, "righteousness.") The Common Lectionary's reading of Isa 61:3-4, 8-9 recounts God's promise to comfort Zion, recompense people, execute covenant fidelity, and bless their descendants. This, in turn, leads to the prophet's praise of God in vv. 10-11. These deeds of compassion are to be historical manifestations of divine justice (v. 8), in the same way that the ministry of Jesus will reveal the power and presence of God in history. Reading this passage during Advent, the church sees the promises of God realized in Christ.

This is the last passage from our treatment of Isaiah that appears in the lectionary. It is appropriate to close with some general observations. It has been evident that the interpretation of these Isaian passages has been influenced by factors entirely extrinsic to their composition and redaction. At times, the liturgical season has been the decisive interpretive factor, especially in the season of Advent and during Passiontide. At other times, explicit dialogue between the Isaian passage and the Gospel has resulted either in an amplification and elucidation of the Gospel, or in a redirection of the Isaian passage. In either case, setting biblical passages in a liturgical context opens interpretive possibilities not available in either historical-critical or canonical-literary approaches. This has the salutary effect of relativizing the claims of one methodology over another, and of reclaiming the very reason these texts have been preserved and studied so assiduously for so long—they are texts of believing communities who see in them something of God's intentions and acts on humanity's behalf. On the other hand, liturgical interpretation is best undertaken with sensitivity to and awareness of historical and canonical concerns. Liturgical interpretation is not license to ignore the hard work of critical exegesis. But neither do critical methods exert hegemony over the meaning and significance of the text. Ideally, methods that are potential rivals can contribute clarity, depth, and breadth to one another. Finally, liturgical interpretation moves beyond the purely descriptive and expository tasks of academic and scholarly interpretation by relating the texts to the lives of believers and proclaiming what the text means, not to original authors, redactors, or canonizers, but to *us*. This move from the hermeneutical to the homiletical is expressly eschewed by the academy but is the raison d'être of liturgical proclamation.

A Bloody Final Judgment: Isaiah 66:6-16

Some not unfamiliar problems affect analysis of ch. 66: Is it an integral composition? And what is its structure? Assessments, as usual, run the gamut from taking the entire chapter as a unit, to seeing it as a compilation of fragments presented as a summary of Third Isaiah, just as ch. 1 served as an introduction to the entire book. In between these outer limits, commentators have seen two, three, and five independent units, some of which are further divided into as many as seven strophes.[40] Since nothing even approaching a consensus is available, we will proceed with a purely descriptive approach.

The opening verses contest, first, the place of worship (66:1-2) and then the nature of acceptable worship (vv. 3-4). In vv. 5-6, God visits upon the people the same attitude they have displayed toward him in worship—disregard. Verses 7-9, using images of birthing, describe YHWH's miraculous and instantaneous re-creation of Zion. This gives rise to rejoicing (v. 10) and provident provision for the needs of her citizens (vv. 11-14). Verse 14 marks the transition from blessing for God's people to punishment for his enemies, a judgment that is described in incendiary and theophanic imagery in 66:15-16. This study's interest is the verbal form **špṭ* in v. 16:

> For with fire YHWH will execute judgment *(nišpāṭ),*
>   and with his sword on all flesh,
> and the slain of YHWH will be many.

Perhaps sensing the unusual use of the Niphal here, 1QIsa[a] has instead the Qal infinitive, *lšpwṭ*. The Niphal, encountered twice already in Isaiah, usually has the sense of reciprocity, that is, entering into judgment together, as in 43:26 and 59:4.[41] The combative aspect of entering into trial is augmented and amplified in 61:6-16 by traditional imagery taken from the more terrifying aspects of theophany (fire, storm-wind, flames) and from warfare (chariots, sword, the slain). These are combined to create a fearsome image of God coming in judgment. Destroying judgment is the inverse of the prosperity described in vv. 11-14a, again typifying the salvation-judgment prophecy that has come to prominence in Third Isaiah.

If, as most commentators believe, 66:17-24 is part of a redactional framework, the body of Third Isaiah proper comes to a close with an image of God exercising judgment against *all flesh*, that is, YHWH's judgment is universal. In the context of the book as a whole, with ch. 1 serving as the introduction, ch. 2 opens with all peoples streaming to Zion where God judges (**špṭ*, 2:4) between kingdoms and imposes terms on many peoples. The more irenic hopes of ch. 2 seem to have been tarnished by the harsh reality of history, and peaceful judgment has been replaced by terrible punishment. What these disparate images both presume, however, is YHWH's role and right as universal judge. The book is thus enclosed by images of YHWH judging the nations; between these scenes of worldwide judgment are spelled out the requirements and expectations of justice as a way of life for Israel and the world.

Conclusions about *Mišpāṭ*/Justice in Third Isaiah

The distribution of the term *mišpāṭ* and the verb *šāpaṭ*, along with their occurrence with either *ṣĕdāqâ* or *ʾên* in Isaiah 56–66, can be plotted in chart form as follows:

Passage	*mišpāṭ*	**Verb** *šāpaṭ*	**Hendiadys**
56:1-8	*mišpāṭ*, v. 1		yes
58:1-14	*mišpāṭ*, v. 2 *mišpāṭîm*, v. 2		yes (with *ṣedeq*)
59:1-8		*ʾên nišpāṭ*, v. 4	yes
	ʾên mišpāṭ, v. 8		
59:9-15a	*mišpāṭ*, v. 9		yes
	mišpāṭ wāʾên, v. 11		
	mišpāṭ, v. 14		yes
59:15b-20	*ʾên mišpāṭ*, v. 15b		
61:4-11	*mišpāṭ*, v. 8		
66:6-16		*nišpāṭ*, v. 16	
Total	9	2	5

The focus in Third Isaiah shifts back to where it was in the first section of the book of Isaiah, that is, to a consideration of justice as it is enacted in the social realm. This is signaled positively by the reintroduction of the hendiadys *mišpāṭ ûṣĕdāqâ* five times, and negatively by the indictment for social sins, culminating in the oft-repeated summary, "There is no justice." Despite the more optimistic longings and hopes found in chs. 60–62, this sad assessment describes the de facto situation of the community struggling with all the hardships of resettlement, competing interests, and sectarian conflicts.

The importance of the theme of social justice is suggested by its prominent placement as the opening verse of Third Isaiah, by its presentation as divine speech, and by its grammatical form as the object of the opening imperatives. While 56:1 serves an important literary function as both a link to the antecedent Isaiah traditions and as an introduction to the concerns of Third Isaiah, it also indicates the changed historical and social setting of the prophet's community. The theological deployment of the theme of justice by Second Isaiah yields to the more pressing social conditions of a community beset by strife, conflict, and injustice. The very form of the divine imperatives makes it clear that justice is to be understood as the course of action undertaken by those who choose to do that in which YHWH delights (56:1-8).

Though Third Isaiah revives the language of social justice that had characterized First Isaiah, he does so with a different understanding. From the outset, justice is considered in light of the covenant and its obligations, particularly the observance of the Sabbath (56:3-8; 58:13-14; 59:21). The opening imperatives to act with justice are immediately set within the context of the covenant and are given their first test case in the perplexing issue "Who can belong to the covenant community?" Third Isaiah's rebuttal of Deuteronomistic positions makes it clear that while proper interpretation of the covenant is in dispute, the covenant itself is of prime importance. The centrality of the covenant is underscored by the fact that a divine prophecy is required to resolve the issue. That resolution comes, not in terms of ethnic origin or physical wholeness, but in terms of observance of the Sabbath and holding fast the conditions of the covenant. The prominence given to the covenant in these opening verses invites a consideration of all that follows in its light. Indeed, the divine command to maintain justice and to do righteousness emerges as a précis of covenant responsibilities. This is new in the Isaianic tradition.

Like his eighth-century counterpart, Third Isaiah inveighs against corruption of the courts (59:4 and perhaps v. 14; cf. 5:23; 10:1-2); neglect of the poor, the hungry, and the homeless (58:6-7, 9-10a; cf. 1:17; 3:14-15); violence (59:3, 7; cf. 1:21; 5:7); deceit, dishonesty, and perjury (59:3, 4; cf. 28:15; 32:7); he also decries corrupt civic leaders (56:9-12; cf. 1:2ff.; 3:13-14), whom he characterizes as blind sentinels, mute watchdogs (56:10), and ignorant shepherds (56:11). The lack of leadership is part of the problem of social chaos, which afflicts the community: in YHWH's own assessment, "There is no one . . . no one to intervene" (59:16; cf. 3:1-8).

This catalogue of social wrongdoing is counterbalanced by some rather generic language for wickedness that succeeds very well in communicating the climate of pervasive and shocking evil, but which leaves the present-day reader with a sense of bewildered curiosity: What are we to make of poisonous vipers' eggs and worthless spiders' webs (59:5-6)? What is the evil to which feet are eagerly running (59:7)? What exactly is the lying speech, deceitful lips, and mischief-making thoughts that are rebuked so frequently (57:4; 59:3, 4, 7, 13; 63:18)? While the language for sin is almost encyclopedic (for example, 59:12-13), the specifics are somewhat lacking in clarity. Compared to the vivid descriptions of First Isaiah, the details in Third Isaiah are shapeless and murky.

In ch. 59, offenses that are primarily social (vv. 1-8) and those that are of a more religious nature (vv. 12-13) are both considered under the same rubric of *sin* and *iniquity* (**ḥṭ*ʾ and **ʿwn*, vv. 2, 12), making the failure to fulfill social and religious obligations a matter not merely of neglect, but of sin. Significantly, sin, whether considered as a transgression against God (59:9-15a) or as immoral conduct in society (59:1-8), results in the same religious estrangement and social disintegration: justice is far from us, and righteousness does not overtake us (59:9; cf. v. 14). Because *justice* and *righteousness* are the harbingers of *deliverance* and *salvation* (56:1), it stands to reason that such widespread social and religious sin results in *justice, salvation,* and *righteousness* all being *far from (*rḥq)* the community (59:9, 11, 14, respectively).

The symbiosis between religious practice and social responsibility lies behind Third Isaiah's attacks on unacceptable cultic practices and expressions of personal piety. It is not that worship and sacrifice in the temple, or acts of fasting and asceticism, are worthless. They are simply incredible and pointless when undertaken to the neglect of moral conduct in social relationships. It is not possible simultaneously to choose both that in which "you" delight (58:3b) and that in which "God" delights (56:4), or to fast while indulging greed and self-serving behavior to the neglect of the poor (58:3-10). Cultic practices cannot substitute for moral behavior; cultic practices and moral conduct must be practiced in tandem.

God's valuation of the importance of justice is indicated both negatively and positively. The fact that "there is no justice" (59:15b) moves YHWH to take up, as of old, his battle gear and to intervene as the Divine Warrior in defense of justice (59:16b-20). Positively, YHWH, in his own voice, affirms the importance of justice in language that is as poignant as it is telling: "I, YHWH, love justice" (61:8). The justice that YHWH loves is one that is to be manifest both in ethical relationships in society ("I hate robbery with wrongdoing," 61:8), and in structures that support the life of the community—hence his desire to restore the ruins, repair the cities, appoint foreigners as domestic help, and provide for the needs of his people (61:4-11).

Finally, God's defense of justice means simultaneously salvation for his people and judgment for their enemies (for example, 59:11). Such judgment is meted out by YHWH exercising twin roles—that of Divine Warrior and Cosmic Judge. It is with an image of YHWH as an awesome and fearful judge that Third Isaiah ends his writings (66:6-16). What reads at face value as a frightful and terrible image of God is, from the point of view of those suffering oppression, violence, and injustice, a majestic tableau of God doing what is necessary to uphold the moral structure of reality, handing out wrath and requital to his enemies but redemption to those who turn to him (cf. 59:18-20), bringing prosperity to his servants but his indignation against his enemies (61:14). God, the universal judge, YHWH, who loves justice, holds in his hands both judgment and salvation. Just as this section of Isaiah opens with a promise of deliverance and salvation for those who observe justice and do righteousness (56:1), it closes with fiery judgment against all who have disregarded those basic imperatives of social and religious life in the community of YHWH.

chapter 6

Justice in Diachronic and Synchronic Perspectives

The goals of this chapter are twofold. First, I will draw together the findings of the previous three chapters dealing with the book of Isaiah in its various parts. Because each of the chapters has its own rather complete summary, it will not be necessary to repeat those findings in detail here. Instead, we will examine these with reference to one another, offering points of comparison and contrast. Second, I will look at how the vocabulary and the theme of justice function in the book as a whole.

Diachronic Perspectives

Because of the importance of the hendiadys *mišpāṭ ûṣĕdāqâ*, it is fitting to begin this review of the diachronic aspects of justice in the book of Isaiah with a review of its use.

The Use of the Hendiadys *mišpāṭ ûṣĕdāqâ* and the Concern for Justice

The evidence gathered throughout this study is suggestive. Where the concern for social justice is predominant, the hendiadys is very much in evidence, that is, in First and Third Isaiah; conversely, where social justice concerns have receded, that is, in Second Isaiah, the hendiadys is entirely absent. However, it is not enough to identify the use of the hendiadys in both First and Third Isaiah as indicative of an equivalent concern for justice enacted in the social realm, for both in content and in context, the expression is employed somewhat differently in the two sections.

1. The Content. In First Isaiah, justice in the social realm is associated with the widely dispersed cultural pattern of concern for the orphan, the widow, and the poor. On their behalf, Isaiah of Jerusalem upbraids the negligence of the rich, the arrogance of the powerful, the greed of the merchants and the propertied class. In Israel, no less than in Mesopotamia or Egypt, the king is expected to defend the rights of the underclasses and to uphold justice. The material content of "justice" in First Isaiah, though perhaps not its underlying theological motivation,[1] is similar to that found throughout the ancient Near East.

In Third Isaiah, the doing of social justice is explicitly linked to the covenant (56:1-8), imparting a particularly Israelite nuance to the imperative of justice. Indeed, the performance of justice results in YHWH's establishing an "everlasting covenant" with the people (61:1-11). By this stage in Israel's history, the covenant tradition is firmly established and, as Third Isaiah, Jeremiah, Ezekiel, Ezra, and Nehemiah all attest, is the basis on which both judgment and restoration are determined.

In both First and Third Isaiah, the performance of justice is associated with cultic observance. In First Isaiah, the use of the cultic technical term "to seek" *(dāraš)* is applied to the pursuit of justice (1:17), underscoring the symbiotic—not antagonistic—relationship between cult and justice. In Third Isaiah, the relationship between cult and justice is expressed more explicitly, as even eunuchs and foreigners who perform justice and observe the covenant are permitted to participate in the offering of sacrifices and to serve as ministers of YHWH (56:6-8). The symbiosis between justice and cult is further explicated in the use of "fasting" as a metaphor for justice performed on behalf of the poor, the oppressed, and the unjustly bound (58:6, 9-10; cf. also 61:1-11).

2. The Context. In First Isaiah, justice is associated primarily with the responsibilities of the ruling classes and with the obligations of wealthy to care for the plight of the poor and vulnerable. The task of "doing justice" is to set aright the social order by responsible governance on the part of the king and the ruling class, and by just social intercourse on the part of the citizenry. The context is expressly political, economic, and legal.

In Third Isaiah, the concern for social justice (*mišpāṭ ûṣĕdāqâ,* 56:1) is also present, but, as discussed above, it is present with a difference. A certain despair over the possibility of a just social order has set in. The seeming impossibility of reestablishing justice is articulated in God's outraged assessment that there is no one to do justice, there is no one to intervene (59:16). In such circumstances, the only one who can set aright the wrongs that afflict society is God. This expectation for a divinely established justice reorients the mandate for the community to do justice more toward the coming of God's salvation and deliverance (56:1) than toward the righting of society as a good and a goal in itself.

Although notable differences are discernible in the use of the hendiadys, its very appearance in the opening and close of the book serves to establish connections between the sections of the book that deal with the people's life in the land of Judah. Its placement in the opening and closing sections of the book also functions like bookends that bracket the distinctive notion of justice in Second Isaiah, that is, justice as an expression of divine sovereignty.

There is one final observation to make about the placement of the hendiadys. Though the hendiadys is found only in First and Third Isaiah, not all the passages in which it occurs in First Isaiah are attributable to that eighth-century prophet. There are three occurrences that this study accepts as later compositions (32:1, 16; 33:5) and two others that are held by other scholars to be later (1:27; 5:16). Some of these verses are dated to the Josianic redaction, others to the postexilic period. What is significant and curious is that even these later compositions are placed in that part of the book of Isaiah that presents—even if only fictively—the eighth-century prophet at work in Judah. The reason for this is not entirely clear. It could be that the nuance of the expression either is tied integrally to the placement of the people in their national homeland or is associated with the historical circumstances of a bygone age. Alternately, it may due to the literary structuring of the book that segregates the two different word pairs in their respective sections of the book, *mišpāṭ ûṣĕdāqâ* in Isaiah 1–39 and *yĕšûʿâ ûṣĕdāqâ* in Isaiah 40–55. For whatever reason, there seems to be more than chance at work in the distribution of the hendiadys that refers to social justice.

We are now ready to turn our attention more broadly to the use of *mišpāṭ* in the three sections of the book of Isaiah.

First Isaiah

In First Isaiah, justice is identified in classic terms: "Cease to do evil! Learn to do good! Seek justice, set aright the ruthless. Do justice for the orphan, argue the case of the widow" (1:16b-17). Similar concerns are reflected in Amos, Hosea, and Micah, and the criteria for just conduct are spelled out in the covenant stipulations of the Pentateuch (for example, Exod 22:22-23 [Eng. 21-22]; Deut 10:18; 24:17-21; 27:19). First Isaiah's understanding of justice embraces social justice (as expressed in the hendiadys *mišpāṭ ûṣĕdāqâ*), right judicial conduct, proper governance, and upright social intercourse. Virtually everyone is either admonished to do, or condemned for not doing, justice: princes (1:23), elders (3:14) and leaders (1:10; 10:2), the Davidic heir (9:1-6 [Eng. 2-7]; 11:1-9; 16:5), and the people at large (1:21-28; 5:1-7). The wealthy in particular are upbraided for their dispossessing the poor of their land (5:8ff). YHWH is the Judge (2:2-5; 33:22) who will bring right judgment (28:17), that is, salvation to the righteous (1:27) and punishment to the wicked (1:28). The king is the particular guarantor of justice. Because of the failure of the king to effect justice in the social realm, the prophet looks forward to an ideal king who will rule in justice and righteousness; because of the people's failure to right the wrongs of the oppressed, the divine Judge will arise to impose the sentence of exile upon the entire nation.

Second Isaiah

In the exilic setting of Second Isaiah, the demands of justice and the possibilities for its execution are changed. The people are captives; what kind of justice can they hope for? The king, the guarantor of justice, is under house arrest and is as powerless as the God of Israel must appear to be to both captors and captives (for example, 40:27-31; 50:2). Who will execute justice on their behalf?

1. Justice in Babylon. In Second Isaiah, the language of social justice is muted. There is no reference to orphans, widows, or the poor; even the hendiadys for "social justice," *mišpāṭ ûṣĕdāqâ,* is absent. Rather than attacking social ills, the prophet confronts his captors' idols. The threat to Yahwistic faith is palpable in that land whose gods have humbled the house of David and destroyed the house of YHWH. The prophet must persuade a crushed people that their God is not powerless to save.

The arena he chooses is that of the courtroom, where YHWH is exalted but the gods of Babylon are excoriated. In that legal setting, the term *mišpāṭ* is often used in its forensic sense to refer to the legal process, the presenting of a case, and the verdict. In the courtroom, we witness a theological and rhetorical tour de force as YHWH makes the case for his sovereignty. Through relentless questioning and incisive argumentation, YHWH's power and majesty are developed, particularly in the themes of creation and redemption. In the process, the theme of justice is developed in two distinctive ways.

a. Justice Is YHWH's

In Second Isaiah, YHWH's unique relationship to justice is asserted in two ways. First, the prophet is adamant that no one has taught YHWH the "path of justice" (40:14): from the time of creation, YHWH alone directs the "path of justice." Second, justice is appropriated by YHWH as "my justice" (51:4). "My justice," along with "my righteousness/deliverance" (46:13; 49:6; 51:5; 51:6; 51:8) and "my salvation" (46:13; 51:5; 51:6; 51:8), are offered as evidence of YHWH's incomparability. Throughout Second Isaiah, the self-asseveration speeches of YHWH are to be understood as rebuttals to the similar speeches of the Babylonian gods. Together with the refrains "I am YHWH" (42:6; 43:3, 15; 44:24; 48:17) and "there is no god besides me" (for example, 42:8; 43:11; 45:6, 18), terms like "my justice," "my salvation," "my glory" (42:8), "my praise" (43:25), and "my [victorious] hand/arm" (41:10; 43:13; 48:13; 51:5, 16), function as avowals of his sovereignty.

Because of the changed social circumstances and the expressly theological context, the problem of "injustice" has distinctly different implications. Because First Isaiah had situated justice in the matrix of royal and social responsibilities, the failure to uphold justice resulted in national judgment: the people are exiled and the house of David is thoroughly abased. In Second Isaiah, however, because justice is situated in a vastly expanded religious and cosmological context, the lack of justice does more than damage social and national order: it compromises the very sovereignty of God. It is not enough, however, to defend the sovereignty of God in the Divine Council or to haul the gods of Babylon into court. If the sovereignty of God is not demonstrated in history, it is moot. Hence, the fate of the nation emerges as a critical concern. As long as the people suffer exile and national homelessness, the sovereignty and power of God are threatened. To defend divine sovereignty, the prophet takes up the issues of salvation (YHWH freeing the people from captivity) and redemption (restoring the people to their land). Thus, for Second Isaiah, justice is more than a matter of social policy, national life, or personal conduct; justice attests to the power and credibility of YHWH as Creator and Savior, indeed, as God. Justice in Second Isaiah is considered more in its cosmic and theological aspects than in its social manifestations; in short, justice is related to the theological issues of incomparability and sovereignty rather than internal social concerns. The restoration of a national homeland and the establishment of a just social order are the historical manifestations of YHWH's power: YHWH alone, and no other, can accomplish these things.

b. The Agents of Justice

In Judah, justice was demanded of all and executed by the king; in Babylon, justice is YHWH's and is executed exclusively by him or by his Servant. With the king held captive and the people powerless, justice must find its champion elsewhere. YHWH himself (40:14; 41:1-5; 43:26-28; 51:1-8; 54:17), or YHWH through his surrogate, the Servant (42:1-4), arises to establish justice. This narrowing of the agency of justice is a response to the changed social situation brought about by the defeat of Judah, the exile of the people, and the functional demise of the monarchy.

Interestingly, as the agency of justice is constricted, its audience is widened: the Servant is to bring his message and ministry to the "coastlands" (42:4; 49:1; 51:5) and the "ends of the earth" (40:28; 45:22; 52:10). This, too, is in keeping with YHWH's sovereignty. Just as it is "too light" a thing for the Servant to be a messenger merely to the "tribes of Jacob" (49:6), it is not enough for YHWH to be God of Israel only: YHWH's sovereignty is universal (51:5; 41:5; 42:10-12, 22; 52:10). YHWH will rule the nations, *his* justice (54:1) will be their light, and the Servant will be his ambassador (42:1ff.; 49:1ff.). In Second Isaiah, justice has its origin in YHWH, and all functions of justice are centralized in God and God's Servant.

Third Isaiah

Once back in the land of Judah, Third Isaiah must deal with concerns similar to those addressed by First Isaiah. This is signaled in the first verse, as the hendiadys for "social justice" makes its reappearance. But there is a difference: social justice is now explicitly tied to the observance of the covenant (56:1-8) and made the basis for the coming of divine deliverance (56:1). Justice in the social realm has implications for more than merely political stability, social harmony, and economic parity: justice is the precondition for God's coming deliverance and salvation. By linking divine salvation to the human performance of justice, the theological and historical realms intersect and the religious and social aspects of justice are brought together. The indissolubility of this link is accomplished most effectively by using the religious image of "fasting" to describe the enactment of social reforms to relieve the poor and the oppressed (58:3-14).

First Isaiah's concern for social justice and Second Isaiah's for the universal religious significance of justice are brought together by Third Isaiah with a sense of urgency.[2] Injustice disrupts the social order and threatens the divine promise of salvation. It is clear that injustice cannot be allowed to stand. But in the absence of a king, and after the failure of the Servant's mission (52:13—53:12), who will establish justice? There is no human agent to be found (59:16; 63:5). So YHWH himself takes up the cause. Now, as of old, he appears as the Divine Warrior breathing vengeance against wrongdoers, oppressors (59:15b-20), and Israel's foreign enemies (for example, Edom, ch. 63). Because the Divine Warrior must give battle to a different kind of enemy—injustice—he requires new armament: a breastplate of righteousness, a helmet of salvation, garments of vengeance, and a mantle of fury (59:17; 63:5). The battle is fierce and bloody (63:1-6), and the prophet concludes the book with an image of YHWH executing judgment (66:16) and leaving the heaped corpses of the slain as carrion for the undying worms and fuel for the unquenchable fire (66:24). Thus, justice in Third Isaiah is similar to First Isaiah in that it is primarily social justice; but the lack of justice is so pervasive and debilitating that no merely human agent can restore it (59:16; 63:5). Building on Second Isaiah's image of YHWH as cosmic sovereign, Third Isaiah recapitulates YHWH's role as the Divine Warrior to be the champion of justice and in so doing moves justice toward a more apocalyptic realization. In battling the forces of injustice, nothing short of divine intervention will establish justice.

Prior to that final, apocalyptic intervention, however, the work of justice is not abandoned entirely: an unnamed individual is anointed to effect release from oppression (61:1ff.). The text tells us little about his work beyond this one passage, though his ministry seems to be taken up by those whom he revives by his healing word (61:3b-6). Though the task is overwhelming and God alone can guarantee the final triumph of justice, God's people are called nevertheless to liberate the captive, heal the brokenhearted, and comfort all who mourn (61:3b-6).

To oversimplify the trajectory, we can summarize: First Isaiah deals with justice primarily in its social aspects, that is, political, legal, economic, societal justice; Second Isaiah treats it from the theological vantage point of divine sovereignty; Third Isaiah links the theological and social aspects in such a way as to enjoin the doing of justice as an obligation of the covenant, but with an expectation that justice can be fully realized only by a divine intervention.

Synchronic Perspectives

Two aspects of the synchronic consideration of the use of *mišpāṭ* in the book of Isaiah have already been discussed in the introduction of this study. There we pointed out (1) the frequency of its occurrence: twenty-two times in First Isaiah, eleven times in Second Isaiah, and nine times in Third Isaiah; forms from the root **špṭ* occur another fifteen times throughout; and (2) how the term and its root verb were located at key literary junctures: the theme of justice or the act of judging is prominently placed in the editorial framework, chs. 1 and 66, as well as at the opening of each division: 2:2-5; 40:12-31; 56:1-8. We will now pursue these issues in greater detail.

YHWH as Judge

Setting aside for the moment Isaiah 1, which serves as an introduction to the entire "vision of Isaiah," the body of the book opens with YHWH judging *(*špṭ)* the nations that stream to Zion (2:2-4), and closes with YHWH judging *(*špṭ)* the nations with fire and sword (66:15-16). The optimism of the irenic vision in 2:2-4 presents judgment primarily from the beneficiaries' point of view: Zion is exalted, the nations are instructed, and weapons of war are converted to peacetime use. The implications of YHWH's judging between nations and peoples (2:4), that is, that some find favorable judgment while others do not, are not spelled out. The book's final act of divine judgment, however, explicates the two sides of judgment: the redeemed, both Israelite and foreigner, will serve YHWH (66:18-21) and enjoy the new heavens and earth (66:22-23); but those who have rebelled (**pšʿ*, 66:24; cf. 1:2) will suffer unending punishment. The book is thus framed by magisterial scenes of YHWH as the divine and universal Judge. As such, the image of YHWH as judge of all the nations reinforces the theological aspect of divine sovereignty that comes to prominence in Isaiah 40–55, and casts into sharp relief those passages in which YHWH brings either Israel or the foreign nations and their gods to trial. YHWH as the ultimate and final arbiter of justice, the one whose right it is to "judge between nations and render judgment for many peoples" (2:4), is thus the majestic figure under whose shadow the entire book is read and under whose rule history itself unfolds. Though the message of the book is oriented to the final exaltation of Zion, Zion's chief resident is its sovereign Lord, YHWH of Hosts. The exaltation and sovereignty of YHWH on both the domestic and the international scenes, as well as on both the historical and the cosmic planes, are the implied and indispensable corollaries to Zion's exaltation. It is thus fitting that the book open and close with scenes of YHWH as divine cosmic Judge.

What is implicit in the use of judicial language in 2:2-4 and 66:1-16 comes to explicit articulation in 33:22, virtually at the very center of the book:[3]

> For YHWH is our judge, YHWH is our lawgiver;
> YHWH is our king: he will save us.

While our interest is in the assertion that YHWH is "judge," the text's interest is revealed in the threefold asyndetic repetition of the divine name, which rivets the reader's attention on the centrality of Israel's God: YHWH alone is the supreme ruler in whom resides all the offices of authority. The use of the pronoun in emphatic position reinforces the intensive focus on YHWH and directs our attention to what he who has supreme authority will do—*he* will save us. The implication of the verse is that authority and rule are directed toward salvation. This single verse thus interlocks three central concerns of the book: proper judging *(*špṭ)*, divine sovereignty *(*mlk)*, and salvation *(*yšʿ)*. At the physical center of the book, the role of YHWH as judge is once again lifted up. His authority is comprehensive, and the proper telos of such authority is explicated—salvation.

The controlling image of YHWH as judge finds its way even into the opening oracle of the introduction in Isaiah 1. After the superscription, the first words of the book are spoken by YHWH. They are a summons to heaven and earth (1:2a) to stand as witness or arbiter to YHWH's dispute against his people (Bovati 1994: 81, 90 with n. 70; 339–40); the complaint is immediately voiced (v. 2b) and then elaborated (vv. 3-4). It is helpful at this point to recall von Waldow's observation that in prophetic legal speeches, even when YHWH appears as accuser or plaintiff, he is always also the judge (von Waldow 1968: 270ff. with notes, and 280ff.). Thus, the presentation of YHWH as sovereign Judge giving voice to his judicial complaint *(rîb)* at the opening of Isaiah 1 is, whether unintentionally or purposefully, perfectly appropriate both to the theme and to the literary structure of the canonical book. What begins as a judicial complaint against his people (1:2ff.) will broaden over the course of the book into a contest against the foreign nations and their gods, the ends of the earth, the cosmological enemies Rahab and Leviathan, and the entire created order: the rebellion (**pšʿ*, 1:2; 66:24) of which Israel is accused and punished will not be tolerated from any quarter, and YHWH's undisputed rule *(*špṭ)* will be definitively established.

The structural and thematic interest of the book of Isaiah in YHWH as judge reinforces this study's focus on the term *mišpāṭ* and its importance to the overall interpretation of the book, a matter to which we now turn.

The Relationship of *Mišpāṭ* to the Major Concerns of the Book

The synchronic importance of *mišpāṭ* can easily be appreciated by considering how it intersects with many of the major themes, concepts, terms, and characters of the book of Isaiah. As the above discussion of YHWH as judge indicates, the relationship between YHWH and *mišpāṭ* is a key concern and provides an appropriate starting point for the next portion of this examination.

1. YHWH and Justice. YHWH's role as judge, strategically placed at the beginning, middle, and end of the book, lifts into prominence his relationship to justice. YHWH's connection to justice pervades the book and is presented from different perspectives. While the various perspectives cannot be considered in isolation from one another, it will be helpful to organize this discussion according to various points of view evident in the text. For the sake of ease in discussion, we will examine YHWH's relationship to justice from human, theological, and divine perspectives.

a. YHWH and Justice from the Human Perspective

The sovereignty of God, argued at length particularly in chs. 40–55, is implied throughout the book by the oft-repeated divine epithet "YHWH of Hosts" (54 times). Itself a title that exalts YHWH, it is surprisingly amplified in a way directly relevant to this study:

> YHWH of Hosts is exalted by justice,
> and the Holy God is sanctified by righteousness. (5:16)

As the presence of the broken hendiadys and the literary context of this passage (5:8-24) make clear, this verse asserts that YHWH is exalted and sanctified in social justice. It is no surprise that YHWH expects the people to act with justice (5:7; cf. also 1:21-28), or that YHWH requires just dealings in society. It would seem enough to say that God finds it acceptable (for example, 56:7; 58:5; 60:7) or is satisfied (for example, 56:4; 62:4) when obligations are fulfilled and divine expectations are met. But this verse asserts more: that YHWH is *exalted* and *sanctified* by acts of social justice. These verbal actions are more at home in the cultic sphere. When one considers the various cultic rites, sacrificial offerings, acts of piety, and hymns of praise available as possible expressions for the praise and exaltation of the deity, the almost pedestrian enactment of justice is surely somewhat startling.

Yet the implication is that acts of social justice have the same effect as hymns and sacrifices of praise. In this way, this verse obliquely reinforces the close ties between authentic worship and social obligations (for example, 1:10-20; 56:1-8; 58:1-14) and likens the performance of social justice to cultic acts that exalt and honor God as holy.

In 5:16, thus, the salutary effect of justice is to exalt YHWH (see also 33:5). As we have seen, the exaltation of God is central to Isaiah 40–55, which repeatedly asserts YHWH's incomparability to the gods of Babylon: the God who had no need to be counseled in the ways of justice (40:14) is exalted and sanctified, that is, set apart from, any presumed rivals by the establishment of justice. Just as YHWH establishes his sovereignty by justice in the divine assembly (40:12-31), 5:16 suggests that his people advance the divine cause of sovereignty by the enactment of justice in the social realm. As such, this verse describes God's relationship to justice from the human point of view: when people enact justice, God is exalted. The implication is that social justice is more than merely a socially practical, politically expedient, or morally required course of action: it is tied to the worship of YHWH as the one true God. While it is up to YHWH to establish his sovereignty in the divine assembly and to humble the gods of Babylon, it is up to his people to prove that sovereignty in the world by acts of justice.

b. YHWH and Justice from a Theological Perspective

The most obvious and significant theological development has already been suggested in the discussion of Second Isaiah above. There we considered how "justice" was enlisted to serve the cause of divine sovereignty. The intimate connection between YHWH and justice, evident already in creation (40:12ff.), and finding expression in new acts of redemption and restoration, imprints upon the very notion of justice an indelible divine stamp, and so thoroughly imbues the notion of justice with a divine component that no discussion of justice that fails to link it to God can be considered complete.

But the theological aspects of justice are not limited to the middle chapters of the book of Isaiah, nor confined to themes of creation and redemption. In 30:18 God's relationship to justice is once again articulated in expressly theological terms:

> Therefore YHWH waits to be gracious to you;
>   and therefore he is lifted up to be compassionate to you;
> *for a God of justice is YHWH;*
>   blessed are all who wait for him.

That God is a God of graciousness and compassion is not a new assertion. Indeed, in some ancient traditions, the very name YHWH is synonymous with "a God compassionate and gracious" (*YHWH ʾēl raḥûm wĕḥannûn*, Exod 34:6-7; see also 2 Kgs 13:23; Ps 86:15). Isa 30:18 asserts that God is gracious and compassionate *because* (*kî*) he is a God of justice. That is to say, divine mercy and kindness, qualities that define the very nature of God (Exod 34:6-7), are expressions of God's justice. Indeed, graciousness and compassion are so integral to divine justice that he is given the title "God of justice": YHWH is Israel's patron and source of justice. From this it follows that the God of compassionate justice requires his people to care for the orphan, the widow, the poor, and the strangers. Deeds of mercy and compassion, whether performed by God for his people, or by his people for the needy, attest to the justice of God.[4] Later theological debates that pit the demands of justice against the requirements of compassion have ignored and even ruptured the essential coherence of justice and compassion in YHWH, the God of justice who is eager to be gracious and who arises to show compassion.

The theological assertion of this verse, that YHWH is a God of justice, defines something essential to the identity of God, and it does so in a very precise way: justice as a divine attribute is how God expresses his essential graciousness and compassion to people. This is not to say that justice is a one-sided act of benevolence. We have seen repeatedly that justice for the oppressed means simultaneously destruction of the oppressors. Divine graciousness and compassion are not acts of sentimental mercy and clemency for all. Divine justice is revealed as compassion for the needy, the oppressed, and the repentant, but it is also punishment and judgment for the wicked. In this way, graciousness and compassion are integral to justice, but they do not exhaust its meaning. Divine justice is equally at home in caring for the bruised reed and protecting the dimly burning wick (42:3) as it is in brandishing the fiery sword of destruction (66:16-24). Traditionally, the theology of justice has been far clearer about the latter than the former. Isaiah 30:18 asserts unambiguously that YHWH is a God of justice, and an essential aspect of divine justice is graciousness and compassion.

c. YHWH and Justice from the Divine Perspective

Finally, God's relationship to justice is expressed more personally, from the divine point of view, in Isa 61:8:

> *For I, YHWH, love justice,*
> I hate robbery with iniquity;
> I shall give their recompense faithfully,
> and an everlasting covenant I shall make with them.

In direct divine speech, this passage gives YHWH's own estimation of the importance and value of justice: YHWH loves it, as much as he hates wrongdoing. In the Hebrew Bible, there are very few passages in which YHWH as speaker declares his love: he loves the remnant of Israel (Jer 31:3; Hos 11:1; 14:5 [Eng. 4]) and he loves Jacob (Mal 1:2). Elsewhere, he is often described in the third person as loving various people and things.[5] Of the things he (third person) loves, the Psalms list *mišpāṭ ûṣĕdāqâ* (33:5) and *mišpāṭ* (37:28). The assertion in Isa 61:8, then, is a rare instance in which YHWH personally declares his love for something other than his people. That suggests the importance of justice to YHWH and the premium he places on it.

YHWH's high regard for, and close association with, justice is indicated in a number of other passages. In Isa 28:17a, YHWH, in his own voice, declares that he will make justice and righteousness the measuring line by which the foundation stone of Zion is laid. Zion, as his temple city, is squared away and set firmly in place by justice, just as elsewhere, his throne is established on justice and righteousness (Pss 89:15 [Eng. 14]; 97:2). On this stone, the city is immovable; without it firmly in place, the city will be washed away (Isa 28:17b-19; cf. Matt 7:24-25).

In 42:1-4, direct divine speech again reinforces the close ties between YHWH and the execution of justice: YHWH personally raises up his Servant and sends him as an ambassador of *mišpāṭ*. Though our treatment of this passage in the context of Second Isaiah identified the term *mišpāṭ* as referring to both the verdict of the preceding trial scene and the contents of that verdict, viz., that the gods are naught and YHWH alone is sovereign, in the context of the entire book, the term *mišpāṭ* takes on the resonances of "justice" more broadly conceived. Indeed, the mission of the Servant as one who works for the social liberation of the oppressed and the righting of wrongs is precisely how the mission of the prophet in Isa 61:1ff. is interpreted.

YHWH's intimate connection to justice, finally, is clear in 51:4, in which YHWH, as it were, takes possession of justice and makes it his own: "my justice." Further, using a metaphor as far-reaching as that found in 28:17, YHWH's justice serves as *a light to the peoples.* On the one hand, this recalls the response to the opening oracle in 2:2-4—after YHWH judges the people and his instruction goes forth to the nations, the house of Jacob is invited to "walk in the light of YHWH" (2:5). There is an intrinsic connection between right judgment and light. On the other hand, when "there is no justice" (59:8, 11), the people grope about like the blind and stumble like those who have no eyes (59:10). Justice is, indeed, the light by which society walks and without which it stumbles about in darkness. The particular light/justice by which peoples and nations are to walk is YHWH's justice, which, as we saw above, is a justice of compassion and graciousness, a justice eager to redress the plight of those who suffer from want, wrong, or oppression. While there is an undeniable theological aspect to divine justice that illuminates the nature of God, the theological component is not directed toward metaphysical speculation but to practical implementation: God is as God does. Thus, "justice" is not merely a divine quality but a divine manifestation. Divine justice is revealed when human justice actuates compassion and graciousness.

While modern commentators look to the broader social and cultural contexts of the ancient Near East to determine the origins and formative influences of Israel's concern for social justice directed toward the orphan and widow, the book of Isaiah has a different approach. "Who taught YHWH the path of justice?" (40:12-14). No one. YHWH is the God of justice; justice belongs to him. He did not consult others, nor did he learn from others how to establish and order the world. Because God alone establishes the path of justice, the prophet looks to YHWH to understand what justice is; nations come to him to learn his ways (2:3). In the context of the book of Isaiah, the teaching about justice, its material content, and its relationship to YHWH are richly described without reference to extrinsic sources.

d. Justice and the Holiness of YHWH

Before concluding this discussion of YHWH and justice, we must return briefly to Isa 5:16. This verse, in addition to describing how it is that the human community exalts YHWH through the enactment of justice in the social realm, also has ties to an important theme throughout the book, namely, the holiness of YHWH. Isaiah's inaugural vision in the temple (ch. 6) presents perhaps the Bible's most transcendent vision of YHWH enthroned in glory. The awesomeness of his glory fills the whole earth and reverberates in the threshold-shaking song of the seraphim acclaiming YHWH as thrice holy. The residual effects of that vision of the all-holy God are found throughout the book in one of Isaiah's favorite, and distinctive, titles of God as "the Holy One of Israel" (twenty-five times).[6] This verse, 5:16, asserts that the transcendence of God's holiness is paradoxically revealed in the imminence of justice enacted in the social realm: the Holy God is sanctified, honored as holy, or shows himself as holy in the practice of justice. Justice reveals and confirms God's holiness, or "otherness"; the converse is also true: injustice impugns his holiness.

Both Ezekiel and Isaiah use the imagery of harlotry to describe Israel's sin against YHWH, but they do so from different perspectives. From Ezekiel's priestly perspective, harlotry refers to the cult defiled and contaminated by idolatry; this impurity compelled YHWH to quit the sanctuary (Ezek 10:9-17; 11:22-25). In Isaiah 1:21-26, the harlotry of Zion is her injustice. From Isaiah's perspective, injustice compelled YHWH to expel his people from Jerusalem and Judah. Just as for Ezekiel impurity and holiness cannot coexist, for Isaiah injustice and holiness are incompatible. For Isaiah, YHWH's holiness is inextricably connected to justice. While the vision of God's holiness (Isaiah 6) is a privilege revealed to a rare few (for example, Moses in Exod 33:17—34:7; Isa 6:1ff.; and Daniel in Dan 7:9-15), that same holiness is made manifest to the eyes of all in acts of justice, which, as we saw above, reveal the graciousness and compassion of God.

2. Justice and Zion. Considered along with Zion in this discussion will also be passages that relate to Jerusalem and, somewhat more broadly, to Judah. The interrelation of Zion, Jerusalem, and Judah, and their centrality to the book of Isaiah, come to light clearly in Sweeney's form-critical examination of the book. He identifies the literary form of the book as "The Vision of Isaiah ben Amoz: Prophetic Exhortation to Jerusalem/Judah to Adhere to YHWH, Isaiah 1:1—66:24." This is divided into two main subunits which he identifies as "Concerning YHWH's plans for worldwide sovereignty at Zion" (1:1—33:24) and "Concerning realization of YHWH's plans for worldwide sovereignty at Zion" (34:1—66:24; Sweeney 1996a: 39–51). The exhortation is addressed to Jerusalem and Judah; its subject matter is the establishment of YHWH's sovereignty at Zion.

The supremacy of Zion is asserted already in 2:2-4. There it is identified with "the mountain of YHWH" and is exalted above all other mountains (2:2).[7] It is not merely a topological supremacy that Zion enjoys, however; it is both the temple city of YHWH and the international hub to which peoples and nations stream. In turn, this political preeminence is rooted in a religious fact: from Zion go forth YHWH's "instruction" and "word" *(tôrâ* and *dābār).* We shall see the significance of *tôrâ* below. At this point, we can say that in 2:3 the two words together refer to the totality of God's revelation made to the world at Zion. Zion is the seat of YHWH's worldwide sovereignty, the place from which effective decrees are issued. But, for the moment, that is a future vision. The present reality is somewhat less flattering.

Zion's first appearance is in 1:8, where "daughter Zion" sits forlorn like a hut in a cucumber field, the chastened city that has tasted punishment because of its sin. That sin is described in 1:21-28. There she is identified as formerly filled with *justice and righteousness*, but now defiled by injustice, which is catalogued in 1:21-23. The assertion of Zion's former glory but present disgrace is also made of Judah at large:

> For the vineyard of YHWH of Hosts is the house of Israel,
> and the people of Judah his pleasant plant.
> He expected justice but found bloodshed,
> righteousness, but found an outcry. (5:7)

The situation in Zion and in Judah is intolerable. In ch. 1, God describes the corrective measures he intends to take for Zion (vv. 24-26), and the means for Zion's restoration are described: "Zion will be redeemed by *justice*, and her returning ones by *righteousness*" (1:27). Zion's reputation as "the faithful city" was based on her being filled with justice and righteousness (1:21); that distinction, lost by murder, corruption, and injustice, will be restored when justice and righteousness once again are resident within her walls (1:26-27). The importance of justice and righteousness to Zion reaches to its very foundations: her foundation stone is measured out by justice and righteousness (28:16-17). Zion is founded on, reputed for, and redeemed by justice.

For this redemption to occur and justice to be reestablished, Zion must be purified and the filth of her corruption washed away (4:2-6). The means by which this will be accomplished are quite specific: the filth and bloodstains will be cleansed by a "spirit of judgment *(mišpāṭ)* and a spirit of fire" (4:4). Judgment is concomitant with redemption; justice and judgment (the same word in Hebrew—*mišpāṭ*) go together. This fiery judgment of Zion as the prelude to restoration at the beginning of the book thus adumbrates the fiery judgment of the world in 66:16, which is the prelude to the new heavens and new earth (66:22-23).

While Zion will be redeemed by the reestablishment of justice in the social sphere, redemption is not wholly a human act. This is suggested in a number of ways. Already in 1:25-26, it is YHWH who restores Zion's judges and counselors, who will presumably reestablish the justice by which Zion is redeemed. Further, 33:5 makes it clear that justice in Zion has its ultimate source in YHWH:

> YHWH is exalted, for he dwells on high;
> he has filled Zion with justice and righteousness.

Justice is YHWH's (51:4), and he is the God of justice (30:18): it is, therefore, his right and proper role to fill the city of his dwelling with justice and righteousness. Yet, apart from the apocalyptic longings that arise late in the Isaianic tradition and elsewhere in the Bible, justice is something that, practically speaking, can be established only by human agents working in society. Justice, which has its source in God, can only be realized by people acting in his name.

When we discuss the redemption of Zion—or of society in any age—it is misguided to argue whether the justice by which it is redeemed is effected by God or by humanity. The book of Isaiah taken as a whole makes it clear that YHWH is the source of justice and that he provisions his temple city, Zion, with justice and righteousness. At the same time, it is through the agency of judges and counselors, leaders and citizens, court officials and merchants that justice is established and upheld. Arguments that are overly confident of human ability, or that look quietistically to God to do it all, are equally unbalanced according to Isaiah. The establishment of justice requires both untiring human effort and a firm rooting in the God of justice. It is despair over human cooperation in the divine plan that leads to visions of God alone establishing a new heavens and a new earth (for example, Isa 66:22-23; 2 Pet 3:13; Rev 21:1ff.). There are times in human history when such a vision has power to console and to sustain hope that is otherwise flickering toward extinction. But most often, ordinary people, imbued with the vision and the power of God, arise to rebuild the ancient ruins and repair the breach (Isa 58:12). In Isaiah, traditions and perspectives that diachronic study places in tension function in tandem when read synchronically and provide the dialectical relationship between divine initiative and human response that lies at the heart of biblical theology.

3. Justice and Torah. In his study of *tôrâ* in the book of Isaiah (1996b: 50–67), Sweeney argues that none of the Isaianic writers prior to the time of Ezra understood the word *tôrâ* in the book of Isaiah (12 times) as referring to the Mosaic covenant. However, "the meaning of *tôrâ* takes on a hermeneutical life of its own when it is considered in relation to its full literary and interpretive context in the final form of the book of Isaiah" (Sweeney 1996b: 63). The use of the word with such modifying terms as "*tôrâ* of YHWH of Hosts" (5:24), "*tôrâ* of our God" (1:10), and "*tôrâ* of YHWH" (30:9), along with other features, moves the term out of its more narrow frame of reference as an "instruction" or "teaching" to Israel into the realm of the Mosaic law directed both toward Israel's life and YHWH's worldwide sovereignty.

> In sum, the book of Isaiah as a whole portrays the revelation of YHWH's Torah to the nations and Israel in analogy to the revelation of Torah to Israel and the nations in the Mosaic tradition.... Whereas the Mosaic tradition portrays this revelation as a means to establish Israel in its own land, the Isaiah tradition portrays the revelation as a means to demonstrate YHWH's world-wide sovereignty and to re-establish Israel in Zion. (Sweeney, 1996b: 65)

In his own thinking, Sweeney seems to have moved from classifying the genre of the book of Isaiah as a "Prophetic Exhortation" (as in his commentary, 1996a) to "Prophetic Torah" (as in 1996b).[8] The overall effect is to heighten the importance and significance of the term *tôrâ*.

In the book of Isaiah, *tôrâ* is identified twice with *mišpāṭ*: 42:4; 51:4.[9] As we have seen in our discussion of 42:1-4, the *mišpāṭ* that the Servant brings forth is the verdict of YHWH's sovereignty. The parallel with *tôrâ* in 42:4, then, is exactly consistent with Sweeney's observations above: *tôrâ* and *mišpāṭ* are directed toward, and are in service to, YHWH's sovereignty.

In 51:4, YHWH's own justice, by which the peoples walk, is once again parallel to *tôrâ*: together *justice* and instruction go forth as light for the peoples. The metaphor of light and the importance of justice were discussed above; Torah serves the same function. Indeed, this is the very thrust of 2:2-4(5), which presents YHWH as the worldwide judge to whom come nations and peoples to receive his *tôrâ* and learn to walk in his ways; the house of Jacob, too, will walk by this light.

When, as Sweeney suggests, *tôrâ* comes to be understood in its Mosaic sense, the significance of *mišpāṭ* is broadened and strengthened. Especially in the late postexilic and intertestamental periods, as *tôrâ* becomes the distinguishing feature of Judaism, the association of *tôrâ* and *mišpāṭ* in 51:4 moves "justice" to the very center of the observant life. This same development had been seen earlier in 56:1-8, where the command to "maintain justice and do righteousness" became the précis of "holding fast the covenant." By identifying *tôrâ* and *mišpāṭ*, then, the Isaianic tradition had prepared the ground for understanding the doing of justice as being at the very heart of observing the law.

*4. Justice and "the Way" (*derek *and* ʾōraḥ*).* Closely associated with the life of *tôrâ* is the metaphor of "the way" *(derek)* or "the path" *(ʾōraḥ)*. In Isa 2:2-4, as YHWH gives his *tôrâ*, the nations express the purpose of their pilgrimage to Zion: "that he may teach us his *ways (*derek)* and we may walk in his *paths*" (**ʾōraḥ*; 2:3). This is the first of 58 occurrences of the word *derek*, "way," in the book of Isaiah.[10] Sometimes it is used in a purely literal sense of "road" or "way," as in "a road to cross on foot" (11:15) or a highway as in "the way of the sea" (8:23 = Eng. 9:1), or "the road to Horonaim" (15:5). Especially in Second Isaiah, the image of the "road" is used to describe Israel's return to Judah from exile. Often, however, "the way" is used metaphorically to refer to one's conduct, one's way of life, as in 2:3; 3:12; 8:11; 30:11; 42:24; 48:17; 55:7; 65:2. Throughout the book of Isaiah, *derek* functions as a major verbal and thematic link. It is amplified by the use of the synonym *ʾōraḥ*, which occurs 8 times, 4 of those times in parallelism with *derek*.

In 42:24, *derek* is parallel with *tôrâ*: not to "walk in the way" is to disobey YHWH's instruction *(tôrâ)*. Refusal to walk in his ways or to obey his instruction results in YHWH's giving Israel over to the despoiler. The totality of the destruction underscores the gravity of the offense. Forsaking YHWH's ways and his instructions—or more broadly, his law—is no trivial matter.

In 59:8, the prophet laments:

> The way of peace they do not know;
> there is no justice in their paths.

For the strife-torn community to know peace, justice is essential. As is well known, the term *šālôm* means more than merely "peace": in this case it refers to the total well-being of the community. The lack of well-being, harmony, and prosperity are explained by the lack of justice. Indeed, when "there is no justice," oppression goes unchecked and evil holds sway. The disastrous effects of injustice, here succinctly described as "no peace," are detailed at length in Isaiah 59.

For there to be peace in their ways, there must be justice in their paths. The "path of justice" *(ʾōraḥ mišpāṭ)* is YHWH's special domain (40:14). When the nations and peoples come to Zion "that he may instruct us in his ways and we may walk in his paths" (2:3), the *ways* and *paths* he teaches include the "path of justice" (40:14), which is integral to YHWH's *tôrâ* (42:4), and to "the way of peace" (59:2).

In 58:2, YHWH exposes the hypocrisy of the people who want to know YHWH's ways *(*derek)* without practicing righteousness, doing justice *(mišpāṭ),* or observing YHWH's righteous judgments *(mišpĕṭê-ṣedeq).* Such a situation is an impossibility: one cannot walk in YHWH's ways without doing justice and righteousness.

Both *derek* and *tôrâ* are used as shorthand for living life in conformity to YHWH's will, later summarized under the terms *law* or *covenant.* And an essential component of both *derek* and *tôrâ* is the command to do justice. From the Isaianic perspective, any discussion of *tôrâ* or "the way" that does not consider *mišpāṭ* as an integral component is incomplete and inadequate. It is not possible to walk in YHWH's way or to live according to his law without doing justice.

5. *Justice and the Servant(s).* As we have seen in some detail, the mission of justice is associated in a particular way with the Servant who appears in Isaiah 40–55 and whose mission is perhaps extended in 61:1ff. The Servant image, situated within the entire book, easily and profitably moves in the direction suggested by Clifford, who considers the individual and the nation as part of a continuous tradition of servants in Scripture. Servants like Abraham (for example, Isa 41:8) and Jacob (for example, 44:1, 2, 21; 48:20), Moses (63:11-12), David (for example, 37:35), Jeremiah, Isaiah, Ezekiel, preexilic kings and prophets, all in some way represent what Israel as a whole is called to be and to do: "All Israel becomes a servant when it embraces the divine will and plan as shown by the individual servants" (Clifford 1992: 499).[11]

On the one hand, Servant Israel is called and charged to bring forth *mišpāṭ* (42:1). In the historical context, that meant the judgment or verdict of YHWH's sovereignty; in the context of the book, as we have seen, *mišpāṭ* includes as well the notion of justice enacted in the social realm. The original sense, however, is not lost, for whenever justice is established, YHWH's sovereignty is asserted and the rule of the God of justice is actualized. Justice is integral both to the mission of Servant Israel and to the rule of YHWH: the success of the former is the revelation of the latter.

On the other hand, *mišpāṭ* is not only something Servant Israel does for YHWH, it is also something from which YHWH protects his servants: "every weapon forged against you shall not succeed, and every tongue that rises against you in judgment (*mišpāṭ*) you shall prove guilty" (54:17a). Such divine care is described as "the heritage of the servants of YHWH" (54:17b). As the tragic case of the Servant proved (Isa 52:13—53:12), divine favor was no reprieve from death. What YHWH promises instead is that "their vindication is from me" (54:17b). In the context of the book, this is the divine promise to every servant of YHWH. Those who are agents of *mišpāṭ* are a "sharp sword and a polished arrow," whose ministry of the word is cutting and incisive; they will be protected by YHWH, who hides the sword in his own hand and protects the arrow in his quiver (49:2). All servants of YHWH can, with confidence, make the words of the Servant their own: "my *mišpāṭ* is with YHWH and my recompense is with my God" (49:4). The controversy over the individual versus collective interpretation that dogs the discussion of the Servant in Second Isaiah is resolved in the context of the book in the way that Clifford and others suggest. This interpretation was already anticipated by Third Isaiah, whose discussion focused exclusively on "the servants" (56:6; 63:17; 65:8, 9, 13, 14, 15; 66:14).[12] Both the commission and the gifts required to fulfill the mission are the inheritance of all who are servants of YHWH.

At its best, kingship had a particular role to exercise in the execution of justice. We conclude our study of the intersection of *mišpāṭ* with the book's major themes by turning now to examine the relationship between *mišpāṭ* and the leadership.

6. *Justice and the Leadership.* The incessant prophetic critique of corrupt leadership is a major concern of the book of Isaiah, and its exposition has occupied a good deal of our attention throughout this study. Whenever the prophets of the book of Isaiah turn their attention to the kingship or the leadership more broadly, an admonition to do justice or a reproach for not doing justice is almost always part of the message, underscoring the essential connection between justice and leadership.

But the view has not been entirely negative. Four passages, taken together, represent an optimistic assessment of the possibilities of just and righteous rule: 9:1-6 (Eng. 2-7); 11:1-9; 16:5; and 32:1. There is no consensus as to the historical origins of these passages—whether they come from Isaiah of Jerusalem or a Josianic or postexilic redaction. What they all share is the view that good government broadly, and royal rule more narrowly, involve the establishment of justice and righteousness. From the prophetic point of view, the material prosperity, economic growth, military strength, or geographic expanse of the country are not the measures of good government or just rule. The criteria are announced at the outset of the book in an address to leaders and people alike (1:10): "seek justice; set aright the ruthless; do justice for the orphan; argue the case of the widow" (1:17). While the people at large are charged with doing justice, it is the leadership in general that bears particular responsibility.

In passages that deal with the obligations of the king in positive terms, the importance of "justice and righteousness" is everywhere evident. The king and his princes are explicitly charged with doing justice (32:1). There, the kind of justice is spelled out in images of protection from disastrous and ruinous forces (32:2-3). The king in particular is charged to "judge the poor in righteousness" (11:4). Ideally, the king doesn't merely accede to the task of justice; rather, he "seeks justice and hastens to do righteousness" (16:5).

The essential connection between justice and rule coalesces around one of the chief symbols of royal rule, the throne. In 9:6 (Eng. 7), the prophet looks to a king who will establish his throne on justice and righteousness. This Isaianic theme reflects a theological tradition that upholds God's election of Zion and David in which the king, as the adopted son of God (Ps 2:6-7), instantiates the rule and the justice of God, whose throne is also established on justice and righteousness (Pss 89:15 [Eng. 14]; 97:2). The throne as the place from which the king executes justice comes under divine oversight as YHWH himself becomes a "spirit of justice for the one who sits over judgment" (28:6).

This focus on justice as a defining feature of kingship makes it entirely understandable that so many commentators have detected royal motifs in their discussion of the Servant in 42:1-4. There the Servant's mission of justice evokes specific echoes of the king's task. But as the role of Servant is distributed to all servants, the expectation to enact justice is similarly distributed. The obligations of the king specifically and the ruling class more generally are in turn responsibilities incumbent upon the nation at large (58:2).

I subscribe to Sweeney's view that the subject matter of the book of Isaiah concerns the establishment of YHWH's worldwide sovereignty at Zion. I have argued that justice is an essential part of divine sovereignty, and that earthly rulers and servants bring divine sovereignty to light in their enactment of social justice. In short, taken synchronically, divine sovereignty and justice form the foundation upon which the imperative for social justice stands, from which kingly rule derives its authority, and by which the reign of God is concretely manifest in history.

Concluding Comments

The above consideration of justice/*mišpāṭ* in relation to some of the major themes and concerns of the book of Isaiah is obviously not exhaustive. Nor has any systematic attempt been made to place the various themes in dialogue with one another. Still, it is abundantly clear that, both diachronically and perhaps even more so synchronically, justice/*mišpāṭ* is a key concern of the book. In a sense, the complex editorial and redactional history itself testifies to the importance of the theme of justice. It is not possible to attribute an acute and passionate interest in social justice to just a handful of Isaianic prophetic figures. Its pervasive presence and obvious development over time and through multiple layers of redaction are eloquent testimony to its enduring appeal and urgent necessity. In this regard, the literary trajectory runs counter to the theological development: whereas increasingly complex social circumstances led savants, seers, and even communities to despair of a competent human agent of justice and to look instead to a decisive divine intervention, narrowing the locus of justice, an ever-increasing group of writers, editors, redactors, and readers continued to pin their hopes to, and envision their future as, a society built on justice. As the agency constricted, the audience expanded.

This examination of justice in the book of Isaiah has shown that justice is not a timeless, transcendent, or immutable concept but is inseparably tied to the social conditions of particular communities in specific circumstances. Each of the three major periods that the book of Isaiah addresses had concerns that were peculiar to its historical and geographic situation. The demands of justice were defined, in part, in response to the injustices that arose from changed circumstances. On the other hand, both the continuity of content throughout the three divisions of the book of Isaiah and YHWH's perennial and inalienable identification with justice indicate that neither is justice entirely relative, created de novo as an ad hoc response to changed circumstances. In this way, the book of Isaiah both represents the best of the conservative impulse to preserve the classic traditions of justice, and embodies a bold innovation to respond to new and changed circumstances. This was most evident in Babylon, where the greatest threat to the community was not the corruption of its leaders or the disarray of its society, but the incursion of Babylonian theology into the sphere of Yahwistic faith. When it looked as if both the nation of Israel and their God had been defeated and consigned to powerlessness, the prophet of the exile drew on traditions that identified YHWH as the God of justice to make his case for YHWH's power to effect a new creation and a new act of deliverance. The language of creation in 40:12ff. is used as prelude to kingship; in turn, the power inherent in kingship is the basis for YHWH's ability to redeem the people from exile. Both creation and redemption are expressions of the sovereignty of God, who alone establishes the paths of justice. The "path of justice" is integral to the course of creation; redemption, too, is based on justice, for Israel had paid the debt for their iniquity. This unabashedly theological engagement of justice had the salutary effect not only of confronting the religious threat posed by idolatry, but of enriching immeasurably Israel's own understanding of justice. YHWH is the God of justice. From this basic belief flows the requirement that YHWH's people—king and Servant, prophets and people alike—"bring forth justice to the nations" and "establish justice on the earth" (42:1, 4). The concern is more than mere social activism, however, for whenever justice is established, the sovereignty of God is manifest.

The theme of justice crosses all time periods of the book and unites all its literary divisions. But it does even more. By one and the same act—the enactment of justice in the social realm—the sovereignty of YHWH is manifest on earth and human society is redeemed. The salutary effects of YHWH's sovereignty fill Zion with justice and move the people to exalt their God. The final words belong most appropriately to the book of Isaiah, which asserts both that *Zion is redeemed by justice* (1:27) and that *YHWH of Hosts is exalted in justice* (5:16).

Abbreviations

AB	Anchor Bible
ABD	D. N. Freedman, ed., *Anchor Bible Dictionary*
ANET	J. B. Pritchard, ed., *Ancient Near Eastern Texts Relating to the Old Testament*
ASV	American Standard Version
BDB	F. Brown, S. R. Driver, and C. A. Briggs, *Hebrew and English Lexicon of the Old Testament*
BETL	Bibliotheca ephemeridum theologicarum lovaniensium
Bib	*Biblica*
BR	*Biblical Research*
BSac	*Bibliotheca Sacra*
BTB	*Biblical Theology Bulletin*
BZ	*Biblische Zeitschrift*
BZAW	Beihefte zur ZAW
CBQ	*Catholic Biblical Quarterly*
EncJud	*Encyclopaedia Judaica*
ExpT	*Expository Times*
GKC	*Gesenius' Hebrew Grammar*, ed. E. Kautzsch, trans. A. E. Cowley
IBC	Interpretation: A Bible Commentary for Teaching and Preaching
IDB	*Interpreter's Dictionary of the Bible*
Int	*Interpretation*
JBL	*Journal of Biblical Literature*
JNES	*Journal of Near Eastern Studies*
JPSV	Jewish Publication Society Version (1988)
JQR	*Jewish Quarterly Review*
JSOT	*Journal for the Study of the Old Testament*
JSOTSup	JSOT—Supplement Series
JTS	*Journal of Theological Studies*
KJV	King James Version of the Bible
LXX	Septuagint

MT	Masoretic Text
NAB	New American Bible
NCB	New Century Bible
NICOT	New International Commentary on the Old Testament
NIV	New International Bible
NJB	New Jerusalem Bible
NJBC	R. E. Brown et al., eds., *New Jerome Biblical Commentary*
NRSV	New Revised Standard Version of the Bible
OTL	Old Testament Library
OtSt	Oudtestamentische Studiën
REB	Revised English Bible
RelEd	*Religious Education*
RevScRel	*Revue des sciences religieuses*
SBL	Society of Biblical Literature
SBLSP	*SBL Seminar Papers*
Sem	*Semitica*
SJOT	*Scandinavian Journal of the Old Testament*
SJT	*Scottish Journal of Theology*
ST	*Studia theologica*
TBT	*The Bible Today*
TEV	Today's English Version
TRu	*Theologische Rundschau*
TToday	*Theology Today*
VT	*Vetus Testamentum*
VTSup	VT Supplements
WW	*Word and World*
ZAW	*Zeitschrift für die alttestamentliche Wissenschaft*

Notes

Introduction

1. These examples, and those in the next few notes, are not exhaustive, merely representative: Genesis 18; 1 Sam 7:17; 8:3, 15; 1 Kgs 3:16-28; 10:9; 1 Chr 18:14; 2 Chr 19:7; Daniel 13; 1 Macc 2:29; 7:18.

2. Isa 1:17; 10:2; Jer 21:12; 22:3; Ezek 18:8; Hos 2:19 (MT 2:21); Amos 5:15; Mic 3:1; Hab 1:4; Zech 7:10; Mal 3:5.

3. Exod 22:22; 23:2, 6; Lev 19:15; Deut 16:19, 20; 24:17; 27:17.

4. Pss 33:5; 37:28; 72:2; 82:3; 89:14 (MT 15); 94:6; 97:2; 99:4; 146:9.

5. Job 8:3; 19:7; 34:12, 17; 37:28; Prov 1:3; 2:8, 9; 17:23; 19:28; Eccl 5:8 (MT 7); Wis 5:18; 8:7; Sir 27:8; 35:22.

1. The Study of Justice in the Bible

1. An approach like that of Young (1992), who translates forty of Isaiah's forty-two occurrences of *mišpāṭ* as "judgment," clearly fails to reckon with the complexity and multivalence of the word.

2. This count is taken from the computer reference tool, *Accordance* (Version 5., 2001), and agrees with Mitchel (1984: 75). The concordance by Even-Shoshan (1990) lists 424 occurrences, omitting the appearance in Gen 14:7, where it is part of a place name. A total of 422 is cited by both BDB and Johnson (1986); Booth (1942) discussed 412 references, after discarding ambiguous references and repetition in dependent passages; Gossai (1993) also cites 412 references.

3. The exceptions are Ruth, Esther, Song of Songs, Joel, Obadiah, Jonah, Nahum, and Haggai.

4. We note with understanding Gossai's omission of Epsztein's *Social Justice in the Ancient Near East and the People of the Bible* (1986). Epsztein's work is a convenient and helpful summary of a broad range of secondary scholarship, but is largely derivative and offers little analysis that is original or new. Much of the ground that he covers somewhat superficially (for example, a mere 14 pages on "Prophecy and Social Justice," with quotes and citations from only the eighth-century prophets) is treated more comprehensively, and with a greater sensitivity both to original sources and to the biblical text, by Weinfeld's book (see below). Otherwise, Gossai's review sketches some of the main trends.

5. Consult the bibliography for Hollenbach 1982; Mallia 1983; Nash 1991; Nysse 1992; Renner 1990; Stek 1978; Sabourin 1981; Míguez Bonino 1987, who deals only with the word *ṣĕdāqâ*.

6. See Weinfeld (1995: 25, n. 1) for references. See also van der Westhuizen (1978: 50–57) and Myers (1968: 98), both of whom also identify *ṣedeq ûmišpāṭ* as a hendiadys.

7. Brongers (1965: 113, with n. 1).

8. Bazak agrees that the expression is a hendiadys but he understands it differently: "'righteousness' is an attribute describing 'justice.' . . . It denotes righteous laws, an honest judiciary and a liberal, flexible interpretation of the law which takes into account considerations of time and place in order to avoid harsh consequences which might correspond to the letter of the law but are obviously morally wrong and contrary to the spirit of the law" (1989: 13). That he argues for a specifically forensic meaning of the term might be explained by the fact that Bazak is a judge in the District Court of Jerusalem. This argument founders, however, on the fact that the hendiadys is often found with the terms reversed (*ṣĕdāqâ ûmišpāṭ,* Isa 32:1; 58:2; Gen 18:19; Ps 33:5; Prov 21:3) with no apparent difference in meaning.

9. Consult the bibliography for Banks (1905); Schwarzschild (1972), who treats *ṣĕdāqâ* as his base word for "justice"; the same is true of Steinmueller and Sullivan (1956), and Beaucamp (1969). For a discussion of the relationship between the legal and ethical aspects of justice, see Falk 1992b.

10. Tellingly, *IDB* has no article on "Justice," only one on "Justification, Justify"; see also Krašovec (1988); Achtemeier's article on "Righteousness" (1962) ends up with "justification," finding evidence in Isaiah for the doctrinal assertion of "imputed righteousness."

11. Consult the bibliography for Hertzberg 1922 and 1923; Berkovits 1969a; Mott 1985; Bazak 1989; Schrey 1955.

12. Consult the bibliography for Brueggemann 1984 and 1998; Carr 1993; Clements 1982; Clifford 1993; Evans 1988; Motyer 1994; Polan 1997; Rendtorff 1996; Seitz 1993b; Sommer 1996.

2. Isaiah: The Prophet(s), the Book, the Commentators

1. It may be noted that Motyer is not alone among contemporaries in holding for the Isaianic authorship of the entire book. Before him is the three-volume commentary of Young (1992). Young's position is this: "The prophet Isaiah himself was the author of the entire book; he himself committed it all to writing, and he was responsible for collecting his messages and placing them in the present book which bears his name" (1992: vol. 1, p. 8). More recent still is the commentary of Oswalt (1986 and 1998). His position: "the essential content of the book has come to us through one human author, Isaiah the son of Amoz. It is he who received the revelations from God and who directed the shape of the book" (1986: 25); the anthological style of the book suggests that "Isaiah himself or those who worked with him" arranged the material according to a theological scheme and added editorial or transitional material (1986: 26).

2. It may be noted that Kaiser is not alone in this entirely late dating. Watts (1985 and 1987) places the book's origins in the Persian period, specifically in

435, during the reign of Artaxerxes I. Miscall (1993) also believes that the book was composed as a unified work in the postexilic period, probably the fifth century.

3. It is ironic that although Sweeney's commentary spends pp. 39–48 arguing that the major divisions of the book are chs. 1–33 and 34–66, the commentary itself is addressed to Isaiah 1–39. While Seitz (1993a: 4–7) was concerned about his own commentary's break at the traditional point and attempted to justify it, no such explanation is found in Sweeney.

4. See, for example, Seitz (1988b: 105), where he acknowledges his debt to historical analysis and its efforts to "locate the text at prior historical moments," or his commentary, where he states his commitment to "do justice to the historical roots of the message of Isaiah, on the one hand, and the present literary context in which that message is found, on the other" (1993a: 4).

5. The terms *diachronic* and *synchronic* may be new to some readers. "Diachronic" literally means "through time." In this approach, historical setting is the determining factor for the meaning of the text. Uncovering or reconstructing the "original setting" of a passage informs the proper meaning of the text. Thus, discovering whether a passage was written by Isaiah during the reign of Ahaz, or added by an editor during the reign of Josiah a hundred years later, affects the very meaning of the text. Diachronic study examines the meaning of a text as it evolves through time. "Synchronic" literally means "with time" and refers to the study of a text as a stable literary work. For example, the threefold division of the book of Isaiah according to historical periods is of little significance in a synchronic reading. The primary context in which to interpret a passage is not the eighth, or sixth, or fifth century B.C.E., but the context of the book as a whole.

6. We may note, however, that not all such historical references have been successfully suppressed, as the mention of Cyrus in Isa 44:28 and 45:1 attests.

7. Boadt advances a methodology for analyzing the poetics of persuasion by which it may be possible to come closer to a text's original oral form and thus closer to the prophet himself. For a more sober assessment of the possibilities of historical reconstruction, especially from poetic texts, see Melugin (1996c: 63–78).

8. From 735–732 B.C.E.: 1:21-26, 27-31; 5:1-24; 6:1-11, 12-13; 7:2-17, 20; 8:1-15; 8:16—9:6 (Eng. 9:7); 15:1b—16:12; 29:15-24; from 724–720 B.C.E.: 5:25-30; 9:7 (Eng. 8)—10:4; 10:5-34; 14:24-27; 17–18; 19:1-17; 29:1-14; from 715–701 B.C.E.: 1:2-9, 10-18; 2:6-19; 3:1-9, 12-15; 3:16—4:1; 14:4b-21, 28-32; 22:1b-14, 15-25; 23:1b-14; 28; 30:1-18; 31; 32:9-14; from 691–689 B.C.E.: 21:1-10, 11-12, 13-17 (Sweeney 1996a: 59).

9. Tate (1996: 45–47) provides a convenient sampling of themes and their proponents; among the themes: Holy One of Israel, Zion/Jerusalem, glory of YHWH, righteousness, remnant, cosmogonic language, Servant of God, exodus, comfort, and iniquity. In addition, we may include: God's plan, former/latter things, and blindness/deafness; and recently, a light to the nations (Clements 1996, 1997).

3. Isaiah 1–39

1. Some commentators (see Willis 1984: 63–77) look to 2 Kgs 16:5 for evidence: "Then Rezin king of Aram and Pekah son of Remaliah king of Israel went up to Jerusalem to wage war; they laid siege against Ahaz but were not able to conquer him." These commentators have suggested that the Syro-Ephraimite incursion resulted in the devastation described in these verses. First, it should be noted that this account in 2 Kings 16 is laconic in the extreme. The fuller account found in 2 Chron 28:5-15 curiously omits references to the size of the forces employed, the place of battle, and the resultant destruction of the land; it focuses instead on the slaughter of 120,000 valiant men of Judah in one day, the widespread plunder, and the capture of 200,000 women and children. Japhet (1993: 900–901) discounts this report as "historically impossible" and "utterly unrealistic." Through an analysis of vocabulary and themes, she concludes that the material is not typical of the Chronicler and probably derives from some other source. It is employed by the Chronicler, however, as a prelude to the main episode of the story—the capture and subsequent return of the Judahites by the Israelites. This reversal, brought about by the intervention of the prophet Oded, highlights the themes of brotherhood and national unity stressed by the Chronicler. The "exaggerated numbers" and "tendentious tone" urge caution in accepting the details of this narrative as factual.

Stacey (1993: 2–3), echoing arguments found in Gray (1912: 12–13), also discounts the Syro-Ephraimite incursion by reasoning that the Israelites of the north would not likely be called "foreigners," and the sacking, looting, and destruction of the land would hardly have won over the Judahites as allies. Further, evidence is scant for the scale of destruction described by Isaiah. Something more than an incursion of the Syro-Ephraimite army into Judah is needed to account for the devastation, which leaves Jerusalem the lone and isolated survivor implied by Isa 1:8. Even granting the conflict and capture described in 2 Chronicles (but curiously absent in 2 Kings), Gray points out that the description falls short of that found in Isaiah (1912: 12–13).

2. This is the position of Kaiser, who, as discussed above, places the entire composition of Isaiah in the exilic and postexilic periods. He sees the wounds described in vv. 5-6 as the result of disciplinary beatings inflicted on the rebellious sons in v. 2; he understands the "head," "heart," and "feet" as an image for "the body of the people" who were smitten by the events of 587. Verse 7 is a flashback to the people left behind in Judah and Jerusalem after the eighteen-month siege of the city by Nebuchadnezzar. In Kaiser's estimation, the events of 701 do not measure up to the level of destruction envisioned in this verse. Kaiser spends some time correlating the image of the lodge in the cucumber field (v. 8) and the destruction suffered by the city in 587, focusing particularly on the tearing down of its walls, which left it open to plunder. Because there is no record of the city being destroyed in 701, these verses, he argues, must pertain to 587 and following.

Three points may be made. First, the record of destruction detailed in Sennacherib's annals (*ANET* 1969: 287), even allowing for their self-serving grandiosity, seems in the view of many commentators (for example, Gray, Sweeney, Wildberger, Clements) to accord well with the terse description in Isa 1:7-8. This is true not only of the general description, but also of the specific vocabulary, which, Machinist contends, is applied directly by Isaiah to the Assyrians in such a way "that the two cannot be dissociated" (1983: 724). Second, the image of a hut in a vineyard or a lodge in a cucumber field is not one of destruction but one of survival—something in fact survives and is left after the siege. It is an image of forlorn isolation with everything surrounding having been removed. This is a potent and poignant image of Hezekiah's Jerusalem left alone in the midst of a land wherein forty-six strong cities and numerous small villages had been destroyed and plundered. Third, the point of 2 Kgs 25:8ff., which Kaiser enlists in support of his argument for the extensive destruction of the city in the events of 587, is exactly that: the city was destroyed and nothing left. Isaiah's description of Jerusalem as a hut in a vineyard implies that something survived, but the description in 2 Kgs 25:8ff. makes it clear that Nebuchadnezzar's army left nothing.

3. For a representative sampling of the redactional makeup of ch. 1 over the past seventy-five years, see Niditch (1980: 509, n. 1). Gray provides a similar summary of scholarship up to and including his time (1912: 3–4). Roberts (1982: 293) also offers a brief survey of five different representative approaches, each situated in a particular historical framework.

4. This fatal ignorance will likewise concern Jeremiah: it is perfectly understandable, then, that Jeremiah's "new covenant" is distinguished not by new provisions, but by its being *known* by all (Jer 31:31-34).

5. See the discussion in Hayes and Irvine (1987: 75). Sweeney (1996a: 80–81) makes the same point but from a different angle: what Isaiah condemns specifically is "false offerings" (*minḥat-šāwʾ*, v. 13). Sweeney goes on to relate 1:10-17 to Hezekiah's cultic reforms (2 Kgs 18:1-8), which served to centralize the cult in Jerusalem as part of his larger military strategy against Assyria. This manipulation of the cult in service to the nation's foreign policy and strategic plans runs counter to Isaiah's fundamental teaching that the nation's survival is dependent upon the promise of God's protection, not on political and military initiatives. From such a perspective, Isaiah "condemns the temple service as false and hypocritical" (1996a: 81).

6. While the traditional translation, "rescue the oppressed," fits the context of other disadvantaged classes, namely, orphans and widows, confronting the ruthless is also contextually appropriate, fulfilling the first imperative, "Cease to do evil."

7. This word pair occurs 20 times in the Hebrew Bible, 17 of those instances in this word order. It occurs another 10 times in the plural, 4 times in the order "orphans and widows." In three instances, one term is plural and the other singular. Of the total 30 times, whether in the singular or plural, 10 instances are found in the prophets (4 times in Isaiah: singular in 1:17, 23; plural in 9:16 [Eng. 17]; 10:2), and 11 times in the book of Deuteronomy.

8. For a discussion of trends in the distinctiveness debate and a contribution to that discussion, see Machinist (1991).

9. In addition to these terms for poverty, van der Ploeg (1950: 236–70) adds three other synonyms for "poor": *rāš, rêq,* and *miskēn.*

10. It may be recalled that in the "entrance liturgy" found in Psalm 24, "those who seek *(dāraš)* him, who seek (Piel of **bqš*) the face of the God of Jacob" (v. 6) must give evidence of their moral purity (v. 4). Gary A. Anderson sees more than parallelism at work in these verses: *dāraš* has the sense described above, one making formal inquiry of God, while **bqš* has the sense of "whoever shows up." Both the needy pilgrim and the impromptu visitor to the shrine must be morally pure to gain admittance. Isaiah raises the stakes from personal morality to social responsibility.

11. Isaiah's religious or theological nuance of *dāraš* is confirmed by its other occurrences in First Isaiah. Its use in 16:5 is closest to that in 1:17: here a faithful ruler is described as one who "seeks justice and is swift to do what is right." There are two instances in which *dāraš* is used of those who "seek the ghosts and familiar spirits" or who consult "idols and the dead" (8:19; 19:3). Twice more the people are reproached for not seeking or consulting YHWH (9:12 [Eng. 13]; 31:1). Finally, in 11:10, on some eschatological day, the nations will seek the root of Jesse, who stands as a signal to the peoples. With the possible exception of this last instance, *dāraš* in First Isaiah is always used in what Wagner (1978: 49) describes as a figurative sense. In four of these instances, it is clearly used in a formal religious sense—to make inquiry of God, or the spirits, etc. Even in four of the remaining six occurrences in the book of Isaiah, the object of the verb *dāraš* is YHWH: 55:6; 58:2; 65:1; 65:10. In 34:16, the people are commanded to "seek and read from the book of YHWH": the book of God's word has become the stand-in for God, the place where his will may be ascertained. And finally, in a nice poetic reversal, God refers to restored Zion as a city "sought out" by God (62:12).

12. See Weinfeld (1995: 25–44). Weinfeld, discussing Isa 1:17, acknowledges the legal context and setting of these verses but describes the practical social consequences of such acts of justice: "the poor and weak should be saved in their struggle with the mighty" (1995: 40–41).

13. See Bovati (1994: 201–5). Bovati, discussing the verb *šāpaṭ* (to judge) and paying particular attention to its verbal parallels, in this case *rîb* (to plead a case), describes the legal procedures by which the righteous, or the unjustly oppressed, are "saved and defended," and conversely, the wicked and unjust oppressors are punished and condemned.

14. See Berkovits (1969a: 188–209). Berkovits roots the demand for justice in God's own concern for those to whom justice is denied (1969a: 191), which results in Berkovits's repeated theological dictum, "The ways of God with men become the laws of God for men" (1969a: 201 and again 209).

15. The Common Lectionary provides for an alternative option for the Proper Sundays. The first reading may be a continuous or semicontinuous reading of an Old Testament book, in which case the correspondence between the assigned readings for a given day is coincidental.

16. Isaiah 1:29-31 seems to be an addition made to the final form of the entire book, helping to round off the symmetry between chs. 1 and 65–66. On the rela-

tionship between chs. 1 and 65–66, see the summary discussion of Sweeney (1988: 21–25), though Sweeney himself holds that 1:29-31 are integral to ch. 1 and not a later addition. For an even more complete discussion, see Carr (1996: 188–218). See also Liebreich (1957: 128–29).

17. Repointing *šeber* as *šibbēr*.

18. Summaries of this long-standing debate are conveniently available. See Wildberger (1991: 85–87), who concludes that the oracle originates with Isaiah of Jerusalem; see also Sweeney (1998: 164–74), who outlines four positions and concludes that "Isa 2:2-4 should be dated after the time of Deutero-Isaiah to the period of the return when Jerusalem was reestablished as YHWH's home . . . [that is,] the late sixth century" (173–74); see also Williamson (1994: 147–48), who describes five approaches to the question of the relationship of 2:2-4 to the Isaianic tradition. Williamson himself eventually concludes that "2:2-4 is roughly contemporaneous with Deutero-Isaiah" and that "the manner in which the two [. . .] relate to one another is that 40–55 has drawn on 2:2-4 rather than the other way round" (152).

19. Clifford (1972: 157), commenting on Isa 2:2-4, describes "the holy mountain . . . [as] the place from where the authoritative word goes out." This is an instance of the more general characterization of the cosmic mountain as the place where "effective decrees are issued" (3). Levenson develops these observations at length (1985: 122–26).

20. The more common verbs used with *milḥāmâ* are: *yṣʾ* (go out, 44x); *bwʾ* (go to, 39x); *ʿlh* (go up to, 30x); *ʿśh* (make, 24x); and *ʿrk* (arrange for, 21x).

21. Bovati (1994: 185) cites the following examples: Gen 16:5; Exod 18:16; Num 35:24; Deut 1:16; Judg 11:27; 1 Sam 24:13, 16; Isa 5:3; Ezek 34:20.

22. So Clements (1980: 46–47); Jensen suggests a date of 735, when Ahaz became a vassal to Tiglath-pileser III (1984: 65); Vawter (1961: 178)takes the mention of "suckling" in v. 4 to refer to Ahaz who was titular regent during Jotham's last years (2 Kgs 16:2); Sweeney dates this specifically to the immediate aftermath of Hezekiah's revolt in 701 (1996a: 109). Stacey takes a minority position and attributes 3:1-7 to a post-Isaianic author (1993: 22). Surprisingly, Hayes and Irvine don't identify a specific historical moment but suggest that Isaiah is here imagining a children's game, "playing ruler" (1987: 88–89).

23. Reading *ʿl* with 1QIsa[a] for MT's *ʾl*.

24. The verb **nkr* with the noun **pny* forms an idiom **nkr pny,* which means "to show partiality" (Deut 1:17; 16:19; Prov 24:23; 28:21).

25. Following the Greek and Syriac, many commentators emend to *ʿammô,* "his people"; for those who do, see Gray (1912: 69), Wildberger (1991: 141–42); on accepting the MT, see Watts (1985: 41).

26. On the as yet unresolved meaning of this term *(*bʿr),* see Wildberger (1991: 142). Gray (1912: 69) proposes "depasture."

27. This is an extension of the ancient principle found, for example, in Exod 22:22-23 (Eng. 22:23-24)—"If you indeed abuse them [orphans and widows], when they cry out to me, I shall surely heed their cry; my anger shall burn, and I will kill you with the sword, and your wives shall become widows and your children orphans."

28. This is the only instance in Isaiah in which *bmšpṭ* is pointed with the definite article, *bammišpāṭ;* cf. 1:27; 3:14; 9:6. Repointing to *bĕmišpāṭ* involves no change in the consonantal text.

29. BDB, 873: the Niphal can mean, in addition to "shew oneself sacred, majestic," to "be honored or treated as sacred."

30. This is the very sentiment expressed in Prov 14:31, using slightly different vocabulary: "The one who oppresses the poor despises his maker, but the one who is gracious to the needy honors him."

31. But see Seitz (1993a: 84–87), who is inclined to understand this passage as the birth of the child promised in 7:14-16.

32. Weinfeld (1995: 9) lists the following biblical verses to demonstrate the association of social reforms with the anointing of the new king and with kingship: 2 Sam 8:15; 1 Kgs 10:9; Isa 9:4 (Eng. 5); 16:5; Jer 22:3, 15; 23:5; 33:15; Ps 72:1-2; Prov 16:12.

33. For the use of "father" as a guardian of the disadvantaged, Bovati further cites Job 31:18; Sir 4:10. See also Gen 45:8, in which Joseph, as "father to Pharaoh," cares for all the hungry and needy of the land. In the Additions to Esther (Greek B 13:6), Haman's role as second in command to the king is described as his being "our second father"; see also Greek Addition E, 16:11.

34. The Roman Lectionary (NAB) translates this phrase as "judgment and justice."

35 BDB, 508, offers for this isolated use of the Piel of **ktb* "busy writers that make a business of writing." A reiterative nuance is as likely. Wildberger proposes this translation of 10:1—"Woe to those who draw up statutes, which are plainly evil, / and eagerly establish decrees which are full of affliction" (1991: 189).

36. Among the texts Bovati cites are Deut 16:19; 24:17; 27:19; 1 Sam 8:3; Exod 23:6; Lam 3:35, 36.

37. For Sweeney's most recent treatment of the Josianic redaction of this passage, which he argues is part of the literary unit that spans 10:5—12:6, see his article (1996c: 103–18).

38. Again, see Wildberger (1991: 465–66) for an extensive listing of those holding for, and those denying, the Isaianic authorship of this passage.

39. Freedman, relying on Dahood's work, understands the particle, *lōʾ*, not as negative but as "asseverative," and translates: "And strictly in accordance with what his eyes see shall he judge, / and strictly in accordance with what his ears hear shall he decide, / so that he may judge with righteousness the poor, / so that he may decide with equity for the meek of the earth" (1971: 536). We may note that such a translation does not affect the desired outcome, but only the means: in either case, the poor are judged justly.

40. Reading *ʿāriṣ* for *ʾereṣ*.

41. Lit., "waistcloth." Many commentators change either the first or the second *ʾēzôr* to *ʾēsûr* (band) or *hăgôr* (belt, girdle).

42. For a treatment of chs. 28–33 considered as a unified literary block of material within, and tied to, the larger book, see Stansell (1996: 68–103).

43. See the article by Lang (1982). Asen, focusing on the image of flower garlands in 28:1, describes how domesticated flowers are indicative of "cultures of luxury" (1996: 75). He goes on to say that those who participated in the *marzēaḥ* were usually the wealthy and the affluent (1996: 77).

44. Asen, examining the image of flowers (and fruits) in Egypt, Canaan, and Greece, arrives at the same conclusion: "The reason for the destruction is rooted in the failure to bring forth the fruit of justice at the gate" (1996: 87).

45. In place of MT's Piel perfect *yissad,* read a Qal participle *yôsēd* with 1QIsa[b]: "I am now laying in Zion a stone." See also Jeppesen (1984: 93–99).

46. This is signaled by three features: (1) verses 15-17 are first-person divine direct discourse, while v. 18 shifts to third-person reference to YHWH; (2) this is followed in vv. 19-26 by second-person (singular and plural) address to the people indicating the prophet's own speech; (3) there is a shift in content from vv. 1-17 with their focus on condemnation and punishment, to vv. 18-26 with their focus on salvation and deliverance (Sweeney 1996a: 386–401).

47. Various candidates are proposed for the "king" mentioned in v. 1. Hayes and Irvine, with their focus on the eighth-century prophet, see v. 1 as an implied criticism of the North's Hoshea and a tribute to the just rule of Hezekiah in Judah (1987: 354–55). Clements (1980: 259–60) and Sweeney (1996a: 409–20) attribute this passage to the Josianic redaction of the book and see Josiah as the king mentioned in v. 1. Seitz interprets ch. 32 in light of chs. 36–39 and understands the king to be Hezekiah (1993a: 228–33). While he explicitly denies that Josiah has any named role whatsoever to play in the book of Isaiah, he is less explicit as to whether the reference to Hezekiah derives from Isaiah or from the placing of the Hezekiah stories at the end of this first part of the book of Isaiah. Watts for the most part bypasses the issue of historical referentiality and sees the passage as a wisdom instruction and translates, "*Suppose* a king should reign with righteousness and *likewise* princes rule with justice. Then . . ." (1985: 410; italics added). The purpose is a "civics lesson" presented sarcastically: everyone knows that justice and righteousness are in fact not in evidence (1985: 412–13).

48. In Isaiah 1–39 *melek* ("king") is found 58 times, and is always used of historical or specific persons: Uzziah, Jotham, Ahaz, Hezekiah, Rezin, Pekah, Tabeel; the kings of Egypt, Assyria, and Babylon, Sargon (20:1), Sennacherib (36:1), Tirhakah of Ethiopia (37:9); the five kings of Hamath, Arpad, Sepharvaim, Hena, and Ivvah (37:13); and generically "kings of the nations" (14:9, 18). God, too, is called "king" (6:5; 33:22), and the term is used as a cipher perhaps for Molech (30:33).

49. The order in 32:1 is actually *ṣedeq ûmišpāṭ,* which Weinfeld considers equivalent (1995: 25–26). Indeed, the fact that the terms can appear in either order with no apparent difference in meaning argues against understanding the two words as referring to different elements, for example, Motyer's principles and actions (1993: 72), or seeing one as qualifying the other in a particular way, for example, Bazak's "justice *marked* by righteousness" (1989: 6).

50. Bovati thinks that 32:7 refers to a "complaint," that is, "the procedure of someone speaking in the name of the law (cf. Isa. 32.7), addressing a judge as judge, that is, as a court of appeal with authority to decide in favor of the one who is (in the) right" (1994: 312). The judicial setting may indeed be included in the villainies contrived against the poor and needy, but such harmful practices are not restricted to the courtroom.

51. Although the hendiadys is not split in form, each word serves as the subject of different verbs; this break between the sentence parts is indicated by the *athnaḥ* that occurs between *mišpāṭ* and *ûṣĕdāqâ*.

52. For a more complete discussion, see Beuken (1992: 78–102).

53. The exhortatory refrain from the Holiness Code is "You shall be holy, for I, the LORD your God, am holy" (Lev 19:2; 20:26; 21:8; also 11:44, 45; 20:7).

54. For example, Bovati's discussion of the legal aspects, Gossai's exclusive focus on the aspect of "relationship," or Hayes and Irvine's tendency to interpret breaches of "justice and righteousness" as violations of the vassal covenant with Assyria are each too narrow.

55. Hanson (1994a); see pp. 34–37 of this study for the excursus on orphans and widows.

4. Isaiah 40–55

1. For a review of scholarship on Second Isaiah see Fohrer (1980: 1–39, 109–32); Schoors (1973: 1–31); Spykerboer (1976: 1–29); Stuhlmueller (1980: 1–29); Tate (1996: 22–56, esp. 38–43); Baltzer (2001: 1–44).

2. Though the forms in this verse *(ṣaddîq ûmôšîaʿ)* are different, they are nonetheless both from the same two roots under discussion, **ṣdq* and **yšʿ*.

3. McKenzie (1968; 1978: xxxviii–lv) provides a convenient summary of interpretations that propose collective, individual, and ideal candidates for the Servant. See also Muilenburg (1956, 5:406–14); a more recent survey is that of Kruse (1978: 3–27).

4. This summary of Duhm's position is that of Mettinger (1983: 9). Among the many responses to Mettinger's monograph, see especially those of Emerton (1981: 626–32); and Hermisson (1984: 209–22).

5. Mettinger 1983, chs. 1, 2, and 3, respectively. The tendency to segregate the Servant Songs from the rest of Second Isaiah is increasingly contested, as, for example, in Beuken (1972: 1–30); see also Wilcox and Paton-Williams (1988: 79–102), who "attempt to relate the four 'Servant Songs' in the prophecies of Deutero-Isaiah . . . more closely to their context" (79).

6. See also Hermisson (1996: 43–68), who sees the individual and collective aspects at work simultaneously. We will have more to say about the "individual vs. collective" interpretations in the discussion of 42:1-4.

7. Mettinger's analysis stumbles particularly over the problem of "innocent Israel" in 52:13—53:12 but "punished Jerusalem" in 50:2. To harmonize these discrepancies, he must identify the innocent Servant of 52:13—53:12 as "a pious rem-

nant" in Israel, whereas in all other instances the Servant is simply Israel. His treatment of 49:1-6 is also problematic: his argument that the infinitives of vv. 5-6 refer to YHWH, not the Servant, is grammatically awkward and unconvincing.

8. For a helpful discussion of the intersection between the theological thought world and the historical circumstances that provide the conceptual background for the Servant Songs, see Hanson (1998: 9–22).

9. See 40:19-20; 41:5-7; 44:9-20. But Spykerboer's study of the polemics against idolatry concludes that the passages in question "are intimately rooted in their context and cannot be separated from it, without disturbing [Deutero-Isaiah's] line of thought" (1976: 185). See also Laato (1990: 207–28), whose structural analysis argues that the Servant Songs and the idol passages are not later additions, but are integral to the composition.

10. See 42:18-25; 46:8, 12-13; 48:12-16, 17-19; 49:7, 8-12, 24-26; 50:3; 51:1-2, 4-8; 51:12-14, 15-16; 54:11-17; 55:6-7. For details of this *qārôb* argument, advanced by Hermisson (1984), see the analysis and critique of Williamson (1994: 22–26).

11. See the discussion in Kaufmann (1970:3–65); for a briefer survey, see Paul D. Hanson (1995: 1–4).

12. The evidence usually advanced for this position includes the following: (1) specific mention of YHWH having delivered Israel over to destruction (42:24; 43:27-28; 47:6); (2) the description of Zion as destroyed and abandoned (49:14, 17, 19; 51:19); (3) frequent references to Babylon or Chaldea (43:14; 47:1, 5; 48:14) and, more specifically, the exhortation for the people to depart from Babylon (48:20; 55:12a); (4) the general and pervasive exodus imagery (for example, 43:16; 51:10), including especially the highway through the desert (40:3-5; 42:16; 43:19; 49:11), all of which presumes that the people are traveling or returning *to* Palestine; (5) the decisive action of YHWH's ingathering of the people from afar (49:22; 51:11); (6) the mention of Cyrus, the Persian conqueror, by name (44:28; 45:1); (7) detailed descriptions of Babylonian cultic practices (for example, 44:9-20; 46:1ff.); (8) the contrast between the "new things" of the present and the "former things," which presumes that those former things are truly in the past (Seitz 1990: 229–47; 1993b: 260–66). All of this argues persuasively for setting Second Isaiah in the mid-sixth century in Babylon.

13. It should be noted that, although Seitz reports this consensus, he is not altogether convinced of it. He raises the possibility that chs. 40–55 might "be better understood as Jerusalemite both in orientation (as many have admitted) and in origin (as most have not)" (1993b: 265). In his article (1992: 501–7), he advances aspects of that argument by raising further questions about the distinction between a Second and a Third Isaiah, a matter we will take up later. In both these articles, and in his commentary (1993a: 240–42), he maintains that the distinction between chs. 1–39 and 40–66 is not primarily historical (preexilic/exilic) or geographical (Judah/Babylon), but literary. According to his analysis, the break comes between chs. 33 and 34 and is structured around the typological theme of "former" and "new" things: Zion's deliverance in 701 is the promise of her ultimate vindication, about to be realized in her return from exile. Thus, the primary concern that

shapes the material is *"God's fundamental, abiding concern for Zion's final triumph and permanent fortification against the nations"* (1993a: 242; italics his). For the position that all of the prophet's message was directed to the Judeans in Judah, see Barstad (1982: 77–87; 1987: 90–110; 1996).

14. Torrey (1928) mounts a sustained and systematic attack against the Babylonian setting of Second Isaiah (and the existence of a Third Isaiah). For a succinct summary of Torrey's argument, see Schramm (1995: 21–31).

15. Seitz (1990); Clifford (1984: 72–74); Scullion (1982: 21–23); also, Cross (1953: 274–78).

16. This is a common view: see, for example, Whybray (1975: 48–51); McKenzie (1978: 15–19); Clifford (1984: 74ff.).

17. Most commentators, following the LXX, omit this phrase. It is supported by 1QIsa[a], though it appears in smaller script.

18. Of the former he asserts that both terms refer to "the proper way (of doing something)," and he cites instances in which *derek* is linked to various nouns to produce such phrases as "the way of life" (Prov 6:23), of "peace" (Isa 59:8), of "understanding" (Prov 9:6), and of "insight" (Prov 21:16). He simply asserts that *ʾōraḥ* is used in exactly the same way in Ps 16:11; Prov 2:19; 5:6; 10:17. He then shows how *derek* can be "taught" (Hiphil of **yrh*), which he argues is equivalent to "to teach" (Piel of **lmd*) in Isa 40:14. Drawing on Isa 28:26, where *mišpāṭ* was used to describe the proper way of planting, and likening *mišpāṭ* to *tĕbûnôt* and *bînâ,* which signify "practical knowledge," Whybray translates *ʾōraḥ mišpāṭ* in Isa 40:14 as "the way of achieving a proper order (in what one does)" (1971: 16–17).

19. The expression *ʾōraḥ mišpāṭ* (as in Isa 40:14) occurs two times: Prov 2:8 and 17:23. In both instances, the noun *ʾōraḥ* is plural, though its parallel in Prov 2:8 is the singular of *derek*. To determine whether the variation between the singular of *ʾōraḥ* in Isa 40:14 and the plural *ʾorḥôt* in these two texts is significant, we can compare Prov 2:8 and 8:20, where the terms for *road, path,* or *way* are singular in one colon and plural in the parallel cola. According to Kugel, such alternation between singular and plural is one of nine or more literary devices in which an author/poet creates "differentiation" rather than "parallelism" between the two cola of a line (1981: 20–21). In this instance, then, the difference between the singular and plural seems to be a matter of style, not substance. These two passages may be taken as equivalent to the singular expression as found in Isa 40:14 and suitable for comparison.

In Prov 8:20, the situation is slightly different, though still informative: the expression is actually *nĕtîbôt mišpāṭ* ("paths of justice"). However, its parallel with *ʾōraḥ-ṣĕdāqâ* ("way of righteousness") puts it in the same semantic range of meaning and can suitably be drawn into the discussion. Along with Prov 2:8-9 and 17:23, it can be helpful in determining the nuance of the term *mišpāṭ*.

20. For a more extended treatment of the relationship between Isaiah 40 and Proverbs 8 see Gosse (1993: 186–93).

21. In his form-critical study of 40:12-31, Melugin (1971: 326–37) classifies 40:12-17 as a "Wisdom disputation."

22. Clifford (1980: 35–48) sees this progression of events in Psalm 89: death of Sea (vv. 10-11 [Eng. 9-10]), establishment of heaven and earth (vv. 12-13 [Eng. 11-12]), victory procession (vv. 14-19 [Eng. 13-18]), appointment of king (vv. 20ff. [Eng. 19ff.]). See also Clifford (1993: 1–17).

23. Clifford credits Prof. Paul Mosca for the comparison of v. 12 and vv. 15-16.

24. This term is best understood in the broader sense of "rulers," as its parallel with *rôzĕnîm* (princes) confirms. This is the only instance in the Hebrew Bible where *šōpēṭ* is used in parallel to *rôzĕnîm,* whose usual partner is "kings" (for example, Judg 5:3; Hab 1:10; Ps 2:2; Prov 8:15; 31:4). The expression "rulers of the earth" *(šōpĕṭê ʾereṣ)* is also found in Pss 2:10 and 148:11 with the same meaning.

25. See, for example, Whybray (1975: 53–54); Hanson (1995: 28). On Ea's counsel to Marduk in his battle with Tiamat, see *Enuma Elish* 2:96–102; on Ea's counsel to Marduk and his role in the creation of humanity, see 6:11-37; on Ea leading the gods in proclaiming Marduk as *Lugal-dimmer-an-ki-a,* "The king of the gods of heaven and earth," see 6:28; for a brief discussion of these passages, see Jacobsen (1976: 179–81).

26. On *mišpāṭ* as a verbal link between chs. 40 and 41, see Hanson (1995: 33–35).

27. According to von Waldow (1968: 259–88), YHWH presiding as judge over the Gentile nations and their gods (41:1-5, 21-29; 43:8-13; 44:6-8) is an innovation of Second Isaiah.

28. On chs. 40 and 41 as the context for understanding 42:1-4, see Beuken, who concludes that "Israel's *mišpāṭ,* violated by the nations, which seem to enjoy the protection of their gods, and apparently disregarded by Yhwh, is the issue at stake throughout Is. xl 12–xli 29" (1972: 23).

29. To these various features may be added those of a priest (so McKenzie 1978: 36–38) and a messenger of the heavenly court (so Watts 1987: 119).

30. For a detailed analysis of the parallels between 41:8-16 and 42:1-6, see Goldingay (1979: 289–99); unlike Hanson, however, he concludes, as do Wilcox and Paton-Williams, that the servant in 42:1-4 is Israel. Mettinger (1983: 28) also situates 42:1-9 in the compositional unit 41:1—42:13 and sees 41:8-13 as a "companion piece" to 42:1-9. As we saw earlier, Mettinger understands the Servant as Israel.

31. We may note here that this word pair occurs again in 51:4. It is also possible to recall Isa 2:2-4, in which *tôrâ* goes forth from Zion, from where YHWH rules *(špṭ)* the nations.

32. Melugin (1976: 99) also examines these references to Egypt's inability to provide security but argues in a different direction, namely, that "the servant will not rely on a crushed reed and thus break it; nor will he depend on and thus extinguish a dimly-burning wick."

33. The LXX of Isa 42:1 identifies the figure as "Jacob/Israel." Its term for "my servant" is *pais mou; pais* means both "child" and "slave." Matthew resolves any ambiguity by using *huios mou,* "my son" (3:17).

34. See, for example, summary discussions in Wilcox and Paton-Williams (1988: 80–82); Scullion (1990: 96–97); Stuhlmueller (1980: 5–6).

35. For a brief but helpful discussion of *pĕᶜullâ,* see Stuhlmueller (1970: 219–20).

36. According to Muilenburg (1956: 404) this "mighty first person" aspect of divine speech, coupled with all "the emphatic use of the second person" speech addressed to Israel, highlights the intimate nature of the "I-Thou" relationship between God and Israel. See also Phillips (1971: 32–51).

37. Whitely argues that the noun *ṣedeq* refers to YHWH's essence and that, in 51:4-6, where it is parallel with *my salvation,* it means more properly "my divine rule" (1972: 475).

38. While some commentators note this curiosity, no explanation is offered; see, for example, Watts (1987: 236); Kutscher (1974: 552); Schwarz (1971: 254–550). Frank Moore Cross (private communication), noting the dots above and below the *ḥet* of *yṣlḥ,* offers the following explanation:

> Sometimes such dots are found where there is a textual disturbance in the text. For example note in 40:8 the dots under *wdrb.* A later hand (that of the *Serek hay-yaḥad* of Cave 1) fills in the words missing owing to haplography. Again, look at 36:4 and 36:7 where pluses over MT are dotted. This manuscript has been worked over a number of times as we can tell from the hands of several correctors of a later date.
>
> It is not out of the question that the manuscript from which 1QIsaa was copied was defective here, and that the scribe thus left a blank space to be filled in later—and never got back. This phenomenon is well attested by blanks in 1QS, which we can now fill in from Cave 4 copies of the work.

39. It may be that the speaker in this oracle is either a member of the heavenly court or even YHWH himself, whose voice explicitly appears in v. 25. Watts, dividing these kinds of verses between choruses of "heavens" and "earth," assigns this verse to "earth."

40. This verse could be spoken by the prophet; the text is not clear.

5. Isaiah 56–66

1. For another assessment of the scholarship, see also Hanson (1979: 32–46; idem, (1987: 253–68). See also P. A. Smith (1995: 22–49), who supports the distinctiveness of chs. 56–66, which are best interpreted in light of the entire book of Isaiah; he identifies two basic strands, or prophetic minds (Third Isaiah 1 and 2), and dates the work between 538 and 515. Brueggemann, too, places these chapters in the early postexilic period: most broadly, between 520 and 444, but most likely soon after 520 (1998b: 164).

2. See the discussion of opinions in Schramm (1995: 115–18) and P. A. Smith (1995: 50–61).

3. For a comprehensive examination of this theme, see Scullion 1971: 333–48.

4. The negative use of *min* (cf. GKC §119v-w), here prefixed to the Piel infinitive construct, reads literally "who keeps the Sabbath, not profaning it." 1QIsa[a] reads *mḥllh,* taking "Sabbath" as feminine; for the details, see Watts 1987: 244.

5. Melamed (1961: 149), sees these terms as a split hendiadys, *ʾĕnôš ben ʾādām*, "the full form of the term for 'human being.'"

6. The verb *ʿāśâ* with *ṣĕdāqâ* as its sole object is found only in Isa 56:1 and 58:2 (Smith 1995: 102, n. 19). Further, the plural imperative *šimrû mišpāṭ* is nowhere else to be found, and the singular imperative with *mišpāṭ* is found only once, in Hos 12:7 (Eng. 6), which commands "observe loving-kindness and justice" (*ḥesed ûmišpāṭ šĕmōr*). The only other instance in which the verb **šmr* is used with the absolute singular of *mišpāṭ* is in Ps 106:3, where the psalmist declares, "happy are they who observe justice [and] the one who does righteousness" (*ʾašrê šōmĕrê mišpāṭ ʿōśēh ṣĕdāqâ*). So in 56:1, the use of the plural of **šmr* with the singular of *mišpāṭ* is unexpected and atypical. While the pairing of the verbs *ʿāśâ* and **šmr* found in 56:1 is very common, especially in Deuteronomy (some 33 times) and Leviticus (some 10 times), the occurrence of the coordinated imperatives is rare (elsewhere only in Ezek 20:19 and 2 Chr 19:7). In Deuteronomy, the two verbs are often used in a modifying, rather than a parallel, relationship signifying "to observe diligently" (for example, Gen 18:19; 2 Sam 8:15; 1 Kgs 10:9; Jer 22:3, 15; 23:5; 33:15; Ezek 18:5; Prov 21:3; 1 Chr 18:14; 2 Chr 9:8).

7. Polan, whose analysis we have followed so far on this point, thinks that the pronouns in v. 2a point to v. 2b only, and argues specifically against seeing *zō(ʾ)t*/this and *bāh*/it as references to either v. 1a only (so Pauritsch 1971), or to both v. 1a and v. 2b (so Muilenburg 1956). While we agree with Polan that the immediate reference is to v. 2b, there is no reason that this dramatically delayed specification must be so limited.

8. Looking to v. 1 for the referent of the pronouns is not only rhetorically possible, it is also grammatically legitimate: just as a feminine noun may be used to refer to classes of ideas and abstracts (GKC §122q), the feminine pronoun can be used—as here—to refer to the verbal idea of a preceding statement (GKC §135p; Joüon 1993: §152b).

9. Because the subject of these verses is the eunuch, it is possible that *yād* ("monument") is used euphemistically for the sexual organ (for example, 2 Sam 18:18; see also BDB, 390, #4.g). The double entendre is continued at the end of v. 5, in which YHWH restores to the eunuch an everlasting name that will not be *cut off.* Schramm (1995: 124 and n. 5) also refers to this and thinks that "the writer is having some fun at the expense of the eunuchs."

10. To this inclusion, Polan (1986: 51–52) adds "the distant parallelism" of *lbwʾ* in v. 1 and *mqbṣ* in v. 8. Throughout his discussion of the "indications of unity in Isaiah 56:1-8" (1997: 44–52), Polan focuses on internal features, rhetorical devices, and the progression of thought that unite the passage. My argument is focused more specifically on the elements of vv. 1-2 that are linked to features in vv. 3-8, arguing against Westermann et al., who separate these two sections.

11. For further discussion of the unity of the passages, see Polan's discussion cited above; also the discussions of P. A. Smith (1995: 50–54) and van Winkle (1997: 234–35).

12. Use of the word "covenant" has been generic, referring to international treaties (28:15, 18; 33:8) or God's covenant with the earth (24:5, the covenant with Noah). It is used somewhat ambiguously to describe the Servant's vocation as a "covenant to the people" (42:6; 49:8). In 54:10, the "covenant of peace" is used alongside other images of compassion, restoration, and fidelity. Finally in 55:3 it refers to a future covenant God will make, like the former covenant of loyalty with David.

13. For the position that Isaiah presumes the covenant tradition, see Eichrodt (1983: 167–88). The argument is largely inferred from Isaiah's use of Zion, cultic, and amphictyonic traditions related to the covenant. Eichrodt argues from silence: "Knowledge of the divine commandments is here taken for granted and does not need to be mentioned" (187). Further, Eichrodt alleges that Isaiah avoids the use of the term "covenant" because of disputed prophetic and popular understandings of the covenant. Rather than engage a theological debate on the nature of the covenant, Isaiah simply addressed himself to the message of impending judgment.

14. Polan (1986: 69–70, with notes). Polan cites the work of Baker (1980: 131) and refers to GKC §155n.

15. Schramm explicitly refutes Duhm's interpretation of 56:1 in a conditional sense ("If you observe justice and do righteousness, then my salvation will come"). Weinfeld (1995: 197) holds the opposite view on 56:1, namely, "that the observance by society of 'justice and righteousness' will bring about the revelation of salvation and righteousness by God." In commenting on 56:1, Weinfeld says that "the vindication of the Lord is made conditional upon the individual's practicing justice and righteousness" (1995: 221). I am inclined to understand the coming of salvation and deliverance as dependent on the doing of justice and righteousness. This view is supported negatively by 59:9-14, which laments that because justice and righteousness are far off, so, too, is salvation.

16. Webster 1997; Webster argues that "we should read the oracle [56:1-8] with primary emphasis on the unlimited efficacy of sabbath and covenant observance—an efficacy that could override even a demand for purity in descent and for physical wholeness."

17. The vocabulary of both the NRSV and the NAB translations is problematic. As the commentary on this passage indicated, the opening expression is the hendiadys "justice and righteousness." The NRSV translates "Maintain justice, do what is right." The NAB translates, "Observe what is right, do what is just," taking *ṣĕdāqâ* to mean "just." For this reason, it also translates the second appearance of *ṣĕdāqâ* in this verse as "justice"—"for my salvation is about to come, my *justice* (*ṣĕdāqâ*) about to be revealed."

18. The further division of this unit into strophes is more complicated. Most (for example, Westermann 1975, Hanson 1979, Whybray 1975, Schramm 1995) consider the first strophe to be. vv. 1-4; P. A. Smith (1995) argues that the division is vv. 1-5; Polan (1986) takes an intermediate position: vv. 1-4 and 6-9a are bridged by v. 5.

19. For a discussion of various translation possibilities for the initial *waw,* see P. A. Smith (1995: 105), who suggests that "yet" conveys the sense of irony of the

prophet's announcing sins to people who appear to be religiously observant. See also Polan (1986: 193).

20. Polan (1986: 173) inexplicably translates *mišpĕṭê-ṣedeq* in the singular, "righteous justice." Scullion (1971: 343) rightly notes that *mišpĕṭê-ṣedeq* means "instructions or ordinances that will set them in the way of *ṣedeq*, external prescriptions such as are listed in vv. 3-4." Elsewhere, Scullion argues, "In 58:2 *sedeq* is determined by *mishpat* in the construct plural and the context to mean instructions that will make the people pleasing to God" (1990: 211). Avishur (1971–1972: 75) points to *mišpaṭ ṣedeq* as an example of a parallel word pair in construct whose meaning "comes from a combination of the meanings of the two component parts"; that is, the meaning of the construct relationship is different from the word pair when it appears as either a hendiadys or in parallel. In the case of *mišpĕṭê-ṣedeq* in 58:2, he translates somewhat woodenly, "the righteousness of justice" (36–37); this ignores the plural form and the obvious meaning of legal ordinances.

21. Scullion (1971: 343) says that "It is not straining the text to see in Is 58,2 a direct reference to the covenant."

22. We are taking the shift from the previous three infinitives absolute to the plural imperfect and the adversative *waw* (*wĕkol-*) to signal the end of the interrogative. Many read the interrogative to the end of the verse. Similarly, many read all of v. 7 as a question. The difference is more stylistic than substantive.

23. The references are those cited in Westermann (1975: 346). For *lip(s)* (*śāpâ*) speaking deceit (*šeqer*), see also Ps 31:19 (Eng. 18); Prov 10:18; 12:22; 17:7; for a *tongue* (*lāšôn*) uttering *wickedness* (*ʿawlâ*) see also Job 6:30. Finally, for a *tongue* (*lāšôn*) speaking *deceit* (*šeqer*), see Prov 12:19. Regarding the language of Isa 59:4b, Scullion (1990: 167) offers the following references: Pss 12:3-4 (Eng. 2-3); 41:7 (Eng. 6); 144(143):8; Muilenburg (1956: 688) cites Ps 7:15 (Eng. 14) and Job 15:35; Westermann (1975: 347) cites in addition Ps 148:11; Ezek 13:8; Zech 10:2; Ps 7:15 (Eng. 14).

24. Bovati (1994: 315, n. 136) says that *qārāʾ* is used with "the juridical nuance of a complaint (or appeal) . . . only in requests addressed to God, not in ones to human tribunals." The context is prayer framed in the language of the court.

25. Bovati (1994: 282) also understands *dabber-šāwʾ* of v. 4b as false testimony.

26. Weinfeld (1995: 30–31) however, is not so literal in his understanding of "road" or "path" imagery; when used with the terms *justice, righteousness, truth,* and *equity,* it refers to just dealings in social conduct; so also Bovati 1994: 192, n. 52.

27. Bovati interprets the images of light and darkness juridically: "Since the break of day is the equivalent of the moment in which judgment in accordance with justice takes place, light becomes the symbol of the victory of law . . . whereas darkness is the framework for images of the dominance or continuance of injustice" (1994: 368).

28. The proposed translation of 59:11b provides the very terminology for the new literary form Hanson identifies as the "salvation-judgment oracle"; see Hanson 1979: 106–7, 119–20.

29. On the meanings of the root **qwh* ("to look for, expect," "to wait for"), see Polan 1986: 278–79.

30. Muilenburg (1956: 693) cites with approval Lagarde's proposed emendation of *dbr-ʿšq* to *dbr-ʿqš*, "speaking deceit," which minimizes further the social aspect of oppression in favor of still more verbal activity. Whybray (1975: 225) also suggests *ʿiqqēš* for *ʿōšeḳ*, "'that which is crooked' (the corresponding verb occurs in verse 8)."

31. Bovati (1994: 230 with n. 20) notes that *town square* "seems to have the force of a law court in Job 29:7 (parallel to 'gate') and in Isa. 59:14 (cf. also Ps 55:12)."

32. For a discussion of the servants in Third Isaiah, see Beuken 1990: 67–87.

33. For similar assessments and sentiments, see Muilenburg 1956: 694; Scullion 1990: 168; Hanson 1979: 123–24; idem 1995: 211–12. Watts (1987: 286ff.), somewhat idiosyncratically, agrees that the "distressing situation" of 59:1-15a has attracted God's attention, but Watts suggests that God's solution is to send Artaxerxes I, clothed in the battle regalia described in 59:17, to rectify the situation.

34. See, for example, Neufeld 1997 and von Rad 1991.

35. Westermann (1975: 296–308) presents a common view of the structure and composition of Third Isaiah and the role of these chapters as the nucleus. See also Hanson 1979: 59–77, and P. A Smith 1995: 26–38.

36. Seitz (1996: 238) posits a genetic relationship between this voice and the prophet who speaks in 49:1-7; 50:4-9. Beuken (1989: 411–42) understands vv. 1-3a as a self-presentation of the speaker as the offspring of the Servant. See also Muilenburg 1956: 708; Westermann 1975: 365–67; Whybray 1975: 239–40; McKenzie 1978: 180–81; Scullion 1990: 178; Hanson 1995: 223–24.

37. Watts (1987: 303), who cites Jer 34:8, 15, 17. Westermann (1975: 366), however, thinks that the liberation of captives refers not to the freeing of the exiles, but to the release of those who have been imprisoned for debt.

38. Notice the threefold repetition of the pattern "this instead of that" in 61:3.

39. Reading *bĕʿawlâ* with the versions. Hanson (1979: 58, note "s") reads with the MT, as does the JPS, "robbery with a burnt offering." In his 1995 commentary, Hanson stays with the NRSV, the base text for the Interpretation series, which reads "robbery and wrongdoing."

40. For a survey of these positions, see Muilenburg 1956: 758. He divides the chapter into two units, vv. 1-16, 17-24. The first unit is further divided into 7 strophes: vv. 1-2, 3-4, 5-6, 7-9, 10-11, 12-14, 15-16. After Muilenburg's commentary we find the following analyses: Westermann (1975), vv. 1-4, 5, 6-16, 17, 18-24; McKenzie (1978), vv. 1-4, 5-24; Hanson (1979), vv. 1-2, 3-4, 5-6, 7-9, 10-11, 12-16 (and a redactional framework: vv. 17-24); Watts (1987), 65:17—66:5, 6-24; Scullion's analysis (1990) takes the chapter as fragments: vv. 1-4, 5, 6, 7-14, 15-16, 17, 18-21, 22, 23, 24; Schramm (1995), vv. 1-17, 18-24.

41. The other usual use of the Niphal is the passive sense, "to be judged," for example, Pss 9:20 (Eng. 19); 37:33; 109:7 (so BDB, 1048, #2). See also Bovati's discussion of the Niphal of **špṭ* (1994: 49), which supports these two general senses. He understands 66:16 in the sense of "being at odds legally with some-

one." He takes the expression "with fire" metaphorically, that is, as the "heat of wrath" (p. 51).

6. Justice in Diachronic and Synchronic Perspectives

1. See "Excursus: Concern for the 'Orphan and Widow'" in ch. 3, especially the discussion of the views of Hanson.

2. Both Rendtorff and Polan have argued that the presence in 56:1 of the two word pairs that were distinctive of First Isaiah *(mišpāṭ ûṣĕdāqâ)* and Second Isaiah *(yĕšûʿâ ûṣĕdāqâ)*, respectively, demonstrates a conscious and deliberate reference to the antecedent Isaiahs.

3. The *Masora parva* indicates that 33:20 is the exact midpoint of the book's total verses.

4. On the intersection of divine graciousness, redemption, and restoration in Second Isaiah, and the people's response to divine graciousness in acts of compassionate justice, see Hanson 1997: 182–83.

5. People include: "your ancestors" (Deut 10:15), Israel (for example, 1 Kgs 10:9; Hos 3:1; 2 Chr 9:8); Solomon (2 Sam 12:24); Cyrus (Isa 48:14). Things he loves: righteous deeds (Ps 11:7); the gates of Zion (Ps 87:2); the righteous (Ps 146:8); the one whom he reproves (Prov 3:12); those who pursue righteousness (Prov 15:9). It is curious to note that in the Psalms, when the verb "to love" *(*ʾhb)* is used of YHWH, it most often occurs as a participle (Pss 11:5; 33:5; 37:28; 87:2; 146:8), just as it does in Isa 61:8.

6. The title is found outside Isaiah only 6 times, in 2 Kgs 19:22; Jer 50:29; 51:5; Pss 71:22; 78:41; 89:19 (Eng. 18).

7. Magonet 1991: 175–81. His structural analysis demonstrates this supremacy pictorially. On the connections between Zion, Sinai, and the cosmic mountain, see especially Levenson 1985: 187–208.

8. For Sweeney's understanding of "Exhortation," "Instruction" and "(Priestly) Torah," see his glossary, 1996a: 520, 522, and 527, respectively.

9. *Tôrâ* is also identified with *ṣedeq* in 42:21 and 51:7.

10. The root **drk* is also used verbally as part of the idioms "to bend the bow" (5:28; 21:15) and "to trample the vineyard" (16:10; 63:3); it also means "staff or rod" (10:24).

11. See also Johnston 1994: 31–40. She sees an Isaianic "servant community" as an alternative to Ezekiel's priestly community centered around the temple.

12. Third Isaiah's only use of the singular "servant" is his reference to God's "servant Moses" (63:11).

Bibliography

Accordance. 2001. *Accordance: Bible Study Software for the Macintosh.* Version 5.0. Vancouver, Wash.: Gramcord Institute.

Achtemeier, Elizabeth. 1962. "Righteousness in the OT." In *IDB* 4:80–85.

———. 1988. "Isaiah of Jerusalem: Themes and Preaching Possibilities." In *Reading and Preaching the Book of Isaiah,* edited by C. R. Seitz, 22–37. Philadelphia: Fortress Press.

Ackroyd, Peter. 1987. "Isaiah I–XII: Presentation of a Prophet." In *Studies in the Religious Tradition of the Old Testament,* 79–104. London: SCM.

Aharoni, Yohanan. 1979. *The Land of the Bible: A Historical Geography,* translated by A. F. Rainey. Philadelphia: Westminster.

Alt, Albrecht. 1953. "Jesaja 8,23—9,6: Befreiungsnacht und Krönungstag." In *Kleine Schriften zur Geschichte des Volkes Israel,* 2:206–25. Munich: Beck.

Amit, Yairah. 1992. "The Jubilee Law—An Attempt at Instituting Social Justice." In *Justice and Righteousness: Biblical Themes and Their Influence,* edited by H. G. Reventlow and Y. Hoffman, 47–59. JSOTSup 137. Sheffield: JSOT Press.

Anderson, Bernhard W. 1976. "Exodus and Covenant in Second Isaiah and Prophetic Tradition." In *Magnalia Dei, the Mighty Acts of God: Essays on the Bible and Archaeology in Memory of G. Ernest Wright,* edited by F. M. Cross et al., 339–60. Garden City, N.Y.: Doubleday.

———. 1988. "The Apocalyptic Rendering of the Isaiah Tradition." In *The Social World of Formative Christianity and Judaism,* edited by J. Neusner et al., 17–38. Philadelphia: Fortress Press.

———. 1994. "The Slaying of the Fleeing, Twisting Serpent: Isaiah 27:1 in Context." In *Uncovering Ancient Stones: Essays in Memory of H. Neil Richardson,* edited by L. M. Hopfe, 3–15. Winona Lake, Ind.: Eisenbrauns.

Asen, Bernhard A. 1996. "The Garlands of Ephraim: Isaiah 28:1-6 and the *marzēaḥ*." *JSOT* 71:73–87.

Auld, A. Graeme. 1980. "Poetry, Prophecy, Hermeneutic: Recent Studies in Isaiah." *SJT* 33:567–81.

Avishur, Yitshak. 1971–1972. "Pairs of Synonymous Words in the Construct State (and Appositional Hendiadys) in Biblical Hebrew." *Sem* 2:17–81.

Baker, D. W. 1980. "Further Examples of the *waw explicativum*." *VT* 20:129–36.

Balentine, Samuel E. 1985. "Prayer in the Wilderness Traditions: In Pursuit of Divine Justice." *Hebrew Annual Review* 9:53–74.

Banks, J. S. 1905. "Justice." In *A Dictionary of the Bible,* edited by J. Hastings, 2:825–26. Edinburgh: T. & T. Clark.

Barr, James. 1961. *The Semantics of Biblical Language.* London: Oxford University Press.

———. 1995. "The Synchronic, the Diachronic and the Historical: A Triangular Relationship?" In *Synchronic or Diachronic? A Debate on Method in Old Testament Exegesis,* edited by J. C. de Moor, 1–14. OtSt 34. Leiden: Brill.

Barré, Michael L. 1985. "Fasting in Isaiah 58:1–12: A Reexamination." *BTB* 15:94–97.

———. 1990. "Amos." In *NJBC,* 209–16. Englewood Cliffs, N.J.: Prentice Hall.

Barstad, Hans M. 1982. "Lebte Deuterojesaja in Judäa?" *Norsk Teologisk Tidsskrift* 83(2):77–87.

———. 1987. "On the So-Called Babylonian Literary Influence in Second Isaiah." *SJOT* 2:90–110.

———. 1994. "The Future of the 'Servant Songs': Some Reflections of the Relationship of Biblical Scholarship to Its Own Tradition." In *Language, Theology, and the Bible: Essays in Honour of James Barr,* edited by S. E. Balentine and J. Barton, 261–70. Oxford: Clarendon.

———. 1996. *The Myth of the Empty Land: A Study in the History and Archaeology of Judah during the "Exilic" Period.* Symbolae Osloenses Supplementum 28. Oslo: Scandinavian University Press.

———. 1997. *The Babylonian Captivity of the Book of Isaiah: "Exilic" Judah and the Provenance of Isaiah 40–55.* Serie B: Skrifter 102. Oslo: Novus.

Bartelt, Andrew H. 1996. *The Book around Immanuel: Style and Structure in Isaiah 2–12.* Winona Lake, Ind.: Eisenbrauns.

Barton, John. 1981. "Ethics in Isaiah of Jerusalem." *JTS* 32:1–18.

———. 1984. *Reading the Old Testament: Method in Biblical Study.* Philadelphia: Westminster.

———. 1995. *Isaiah 1–39.* Old Testament Guides. Sheffield: Sheffield Academic.

———. 1997. "Ethics in the Book of Isaiah." In *Writing and Reading the Scroll of Isaiah: Studies of an Interpretive Tradition,* edited by C. C. Broyles and C. A. Evans, 67–77. VTSup 70. Leiden: Brill.

Bastiaens, Jean, Wim Beuken, and Ferenc Postma. 1984. *Trito-Isaiah: An Exhaustive Concordance of Isa. 56–66.* Amsterdam: Free University Press.

Bazak, Jacob. 1989. "The Meaning of the Term 'Justice and Righteousness' in the Bible." *Jewish Law Annual* 8:5–13.

Beaucamp, E. 1969. "La Justice en Israël." In *Populus Dei,* vol. 1: *Israel,* 201–35. Rome: Communio.

Becker, Uwe. 1999. "Jesajaforschung (Jes 1–39)." *TRu* 64:1–37.

Bellinger, William H., and William R. Farmer, eds. 1998. *Jesus and the Suffering Servant: Isaiah 53 and Christian Origins.* Harrisburg, Pa.: Trinity Press International.

Ben Zvi, Ehud. 1991. "Isaiah 1,4-9, Isaiah, and the Events of 701 BCE in Judah: A Question of Premise and Evidence." *SJOT* 5:95–111.

Berkovits, Eliezer. 1969a. "The Biblical Meaning of Justice." *Judaica* 18:188–209.

———. 1969b. "*Ṣedeq* and *Ṣ*ᵉ*daqah.*" In *Man and God: Studies in Biblical Theology,* 292–348. Detroit: Wayne State University Press.

Beuken, Willem A. M. 1972. "*Mišpāṭ:* The First Servant Song and Its Context." *VT* 22:1–30.

———. 1989. "Servant and Herald of Good Tidings: Isaiah 61 as an Interpretation of Isaiah 40–55." In *Le Livre d'Isaïe: Les Oracles et Leurs Relectures Unité et Complexité de l'Ouvrage,* edited by J. Vermeylen, 411–42. BETL 81. Leuven: Peeters.

———. 1990. "The Main Theme of Trito-Isaiah: The 'Servants of YHWH.'" *JSOT* 47:67–87.

———. 1991. "Isaiah Chapters LXV–LXVI: Trito-Isaiah and the Closure of the Book of Isaiah." In *Congress Volume: Leuven 1989,* edited by J. A. Emerton, 204–21. Leiden: Brill.

———. 1992. "Isaiah 34: Lament in Isaianic Context." *Old Testament Essays* 5.1:78–102.

———. 1995. "Isaiah 28: Is It Only Schismatics That Drink Heavily? Beyond the Synchronic versus Diachronic Controversy." In *Synchronic or Diachronic? A Debate on Method in Old Testament Exegesis,* edited by J. C. de Moor, 15–38. OtSt 34. Leiden: Brill.

Boadt, Lawrence. 1997. "The Poetry of Prophetic Persuasion: Preserving the Prophet's Persona." *CBQ* 59:1–21.

Booth, Osborne. 1942. "The Semantic Development of the Term *mišpāṭ* in the Old Testament." *JBL* 61:105–10.

Bovati, Pietro. 1989. "Le Langage Juridique du Prophète Isaïe." In *Le Livre d'Isaïe: Les Oracles et Leurs Relectures Unité et Complexité de l'Ouvrage,* edited by J. Vermeylen, 177–96. BETL 81. Leuven: Peeters.

———. 1994. *Re-Establishing Justice: Legal Terms, Concepts and Procedures in the Hebrew Bible.* JSOTSup 105. Sheffield: JSOT Press.

Bright, John. 1981. *A History of Israel.* 3rd ed. Philadelphia: Westminster.

Brongers, Hendrick Antoine. 1965. "Merismus, Synekdoche und Hendiadys in der Bibel-Hebräischen Sprache." *Oudtestamentische Studiën* 14:100–114.

Brown, Raymond E. 1979. *The Birth of the Messiah.* Garden City, N.Y.: Image.

Brown, William P. 1990. "The So-Called Refrain in Isaiah 5:25-30 and 9:7—10:4." *CBQ* 52:432–43.

Broyles, Craig C., and Craig A. Evans, eds. 1997. *Writing and Reading the Scroll of Isaiah: Studies of an Interpretive Tradition.* VTSup 70. Leiden: Brill.

Brueggemann, Walter. 1984. "Unity and Dynamic in the Isaiah Tradition." *JSOT* 29:89–107.

———. 1998a. *Isaiah 1–39.* Westminster Bible Companion. Louisville: Westminster John Knox.

———. 1998b. *Isaiah 40–66.* Westminster Bible Companion. Louisville: Westminster John Knox.

Candelaria, Michael. 1983. "Justice: Extrapolations from the Concept *Mishpat* in the Book of Micah." *Apuntes* 3.4:75–82.

Carr, David M. 1993. "Reaching for Unity in Isaiah." *JSOT* 57:61–80.

———. 1996. "Reading Isaiah from Beginning (Isaiah 1) to End (Isaiah 65–66): Multiple Modern Possibilities." In *New Visions of Isaiah,* edited by R. F. Melugin and M. A. Sweeney, 188–218. JSOTSup 214. Sheffield: Sheffield Academic.

Carroll, R. P. 1978. "Inner Tradition Shifts in Meaning in Isaiah 1–11." *ExpT* 89:301–4.

Catholic Church. 1994. *Catechism of the Catholic Church.* Vatican City: Liberia Editrice Vaticana.

Ceresko, Anthony R. 1994. "The Rhetorical Strategy of the Fourth Servant Song (Isaiah 52:13—53:12): Poetry and the Exodus–New Exodus." *CBQ* 56:42–55.

Childs, Brevard S. 1979. *Introduction to the Old Testament as Scripture.* Philadelphia: Fortress Press.

———. 1986. *Old Testament Theology in a Canonical Context.* Philadelphia: Fortress Press.

———. 1993. *Biblical Theology of the Old and New Testaments: Theological Reflection on the Christian Bible.* Minneapolis: Fortress Press.

Clements, R. E. 1965. *Prophecy and Covenant.* Studies in Biblical Theology 1/43. London: SCM.

———. 1980. *Isaiah 1–39.* NCB. Grand Rapids: Eerdmans.

———. 1982. "The Unity of the Book of Isaiah." *Int* 36:117–29.

———. 1985. "Beyond Tradition-History: Deutero-Isaianic Development of First Isaiah's Themes." *JSOT* 31:95–113.

———. 1996. "A Light to the Nations: A Central Theme of the Book of Isaiah." In *Forming Prophetic Literature: Essays on Isaiah and the Twelve,* edited by J. W. Watts and P. R. House, 57–69. JSOTSup 235. Sheffield: Sheffield Academic.

———. 1997. "'Arise, Shine, For Your Light Has Come': A Basic Theme of the Isaianic Tradition." In *Writing and Reading the Scroll of Isaiah: Studies of an Interpretive Tradition,* edited by C. C. Broyles and C. A. Evans, 441–54. VTSup 70. Leiden: Brill.

Clifford, Richard. 1972. *The Cosmic Mountain in Canaan and the Old Testament.* Harvard Semitic Monographs 4. Cambridge: Harvard University Press.

———. 1980. "Psalm 89: A Lament over the Davidic Ruler's Continued Failure." *Harvard Theological Review* 3:35–48.

———. 1984. *Fair Spoken and Persuading: An Interpretation of Second Isaiah.* New York: Paulist.

———. 1992. "Isaiah, Book of (Second Isaiah)." In *ABD* 3:490–501.

———. 1993. "The Unity of the Book of Isaiah and Its Cosmogonic Language." *CBQ* 55:1–17.

———. 1994. *Creation Accounts in the Ancient Near East and in the Bible.* CBQ Monograph Series 26. Washington, D.C.: Catholic Biblical Association.

Clines, David J. A. 1976. *I, He, We, They—A Literary Approach to Isa 53.* JSOTSup 1. Sheffield: JSOT Press.

Coggins, Richard J. 1996. "New Ways with Old Texts: How Does One Write a Commentary on Isaiah?" *ExpT* 107:362–67.

———. 1998. "Do We Still Need Deutero-Isaiah?" *JSOT* 81:77–92.

Conrad, Edgar W. 1991. *Reading Isaiah.* Minneapolis: Fortress Press.

Consultation on Common Texts (Association). 1992. *The Revised Common Lectionary.* Nashville: Abingdon.

Crenshaw, James L. 1970. "Popular Questioning of the Justice of God in Ancient Israel." *ZAW* 82:380–95.

Cross, Frank Moore. 1953. "The Council of Yahweh in Second Isaiah." *JNES* 12:274–77.

———. 1973. *Canaanite Myth and Hebrew Epic.* Cambridge: Harvard University Press.

Crossan, John Dominic. 1994. "The Infancy and Youth of the Messiah." In *The Search for Jesus: Modern Scholarship Looks at the Gospels,* 59–81. Washington, D.C.: Biblical Archaeology Society.

Culver, Robert D. 1980. "שָׁפַט (*šhāpaṭ*)." In *Theological Wordbook of the Old Testament,* edited by R. L. Harris, 2:947–49. Chicago: Moody.

Dalley, Stephanie. 1991. *Myths from Mesopotamia: Creation, the Flood, Gilgamesh, and Others.* Oxford: Oxford University Press.

Daniels, Dwight R. 1987. "Is There a 'Prophetic Lawsuit' Genre?" *ZAW* 99:339–60.

Darr, Kathryn Pfisterer. 1994. "Two Unifying Female Images in the Book of Isaiah." In *Uncovering Ancient Stones: Essays in Memory of H. Neil Richardson,* edited by L. M. Hopfe, 17–30. Winona Lake, Ind.: Eisenbrauns.

Donahue, John. R. 1971. "Tax Collectors and Sinners: An Attempt at Identification." *CBQ* 33:39–61.

———. 1992. "Tax Collector." In *ABD* 6:337–38.

Doorly, William J. 1992. *Isaiah of Jerusalem: An Introduction.* New York: Paulist.

Duhm, Bernhard. 1922. *Das Buch Jesaia.* Handkommentar zum Alten Testament. Göttingen: Vandenhoeck & Ruprecht.

Eichrodt, Walther. 1983. "Prophet and Covenant: Observations on the Exegesis of Isaiah." In *Proclamation and Presence,* edited by J. I. Durham and J. R. Porter, 167–88. Macon, Ga.: Mercer University Press.

Eissfeldt, Otto. 1966. *The Old Testament: An Introduction,* translated by Peter R. Ackroyd. New York: Harper & Row.

Elliger, Karl. 1966. "Der Begriff 'Geschichte' bei Deuterojesaja." In *Kliene Scriften zum Alten Testament,* 199–210. Theologische Bücherei 32. München: Kaiser. (Orig. art. 1953).

Emerton, John. A. 1981. "Review of 'A Farewell to the Servant Songs: A Critical Examination of an Exegetical Axiom,' by T. N. D. Mettinger." *Bibliotheca orientalis* 48:626–32.

———. 1993. "The Historical Background of Isaiah 1:4-9." In *Eretz-Israel* 24: *Archaeological, Historical, and Geographical Studies: Avraham Malamat Volume,* edited by S. Ahituv and B. A. Levine, 34–40. Jerusalem: Israel Exploration Society.

Epzstein, Léon. 1986. *Social Justice in the Ancient Near East and the People of the Bible,* translated by J. Bowden. London: SCM.

Evans, Craig A. 1988. "On the Unity and Parallel Structure of Isaiah." *VT* 38:129–47.
Even-Shoshan, A. 1990. *A New Concordance of the Bible.* Jerusalem: Sivan.

Falk, Ze᾿ev. 1960a. "Hebrew Legal Terms." *Journal of Semitic Studies* 5:350–54.
———. 1960b. "Two Symbols of Justice." *VT* 10:72–74.
———. 1992. "Law and Ethics in the Hebrew Bible." In *Justice and Righteousness: Biblical Themes and Their Influence,* edited by H. G. Reventlow and Y. Hoffman, 82–90. JSOTSup 137. Sheffield: JSOT Press.
Farmer, William R. 1994. "The Role of Isaiah in the Development of the Christian Canon." In *Uncovering Ancient Stones: Essays in Memory of H. Neil Richardson,* edited by L. M. Hopfe, 217–22. Winona Lake, Ind.: Eisenbrauns.
Fensham, F. C. 1962. "Widow, Orphan and the Poor in Ancient Near Eastern Legal and Wisdom Literature." *JNES* 21:129–39.
Ferguson, Henry. 1888. "The Verb *špṭ*." *JBL* 8:130–36.
Fitzmyer, Joseph A. 1981–1985. *The Gospel According to Luke: Introduction, Translation, and Notes.* AB 28, 28A. Garden City, N.Y.: Doubleday.
Fohrer, Georg. 1962. "Jesaja 1 als Zusammenfassung der Verkündigung Jesajas." *ZAW* 74:251–80.
———. 1980. "Neue Literatur zur alttestamentlichen Prophetie (1961–1970), 5: Jesaja; 6: Deutero- und Tritojesaja." *TRu* 45:1–39.
Franke, Chris. A. 1996. "Reversals of Fortune in the Ancient Near East: A Study of the Babylon Oracles in the Book of Isaiah." In *New Visions of Isaiah,* edited by R. F. Melugin and M. A. Sweeney, 104–23. JSOTSup 214. Sheffield: Sheffield Academic.
Freedman, David Noel. 1971. "Is Justice Blind? [Isa 11:3f.]." *Bib* 52:536.
Frey, Christopher. 1992. "The Impact of the Biblical Idea of Justice on Present Discussions of Social Justice." In *Justice and Righteousness: Biblical Themes and Their Influence.* 91–104. Edited by H. G. Reventlow and Y. Hoffman. JSOTSup 137. Sheffield: JSOT Press.

Gelston, A. 1992. "Universalism in Second Isaiah." *JTS* 43:377–98.
Giménez, José Maria Bernal. 1984. "El Siervo Como Promesa de '*mišpaṭ*': Estudio biblico del termino '*mišpaṭ*' en Is 42,1-4." In *Palabra Y Vida,* edited by A. Vargas-Machuca and G. Ruiz, 77–85. Madrid: Universidad Pontificia Comillas Madrid.
Goldingay, John. 1979. "The Arrangement of Isaiah XLI–XLV." *VT* 29:289–99.
———. 1998. "Isaiah i 1 and ii 1." *VT* 48:326–32.
———. 1999. "The Compound Name in Isaiah 9:5(6)." *CBQ* 61:239–44.
Gossai, Hemchand. 1993. *Justice, Righteousness, and the Social Critique of the Eighth-Century Prophets.* New York: Lang.
Gosse, Bernard. 1993. "La création en Proverbes 8, 12-31 et Isaïe 40, 12-24." *La nouvelle revue théologique* 115:186–93.
Graffy, Adrian. 1979. "The Literary Genre of Isaiah 5,1-7." *Bib* 60:400–409.
Gray, George Buchanan. 1912. *A Critical and Exegetical Commentary on the Book of Isaiah: I–XXXIX.* International Critical Commentary. Edinburgh: T. & T. Clark.

Hammershaimb, Erling. 1966. *Some Aspects of Old Testament Prophecy from Isaiah to Malachi.* Copenhagen: Rosenkilde og Bagger.

Hanson, Paul D. 1979. *The Dawn of Apocalyptic.* Rev. ed. Philadelphia: Fortress Press.

———. 1986. "The Servant Dimension of Pastoral Ministry in Biblical Perspective." In *The Pastor as Servant,* edited by E. E. Shelp and R. H. Sunderland, 3–19. New York: Pilgrim.

———. 1987. *The People Called: The Growth of Community in the Bible.* San Francisco: Harper and Row.

———. 1994a. "The Ancient Near Eastern Roots of Social Welfare." In *Through the Eye of a Needle: Judeo-Christian Roots of Social Welfare,* edited by E. A. Hanawalt and C. Lindberg, 7–28. Kirksville, Mo.: Thomas Jefferson University Press.

———. 1994b. "Second Isaiah's Eschatological Understanding of World Events." *Princeton Seminary Bulletin, Supplementary Issue* 3:17–25.

———. 1995. *Isaiah 40–66.* IBC. Louisville: John Knox.

———. 1997. "Divine Power in Powerlessness: The Servant of the Lord in Second Isaiah." In *Power, Powerlessness, and the Divine: New Inquiries in Bible and Theology,* edited by C. L. Rigby, 179–98. Scholars Press Studies in Theological Education. Atlanta: Scholars.

———. 1998. "The World of the Servant of the Lord in Isaiah 40–55." In *Jesus and the Suffering Servant: Isaiah 53 and Christian Origins,* edited by W. H. Bellinger and W. R. Farmer, 9–22. Harrisburg, Pa.: Trinity Press International.

Hare, Douglas R. A. 1993. *Matthew.* IBC. Louisville: John Knox.

Hartman, Louis F. 1965. "Justice." In *Encyclopedic Dictionary of the Bible,* 1251–55. New York: McGraw-Hill.

Hayes, John H., and Stuart A. Irvine. 1987. *Isaiah, the Eighth Century Prophet: His Times and His Preaching.* Nashville: Abingdon.

Hermisson, Hans-Jürgen. 1984. "Review of 'A Farewell to the Servant Songs: A Critical Examination of an Exegetical Axiom,' by T. N. D. Mettinger." *TRu* 49:209–22.

———. 1996. "Gottesknecht und Gottes Knechte. Zur ältesten Deutung eines deuterojesjanischen Themas." In *Geschichte-Tradition-Reflexion: Festschrift für Martin Hengel zum 70. Geburtstag,* edited by H. Canik et al., 43–68. Tübingen: Mohr/Siebeck.

Herntrich, Volkman. 1965. "The OT Term מִשְׁפָּט," s.v. "κρινω." In *Theological Dictionary of the New Testament,* edited by G. Kittel, 3:923–33. Grand Rapids: Eerdmans.

Hertzberg, Hans Wilhelm. 1922. "Die Entwicklung des Begriffes מִשְׁפָּט im AT." *ZAW* 40:256–87.

———. 1923. "Die Entwicklung des Begriffes מִשְׁפָּט im AT." *ZAW* 41:16–76.

Heschel, Abraham J. 1969. *The Prophets.* New York: Harper & Row.

Holladay, William L. 1978. *Isaiah: Scroll of a Prophetic Heritage.* New York: Pilgrim.

Hollenbach, David. 1982. "The Politics of Justice." *TToday* 38:489–93.

Honeyman, A. M. 1952. "Merismus in Biblical Hebrew." *JBL* 71:11–18.

Hood, Robert. E. 1982. "Social Justice from the Prophetic Point of View." In *The Future of Jewish-Christian Relations,* edited by N. H. Thompson and B. K. Cole, 3–43. Schenectady, N.Y.: Character Research.

Hoppe, Leslie. J. 1994. "Messianism in Isaiah." *TBT* 32:213–17.

———. 1997. "A Refuge for the Poor." *TBT* 35:210–15.

Irani, K. D., and Morris Silver, eds. 1995. *Social Justice in the Ancient World.* Westport, Conn.: Greenwood.

Jacobsen, Thorkild. 1976. *The Treasures of Darkness: A History of Mesopotamian Religion.* New Haven: Yale University Press.

Janzen, J. Gerald. 1994. "On the Moral Nature of God's Power: Yahweh and the Sea in Job and Deutero-Isaiah." *CBQ* 56:458–78.

Japhet, Sara. 1993. *I and II Chronicles: A Commentary.* OTL. Louisville: Westminster John Knox.

Jensen, Joseph. 1984. *Isaiah 1–39.* Old Testament Message 8. Wilmington, Del.: Glazier.

Jeppesen, Knud. 1984. "The Cornerstone (Isa. 28:16) in Deutero-Isaianic Rereading of the Message of Isaiah." *ST* 38:93–99.

Jeremias, Jörg. 1972. "*Mišpaṭ* im ersten Gottesknechtslied (Jes 42:1-4)." *VT* 22:31–42.

Johnson, B. 1986. "מִשְׁפָּט." In *Theologisches Wörterbuch zum Alten Testament,* edited by G. Johannes Botterweck, 5:93–107. Stuttgart: Kohlhammer.

Johnston, Ann. 1994. "A Prophetic Vision of an Alternative Community: A Reading of Isaiah 40–55." In *Uncovering Ancient Stones: Essays in Memory of H. Neil Richardson,* edited by L. M. Hopfe, 31–40. Winona Lake, Ind.: Eisenbrauns.

Johnstone, W. 1969. "Old Testament Expressions in Property Holding." *Ugaritica* 6:308–17.

Jones, Douglas. 1955. "The Traditio of the Oracles of Isaiah of Jerusalem." *ZAW* 67:226–46.

Joüon, Paul. 1993. *A Grammar of Biblical Hebrew.* Roma: Editrice Pontificio Instituto Biblico.

Kaiser, Otto. 1974. *Isaiah 13–39,* translated by R. A. Wilson. OTL. Philadelphia: Westminster.

———. 1983. *Isaiah 1–12,* translated by J. Bowden. OTL. Philadelphia: Westminster.

Kang, Sa-Moon. 1989. *Divine War in the Old Testament and in the Ancient Near East.* BZAW 177. Berlin: de Gruyter.

Kapelrud, Arvid S. 1982. "The Main Concern of Second Isaiah." *VT* 32:50–58.

Kaufmann, Yehezkel. 1960. *The Religion of Israel: From Its Beginnings to the Babylonian Exile.* Chicago: University of Chicago Press.

———. 1970. *The Babylonian Captivity and Deutero-Isaiah.* New York: Union of American Hebrew Congregations.

Kendall, Daniel. 1984. "The Use of *Mišpaṭ* in Isaiah 59." *ZAW* 96:391–405.

Kiesow, Klaus. 1990. "Deuterjesaja—ein Neuanfang in der Glaubenskrise." *Bibel und Liturgie* 63:33–36.

Knierim, Rolf P. 1995. "Justice in Old Testament Theology." In *The Task of Old Testament Theology: Substance, Method, and Cases—Essays*, 86–122. Grand Rapids: Eerdmans.

Knight, Douglas A., and Peter J. Paris, eds. 1989. *Justice and the Holy: Essays in Honor of Walter Harrelson.* Homage Series. Atlanta: Scholars.

Koch, Klaus. 1983. *The Prophets: The Assyrian Period,* translated by M. Koch. Philadelphia: Fortress Press.

———. 1983. *The Prophets: The Babylonian and Persian Periods,* translated by M. Koch. Philadelphia: Fortress Press.

Koole, Jan L. 1997. *Isaiah 40–48.* 2 vols. Kampen: Kok Pharos.

———. 1998. *Isaiah 49–55.* Leuven: Peeters.

Korpel, Marjo C. A. 1999. "Second Isaiah's Coping with the Religious Crisis: Reading Isaiah 40 and 55." In *The Crisis of Israelite Religion: Transformation of Religious Tradition in Exilic and Post-Exilic Times,* edited by B. Becking and M. C. A. Korpel, 90–105. OtSt 42. Leiden: Brill.

Krašovec, Jože. 1988. *La Justice (ṢDQ) de Dieu dans la Bible Hébraïque et l'Interprétation Juive et Chrétienne.* Orbis biblicus et orientalis 76. Göttingen: Vandenhoeck & Ruprecht.

Kruse, C. C. 1978. "The Servant Songs: Interpretive Trends since C. R. North." *Studia biblica et theologica* 8:3–27.

Kugel, James L. 1981. *The Idea of Biblical Poetry: Parallelism and Its History.* New Haven: Yale University Press.

Kuntz, J. Kenneth. 1982. "The Contribution of Rhetorical Criticism to Understanding Isaiah 51:1-16." In *Art and Meaning: Rhetoric in Biblical Literature,* edited by D. J. A. Clines et al., 140–71. JSOTSup 19. Sheffield: JSOT Press.

———. 1997. "The Form, Location, and Function of Rhetorical Questions in Deutero-Isaiah." In *Writing and Reading the Scroll of Isaiah: Studies of an Interpretive Tradition,* edited by C. C. Broyles and C. A. Evans, 212–42. VTSup 70. Leiden: Brill.

Kutscher, Edward Y. 1974. *The Language and Linguistic Background of the Isaiah Scroll (I Q Isa[a]).* Studies on the Texts of the Desert of Judah 6. Leiden: Brill.

Kuyper, Lester. J. 1977. "Righteousness and Salvation." *SJT* 30:233–52.

Laato, Antti. 1990. "The Composition of Isaiah 40–55." *JBL* 109:207–28.

———. 1998. *"About Zion I Will Not Be Silent": The Book of Isaiah as an Ideological Unity.* Coniectanea biblica: Old Testament Series 42. Stockholm: Almqvist & Wiksell.

Lambrecht, J. 1988. "Righteousness in the Bible and Justice in the World." *Theologica Evangelica* 21:6–13.

Laney, J. Carl. 1981. "The Role of the Prophets in God's Case against Israel." *BSac* 138:313–25.

———. 1990. "The Prophets and Social Concern." *BSac* 147:32–43.

Lang, Bernhard. 1982. "The Social Organization of Peasant Poverty in Biblical Israel." *JSOT* 24:47–63.

Lau, Wolfgang. 1994. *Schriftgelehrte Prophetie in Jes 56–66: Eine Untersuchung zu den literarischen Bezügen in den letzten elf Kapiteln des Jesajabuches.* BZAW 225. Berlin: de Gruyter.

Levenson, Jon D. 1985. *Sinai and Zion: An Entry into the Jewish Bible.* New Voices in Biblical Studies. Minneapolis: Winston.

———. 1992. "Zion Traditions." In *ABD* 6:1098–1102.

———. 1993. "The Hebrew Bible, the Old Testament, and Historical Criticism." In *The Hebrew Bible, the Old Testament, and Historical Criticism: Jews and Christians in Biblical Studies,* 1–32. Louisville: Westminster John Knox.

Liebreich, Leon J. 1956. "The Compilation of the Book of Isaiah." *JQR* 46:259–77.

———. 1957. "The Compilation of the Book of Isaiah." *JQR* 47:114–38.

Lind, Millard C. 1984. "Monotheism, Power and Justice in Is 40–55." *CBQ* 46:432–46.

———. 1997. "Political Implications of Isaiah 6." In *Writing and Reading the Scroll of Isaiah: Studies of an Interpretive Tradition,* edited by C. C. Broyles and C. A. Evans, 317–38. VTSup 70. Leiden: Brill.

Lindsey, F. Duane. 1982a. "The Call of the Servant in Isaiah 42:1-9." *BSac* 139:12–31.

———. 1982b. "The Commission of the Servant in Isaiah 49:1-13." *BSac* 139:129–45.

———. 1982c. "The Commitment of the Servant in Isaiah 50:4-11." *BSac* 139:216–29.

———. 1982d. "The Career of the Servant in Isaiah 52:13—53:12." *BSac* 139:312–29.

Machinist, Peter. 1983. "Assyria and Its Image in the First Isaiah." *Journal of the American Oriental Society* 103:719–37.

———. 1991. "The Question of Distinctiveness in Ancient Israel: An Essay." In *Ah, Assyria: Studies in Assyrian History and Ancient Near Eastern Historiography Presented to Hayim Tadmor,* edited by M. Cogan and I. Eph'al, 196–212. Scripta Hierosolymitana 33. Jerusalem: Magnes.

Mafico, Temba L. J. 1992. "Just, Justice." In *ABD* 3:1127–29.

Magonet, Jonathan. 1982. "Isaiah 2:1—4:6, Some Poetic Structures and Tactics." *Amsterdamse Cahiers voor Exegese en bijbelse theologie* 3:71–85.

———. 1991. "Isaiah's Mountain or the Shape of Things to Come." *Prooftexts* 11:175–81.

Malchow, Bruce V. 1982. "Social Justice in the Wisdom Literature." *BTB* 12:120–24.

———. 1984. "Social Justice in the Israelite Law Codes." *WW* 4:299–306.

———. 1996. *Social Justice in the Hebrew Bible: What Is New and What Is Old.* Collegeville, Minn.: Liturgical.

Mallia, Bernard. 1983. "Social Justice: A Biblical Dimension [2 parts]." *African Ecclesiastical Review* 25:33–41; 109–13.

Matthews, Victor H. 1991. "The King's Call to Justice." *BZ* 35:204–16.

Mays, James Luther. 1969. *Amos*. OTL. Philadelphia: Westminster.
———. 1983. "Justice: Perspectives from the Prophetic Tradition." *Int* 37:5–17.
Mays, James Luther, David L. Petersen, and Kent Harold Richards, eds. 1995. *Old Testament Interpretation: Past, Present, and Future: Essays in Honor of Gene M. Tucker*. Nashville: Abingdon.
McKenzie, John L. 1965. "Righteous, Righteousness." In *Dictionary of the Bible*, 739–43. Milwaukee: Bruce.
———. 1978. *Second Isaiah*. AB 20. Garden City, N.Y.: Doubleday.
Melamed, Ezra Zion. 1945. "Hendiadys in the Bible." *Tarbiz* 16:173–89.
———. 1961. "Break-up of Stereotype Phrases as an Artistic Device in Biblical Poetry." In *Studies in the Bible*, edited by C. Rabin, 8:115–53. Jerusalem: Magnes.
Melchert, Charles F. 1990. "Creation and Justice among the Sages." *RelEd* 85:368–81.
Melugin, Roy F. 1971. "Deutero-Isaiah and Form Criticism." *VT* 21:326–37.
———. 1976. *The Formation of Isaiah 40–55*. BZAW 141. Berlin: de Gruyter.
———. 1991. "The Servant, God's Call, and the Structure of Isaiah 40–48." In *SBLSP* vol. 30, 21–30. Atlanta: Scholars.
———. 1996a. "Introduction." In *New Visions of Isaiah*, edited by R. F. Melugin and M. A. Sweeney, 282–305. JSOTSup 214. Sheffield: Sheffield Academic.
———. 1996b. "Figurative Speech and the Reading of Isaiah 1 as Scripture." In *New Visions of Isaiah*, edited by R. F. Melugin and M. A. Sweeney, 282–305. JSOTSup 214. Sheffield: Sheffield Academic.
———. 1996c. "Prophetic Books and the Problems of Historical Reconstruction." In *Prophets and Paradigms: Essays in Honor of Gene M. Tucker*, edited by S. B. Reid, 63–78. JSOTSup 229. Sheffield: Sheffield Academic.
Mettinger, Tryggve N. D. 1983. *A Farewell to the Servant Songs: A Critical Examination of an Exegetical Axiom*. Scripta minora 3. Lund: Gleerup.
Míguez Bonino, José. 1987. "The Biblical Roots of Justice." *WW* 7:12–21.
Mihelic, Joseph L. 1966. "The Concept of God in Deutero-Isaiah." *BR* 11:29–41.
Miller, James Maxwell, and John H. Hayes. 1986. *A History of Ancient Israel and Judah*. Philadelphia: Westminster.
Miller, Patrick D. 1968. "The Divine Council and the Prophetic Call to War." *VT* 18:100–107.
———. 1986. "When the Gods Meet: Psalm 82 and the Issue of Justice." *Journal for Preachers* 9:2–5.
———. 1995. "The World and Message of the Prophets: Biblical Prophecy in Its Context." In *Old Testament Interpretation: Past, Present, and Future: Essays in Honor of Gene M. Tucker*, edited by J. L. Mays et al., 97–112. Nashville: Abingdon.
Miscall, Peter D. 1993. *Isaiah*. Readings. Sheffield: JSOT Press.
Mitchel, Larry A. 1984. *A Student's Vocabulary for Biblical Hebrew and Aramaic*. Grand Rapids: Zondervan.
Moor, Johannes C. de, ed. 1995. *Synchronic or Diachronic? A Debate on Method in Old Testament Exegesis*. OtSt 34. Leiden: Brill.
Morris, Leon. 1959. "Judgment and Custom." *Australian Biblical Review* 7:72–74.

Mott, Stephen C. 1985. "Justice." In *Harper's Bible Dictionary,* edited by P. J. Achtemeier, 519–20. San Francisco: Harper & Row.

Motyer, Alec. 1993. *The Prophecy of Isaiah: An Introduction and Commentary.* Downers Grove, Ill.: InterVarsity.

———. 1994. "Three in One or One in Three: A Dipstick into the Isianic Literature." *Churchman* 108:22–36.

Muilenburg, James. 1953. "A Study in Hebrew Rhetoric: Repetition and Style." In *Congress Volume: Copenhagen,* 97–111. VTSup 1. Leiden: Brill.

———. 1956. "Isaiah 40–66." In *Interpreter's Bible* 5:381–773. Nashville: Abingdon.

Myers, Edward P. 1986. "Interpreting Figurative Language." In *Biblical Interpretation: Principles and Practices,* edited by F. F. Kearley et al., 91–100. Grand Rapids: Baker.

Nardoni, Enrique. 1997. *Los que buscan la justicia: Un estudio de la justicia en el mundo biblico.* Estella: Verbo Divino.

Nash, Peter T. 1991. "The Old Testament Speaks of Power, Race, and Justice: Does Anyone Care to Listen?" *Lutheran Theological Seminary Bulletin* 71:4–15.

Neufeld, Thomas R. Yoder. 1997. *"Put on the Armour of God": The Divine Warrior from Isaiah to Ephesians.* JSNTSup 140. Sheffield: Sheffield Academic.

Niditch, Susan. 1980. "The Composition of Isaiah 1." *Bib* 61:509–29.

Nielsen, Kirsten. 1979. "Das Bild Gerichts (*Rib*-Pattern) in Jes, I–XII." *VT* 29:309–24.

Nysse, Richard W. 1992. "Moral Discourse on Economic Justice: Considerations from the Old Testament." *WW* 12:337–44.

Oliver, Hannes. 1996. "God as Friendly Patron: Reflections of Isaiah 5:1-7." *In die Skriflig* 30:293–304.

Olley, John W. 1977. *"Righteousness" in the Septuagint of Isaiah: A Contextual Study.* Septuagint and Cognate Studies Series 8. Missoula, Mont.: Scholars.

Oswalt, John N. 1986. *The Book of Isaiah: Chapters 1–39.* NICOT. Grand Rapids: Eerdmans.

———. 1998. *The Book of Isaiah: Chapters 40–66.* NICOT. Grand Rapids: Eerdmans.

Padilla, C. René. 1985. "The Fruit of Justice Will Be Peace." *Transformation* 2:2–4.

Parker, Simon B. 1994. "The Lachish Letters and Official Reactions to Prophecies." In *Uncovering Ancient Stones: Essays in Memory of H. Neil Richardson,* edited by L. M. Hopfe, 65–78. Winona Lake, Ind.: Eisenbrauns.

Patterson, Richard D. 1973. "The Widow, the Orphan, and the Poor in the Old Testament and the Extra-Biblical Literature." *BSac* 130:223–35.

Pauritsch, Karl. 1971. *Die neue Gemeinde: Gott sammelt Ausgestossene und Arme (Jesaia 56-66). Die Botschaft des Tritojesaia-Buches literar-, form-, gattungskritisch und redaktionsgeschichtlich untersucht.* Analecta biblica, 47. Rome: Biblical Institute Press.

Pedersen, Johannes. 1926. *Israel: Its Life and Culture.* Vol. 1-2. London: Oxford University Press.

Phillips, Morgan L. 1971. "Divine Self-Predication in Deutero-Isaiah." *BR* 16:32–51.

Plöger, Otto. 1968. *Theocracy and Eschatology,* translated by S. Rudman. Oxford: Blackwell.

Polan, Gregory J. 1986. *In the Ways of Justice toward Salvation: A Rhetorical Analysis of Isaiah 56–59.* New York: Lang.

———. 1997. "Still More Signs of Unity in the Book of Isaiah: The Significance of Third Isaiah." In *SBLSP* vol. 36, 224–33. Atlanta: Scholars.

Porteous, Norman W. 1949. "Ritual and Righteousness: The Relation of Ethics to Religion in the Prophetic Literature." *Int* 3:400–414.

Rad, Gerhard von. 1965. *Old Testament Theology,* vol. 2: *The Theology of Israel's Prophetic Traditions,* translated by D. Stalker. San Francisco: Harper & Row.

Renaud, Bernard. 1977. "La Mort du Juste, Entrée dans la Paix (Is., 57,1-2)." *RevScRel* 51:3–21.

———. 1990. "La mission du Serviteur en Is 42,1-4." *RevScRel* 64:101–13.

Rendtorff, Rolf. 1993a. "The Composition of the Book of Isaiah." In *Canon and Theology,* translated by M. Kohl, 146–69. Minneapolis: Fortress Press.

———. 1993b. "Isaiah 56:1 as a Key to the Formation of the Book of Isaiah." In *Canon and Theology,* edited by M. Kohl, 181–89. Minneapolis: Fortress Press.

———. 1996. "The Book of Isaiah: A Complex Unity. Synchronic and Diachronic Reading." In *New Visions of Isaiah,* edited by R. F. Melugin and M. A. Sweeney, 32–49. JSOTSup 214. Sheffield, Eng.: Sheffield Academic.

Renner, J. T. Erich. 1990. "Justice and Human Rights: Some Biblical Perspectives." *Lutheran Theological Journal* 24:3–10.

Reventlow, Henning Graf, and Yair Hoffman, eds. 1992. *Justice and Righteousness: Biblical Themes and Their Influence.* JSOTSup 137. Sheffield: JSOT Press.

Roberts, J. J. M. 1982. "Form, Syntax and Redaction in Isaiah 1:2-20." *Princeton Seminary Bulletin* 3:293–306.

———. 1983. "The Divine King and the Human Community in Isaiah's Vision of the Future." In *The Quest for the Kingdom of God: Studies in Honor of George E. Mendenhall,* edited by H. B. Huffmon et al, 127–36. Winona Lake, Ind.: Eisenbrauns.

Robinson, Gnana. 1976. "Justice in the Old Testament." In *Where Is Justice?* edited by A. Frenz, 1–7. Arasaradi, Madurai, India: Tamilnadu Theological Seminary.

Rodd, C. S. 1972. "'Shall Not the Judge of All the Earth Do What Is Just?' (Gen 18:25)." *ExpT* 83:137–39.

Rofe, Alexander. 1985. "Isaiah 66:1-4: Judean Sects in the Persian Period as Viewed by Trito-Isaiah." In *Biblical and Related Studies Presented to Samuel Iwry,* edited by Ann Kort and Scott Morschauser, 215-18. Winona Lake, Ind.: Eisenbrauns.

Sabourin, L. 1981. "The Bible and Social Justice." *Religious Studies Bulletin* 1.3:66–74.

Salvini, Giovanni 1996. "La Città Fondata sulla Guistizia: Reflessioni sul Valore del Terma Guistizia nel Deuterisaia." *Vivens homo* 7:191–218.

Scaria, K. J. 1978. "Social Justice in the Old Testament." *Bible Bhashyam* 4:163–92.

Schmitt, John J. 1997. "The City as Woman in Isaiah 1–39." In *Writing and Reading the Scroll of Isaiah: Studies of an Interpretive Tradition,* edited by C. C. Broyles and C. A. Evans, 95–119. VTSup 70. Leiden: Brill.

Scholnick, Silvia Huberman. 1982. "The Meaning of *Mishpat* in the Book of Job." *JBL* 101:521–29.

Schoors, Antoon. 1973. *I Am God Your Saviour: A Form-Critical Study of the Main Genres in Is. XL–LV.* VTSup 24. Leiden: Brill.

Schramm, Brooks. 1995. *The Opponents of Third Isaiah: Reconstructing the Cultic History of the Restoration.* JSOTSup 193. Sheffield: Sheffield Academic.

Schrey, Heinz-Horst. 1955. *The Biblical Doctrine of Justice and Law.* London: SCM.

Schwartz, Baruch J. 1998. "Torah from Zion: Isaiah's Temple Vision (Isaiah 2:1-4)." In *Sanctity of Time and Space in Tradition and Modernity,* edited by A. Houtman et al., 11–26. Jewish and Christian Perspectives Series 1. Leiden: Brill.

Schwarz, Günther. 1971. "'Kliene Waffe . . .' (Jes 54, 17a)?" *BZ* 15(2):254–55.

Schwarzschild, Steven S. 1972. "Justice." In *EncJud* 10:476–77.

Scott, R. B. Y. 1957. "Biblical Research and the Work of the Pastor: Recent Study in Isaiah 1–39." *Int* 11:259–68.

Scott, Timothy. 1997. "Hope for Redemption." *TBT* 35:222–28.

Scullion, John J. 1971. "*Ṣedeq-Ṣedaqah* in Isaiah cc. 40–66 with Special Reference to the Continuity of Meaning between Second and Third Isaiah." *Ugarit-Forschungen* 3:335–48.

———. 1982. *Isaiah 40–66.* Old Testament Message 12. Wilmington, Del.: Glazier.

Seitz, Christopher R. 1988a. "The One Isaiah/The Three Isaiahs." In *Reading and Preaching the Book of Isaiah,* edited by C. R. Seitz, 13–22. Philadelphia: Fortress Press.

———.1988b. "Isaiah 1–66: Making Sense of the Whole." In *Reading and Preaching the Book of Isaiah,* edited by C. R. Seitz, 105–26. Philadelphia: Fortress Press.

———. 1990. "The Divine Council: Temporal Transition and New Prophecy in the Book of Isaiah." *JBL* 109:229–47.

———. 1992. "Isaiah, Book of (Third Isaiah)." In *ABD* 3:501–7.

———. 1993a. *Isaiah 1–39.* IBC. Louisville: John Knox.

———. 1993b. "On the Question of Divisions Internal to the Book of Isaiah." In *SBLSP,* vol. 32, 260–66. Atlanta: Scholars.

———. 1996. "How Is the Prophet Isaiah Present in the Latter Half of the Book? The Logic of Chapters 40–66." *JBL* 115:219–40.

Silberman, Lou H. 1972. "God: Justice and Mercy of God." In *EncJud* 7:669–70.

Silva, Moises. 1994. *Biblical Words and Their Meaning: An Introduction to Lexical Semantics.* Grand Rapids: Zondervan.

Sloyan, Gerard S. 1988. *John.* IBC. Atlanta: John Knox.

Smith, P. A. 1995. *Rhetoric and Redaction in Trito-Isaiah: The Structure, Growth and Authorship of Isaiah 56–66.* VTSup 62. Leiden: Brill.

Smith, Ralph L. 1991. "A Selected Bibliography on Isaiah." *Southwestern Journal of Theology* 34:63–66.

Snaith, Norman H. 1944. "The Righteousness of God." In *The Distinctive Ideas of the Old Testament,* 51–78. London: Epworth.

Sommer, Benjamin D. 1996. "Allusions and Illusions: The Unity of the Book of Isaiah in Light of Deutero-Isaiah's Use of Prophetic Tradition." In *New Visions of Isaiah,* edited by R. F. Melugin and M. A. Sweeney, 156–86. JSOTSup 214. Sheffield: Sheffield Academic.

Spykerboer, Hendrik Carel. 1976. *The Structure and Composition of Deutero-Isaiah with Special Reference to the Polemics against Idolatry.* Meppel: Krips Repro.

Stacey, David. 1993. *Isaiah: Chapters 1–39.* Epworth Commentary Series: Old Testament. London: Epworth.

Stager, Lawrence E. 1985. "The Archaeology of the Family in Ancient Israel." *Bulletin of the American Schools of Oriental Research* 260:1–35.

Stansell, Gary. 1996. "Isaiah 28–33: Blest Be the Tie That Binds (Isaiah Together)." In *New Visions of Isaiah,* edited by R. F. Melugin and M. A. Sweeney, 68–103. JSOTSup 214. Sheffield: Sheffield Academic.

Steinmueller, John E., and Kathryn Sullivan. 1956. "Justness of God." In *Catholic Biblical Encyclopedia: Old Testament,* 608–10. New York: Wagner.

Stek, John H. 1978. "Salvation, Justice and Liberation in the Old Testament." *Calvin Theological Journal* 13:133–65.

Strolz, Walter. 1981. "The Unique One: The Uniqueness of God according to Deutero-Isaiah." In *Standing before God: Studies on Prayer in Scriptures and in Tradition with Essays,* edited by A. Finkel and L. Frizzell, 257–66. New York: Ktav.

Struik, Félix. 1991. "Justicia Integral: El mensaje social de los profetas pre-exílicos." *Biblia y fe* 17:171–93.

Stuhlmueller, Carroll. 1970a. *Creative Redemption in Deutero-Isaiah.* Analecta biblica 43. Rome: Biblical Institute.

———. 1970b. "Yahweh-King and Deutero-Isaiah." *BR* 15:32–45.

———. 1980. "Deutero-Isaiah: Major Transitions in the Prophet's Theology and in Contemporary Scholarship." *CBQ* 42:1–29.

Sweeney, Marvin A. 1987. "Structure and Redaction in Isaiah 2–4." *Hebrew Annual Review* 11:407–22.

———. 1988. *Isaiah 1–4 and the Post-Exilic Understanding of the Isaianic Tradition.* BZAW 171. Berlin: de Gruyter.

———. 1993. "The Book of Isaiah in Recent Research." *Currents in Research: Biblical Studies* 1:141–62.

———. 1995. "Formation and Form in Prophetic Literature." In *Old Testament Interpretation: Past, Present, and Future: Essays in Honor of Gene M. Tucker,* edited by J. L. Mays et al., 113–26. Nashville: Abingdon.

———. 1996a. *Isaiah 1–39: With an Introduction to Prophetic Literature.* FOTL 16. Grand Rapids: Eerdmans.

———. 1996b. "The Book of Isaiah as Prophetic Torah." In *New Visions of Isaiah,* edited by R. F. Melugin and M. A. Sweeney, 50–67. JSOTSup 214. Sheffield: Sheffield Academic.

———. 1996c. "Jesse's New Shoot in Isaiah 11: A Josianic Reading of the Prophet Isaiah." In *Gift of God in Due Season: Essays on Scripture and Community in Honor of James A. Sanders*, edited by R. D. Weis and D. M. Carr, 103–18. JSOTSup 225. Sheffield: Sheffield Academic.

Talmon, Shemaryahu. 1962. "DSIa as a Witness to Ancient Exegesis of the Book of Isaiah." *Annual of the Swedish Theological Institute* 1:62–72.

Tate, Marvin E. 1996. "The Book of Isaiah in Recent Study." In *Forming Prophetic Literature: Essays on Isaiah and the Twelve in Honor of John D. W. Watts*, edited by J. W. Watts and P. R. House, 22–56. JSOTSup 235. Sheffield: Sheffield Academic.

Tomasino, Anthony J. 1993. "Isaiah 1.1—2.4 and 63–66, and the Composition of the Isaianic Corpus." *JSOT* 57:81–98.

Torrey, Charles Cutler. 1928. *The Second Isaiah.* New York: Scribner.

van der Ploeg, J. 1950. "Les Pauvres d'Israël et Leur Piété." *Old Testament Studies* 7:236–70.

van der Westhuizen, J. P. 1978. "Hendiadys in Biblical Hymns of Praise." *Sem* 6:50–57.

Vanes, Rowland. 1979. "Some Biblical Concepts of Justice." *South East Asia Journal of Theology* 20:45–48.

van Ruiten, Jacques, and M. Vernesse, eds. 1997. *Studies in the Book of Isaiah: Festschrift Willem A. M. Beuken.* BETL 132. Leuven: Leuven University Press.

van Uchelen, N. A. 1981. "Isaiah I:9—Text and Context." OtSt 21:155–63.

van Winkle, D. W. 1997. "Isaiah LVI 1-8." In *SBLSP* vol. 36, 234–52. Atlanta: Scholars.

Vawter, Bruce. 1961. "Isaiah ben Amoz." In *The Conscience of Israel: Pre-exilic Prophets and Prophecy*, 162–207. New York: Sheed & Ward.

Vermeylen, Jacques. 1989. "L'Unité du Livre d'Isaïe." In *Le Livre d'Isaïe: Les Oracles et Leurs Relectures Unité et Complexité de l'Ouvrage*, edited by J. Vermeylen, 177–96. BETL 81. Leuven: Peeters.

Vijayakumar, J. 1983. "Factors Causing Poverty and Oppression in Eighth Century Israel and the Prophetic Response (Abstract)." *Bangalore Theological Forum* 15:59–60.

———. 1991. *Holy War in Ancient Israel*, translated by M. J. Dawn. Grand Rapids: Eerdmans.

Vriezen, Theodorus Christiaan. 1962. "Essentials of the Theology of Isaiah." In *Israel's Prophetic Heritage*, edited by B. W. Anderson and W. Harrelson, 128–46. New York: Harper.

Wagner, S. 1978. "דָרַשׁ *dārash;* מִדְרָשׁ *midrāsh.*" In *Theological Dictionary of the Old Testament*, edited by G. J. Botterweck and H. Ringgren, 3:293–307. Grand Rapids: Eerdmans.

Waldow, H. Eberhard von. 1968. "The Message of Deutero-Isaiah." *Int* 22:259–87.

———. 1970. "Social Responsibility and Social Structure in Early Israel." *CBQ* 32:182–204.

Walsh, Jerome T. 1993. "Summons to Judgment: A Close Reading of Isaiah LXI 1–20." *VT* 43:351–71.

Waltke, Bruce K., and M. O'Connor. 1990. *An Introduction to Biblical Hebrew Syntax.* Winona Lake, Ind.: Eisenbrauns.

Watts, James W., and Paul R. House, eds. 1996. *Forming Prophetic Literature: Essays on Isaiah and the Twelve in Honor of John D. W. Watts.* JSOTSup 235. Sheffield: Sheffield Academic.

Watts, John W. D. 1985. *Isaiah 1–33.* Word Biblical Commentary 24. Waco, Tex.: Word.

———. 1987. *Isaiah 34–66.* Word Biblical Commentary 25. Waco, Tex.: Word.

Webster, Edwin C. 1997. "Response (to Gregory Polan's 'Still More Signs of Unity'): Word Pairs in Third Isaiah." SBL Annual Conference. San Francisco.

Weil, H.-M. 1940. "Exégèse d'Isaie, III, 1-15." *Revue biblique* 49:76–85.

Weinfeld, Moshe. 1982. "'Justice and Righteousness' in Ancient Israel against the Background of 'Social Reforms' in the Ancient Near East." In *Mesopotamien und seine Nachbarn,* 2:491–519. 2nd ed. Berliner Beiträge zum Vorderen Orient 1. Berlin: Reimer.

———. 1983. "Divine Intervention in War in Ancient Israel and in the Ancient Near East." In *History, Historiography and Interpretation: Studies in Biblical and Cuneiform Literatures,* edited by H. Tadmor and M. Weinfeld, 121–47. Jerusalem: Magnes.

———. 1992. *Deuteronomy and the Deuteronomistic School.* Reprint. Winona Lake, Ind.: Eisenbrauns.

———. 1992. "'Justice and Righteousness'—משפט וצדקה—The Expression and Its Meaning." In *Justice and Righteousness: Biblical Themes and Their Influence,* edited by H. G. Reventlow and Y. Hoffman, 228–46. JSOTSup 137. Sheffield: JSOT Press.

———. 1995. *Social Justice in Ancient Israel and in the Ancient Near East.* Minneapolis: Fortress Press.

Weingreen, Jacob. 1959. *A Practical Grammar for Classical Hebrew.* Oxford: Clarendon.

Westbrook, Raymond. 1993. "Social Justice in the Ancient Near East." In *Social Justice in the Ancient World,* edited by K. D. Irani and M. Silver, 149–64. Contributions in Political Science 354. Westport, Conn.: Greenwood.

Westermann, Claus. 1960. "Die Begriffe für Fragen und Suchen im Alten Testament." *Kerygma und Dogma* 6:2–30.

———. 1975. *Isaiah 40–66,* translated by D. M. G. Stalker. OTL. Philadelphia: Westminster.

Whitley, Charles Francis. 1972. "Deutero-Isaiah's Interpretation of *Ṣedeq.*" *VT* 22:469–75.

Whybray, R. N. 1971. *The Heavenly Counsellor in Isaiah xl 13-14.* Society for Old Testament Study Monograph Series 1. Cambridge: Cambridge University Press.

———. 1975. *Isaiah 40–66.* NCB. London: Oliphants.
Wilcox, Peter, and David Paton-Williams. 1988. "The Servant Songs in Deutero-Isaiah." *JSOT* 42:79–102.
Wildberger, Hans. 1982. *Jesaja 28–39: Das Buch, der Prophet und seine Botschaft.* Biblischer Kommentar 10/3. Neukirchen-Vluyen: Neukirchener.
———. 1991. *Isaiah 1–12,* translated by T. H. Trapp. Continental Commentary. Minneapolis: Fortress Press.
———. 1997. *Isaiah 13–27,* translated by T. H. Trapp. Continental Commentary. Minneapolis: Fortress Press.
Willey, Patricia Tull. 1992. "Repairing the Breach: A Meditation on Isaiah 58." *Church and Society* 83:10–21.
———. 1997. *Remember the Former Things: The Recollection of Previous Texts in Second Isaiah.* SBL Dissertation Series 161. Atlanta: Scholars.
Williamson, H. G. M. 1994. *The Book Called Isaiah: Deutero-Isaiah's Role in Composition and Redaction.* Oxford: Clarendon.
———. 1995. "Synchronic and Diachronic in Isaian Perspectives." In *Synchronic or Diachronic? A Debate on Method in Old Testament Exegesis,* edited by J. C. de Moor, 211–26. OtSt 34. Leiden: Brill.
———. 1997. "Relocating Isaiah 1:2-9." In *Writing and Reading the Scroll of Isaiah: Studies of an Interpretive Tradition,* edited by C. C. Broyles and C. A. Evans, 263–77. VTSup 70. Leiden: Brill.
———. 1998. *Variations on a Theme: King, Messiah, and Servant in the Book of Isaiah.* Didsbury Lectures 1997. Carlisle, U.K.: Paternoster.
Willis, John T. 1984. "The First Pericope in the Book of Isaiah." *VT* 34:63–77.
———. 1985. "An Important Passage for Determining the Historical Setting of a Prophetic Oracle—Isaiah 1.7-8." *ST* 39:151–69.
Wolterstorff, Nicholas P. 1991. "Justice as a Condition of Authentic Liturgy." *TToday* 48:6–21.

Yee, Gale A. 1981. "A Form-Critical Study of Isaiah 5:1-7 as a Song and a Juridical Parable." *CBQ* 43:30–40.
Young, Edward J. 1992. *The Book of Isaiah.* 3 vols. Reprint. Grand Rapids: Eerdmans.

Index of Biblical References

Verse numbers are given according to the Hebrew numbers. References in the text that indicate a verse and its following verse(s) are listed in this index under the initial verse (for example, 2:2ff. is listed as 2:2). Half verses are listed under the verse number without the half-number designation (for example, 50:4b is listed as 50:4). Primary passages and their main discussions are indicated in bold.